PRINCIPLES OF CONFLICT ECONOMICS

Conflict economics contributes to an understanding of violent conflict in two important ways. First, it applies economic analysis to diverse conflict activities such as war, arms races, and terrorism, showing how they can be understood as purposeful choices responsive to underlying incentives. Second, it treats appropriation as a fundamental economic activity, joining production and exchange as a means of wealth acquisition. Drawing on a half-century of scholarship, this book presents a primer on the key themes and principles of conflict economics. Although much work in the field is abstract, the book is made accessible to a broad audience of scholars, students, and policy makers by relying on historical data, relatively simple graphs, and intuitive narratives. In exploring the interdependence of economics and conflict, the book presents in novel ways current perspectives on conflict economics and offers new insights into the economic aspects of violence.

Charles H. Anderton is Professor of Economics at the College of the Holy Cross, Worcester, Massachusetts, where he has taught since 1986. He coedited the volume *Economics of Arms Reduction and the Peace Process* with Walter Isard in 1992. A former North American editor of the journal *Defence and Peace Economics*, Professor Anderton's research has appeared in journals such as *Economic Inquiry*, *Journal of Economic Behavior and Organization*, *Journal of Conflict Resolution*, *Conflict Management and Peace Science*, and *Peace Economics, Peace Science, and Public Policy*, as well as in the *Handbook of Defense Economics*, volumes 1 and 2.

John R. Carter is Professor of Economics at the College of the Holy Cross, Worcester, Massachusetts, where he has served on the faculty since 1976. A former Chair of the Department of Economics, Professor Carter received the Holy Cross Distinguished Teaching Award in 1992. His research has appeared in journals such as the *Review of Economics and Statistics*, *Journal of Law and Economics*, *Journal of Economic Perspectives*, *Journal of Economic Behavior and Organization*, *Defence and Peace Economics*, *Journal of Peace Research*, and *Public Choice*, as well as in the *Handbook of Defense Economics*, volume 2.

Principles of Conflict Economics

A Primer for Social Scientists

CHARLES H. ANDERTON
College of the Holy Cross

JOHN R. CARTER
College of the Holy Cross

CAMBRIDGE UNIVERSITY PRESS
Cambridge, New York, Melbourne, Madrid, Cape Town, Singapore, São Paulo, Delhi

Cambridge University Press
32 Avenue of the Americas, New York, NY 10013-2473, USA

www.cambridge.org
Information on this title: www.cambridge.org/9780521698658

First published 2009

Printed in the United States of America

A catalog record for this publication is available from the British Library.

Library of Congress Cataloging in Publication data
Anderton, Charles H.
Principles of conflict economics : a primer for social scientists /
Charles H. Anderton, John R. Carter.
p.   cm.
Includes bibliographical references and index.
ISBN 978-0-521-87557-8 (hardback) – ISBN 978-0-521-69865-8 (pbk.)
1. Social conflict.   2. Arms control – Economic aspects.
3. Disarmament – Economic aspects.   4. Peace.
I. Carter, John R.   II. Title.
HM1121.A53 2009
303.6′6–dc22   2008052036

ISBN 978-0-521-87557-8 hardback
ISBN 978-0-521-69865-8 paperback

To Our Families

Contents

Figures

Tables

Preface

Now the earth was corrupt in God's sight and was full of violence.

Genesis 6:11

Throughout recorded history, violent conflict has been a conspicuous aspect of the human experience. In recent decades, terrorism, civil strife, nation-state warfare, and the proliferation of weapons of mass destruction have dominated the headlines. It might at first appear that economics has little to say about such realms of conflict. After all, most economics textbooks restrict their attention to the behavior of consumers, producers, and governments operating peacefully in secure environments. Fortunately, however, the rapidly developing field of conflict economics can contribute greatly to an understanding of conflict in two important ways. First, conflict economics rigorously applies the concepts, principles, and methods of economics to the study of diverse conflict activities. Second, conflict economics treats appropriation as a fundamental economic activity, revealing how conflict both shapes and is shaped by the traditional economic activities of production and trade.

This book provides the reader with an accessible overview of the basic principles and major themes of conflict economics. Following an introduction to the field in Chapter 1, Chapters 2 through 4 survey many of the economic concepts and methods applied in subsequent chapters. These chapters will be useful to readers who either have no formal training in economics or would like to review economic principles with a focus on conflict. Chapters 5 through 11 explore major topics in conflict economics, including the bargaining theory of war; conflict between states; civil war and genocide; terrorism; the geography and technology of conflict; arms rivalry, proliferation, and arms control; and alliance behavior. These chapters provide a balanced mix of theoretical and empirical content. Chapter 12 is more theoretical and treats appropriation as a fundamental economic activity, joining production and trade as a means of wealth acquisition. Bibliographic notes are provided at the ends of chapters to help readers who want to pursue topics in greater depth. Two appendixes are also available – a primer on statistical analysis and a bargaining model of conflict.

Given our training and background, we concentrate on economic aspects of conflict. Although we recognize and incorporate contributions from various disciplines, especially political science, we defer to specialists in other fields to convey those contributions more thoroughly. Our emphasis on economic aspects of conflict can be valuable to both economists and non-economists. For economists, the book shows numerous ways in which economic methods can be applied to conflict issues. Moreover, the book's treatment of conflict as a fundamental category of economic activity will help economists reduce the gap that now exists between textbook models of peaceful production and exchange and real economies subject to potential or actual violence. The book should also appeal to those with backgrounds in fields other than economics. Non-economists are naturally drawn to incorporate economic variables in their studies of conflict, and our book offers coverage of such variables from the perspective of the economist. Also, many models and methods central to conflict economics (e.g., rational choice theory, game theory, and econometrics) are of growing importance in disciplines other than economics.

Much of the academic work in conflict economics is theoretical and abstract, but we take steps to increase the accessibility of the text. In addition to the overview of economic fundamentals in Chapters 2 through 4, the book contains extensive coverage of conflict data, intuitive narratives, relatively simple algebra and graphs, and summaries of empirical evidence on conflict phenomena. Furthermore, the book is organized so that the more accessible chapters occur early and the more difficult chapters later. The book should be useful to scholars, policy makers, and practitioners from a variety of disciplines and backgrounds, including economics, political science, international relations, peace studies, military sciences, and public policy. It should likewise be suitable in undergraduate or beginning-level graduate courses on the economics of conflict and in courses on war and peace at universities and military service schools.

The social science literature on conflict is massive. Hence, we are selective in the topics covered, theories emphasized, empirical articles reviewed, and bibliographic notes provided. The particular empirical articles that we choose to review are selected because they are relatively recent and highlight the importance of economic variables in conflict analysis. Thus, we do not necessarily choose seminal empirical studies for review, nor do our summaries of results necessarily reflect ongoing empirical controversies within topic areas. Finally, although the book covers issues pertinent to many contemporary conflicts such as those in Iraq, Afghanistan, and Sudan-Darfur, we do not attempt to focus the book on current events and policy debates. Instead, our goal is to emphasize principles of conflict economics that will be as useful in exploring conflicts yet to emerge as they are in studying historical and contemporary events.

Over the years, many scholars have shaped our thinking about conflict economics and encouraged our attempts to contribute to the field. We regret that we can mention only a few, but they include Jurgen Brauer, Keith Hartley, Jack Hirshleifer, Michael Intriligator, Walter Isard, and Todd Sandler. We also wish to acknowledge our former students, especially those in Experimental Microeconomics and Economics of Peace, Conflict, and Defense, both upper-level courses taught in the Department of Economics at the College of the Holy Cross. Their questions and comments have contributed greatly to our understanding of pedagogy in general and conflict economics in particular.

We are indebted to Scott Parris at Cambridge University Press for encouragement and advice over the course of the project; to the production staff at Cambridge University Press for their excellent work; to Daniel Arce, Jurgen Brauer, and several anonymous reviewers for extensive and insightful comments on various drafts; to Roxane Anderton for help with citations; to Erin Wall (College of the Holy Cross, 2006) for research assistance funded by the May and Stanley Smith Charitable Trust Summer Research Assistant Program; to the College of the Holy Cross for timely research leaves; and to Nancy Baldiga, Miles Cahill, Robert Frank, George Kosicki, and Todd Sandler for generous letters of support. We are especially grateful to our wives, Roxane Anderton and Gloria Carter, for their love and understanding, without which this book would not have been possible.

Introduction: Definition and Scope of Conflict Economics

For many people, in many places, violent or potentially violent conflict is part of the human experience. Headline stories of civil strife, insurgency, nation-state warfare, terrorism, and the proliferation of weapons of mass destruction document the prevalence of conflict as a basic fact of life. Less dramatic indications of conflict include deadbolt locks, gated residential communities, electronic security systems, and handgun sales, to name a few. At first blush, it might appear that economics has little if anything to say about life's harder side. Economics textbooks typically restrict their attention to the peaceful behavior of consumers, producers, and governments in the marketplace. Thus, it might seem that potential and actual violence over resources, goods, and political power lie outside the domain of economics. But this is a misperception, as is demonstrated by the rapidly developing field of conflict economics.

1.1. What Is Conflict Economics?

Conflict economics has two defining characteristics. First, it maintains that the concepts, principles, and methods of economics can be fruitfully applied to the study of conflict activities. Thus, diverse phenomena like war, arms races, alliances, and terrorism are analyzed and understood as outcomes of purposeful choices responsive to changes in underlying incentives. As just one example, economics explains how consumers shift purchases from one good (say orange juice) toward another (say grape juice) when the price of one rises relative to that of the other. Similar economic forces are at work in many conflict settings: when one type of weapon is constrained by arms control, another type is substituted; when political targets are hardened, terrorists turn to less costly civilian targets;

and when entrepreneurs of local violence lose access to land mines, they employ young males armed with assault rifles.

But conflict economics is more than the application of economics to conflict. It also involves a gradual reconstruction of the core of economic theory to take account of conflict. Conflict of the sort considered in this book ultimately involves intended or realized appropriation, where the term "appropriation" refers to a taking that rests on force or the threat of force. As its second defining characteristic, conflict economics treats appropriation as a fundamental economic activity, joining production and exchange as a means of acquiring wealth. Traditional economic models assume that economic behavior is peaceful. Yet in real economies, conflicts over goods and resources abound. Conflict economics seeks to close this gap between theory and reality. Thus, a range of appropriative activities has been modeled, including resource conflicts, piracy, and extortion. These models reveal how conflict both shapes and is shaped by the traditional economic activities of production and exchange.

For the purposes of this book, we define conflict economics as (1) the study of violent or potentially violent conflict using the concepts, principles, and methods of economics and (2) the development of economic models of appropriation and its interaction with production and exchange activities. By including the qualifier that conflict on some level be violent, the definition intentionally excludes the analysis of ordinary market competition and, more tentatively, activities like litigation and rent seeking. Clearly included by the definition is the study of what might be called macro conflict, comprising interstate conflict (e.g., war between states), intrastate conflict (e.g., civil war, domestic terrorism), and extra-state conflict between states and external non-state actors (e.g., international terrorism, colonial wars). Also included is the study of micro conflict, meaning conflict activities among private persons and organizations (e.g., theft, extortion, human trafficking). In the next section, we begin to document empirically the enormity of conflict in the human experience.

1.2. A Look at Conflict Large and Small

Macro Conflict

Interstate, intrastate, and extra-state conflicts are the primary subject matter in conflict economics. Based on data from the Correlates of War

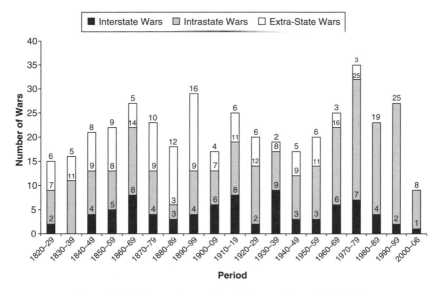

Figure 1.1. War onsets per decade by war type, 1820–2006.
Sources: Sarkees (2000) for 1820–1989 data; Uppsala Conflict Data Program (UCDP) and International Peace Research Institute, Oslo (PRIO) and Gleditsch, Wallensteen, Eriksson, Sollenberg et al. (2002) for 1990–2006 data.

(COW) Project, Uppsala Conflict Data Program (UCDP), and International Peace Research Institute, Oslo (PRIO), Figure 1.1 shows the frequency of interstate, intrastate, and extra-state war onsets from 1820 to 2006. War onsets are wars initiated during the time periods indicated. Figure 1.1 shows that there were 408 war onsets of all types in the international system from 1820 to 2006. About half of the wars were intrastate (221, or 54.2%), followed by extra-state (106, or 26.0%) and interstate (81, or 19.9%). Figure 1.1 also shows that there were more interstate and intrastate wars in the 1900–99 period relative to 1820–99 (50 and 143 compared to 30 and 70), but fewer extra-state wars (35 compared to 71). Over the past five decades, intrastate wars have become more frequent while extra-state wars have diminished significantly. According to Sarkees, Wayman, and Singer (2003), the decline in extra-state wars is due to the reduction in the numbers of colonies and dependencies in the international system.

Figure 1.2 depicts the worldwide frequency of international and domestic terrorist incidents combined for the period 1970–2004. Domestic terrorism "is perpetrated within the boundaries of a given nation by nationals from that nation," while international terrorism involves "the

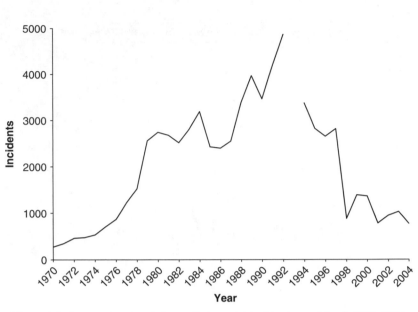

Figure 1.2. International and domestic terrorist incidents combined, 1970–2004.
Note: Data for 1993 are missing.
Sources: LaFree and Dugan (2006, 2007a).

interests and/or nationals of more than one country" (LaFree, Dugan, Fogg, and Scott 2006, pp. 5 and 22). Figure 1.2 suggests two observations. First, no upward (linear) trend is evident in the incident series for the full time period. Second, terrorist incidents around the globe were far more numerous in the 1980s and early 1990s relative to the latest years in the sample. However, in recent years the number of casualties per incident (not shown) has been rising (Enders and Sandler 2000).

Although scholars distinguish interstate, intrastate, and extra-state conflict, some conflicts fit two or even all three of the categories. For example, the post–Gulf conflict in Iraq began in March 2003 as an interstate war between Iraq and a coalition of states led by the United States. Following the official end of major combat operations in May 2003, the United States and its allies began a transitional occupation until the Iraqi Transitional Government was installed in January 2005. This was followed by violent conflict between irregular armed forces on one side and the new Iraqi state and the US-led coalition on the other. Since the irregular forces encompass both Iraqis and foreign forces putatively associated with al Qaeda, this stage of the conflict in Iraq is both intrastate and extra-state in nature.

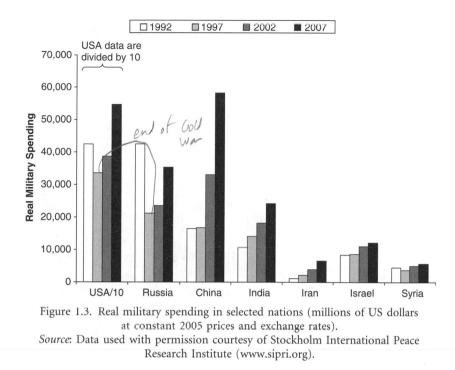

Figure 1.3. Real military spending in selected nations (millions of US dollars at constant 2005 prices and exchange rates).
Source: Data used with permission courtesy of Stockholm International Peace Research Institute (www.sipri.org).

The macro conflicts summarized in Figures 1.1 and 1.2 involve three types of economic costs. First, when nations and groups allocate resources to conflict, alternative goods that could be produced with those resources, such as food and clothing, are forgone. This economic cost is borne even when the conflict activities are purely defensive and no violence occurs. Second, when violence does occur, goods and resources (including human lives) are destroyed, causing current and future consumption and production to be sacrificed. Third, threatened or realized violent conflict causes some present and future production and exchange activities to be rendered uneconomical and hence lost. Collier (1999, p. 171) characterizes the three economic costs of conflict as diversion, destruction, and disruption. The next three figures provide some sense of the nature and magnitude of these economic costs of conflict within the international system.

Figure 1.3 shows real (inflation-adjusted) military expenditures for selected nations in 1992, 1997, 2002, and 2007. These expenditures serve as a proxy for the direct diversion of resources associated with potential or actual conflict involving nation-states. The years 1992 and 1997 reflect conditions following the end of the Cold War rivalry between the United States and the

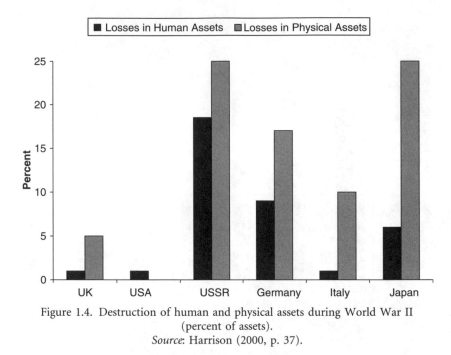

Figure 1.4. Destruction of human and physical assets during World War II
(percent of assets).
Source: Harrison (2000, p. 37).

Soviet Union in 1989 and the 1990/91 Gulf War. The decline in real military spending for the United States and Russia from 1992 to 1997 is consistent with a hoped for "peace dividend" following the Cold War. The years 2002 and 2007 follow the September 11, 2001, terrorist attacks on the United States. The substantial increase in real military spending for the United States from 1997 to 2007 suggests that the terrorism threat squelched any continued peace dividend. Note that Figure 1.3 also shows upward trends in real military spending for several nations in South Asia and the Middle East.

Estimates of the destruction of human and physical assets for selected states involved in World War II are presented in Figure 1.4. The figure shows the destruction of human lives as a percentage of the working-age population and the destruction of physical assets as a percentage of national wealth (or industry fixed assets in the cases of Germany and Italy). Human destruction ranged from one percent for the United Kingdom and the United States to as high as 19 percent for the USSR. Physical asset destruction ranged from zero percent for the United States to 25 percent for the USSR and Japan.

Figure 1.5 shows the United States' real merchandise trade (exports plus imports) with Germany and Japan before, during, and after World War II. Notice how trade is driven to zero or near zero during the war and

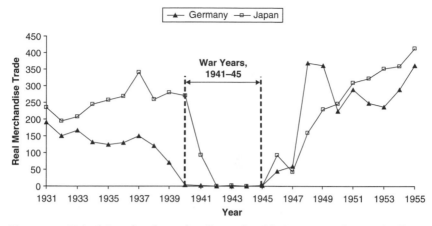

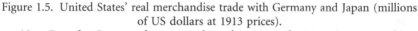

Figure 1.5. United States' real merchandise trade with Germany and Japan (millions of US dollars at 1913 prices).
Note: Data for Germany from 1952 through 1955 are for West Germany only.
Source: Anderton and Carter (2003, pp. 302–303).

Disruption

rebounds with the restoration of peace. Figure 1.5 is but one example of how conflict disrupts economic activity, in this case trade.

Figure 1.6 depicts the cost for 2007 of selected multilateral peace missions by location and by the sponsoring intergovernmental organization (IGO). Several observations follow. First, numerous IGOs, such as the United Nations (UN) and the North Atlantic Treaty Organization (NATO), undertake peace missions. Second, some missions involve multiple IGOs, such as the Organization of Security and Cooperation in Europe (OSCE) and NATO in Kosovo and the African Union (AU) and the UN in Sudan. Third, peace is costly. For example, the annual cost of peace missions exceeds $1 billion both in the Democratic Republic of Congo and in Sudan. According to the Stockholm International Peace Research Institute, the annual cost of all multilateral peace missions in 2007 was $7.5 billion. While war clearly entails economic costs, Figure 1.6 documents that substantial resources are invested to establish or maintain peace in many nations and regions. *Peace is costly*

Micro Conflict

Common theft, piracy of merchant ships, and human trafficking are but a few examples of appropriation possibilities at work in modern economies at the micro level. Figure 1.7 shows real (inflation-adjusted)

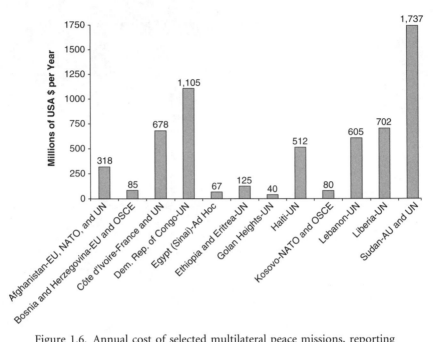

Figure 1.6. Annual cost of selected multilateral peace missions, reporting
year 2007.
Notes: AU – African Union, EU – European Union, NATO – North Atlantic Treaty
Organization, OSCE – Organization of Security and Cooperation in Europe,
UN – United Nations. The EU cost for Bosnia and Herzegovina is the sum
of the EU Police Mission and the EU Military Operation.
Source: Data used with permission courtesy of Stockholm International Peace
Research Institute (www.sipri.org).

expenditures on defense against crime (police protection, correction, and
judicial and legal activities) by federal, state, and local governments in the
United States (measured on the left axis). Also shown is the real lost value
associated with property crimes such as robbery, burglary, larceny,
and motor vehicle theft in the United States (measured on the right axis).
Figure 1.8 shows the total number of actual and attempted pirate attacks
against merchant ships worldwide from 1998 to 2007. In 2007, a disproportionate number of pirate attacks occurred in the waters of South Asia
(Indonesia – 43, Bangladesh – 15, India – 11, Malaysia – 9) and Africa
(Nigeria – 42, Somalia – 31, Gulf of Aden/Red Sea – 13) (ICC International
Maritime Bureau 2007, pp. 5–6). Attacks against ships in the Malacca Straits
were much less frequent than in the early 2000s, due in part to increased
naval patrols by Indonesia, Malaysia, and Singapore, and in part to the
adoption of new merchant defense technologies, including electrified fences

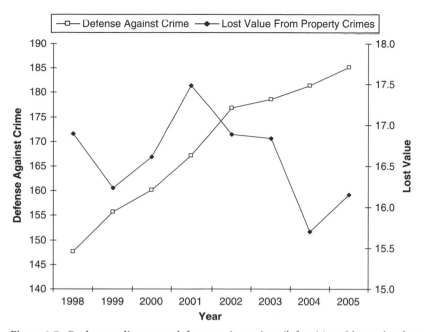

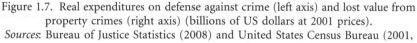

Figure 1.7. Real expenditures on defense against crime (left axis) and lost value from property crimes (right axis) (billions of US dollars at 2001 prices).
Sources: Bureau of Justice Statistics (2008) and United States Census Bureau (2001, 2003, 2006, 2008).

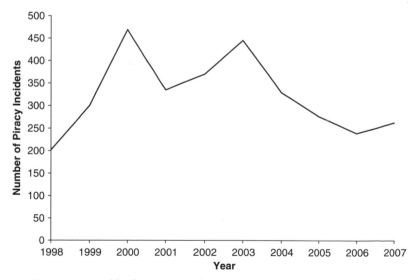

Figure 1.8. Worldwide pirate attacks against merchant ships, 1998–2007.
Source: ICC International Maritime Bureau (2006, 2007).

Table 1.1. *Victims of human trafficking worldwide.*

	US Government Study	International Labour Organization Study
Number of Victims	600,000–800,000 trafficked across borders in 2003	At least 2.45 million trafficked internationally and internally, 1995–2004
Type of Exploitation		
Commercial sex	66%	43%
Economic or forced labor	34%	32%
Mixed and other		25%
Gender and Age		
Females	80%	80%
Minors	50%	40%

Source: United States Government Accountability Office (2006, p. 12).

and unmanned aerial vehicles. Lastly, Table 1.1 provides information on victims of human trafficking, which is "a worldwide form of exploitation in which men, women, and children are bought, sold, and held against their will in slave-like conditions" (United States Government Accountability Office 2006, p. 1). As shown, an estimated 2.45 million people were trafficked over the 1995–2004 period, with a high percentage of victims being females and minors.

1.3. Methodology of Conflict Economics

Conflict and Economics

Conflict and economics combine naturally in four distinct ways that we draw on throughout this book. First, conflict is a choice. Economics is defined as the study of choices that people make under conditions of scarcity. Because conflict involves choices among various violent and non-violent alternatives, the concepts, principles, and methods of economics apply directly to a wide range of conflict activities. Second, conflict affects economic outcomes. As shown earlier, war seriously diminished trade between the United States and Germany and Japan during World War II. Other economic variables disrupted by conflict include production, capital and labor migration, investment, and growth. Third, economic variables affect conflict. Trade, foreign direct investment, growth, income, and resource endowments can affect the likelihood and duration of conflicts. Fourth, conflict in the form of appropriation is a fundamental mode of wealth acquisition. While economists typically emphasize production and trade, conflict often involves the allocation of resources to acquire the holdings of others. Hence, appropriation is a means of wealth acquisition coequal with production and trade as a fundamental economic activity.

Rationality and Equilibrium

Like other scholarly disciplines, economics is distinguished by its analytical concepts and organizing principles. Analytical concepts are just terms that categorize and refer to abstract aspects of the phenomena studied. Examples already encountered here include scarcity, cost, production, and trade. Organizing principles are the systematic and general means by which the analytical pieces are brought together to yield predictions and explanations. Paramount in economics are the organizing principles of rationality and equilibrium. Actors are assumed to be rational, meaning that they have consistent preferences and choose from among the best alternatives available to them. The choices in turn are assumed to adjust and combine in ways that yield equilibrium outcomes. An equilibrium is a coordination among the actors' choices so that no single actor has an incentive to change his or her choice. For example, a market is said to be in equilibrium when the quantity that consumers want to buy just balances the quantity that producers want to sell at the current price.

The rationality assumption has been subject to criticism, sometimes from within economics but more often from the other social sciences. For discussion and debate about the assumption, see the bibliographic notes at the end of this chapter. Here we are content to make three points. First, the assumption of rationality by itself says nothing about either the origin or the content of preferences. The formation of the preferences of violence-producing individuals and organizations is an important question studied by a variety of disciplines. Although most models of conflict assume self-interested preferences, it might prove useful in some cases to assume other-regarding preferences involving malevolence or concerns of fairness or reciprocity. Second, in this book we often assume that groups (including nations) behave as if they have well-defined preferences. We believe that this assumption is useful in many cases, but it is not without problems as documented in economics, political science, and psychology. Third, we expect to see continued refinements and alternatives to the rationality assumption that will advance our understanding of human behavior in general and conflict in particular. Evolutionary models, wherein actors are assumed to imitate or learn successful choices, are especially promising for the study of long-lasting conflicts.

Quantitative Methods

Economics, like other social sciences, requires interplay between theory and observation, or, in practice, between models and empirical tests. The models tend to be mathematical, because the organizing principles of rationality and equilibrium are themselves mathematical. Rationality is formalized as a constrained optimization problem, whereby an actor maximizes an objective (e.g., territory controlled) subject to one or more constraints. Equilibrium is a solution to a set of simultaneous equations. Fortunately, the logic of conflict models can often be conveyed verbally together with relatively straightforward algebra and graphs. Because the outcomes of conflict depend on the choices of multiple actors, there arises what is called strategic interdependence, meaning that the best choice for one actor depends on the choices of others. To allow for this interdependence, conflict models are often constructed using the principles of game theory, a branch of mathematics that is now prominent in both the natural and the social sciences. Again, the basics of game theory can be presented with relatively modest demands in terms of mathematics.

Models of conflict are tested empirically using standard methods of statistical inference. The sources of data for various forms of conflict are rapidly growing in this age of information. Large panels of cross-country data now permit scholars to conduct epidemiological studies, wherein the risks of interstate, intrastate, or extra-state conflict are estimated based on socioeconomic and geopolitical variables, much like studies in medicine estimate risk factors for cancer and other diseases. Most of the data used in studies of conflict are naturally occurring, meaning that they result from historical events and are collected and disseminated by various organizations. With the growth of game theoretic models of conflict, data are also being generated with increasing frequency using experimental methods in controlled laboratory settings.

Multidisciplinary Nature of Conflict Economics

Many conflict activities have important political, sociological, and psychological aspects. The central purpose of conflict economics is to promote an understanding of the economic nature, causes, and consequences of conflict. Conflict economics informs and is informed by other disciplines. At numerous places in this book we draw on literature from other disciplines, especially political science.

1.4. Organization of Book

We have defined conflict economics as the economic analysis of conflict together with the development of models of appropriation. The remainder of the book is organized in accordance with this definition. Chapters 2 through 4 provide grounding in the economic concepts, principles, and methods that are utilized throughout the book. Chapter 5 presents a simple bargaining model of conflict and provides a transition to conflict economics proper. Chapters 6 through 11 apply economic analysis to historical and contemporary conflict topics, including war between and within states, terrorism, spatial and technological aspects of conflict, arms rivalry, proliferation, arms control, and alliance behavior. Chapter 12 introduces appropriation possibilities into mainstream production and trade theory. At the end of each chapter we include bibliographic notes whereby the interested scholar, student, or practitioner can explore the field in more depth. Appendix A offers a brief review of statistical methods, and Appendix B presents a bargaining model of conflict.

1.5. Bibliographic Notes

Insightful perspectives on the economics of peace and war were developed by well-known economists in the eighteenth, nineteenth, and early twentieth centuries (see Goodwin 1991 and Brauer 2003 for overviews). The widespread application of formal economic models to the study of conflict began largely during the Cold War, when attention was drawn to various aspects of international conflict. The resulting scholarship was called alternatively peace economics or defense economics. Peace economics focused on the causes of violence and ways that violence can be avoided, managed, or resolved, while defense economics also addressed questions of weapons production and resource allocation in war. Richardson (1960a, 1960b), Schelling and Halperin (1961), Boulding (1962), and Isard (1969) provided classic works in peace economics, as did Hitch and McKean (1960) and Peck and Scherer (1962) in defense economics. Also important were Schelling (1960, 1966) on strategic behavior and game theory, Olson and Zeckhauser (1966) and Sandler and

Cauley (1975) on alliance behavior, McGuire (1965) and Intriligator (1975) on arms rivalry, Tullock (1974) on intrastate conflicts, and Benoit (1973) on defense expenditures and economic growth in developing countries. Defense and peace economics has since expanded to include such topics as civil wars, peacekeeping and peace enforcement, the arms trade, proliferation of weapons of mass destruction, terrorism, economic interdependence and conflict, and the appropriation and defense of wealth. Key contributions in these and other topics are available in the edited volumes of Hartley and Sandler (1995, 2001) and Sandler and Hartley (2003, 2007).

Emphasis in this book is primarily on topics in macro conflict. Under the heading of micro conflict, formal treatment of the economics of crime is well developed. See, for example, Becker (1968) and the collected papers in Ehrlich and Liu (2006). The study of other micro topics is more dispersed. On human trafficking, see Laczko and Gozdziak (2005).

Conflict economics is part of a broader social scientific study of conflict. An excellent overview of the historical development of the social scientific study of interstate conflict is provided by Singer (2000). Sambanis (2002) reviews the development of the social scientific study of intrastate conflicts, while Enders and Sandler (2006a) do the same for terrorism.

Central to most economic analysis of conflict is the assumption that actors are rational. Introductions to the rational choice model can be found in intermediate microeconomics textbooks. More formal statements are available in Kreps (1990) and Mas-Colell, Whinston, and Green (1995). For a sampling of the debate surrounding the rationality assumption in economics, see Hirshleifer (1985), Binmore and Samuelson (1994), and Kahneman (2003), and in political science see Brown, Coté, Lynn-Jones, and Miller (2000), Quackenbush (2004), and Vahabi (2004).

Production Possibilities and the Guns versus Butter Trade-Off

Modern economies are highly complex. In the United States economy in 2006, for example, 145.8 million workers combined their labor with $23.1 trillion worth of capital to produce $13.2 trillion worth of goods and services. Fortunately, the concepts and principles that guide economists' understanding of economic activity are relatively simple. In this chapter we explain selected aspects of the economics of production such as the production function, scarcity, production possibilities, opportunity cost, efficiency, comparative advantage, and gains from trade. We then apply these principles to better understand the economic costs of conflict, the effects of defense spending on economic growth, and the depressed state of North Korea's militarized economy.

2.1. Production Possibilities Model

Production Function

Assume that an economy produces two types of goods: military (M) and civilian (C). Military goods include tanks, fighter aircraft, and the like, while civilian goods encompass food, clothing, shelter, and so on. In economics, military goods are often called "guns," while civilian goods are called "butter." The production of military and civilian goods requires inputs such as labor (L) and capital (K), where the latter refers to physical assets like buildings and machines. A production function specifies the maximum amount of a good that can be produced with any given combination of inputs under the current state of technology. Technology is the scientific and organizational knowledge available to transform inputs into outputs. Production functions for M and C can be summarized algebraically as:

$$M = f(L_M, K_M) \tag{2.1}$$

$$C = g(L_C, K_C), \tag{2.2}$$

where L_M and K_M are labor and capital inputs in military production and L_C and K_C are the same for civilian production.

Equations (2.1) and (2.2) represent production functions in general functional form, but economists often work with specific functional forms. The most famous specific production function in economics is the Cobb-Douglas function, which for M and C can be written:

$$M = AL_M^a K_M^\beta \tag{2.3}$$

$$C = \tilde{A}L_C^a K_C^b. \tag{2.4}$$

In equations (2.3) and (2.4), the A and $\tilde{A}$ terms are positive constants representing the state of technology in the production of military and civilian goods. The positive parameters a, β, a, and b capture the productive capability of the inputs. The parameters for production functions often can be estimated statistically using historical data, but for our purposes a numerical example is sufficient to understand the functions. Suppose $A = 50$, $a = 0.5$, and $\beta = 0.5$ in equation (2.3). If labor and capital inputs are $L_M = 100$ hours and $K_M = 9$ units, then military output would be $M = 50(100)^{0.5}(9)^{0.5} = 1,500$ units.

Two well-known production concepts are marginal product and returns to scale. Marginal product is the change in output that occurs when one unit of a given input is added, holding other inputs constant. In mathematical terms, it is the partial derivative of output with respect to the given input. For example, using the Cobb-Douglas production function for military goods, the marginal product of labor is $\partial M / \partial L_M = aAL_M^{a-1} K_M^\beta$. Given parameter values $A = 50$, $a = 0.5$, and $\beta = 0.5$ and the input values $L_M = 100$ and $K_M = 9$, the marginal product of labor in the military industry is $MP_{L_M} = 7.5$. This means that if labor input is increased by one hour (holding capital fixed), military output will rise by 7.5 units. According to the law of diminishing returns, as the amount of an input increases (holding the other input fixed), after some point its marginal productivity will diminish. For example, if L_M is raised to 144 and K_M held fixed at 9, the marginal product of labor in the military industry diminishes from 7.5 to 6.25 units. Note that this means that even though the *total* output is now larger, the *addition* to the output is now smaller. Now consider increasing both inputs at the same time. For example, suppose both inputs are doubled, so that output becomes $M = 50(200)^{0.5}(18)^{0.5} =$ 3,000 units. Doubling both inputs causes output to exactly double, which is known as constant returns to scale. For the Cobb-Douglas production function, constant returns to scale exists when $a + \beta = 1$. If $a + \beta > 1$, doubling inputs causes output to more than double, which is known as increasing returns to scale. If $a + \beta < 1$, doubling inputs causes output to less than double, which is called decreasing returns to scale.

Production Possibilities Frontier

In economics, the fundamental fact of nature is scarcity, whereby individuals, groups, and nations have limited resources and technology to produce goods and services to meet peoples' virtually unlimited wants. Assume that the labor and capital employed in the military and civilian sectors equal the total labor and capital available to the economy, L and K:

$$L - L_M + L_C \tag{2.5}$$
$$K = K_M + K_C. \tag{2.6}$$

The scarcity of labor and capital is reflected in equations (2.5) and (2.6), while the technological limits to production of goods for given input combinations are implied by the production functions (2.3) and (2.4). Technological limitations in production and scarcity of inputs imply a production possibilities frontier (PPF) such as that shown in Figure 2.1. Points on or within the PPF constitute the attainable region, which includes all combinations of guns (M) and butter (C) that are possible to produce within an economy.

The PPF in Figure 2.1 depicts the fundamental notion of scarcity in two ways. First, all combinations of guns and butter above the PPF lie in the unattainable region, meaning they cannot be produced given the available resources and technology. Second, the slope of the PPF is negative, meaning there exists a production trade-off between the two goods. At any point on the PPF, say point A, the only way to obtain more guns (moving to point B, say) is to give up some butter. When production is on the frontier, gaining more of one good requires giving up or forgoing some of the other good. This trade-off is captured by the concept of opportunity cost. In Figure 2.1, the opportunity cost of an increase in guns from m^1 to m^2 is the $c^1 - c^2$ units of butter given up. Note that the PPF in Figure 2.1 is bowed out. This indicates that the opportunity cost of a good will increase

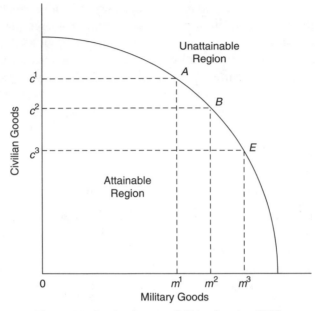

Figure 2.1. Production possibilities frontier (PPF).

as more of the good is acquired. For example, in moving from point B to point E, even more units of butter must be given up for an equal increment of guns than when moving from point A to point B. Economists believe that PPFs are usually bowed out because resources shifted from the production of one good to another tend not to be equally adaptable.

As depicted by the PPF, many alternative production points exist; hence, choice is inescapable. Among the thousands of goods and services that might be produced in a modern economy, decisions must somehow be made about what quantities of which goods will be produced, what combinations of inputs will be used, where the goods will be produced, how the goods will be distributed, and how all of these things will be coordinated and adjusted as technology, resources, and peoples' preferences change over time. Different nations have different economic systems for addressing these issues. In the United States and many European nations, there is substantial private ownership of property and a reliance on markets (supply and demand) to coordinate economic activity. In North Korea and Cuba, most property is not privately owned, and economic activity is directed by state central planning. Other economies have somewhat limited private property yet a significant role for markets (e.g., China).

Figure 2.1 can also be used to understand the concepts of productive and allocative efficiency. Productive efficiency occurs when inputs are fully employed, so that equations (2.5) and (2.6) hold, and maximum output is produced from those inputs based on available technology, so that equations (2.3) and (2.4) hold. When productive efficiency is achieved, the economy operates at some point on the PPF. If the economy fails to employ all resources fully and productively, then it operates at a point inside the PPF, which is called productive inefficiency. Allocative efficiency, also known as Pareto efficiency, occurs when it is not possible to improve one individual's or group's well-being without hurting another's. For example, suppose the economy is operating at point *B* in Figure 2.1, which is productively efficient. Now assume that the movement from point *B* to point *A* makes everyone better off, but that any further move from point *A* will leave at least one person worse off. This would imply that *B* is productively efficient but not allocatively efficient, whereas *A* is both productively and allocatively efficient.

Specialization and Trade in the Production Possibilities Model

The authors of this book produce teaching and research services, and maybe a few vegetables from gardening, but they consume hundreds of other products. Our case is typical of workers in modern economies who specialize in the production of one or a few items and then trade their specialized output (with money facilitating exchange) for the goods they consume. Specialized production and trade is a fundamental aspect of economic life, not only for individuals but also for nations.

In Figure 2.2 we depict specialized production and trade using the production possibilities model. Recall that along a PPF there exists a trade-off between one good and another. This trade-off is internal to the country; that is, within the country's own production possibilities, it can trade off one good for another as reflected in the slope of its PPF. But there is another possibility available to the country; namely, it can trade some of its output with another country. This is an external exchange possibility. In Figure 2.2 we draw a curved line, known as an indifference curve, tangent to the PPF. We will discuss indifference curves in more detail in Chapter 3, but for now it is sufficient to say that points along any given indifference curve generate a fixed level of well-being or utility, and that the higher the indifference curve, the greater the well-being or utility. In Figure 2.2, if the nation produces goods only for itself and does not trade, the highest attainable indifference curve is the one that is tangent to the PPF (labeled *aa*), say at point *A*. Point *A*

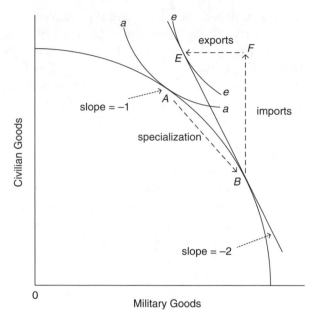

Figure 2.2. Specialized production and trade.

is known as an autarky optimum, because it is where the country would produce to maximize its material well-being in the absence of any external trade. Assume the opportunity cost of military goods in the neighborhood of point *A* equals −1, meaning that the production of an additional unit of *M* would cost one unit of *C* forgone. But suppose that prices on world markets are such that one unit of *M* could exchange for *two* units of *C*. This external terms-of-trade is represented by the line with slope −2 drawn tangent to the PPF at point *B*. With external trade, the country can achieve a higher indifference curve and therefore a higher level of well-being by following an "economic two-step." First, it specializes more in the production of *M* by moving its production point from *A* to *B*. Second, it trades away some *M* in return for some *C*, arriving at a final consumption point *E* on the higher indifference curve *ee*. The distance *FE* represents the country's exports of *M*, while *BF* represents its imports of *C*.

Figure 2.2 shows that specialized production and trade allow the country to consume more goods and services than it could produce in isolation. At consumption point *E*, the country is consuming a bundle of goods that lies outside the PPF. Although *E* is an unattainable production point, it is not an unattainable consumption point because of the opportunity presented by external trade. When specializing in a product (good *M* in this case) that is more valued on world markets relative to the opportunity cost of producing it in isolation, the country is operating according to what is known as its comparative advantage. Such specialization increases the value of the country's production and, through trade, allows the country to reach a higher indifference curve. The increase in the indifference curve from *aa* to *ee* is a graphical representation of the gains from trade.

Economic Growth in the Production Possibilities Model

Over time, most economies experience an increase in the amount of goods and services that are produced as more labor and capital and better technology become available. This is known as economic growth. For example, since the early 1940s, a growing proportion and number of women have entered the work force in the United States, contributing to its post–World War II growth in gross domestic product (GDP). In some countries, such as Afghanistan prior to the fall of the Taliban in 2002, women have been discouraged or forbidden from paid employment, which tends to depress GDP growth. When new resources or technology become available, the PPF moves outward, causing some previously unattainable production points to become attainable. The PPF does not necessarily shift out equally along the two axes. If resources or technological developments are biased in favor of, say good C, the PPF would shift out more along the C axis than the M axis. Note also that the PPF can shift in, which constitutes negative economic growth. For example, Hurricane Katrina destroyed lives and capital stock in New Orleans and Southern Mississippi in 2005, causing the PPFs for these local economies to shift inward.

2.2. Applications

Economic Costs of Conflict

In Chapter 1 we indicated that violent conflict involves economic costs of three sorts: diversion of resources to defense, destruction of goods and resources, and disruption of present and future economic activities. Figure 2.3 illustrates these three types of costs in the production possibilities model. Conflict typically leads to an increase in military production as a proportion of overall production. In panel (a), the increase in military goods relative to civilian goods causes the production point in the economy to move from say A to B. In this case, the increase in "guns" from m^1 to m^2 occurs at the expense of "butter," which declines from c^1 to c^2. In

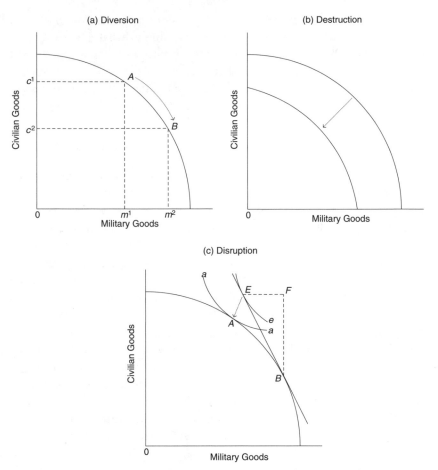

Figure 2.3. Economic diversion, destruction, and disruption from violent conflict.

panel (b), the destruction of goods, capital, and people through violent conflict causes production possibilities to shrink, reflected by the inward shift of the PPF. In this example, violent conflict leads to negative economic growth. In panel (c), disruption of trade by conflict leads to a decline in material well-being. Initially, the country produces at point B, exports FE units of M, imports BF units of C, and reaches indifference curve ee at consumption point E. Assume now that trade ceases with conflict. This causes the country to operate in autarky at point A, with reduced consumption of each good and a lower level of utility shown by indifference curve aa.

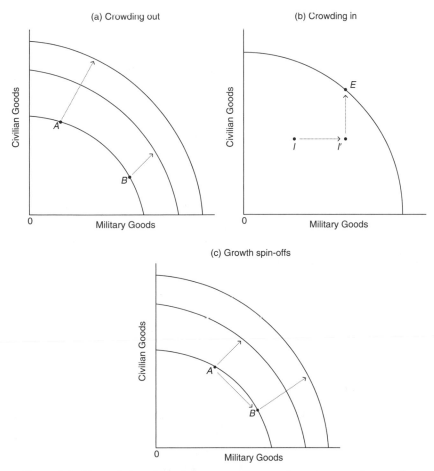

Figure 2.4. Channels by which defense spending can impact economic growth.

Defense Spending and Economic Growth

There are multiple channels by which defense spending can impact a nation's economic growth. Figure 2.4 considers three of the major channels: (a) crowding out, (b) crowding in, and (c) growth spin-offs. In panel (a), assume that the preponderance of a nation's investment goods (i.e., new machines and factories) is embodied in civilian goods *C*. If the nation operates at point *A*, it will have a relatively large amount of investment goods this year leading to a relatively large capital stock next year and a correspondingly higher PPF. If the nation operates at point *B*, however, it will have a relatively small amount of investment goods this year, leading to a relatively small capital stock next year and a correspondingly lower PPF. Thus, when the nation chooses more military goods (point *B* rather than point *A*), it crowds out or dampens capital accumulation, leading to diminished economic growth. In panel (b), assume that the nation is initially operating at inefficient point *I*, perhaps because the country is experiencing a recession with underutilized labor and capital. In this case, increased defense spending can stimulate economic activity, moving production from *I* to *I'*, for example. The increase in production of military goods raises the incomes of workers and owners in the military sector. These income earners will spend some of their increased income on civilian goods, causing civilian goods production to rise from *I'* to *E* via a multiplier effect. This stimulation of civilian production is called crowding in. Panel (c) looks like panel (a) except that the arrow from point *B* is now longer than the arrow from point *A*. Suppose that greater defense spending leads to what are called growth spin-offs, such as increases in education and advances in technology. If this is the case, the diversion of resources to military goods when moving from *A* to *B* can cause the future PPF to be further out than otherwise.

Following the end of the Cold War in 1989, the defense spending–economic growth relationship was of particular interest because it was thought that defense spending would fall throughout the world. Many scholars expected a "peace dividend" in the form of greater economic growth, based on the view that defense spending dampens economic growth as shown in panel (a). Other scholars warned that cuts in defense spending could have a recessionary impact or could dampen technological development as suggested by panels (b) and (c). Of course, the multiple channels by which defense spending can affect economic growth are not mutually exclusive. For example, consistent with panel (b), it is possible that cuts in real US defense spending from 1989 to 1991 could have contributed to the recession of 1990–91. On the other hand, consistent with panel (a), the resources freed up from cuts in US defense spending may have been partly responsible for the rapid economic growth experienced by the United States in the later 1990s. As briefly reviewed in this chapter's bibliographic notes, empirical evidence on the relationship between defense spending and economic growth is mixed.

North Korea

The Korean demilitarized zone (DMZ), established after the Korean War (1950–53), serves as a buffer zone separating North and South Korea. Despite attempts at reconciliation, the DMZ is one of the world's most

Table 2.1. *Economic and military data for North Korea, South Korea, and the United States, 2007.*

	North Korea	South Korea	United States
Economic Variables			
Gross domestic product (GDP)	$40.0 billion	$1,206.0 billion	$13.9 trillion
GDP per capita	$1,900	$24,600	$46,000
Military spending as % of GDP	22.9%	2.7%	4.1%
Armed Forces			
Active armed forces	1,106,000	687,700	27,114
Active paramilitary forces	189,000	4,500	0
Weapons			
Main battle tanks	3,500	2,330	116
Artillery	17,900	10,774	45
Surface-to-air missiles	10,000	1,090	1 battalion
Tactical submarines	63	12	0
Principal surface combatants	8	44	0

Notes: North Korea's military spending as a percentage of GDP is for 2003. GDP and GDP per capita data are at purchasing power parity. US armed forces and weapons data are for the Korean Peninsula only.

Sources: Central Intelligence Agency (2008) for economic variables, and International Institute for Strategic Studies (2008) for armed forces and weapons.

militarized areas, with close to two million troops (including approximately 27,000 US troops) and a large stock of pre-positioned military equipment ready for immediate deployment should hostilities break out. The tension on the Korean Peninsula is heightened by North Korea's long-range missile capabilities and its continuing research into nuclear, biological, and chemical weapons. On October 9, 2006, North Korea claimed that it had successfully detonated a nuclear device. Ongoing efforts to resolve the status of North Korea's nuclear weapons and energy programs have occurred in the context of the "six-party talks" (North Korea, China, Japan, Russia, South Korea, and the United States).

Table 2.1 summarizes selected economic and military data for North and South Korea and for the South's ally, the United States. The data on armed forces and conventional weapons for the United States represent US deployment on the Korean Peninsula. Three summary observations follow. First, North Korea's national output or gross domestic product (GDP) in 2007 was less than 4 percent of South Korea's GDP. On a per person basis, North Korea produced only $1,900 worth of goods and services in 2007, whereas South Korea created $24,600. These figures are striking because North Korea's per capita GDP and economic growth rate were greater than the South's in the years immediately after the Korean War (Kim 2003, p. 77). The stagnation of North Korea's production is all the more shocking given that approximately 2.5 million of its people starved to death between 1995 and 1997 (Natsios 2001, pp. 212–215). Second, North Korea's defense burden is extraordinarily high. In 2003, North Korea devoted 22.9 percent of its GDP to military spending. To put that figure in perspective, data elsewhere for 2003 show that only three other countries, Afghanistan, Eritrea, and Oman, had defense burdens exceeding 10 percent (Stockholm International Peace Research Institute 2007, pp. 317–323). Despite widespread famine in the 1990s and on-going problems with food provision, North Korea continues to deploy over one million troops and a substantial number of weapons. Third, the 189,000 paramilitary forces actively deployed in North Korea is a huge number compared to the number deployed by the South. Although North Korea fears its external enemies, its leaders also fear internal unrest, as evidenced by the large number of paramilitary forces.

We can use the production possibilities model to explore three elements that have contributed to North Korea's severe economic and humanitarian problems: high defense burden, sclerotic central planning, and paucity of external trade. As shown in Figure 2.4(a), a high defense burden leads to resource diversion along a production possibilities frontier. If crowding out of capital accumulation outweighs crowding in and growth spin-offs from defense, then a high defense burden will stifle growth and possibly even shift the production possibilities frontier inward (negative growth). A second source of economic decay in North Korea is communist central planning. When a few leaders attempt to answer for a large population the vastly complex questions of what will be produced, who will produce it, and who will receive it, economic stagnation eventually emerges. Central planning tends to stifle movements of labor and capital into new industries and locations, causing an economy to operate at an inefficient point inside the PPF, such as point *I* in Figure 2.4(b). Moreover, when the distribution of the fruits of new investments is determined by central planners, initiative and innovation can be stunted, causing the PPF to grow more slowly than it would otherwise. Third, as a somewhat insular economy, North Korea has pursued comparatively little external trade. For example, exports in 2003 as a percentage of GDP were estimated to be 5.3 percent for North Korea as compared to 23.5 percent for South Korea. As we saw in Figure 2.2, external trade allows a state to consume goods and services beyond what it is able to produce in isolation. To the extent that North Korea pursues little trade, it ends up on an unnecessarily low indifference curve much like *aa* in Figure 2.3(c).

2.3. Bibliographic Notes

Production function concepts in general and the Cobb-Douglas production function in particular are covered in intermediate microeconomics texts (e.g., Nicholson and Snyder 2008). Graphical presentations of the production possibilities model are available in economics principles texts (e.g., Mankiw 2007), with more advanced treatments in many intermediate microeconomics books (e.g., Pindyck and Rubenfeld 2009). Principles texts generally cover comparative advantage and the gains from trade, but few do so using the production possibilities model. For coverage of these topics in a production possibilities framework, see intermediate microeconomics texts (e.g., Pindyck and Rubenfeld 2009, Waldman 2009) or international trade texts (e.g., Krugman and Obstfeld 2009). Virtually all principles and intermediate texts in macroeconomics cover economic growth (see, e.g., Hall and Papell 2005, Taylor and Weerapana 2009).

Benoit's (1973) path-breaking study of the effects of defense spending on economic growth stimulated a vast literature. Based on a sample of 44 developing countries over the 1950–65 period, Benoit (1973, p. xix) concluded that the more that countries "spent on defense, in relation to the size of their economies, the faster they grew – and vice versa." Since Benoit, studies have employed more sophisticated models and methods, included developed economies in the samples, and considered more channels by which defense spending might affect growth (see, e.g., Deger and Sen 1995, Ram 1995, Aslam 2007). In a review of the literature, Dunne, Smith, and Willenbockel (2005) conclude that defense spending is a significant determinant of economic growth (positive in some studies, negative in others) in the conflict economics literature but not in the mainstream growth literature. They attribute the mixed message from the two literatures to the use of different theoretical models.

For recent studies of North Korea's economy and security, see Kim (2003) and Cha and Kang (2005). For an in-depth analysis of North Korea's 1995–97 famine, see Natsios (2001). Han (2005) provides an overview of North Korea's food problems.

3

Rational Choice and Equilibrium

Economic analysis of conflict normally rests on either or both of two organizing principles, namely, rationality and equilibrium. Rationality pertains to how actors choose purposefully among alternatives, while equilibrium involves how the choices of different actors are coordinated. We highlight the two principles by reviewing in turn the economic models of consumer choice and supply and demand. Along the way, we explore several issues in conflict economics, including the fungibility of foreign aid and military goods, the ban on land mines, the difficulties of controlling small arms trade, and the liberal peace hypothesis.

3.1. Rational Choice Model

Rational choice theory assumes that an actor has consistent preferences over alternatives and chooses from among the best alternatives available. The actor might be a consumer, producer, voter, politician, insurgent, terrorist, nation-state, or any number of other entities. Here we sketch a basic consumer choice model, so we assume that the actor is a consumer. Specifically, we suppose that the consumer chooses among alternative combinations or baskets of two commodities labeled X (say food) and Y (say housing). He operates with a fixed income I per day, which he spends completely on the two commodities at prices P_X and P_Y. His rational choice problem is to choose the most preferred basket that he can afford given his budget. The two basic elements of the problem are then his preferences and his budget constraint, which we can treat separately before combining them to determine his optimal choice.

Preferences

Rational choice assumes that preferences over alternatives are complete and transitive. Completeness means that when comparing any two alternative

28

baskets *a* and *b*, our consumer can determine whether he prefers *a* to *b*, prefers *b* to *a*, or is indifferent between *a* and *b*. Transitivity means that his various comparisons of this sort are consistent with one another. For example, given three alternative baskets *a*, *b*, and *c*, if he prefers *a* to *b* and *b* to *c*, then it is assumed that he prefers *a* to *c*. Similarly, if he is indifferent between *a* and *b* and between *b* and *c*, then he is indifferent between *a* and *c*. Putting completeness and transitivity together, rationality assumes that our consumer has a subjective ordering over all baskets, with more preferred baskets ranked higher, less preferred baskets ranked lower, and possible ties of indifference along the way. Notice that this rank ordering is independent of his budget constraint; hence it tells us which baskets he would most like to have without consideration of cost. Analytically, we can represent the rank ordering in two essentially equivalent ways, graphically with indifference curves and algebraically with utility functions.

Indifference Curves
An indifference curve for our consumer is a locus of points representing alternative baskets among which he is indifferent. A full collection of indifference curves is called an indifference map and represents his complete rank ordering of preferences. In Figure 3.1 we show just three of what would be an

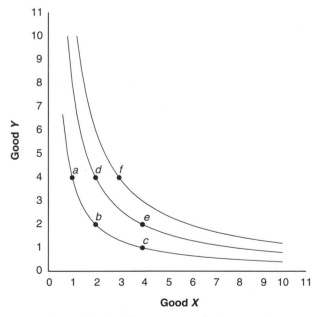

Figure 3.1. Indifference curves for two goods.

infinite number of curves in our consumer's indifference map. In drawing
the curves we have assumed that both commodities are strictly goods for our
consumer, meaning that he always prefers more of each. In later chapters we
will have occasion to consider cases in which one of the commodities, say X,
is a bad, so that the consumer prefers to have less of X rather than more.

The figure depicts several properties of indifference curves. First, points
on an indifference curve are equally preferred by definition. Thus, for
example, baskets a (with $X = 1$ and $Y = 4$) and c (with $X = 4$ and $Y = 1$)
are equally preferred. Second, points on higher indifference curves are
more preferred, because the commodities are goods and preferences are
transitive. For example, according to these hypothetical indifference
curves, basket f (with $X = 3$ and $Y = 4$) is preferred to basket e (with $X = 4$
and $Y = 2$). Third, although indifference curves can squeeze together or
spread apart, they most certainly cannot intersect, because preferences are
transitive and hence consistent.

As a fourth property, notice that in Figure 3.1 the indifference curves
slope downward. Because both commodities are goods, our consumer is
willing to substitute between the two goods, that is, to give up some of one
good in return for more of the other good. Consider baskets a, b, and c,
which all lie on the same indifference curve. Because our consumer would
be neither better off nor worse off, we know that he would be just willing to
move from basket a to basket b, that is, to give up 2 units of Y for 1 added
unit of X. Likewise, he would be just willing to move from a to c, that is, to
give up 3 units of Y for 3 added units of X. In this manner, we can generate
various descriptions of our consumer's willingness to substitute between X
and Y, beginning from basket a. We standardize these descriptions by
focusing on the slope of his indifference curve at point a. Assume that a
precise measurement of the slope at a shows $\Delta Y/\Delta X = -4/1 = -4$. This
then means that beginning from basket a, our consumer is just willing to
substitute between X and Y at a rate of $4Y$ per unit of X. For convenience,
we drop the minus sign and define the marginal rate of substitution (or
MRS) between X and Y at any given point as the absolute value of the slope
of the indifference curve at that same point. Because the MRS measures the
amount of Y that our consumer is just willing to give up per added unit of
X, we can think of the MRS as a measure of his subjective value of X in
terms of Y. So at point a, for example, we can say that his subjective value
of a unit of X is equivalent to $4Y$. Notice that the shape of the indifference
curve through a indicates that the MRS diminishes with rightward
movements along the curve. For example, the absolute slope and hence the
subjective value of X is smaller at point c than at point a.

Table 3.1. *Utilities assigned by the function*
$U = xy.$

Basket	Quantities (x,y)	Utility $U = xy$
a	(1,4)	4
b	(2,2)	4
c	(4,1)	4
d	(2,4)	8
e	(4,2)	8
f	(3,4)	12

Utility Functions

A utility function is a numerical rule that preserves the rank ordering of preferences. In particular, it is a function that assigns higher numbers to more preferred baskets, lower numbers to less preferred baskets, and equal numbers to equally preferred baskets. Thus a utility function can be thought of simply as a rule according to which baskets on higher indifference curves are assigned higher numbers, where these numbers are called utilities. Suppose our consumer has preferences over X and Y as depicted in Figure 3.1. Now consider the following algebraic utility function $U = xy$, which assigns to any basket a utility equal to the product of the respective quantities of goods X and Y. This is an example of what is called a Cobb-Douglas utility function, which has the general form $U = x^\alpha y^\beta$, with the exponents in this case both equal to one. Is this a valid utility function for our consumer's preferences? That is, does it correctly preserve his rank ordering over alternative baskets?

In Table 3.1, we show how the utility function assigns numbers to the various baskets labeled in Figure 3.1. Notice that the utilities assigned to baskets a, b, and c are all equal, correctly indicating that the baskets are equally preferred. Likewise, the utilities assigned to baskets d and e are equal, showing that these baskets are equally preferred. Lastly, notice that the utility of 12 assigned to f is greater than the utility of 8 assigned to d and e, which is greater than the utility of 4 assigned to a, b, and c, correctly indicating that baskets on higher indifference curves are more preferred. In this way we can confirm that the utility function $U = xy$ is indeed a valid utility function for our consumer, because it accurately preserves his rank ordering of preferences.

The utility function $U = xy$ correctly represents one set of preferences, in particular those depicted by the indifference map in Figure 3.1. If our

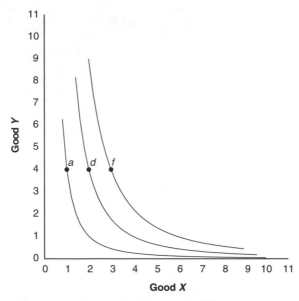

Figure 3.2. Comparatively steeper indifference curves.

consumer had different preferences, they necessarily would be represented by a different utility function. Suppose, for example, that our consumer's preferences change so that in general his subjective valuation of X in terms of Y is now greater. Then his preferences might look like those depicted in Figure 3.2. Notice that his indifference curves through points a, d, and f are now steeper than are the curves through the same three points in Figure 3.1, thus showing higher marginal rates of substitution between X and Y. Because his preferences have changed, so too has his utility function. His new preferences are accurately represented by the utility function $U = x^2 y$, as the reader can confirm with numerical computations similar to those in Table 3.1. Notice that the exponent on the quantity of good X is now higher, which reflects his higher subjective valuation of X in terms of Y.

Budget Constraint

Our consumer is not free to choose just any basket of X and Y, but rather only those baskets that he can afford given his income I and the market prices P_X and P_Y. Assuming he spends all of his available income, we can write his budget constraint as the equation $P_X x + P_Y y = I$, which in words says that his expenditures on X plus his expenditures on Y must equal his available income. Solving for y, we can write $y = (I/P_Y) - (P_X/P_Y)x$, which when graphed will

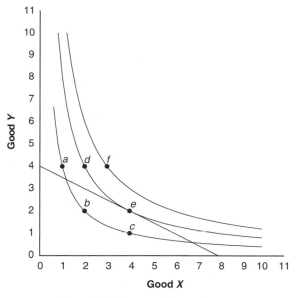

Figure 3.3. Consumption optimum.

plot as a straight line. The vertical intercept is I/P_Y, which is the maximum amount of Y that can be purchased if all income is spent on Y. The slope is $-(P_X/P_Y)$, which is the negative of the relative price of X in terms of Y. Points on the budget line represent baskets that our consumer is just able to afford.

Suppose, for example, that our consumer has an income of $I = \$4$ per day and faces prices of $P_X = \$0.50$ and $P_Y = \$1.00$. The maximum amount of Y that he can purchase is $I/P_Y = \$4/\$1 = 4$, which fixes the vertical intercept of the budget constraint at $4Y$. For the slope, we need the relative price of X, meaning the number of units of Y that our consumer would necessarily forgo if he purchased 1 added unit of X. One unit of X costs \$0.50, which could be used alternatively to purchase one-half unit of Y. Thus, the relative price of X is $P_X/P_Y = \$0.50/\$1 = 0.5$ units of Y, so that the slope of the budget constraint is -0.5. In Figure 3.3 we plot the resulting budget line, which shows all of the baskets that our consumer can afford. Also shown are the earlier indifference curves from Figure 3.1 for the original preferences.

Optimal Choice

Our consumer's choice problem is to choose the most preferred basket given his budget. Because his preferences can be represented with either an indifference map or a utility function, we can model the problem in either of two ways: as a geometric task of reaching the highest indifference curve along his budget line, or as a calculus exercise of maximizing utility subject to his budget constraint. Here we take the former approach, which is comparatively straightforward using Figure 3.3. Our consumer is free to choose any basket within his budget. Because baskets on higher indifference curves are more preferred, he would want to choose the basket lying on the highest indifference curve along his budget line. As shown, his consumption optimum occurs at basket e, which consists of $4X$ and $2Y$. Notice that the indifference curve passing through e is just tangent to his budget line. Hence, at the optimum, his MRS (the absolute slope of the indifference curve) is equal to the relative price of X (the absolute slope of the budget line). This means that the amount of Y that he is just willing to give up to consume his marginal unit of X is equal to the amount of Y that he must give up to purchase that unit of X. At any other point along his budget line, either his subjective value of X would exceed the cost of X in terms of Y, so he would want to buy more X, or the subjective value would be less than the cost, and he would want to buy less X.

Individual Demand

The amounts of X and Y included in the consumption optimum are called the quantities demanded of X and Y, respectively. In the example in Figure 3.3, our consumer's quantities demanded are $4X$ and $2Y$. To extend the analysis without getting into more detail than needed, we focus now on the quantity demanded of just one of the goods, in particular that of X. Holding our consumer's preferences constant, if for some reason his budget line changes, so too will his optimum and hence his quantity demanded of X. The systematic relationship between his quantity demanded of X and the income and price parameters of his budget line is called his demand function for X. In exploring the demand function, we will restrict our attention to how quantity demanded changes when either income or the price of X changes. Also, to simplify, we will develop our graphical analysis more generally, without use of explicit numerical values.

Change in Income
We begin by considering the question of what happens to quantity demanded of X if income increases, holding preferences and prices constant. If X is a good, so that more is preferred to less, ordinarily we expect

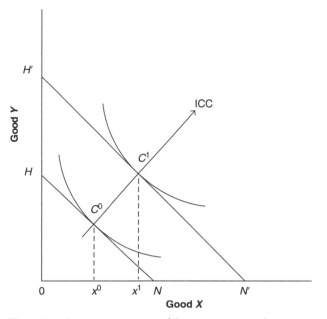

Figure 3.4. Income response and income-consumption curve.

the quantity demanded to increase when income increases. In Figure 3.4 we show our consumer's initial situation with budget line *HN*, consumption optimum C^0, and quantity demanded x^0. When his income increases, the vertical intercept of his budget line rises, because the maximum amount of *Y* that he can purchase is now higher. The slope of the budget line is unchanged, however, because the relative price of *X* is unchanged. Thus, his budget line shifts upward to a new parallel budget line denoted $H'N'$, resulting in a new optimum C^1. The line that traces out the movement in the consumption optimum is called the income-consumption curve (or ICC), which by convention points in the direction of higher utility. As anticipated, the increase in income results in an increase in quantity demanded from x^0 to x^1. Because this is the ordinary case, we say that *X* is a normal good for our consumer. Some goods, however, can be inferior, meaning that quantity demanded can actually decrease with an increase in income. An example for our consumer might be bus transportation. Over higher ranges of income, he might choose less transportation by bus, perhaps because he could now afford more travel by car. If *X* was indeed an inferior good, then in Figure 3.4 the new consumption optimum C^1 would lie somewhere to the left of C^0, causing the ICC to point toward the northwest.

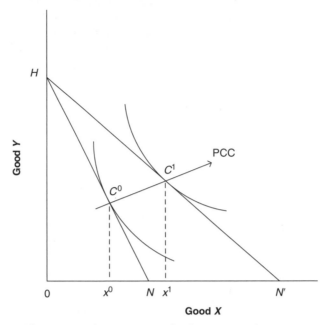

Figure 3.5. Price response and price-consumption curve.

Change in Price

We are ready now to consider the key question of what happens to quantity demanded of X if the price of X decreases, holding preferences, income, and the price of Y constant. According to the law of demand, we expect price and quantity demanded to move in opposite directions. Thus, we expect quantity demanded to increase when price decreases. Figure 3.5 illustrates the law of demand. Assume initially that the price of X is P_X^0, which generates budget line HN, consumption optimum C^0, and quantity demanded x^0. Suppose now that the price decreases to P_X^1. The vertical intercept of the budget line remains fixed, because neither income nor the price of Y changes. The relative price of X falls, however, causing the absolute slope of the budget line to decrease. Thus, our consumer's budget line rotates outward to HN', resulting in a new optimum C^1. The line that traces out the movement in the consumption optimum is called the price-consumption curve (or PCC), which like the ICC points in the direction of higher utility. In accordance with the law of demand, the decrease in the price of X results in an increase in quantity demanded from x^0 to x^1.

    To focus on the relationship between price and quantity demanded, we can draw information from the PCC to construct our consumer's demand

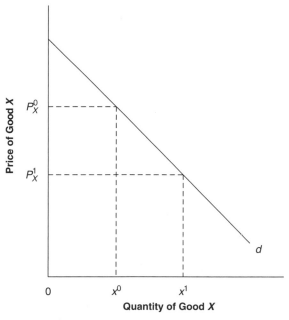

Figure 3.6. Individual demand curve.

curve for X shown in Figure 3.6. For example, from budget line HN and optimum C^0 in Figure 3.5 we can take the price P_X^0 and the corresponding quantity demanded x^0, which yields one point on his demand curve in Figure 3.6. Similarly, from HN' and optimum C^1 we can take the price P_X^1 and the quantity x^1, which yields a second point on his demand curve. Repeating the process at other optimums along the PCC, we can generate our consumer's complete demand curve, which shows the quantity demanded for any given price of X, holding income and the price of Y constant. Notice the preceding ceteris paribus clause. If income or the price of Y were to change, then the PCC in Figure 3.5 and hence the demand curve in Figure 3.6 would change. For example, assuming that X is a normal good, an increase in our consumer's income would cause his entire demand curve to shift to the right, indicating a larger quantity demanded at any given price.

Substitution and Income Effects
According to the law of demand, we expect quantity demanded to increase when price decreases, other things equal. Economic theory identifies two distinct causes for the change in quantity demanded. First, the decrease in the price of X makes X relatively cheaper, thereby creating an incentive to

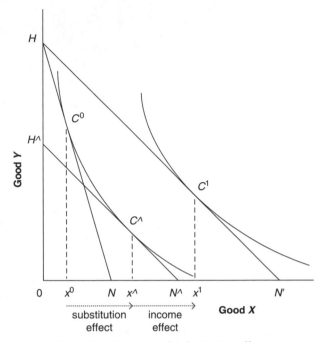

Figure 3.7. Income and substitution effects.

substitute more of X for the other good Y. Second, the fall in the price of X generates an increase in real income, that is, in the purchasing power of our consumer's nominal income I; this in turn creates an incentive to demand more X, assuming that X is a normal good. These two sources of change in quantity demanded are called the substitution and income effects, which we illustrate in Figure 3.7. Initially, the price of X is P_X^0, which generates budget line HN, consumption optimum C^0, and quantity demanded x^0. Suppose the price of X decreases to P_X^1, which produces budget line HN', consumption optimum C^1, and quantity demanded x^1. The change in quantity demanded from x^0 to x^1 can now be decomposed into the underlying substitution and income effects.

   To first isolate the substitution effect, imagine that nominal income is somehow withdrawn hypothetically from our consumer until the best that he can do is to secure his original level of utility despite the lower price P_X^1. Graphically, this means shifting his final budget line HN' back in a parallel manner to $H\wedge N\wedge$, thereby generating hypothetical optimum $C\wedge$ and hypothetical quantity demanded $x\wedge$. Compared to the initial budget line HN, the hypothetical budget line $H\wedge N\wedge$ is less steep, thus showing the decreased relative price of X. At the same time, between the initial optimum C^0 and the hypothetical optimum $C\wedge$, our consumer's utility is the same, meaning in that respect that his real income is unchanged. Therefore, the change in quantity demanded from x^0 to $x\wedge$ must be due entirely to the decrease in the relative price of X and thus measures the substitution effect.

To get at the income effect, suppose that the hypothetically withdrawn income is now returned to our consumer. His hypothetical budget line $H\wedge N\wedge$ shifts parallel out to his final budget line HN', yielding his final optimum C^1 and final quantity demanded x^1. The two budget lines are equally steep, thus showing no change between them in the relative price of X. At the same time, between the hypothetical optimum $C\wedge$ and the final optimum C^1, our consumer's utility is higher, meaning in that respect that his real income is increased. Therefore, the change in quantity demanded from $x\wedge$ to x^1 must be due entirely to the increase in real income and thus measures the income effect.

The decomposition shows that the total change in quantity demanded $(x^1 - x^0)$ is the sum of a substitution effect $(x\wedge - x^0)$, which is due to a change in relative price, and an income effect, $(x^1 - x\wedge)$, which is due to a change in real income. We conclude the analysis with two subtle but important points. The first is that given the assumptions of the consumer choice model, the substitution effect will always move quantity demanded in the direction opposite to that of the price change. This result is referred to as the substitution principle: when price decreases, there is always created the incentive to substitute toward the good; when price increases, there is always created the incentive to substitute away from the good. This principle ultimately provides the basis for the law of demand, which brings us to our second point. In Figure 3.7 we have assumed that X is a normal good, so that the income effect reinforces the substitution effect. If X was an inferior good, the arrangement of indifference curves would instead place the final optimum C^1 to the left of $C\wedge$, meaning that the income effect would decrease quantity demanded, while the substitution effect would still increase quantity demanded as required by the substitution principle. The reader might then ask whether the income effect for an inferior good could more than offset the substitution effect, thereby setting up a violation of the law of demand. As a theoretical possibility, the answer is a surprising yes; as an empirical probability, the answer is almost always no. The law of demand has been observed with such regularity that the dominance of the substitution effect can be asserted with high confidence. Indeed, it is the regularity of the law of demand that accounts for why the inverse relationship between price and quantity earns such special status, that of a scientific law.

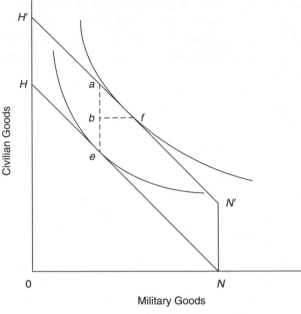

Figure 3.8. Fungibility of foreign aid.

Applications

Arms and the Fungibility of Foreign Aid

Many governments and nongovernmental organizations provide humanitarian aid to nations suffering from war and its aftermath. One of the major challenges is how to prevent aid from inadvertently stimulating the recipient's acquisition of military goods. This is an example of the fungibility problem whereby the aid recipient reduces the allocation of indigenous income to the sector receiving aid and increases the allocation of income to one or more other sectors. Here we use the rational choice model to depict an aid recipient's incentive to increase its military goods, even when the aid package is designed to strictly support nonmilitary activities.

Figure 3.8 shows the effects of pure civilian aid on the recipient's allocation of resources between military and civilian goods. Think of the aid as food, clothing, or medical supplies earmarked for nonmilitary purposes. The recipient might be a nation or a non-state group, while the donor might be an intergovernmental organization (IGO) like the United Nations, a nongovernmental organization (NGO) like the Red Cross, or a sympathetic foreign government. In the figure, the recipient's consumption optimum without aid occurs at point *e* on budget line *HN*. When the donor supplies *ae* units of civilian goods as aid, the recipient's budget line shifts up by that same vertical distance. The new consumption optimum occurs at point f on budget line $H'N'N$. Notice that the aid package, though purely civilian, has served to increase the amount of military goods consumed. In Figure 3.8, the aid package of ae units of civilian goods has made it possible for the recipient to reduce its own acquisition of civilian goods by ab, thereby freeing up enough income to purchase bf additional units of military goods.

Land Mines and the Substitution Principle

We have introduced the rationality principle in the context of consumer choice, but as noted earlier, actors in rational choice models can take on a variety of identities. For example, most economic theory assumes that producers, like consumers, are rational. In particular, producers are assumed to minimize cost for any given output or to maximize output for any given cost. The parallels between consumer choice models and producer choice models are abundant and close, as we illustrate with the following application dealing with land mines.

The use of land mines in various interstate and civil wars around the world has caused not only severe civilian casualties but also serious economic dislocations, including the abandonment of fertile farmlands due to fear of mines (Merrouche 2008). In order to control the proliferation of land mines, the Antipersonnel Mine-Ban Treaty (also known as the Land Mine Treaty or the Ottawa Convention) was entered into force in 1999; it has a current membership of 156 nations. To the extent that the treaty is effective, its direct impact is to reduce the supply of land mines and thus raise the price to nonsignatories.

In Figure 3.9 we assume that a rebel organization in a civil war attempts to maximize the amount of territory it controls by allocating a fixed income between two military inputs – land mines and young males armed with assault rifles. Given associated input prices, the fixed income generates a cost constraint, as shown in either panel by the budget line HN. Also shown are representative isoquants, as they are called in production theory. An isoquant is a locus of points showing alternative input combinations that can be used to produce the same amount of output, in this case territory controlled. Isoquants in many ways are analogous to indifference curves. For example, higher isoquants correspond to larger outputs, and isoquants ordinarily slope downward. The rebel organization is free to choose any combination of inputs within its budget. In order to maximize the territory controlled, it chooses an input combination lying on the highest isoquant along its budget line, as shown by point e in either panel.

Now suppose that the Land Mine Treaty is successful in raising the price of mines, which in either panel causes the rebels' budget line to rotate inward to *HN'*. In accordance with the law of demand, and consistent with the aims of the treaty, the rebels respond to the price increase by reducing their use of land mines at the new optimum *f*. Driving the response is the substitution principle, whereby the higher price of land mines creates an incentive to substitute away from mines in favor of young males with assault rifles. What distinguishes the two panels of Figure 3.9 is the strength of this substitution. In panel (a), the substitution effect is assumed to be relatively small, implying limited substitutability between land mines and young males. As a result, the decrease in mines is comparatively small. This means that when the limited cutback in mines is combined with the higher cost per mine, the rebels' expenditures on land mines actually increase. Given their budget constraint, this in turn leads the rebels to decrease also their use of young males. Alternatively, in panel (b), the substitution effect is assumed to be relatively large, implying easier substitutability between land mines and young males. As a consequence, the decrease in mines is comparatively large. However, as an unintended consequence, the rebels in this case actually increase their use of young males with assault rifles. Despite the higher cost per mine, the decrease in the number of mines is large enough to cause expenditures on land mines to fall. This decrease in land mine expenditures then frees up income and permits the rebels to finance an increase in the use of young males. In brief, the substitution principle in Figure 3.9 sets up a dilemma: the more responsive the rebels are to the increased price of mines, the more likely it is that the treaty will have what are perhaps unintended consequences in

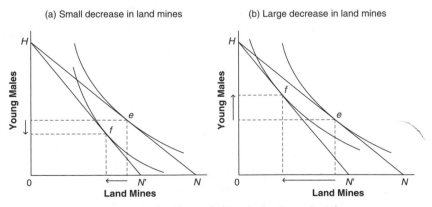

Figure 3.9. Land mines and the substitution principle.

the increased use of other weapons. However, both panels show that the rebel group will end up on a lower isoquant. Hence, regardless of the strength of the substitution between land mines and young males, the higher cost of land mines reduces the territory controlled by the rebels, other things equal.

3.2. Supply, Demand, and Market Equilibrium

Markets typically consist of large numbers of buyers and sellers. The buyers and sellers make hundreds and thousands of choices independently, and yet somehow a consistency of choices emerges. Most of the time, the consumers can buy what they want, based on their incomes and the prices paid, and the producers can sell what they want, based on their costs and the prices received. Market incentives on both sides cause participants to adjust their choices to a point that permits their consumption and production plans to be realized. In economic analysis, this point is called an equilibrium, and it arises systematically from the forces of market supply and demand.

Supply and Demand

Figure 3.10 depicts the demand and supply conditions in a hypothetical market for cereal. The demand curve D shows at any given price the

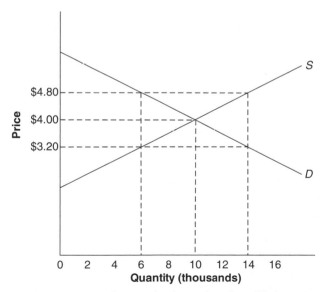

Figure 3.10. Market supply, demand, and equilibrium.

corresponding quantity demanded per week by consumers, holding preferences, incomes, and other prices fixed. The negative slope depicts the law of demand, according to which price and quantity demanded are inversely related. When the price per box of cereal is $4.80, for example, the corresponding quantity demanded in the market is shown to be six thousand boxes per week. If the price falls to $3.20, quantity demanded increases to 14 thousand, as consumers direct more of their consumption toward cereal, which now provides a relatively cheaper breakfast. It is important to recognize that if one of the other variables in the demand relationship changes, then the entire demand curve will shift its position. For example, if cereal is a normal good and incomes rise, then demand for cereal will increase. This means that the demand curve will shift to the right, indicating that at any given price consumers are now willing to buy a larger quantity. Similarly, an increase in the price of a substitute good like eggs will increase the demand for cereal, meaning again that the entire demand curve will shift to the right, as consumers substitute away from relatively more expensive eggs at breakfast. Working in the opposite direction, an increase in the price of a complement good like milk will tend to decrease the demand for cereal, shifting the demand curve to the left, as consumers move away from the consumption of milk used with cereal.

The supply curve S in Figure 3.10 shows at any given price the corresponding quantity supplied by producers, holding technology and input prices fixed. The positive slope depicts the law of supply, according to which price and quantity supplied are directly related. Producers are profit maximizers and thus are willing to supply only those units of output that generate profit. In Figure 3.10, for example, if the price per box of cereal is $3.20, producers are willing to supply six thousand but only six thousand boxes of cereal; thus we can infer that boxes of cereal beyond that quantity are too costly to produce at that price. If, however, the price rises to $4.80, some of those more costly units become profitable, causing quantity supplied to increase now to 14 thousand boxes. As on the demand side, changes in one of the other variables in the supply relationship will cause the entire supply curve to shift. For example, if a technological improvement lowers costs, then more units of output can be profitably produced; as a result, the supply of cereal will increase, meaning that the entire supply curve will shift to the right. Working in the opposite direction, if the price of an input like grain increases, then costs will be higher and supply will decrease, meaning that the supply curve will shift to the left.

Market Equilibrium

An equilibrium can be thought of generally as a resting point that occurs when opposing forces are in balance. In the context of a competitive market, it is a price at which the plans of both buyers and sellers can be realized. Given an equilibrium price, consumers are able to buy those quantities they want to consume, and producers are able to sell those quantities they want to produce. Hence, it is a price at which quantity demanded equals quantity supplied in the market.

Figure 3.10 illustrates how the forces of supply and demand tend to generate a market equilibrium. To begin, suppose that the price of cereal is $4.80 per box. As shown in Figure 3.10, the quantity supplied is 14 thousand boxes per week, while the quantity demanded is six thousand. This means that of the 14 thousand boxes that producers plan to sell, consumers are willing to buy only six thousand. The surplus of eight thousand boxes that are planned but unsold constitutes an excess supply of cereal. This excess supply signals to producers that the price is too high and creates an incentive for them to decrease the price of cereal. The incentive continues until the price is cut to $4.00 per box. At this price, consumers have increased their quantity demanded to 10 thousand boxes and are able to buy 10 thousand boxes; on the other side, producers have decreased their quantity supplied to 10 thousand boxes and are able to sell 10 thousand boxes. Because the plans of both buyers and sellers are realized, there is no further incentive for change, meaning that $4.00 is the equilibrium price. The same result occurs if the price begins below $4.00. For example, suppose that the price is $3.20, so that consumers plan to buy 14 thousand boxes but producers are willing to sell only six thousand boxes. The shortage of eight thousand boxes constitutes an excess demand for cereal and creates an incentive for producers to raise the price. As the price is raised, the quantity supplied increases and the quantity demanded decreases until equilibrium is reached at the price of $4.00.

Comparative-Static Analysis

The supply and demand model provides a simple but powerful method for explaining and predicting market responses to changes in underlying variables. The method is called comparative-static analysis because it involves the comparison of equilibriums before and after a fundamental change affecting the market. As just one example, suppose that the price of grain falls significantly, perhaps because of an unusually large bumper crop. The effect on the market for cereal is depicted in Figure 3.11. Given

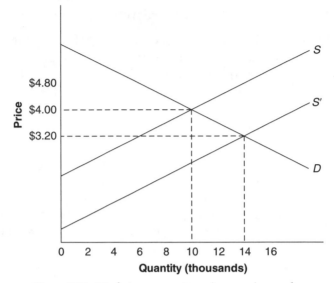

Figure 3.11. Market response to an increase in supply.

demand D and supply S, the initial equilibrium is at a price of $4.00 and a corresponding quantity of 10 thousand boxes. If the price of grain drops, then the cost of producing cereal is reduced. This in turn increases the profitability of cereal production, causing producers to increase their supply. In Figure 3.11 this is shown by the rightward shift of the supply curve from S to S'. Because the price of grain has no direct bearing on consumers' demand for cereal, the demand curve remains unchanged at D. This means that with the same demand D but increased supply S', there exists an excess supply at the original price of $4.00. Consequently, producers are led to cut price so as to encourage consumers to increase their quantity of cereal demanded. When the various adjustments are complete, a new equilibrium emerges with a price of $3.20 and quantity of 14 thousand boxes. Thus, the comparative-static analysis shows that the fall in the price of grain will cause the price of cereal to decrease and the quantity of cereal to increase. Comparative-static analyses proceed similarly for changes involving decreased supply, increased demand, and decreased demand.

Applications

Difficulty of Small Arms Control

Weapons in the contemporary international system fall into three categories: (1) major conventional weapons, such as tanks and fighter aircraft,

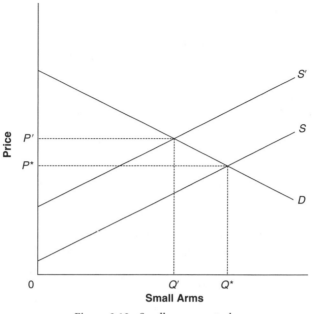

Figure 3.12. Small arms control.

(2) weapons of mass destruction, which include nuclear, biological, chemical, and radiological weapons, and (3) small arms and light weapons, such as assault rifles and improvised explosive devices (known as roadside bombs). Although the data on small arms are relatively sparse, scholars generally agree that in recent decades far more people (including civilians) have been killed by small arms than by major conventional weapons and weapons of mass destruction combined. Hence, efforts to control the production and sale of small arms have been growing among international and regional organizations, nations, and nongovernmental organizations (see Chapter 10 for examples of small arms control organizations and protocols). According to the Small Arms Survey (2004), at least 1,249 companies across more than 90 countries were involved in some aspects of small arms and light-weapons production in 2003. The sizeable number of small arms producers and locales, along with economic incentives in the arms market, makes control of small arms difficult.

Figure 3.12 shows a simple supply and demand model for small arms. The model might apply to the world or to a particular region such as the Middle East or the Horn of Africa. The arms in question might be small arms broadly conceived or a particular class of weapons such as assault rifles. Assume initially that the market is at a long-run equilibrium with price P^* and quantity Q^*, such that arms producers are just able to cover costs and hence earn normal profits on the sale of small arms. Suppose now that an arms control agreement places output restraints on some small arms producers, causing supply to decrease from S to S' in Figure 3.12. The result is that the equilibrium price rises to P' and the equilibrium quantity falls to Q'. The supply restraint appears effective, but the new equilibrium is only a short-run outcome. If the underlying cost conditions of arms producers are unchanged, then the higher price P' reflects an above-normal profit opportunity for the production of small arms. Hence, firms restricted by the agreement have the incentive to secretly increase output, unrestricted firms are eager to expand production, and new firms are drawn to enter the small arms business. The result over the long run is that the supply curve will tend to shift back to its original position until the industry is returned to normal profitability again with price P^* and quantity Q^*. The lesson suggested by the model is that small arms restraints that do not increase producers' costs generate powerful economic incentives that tend to diminish the effectiveness of the restraints over time.

Liberal Peace Hypothesis

According to the liberal peace hypothesis, salient trade between two nations makes it less likely they will fight each other, everything else the same. Figure 3.13 presents a theoretical rationale for the liberal peace

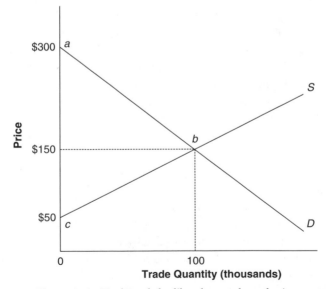

Figure 3.13. Trade and the liberal peace hypothesis.

hypothesis based on the supply and demand model. For simplicity, we assume bilateral trade between two nations A and B. In this context, the demand curve D represents nation A's demand for imports from nation B, and the supply curve S represents nation B's supply of exports to nation A. Since A's imports equal B's exports in a two-nation model, we can measure the quantity of trade as a single variable on the horizontal axis. For the hypothetical demand and supply curves in Figure 3.13, trade equilibrium occurs at a price of $150 and a quantity of 100 thousand.

At this equilibrium the associated aggregate gains from trade for A and B equal the area of triangle *abc*. To understand the gains-from-trade triangle, it is helpful to see that demand and supply curves can be read not only horizontally but also vertically. If read horizontally, the demand curve in Figure 3.13 shows that when the price is $150, nation A is willing to import units of trade up to and including the 100 thousandth unit. This means that the highest price A is willing to pay for the 100 thousandth unit, and hence A's subjective valuation of that unit, is $150. The same logic implies more generally that the vertical distance up to the demand curve shows A's subjective valuation for any given unit of trade. Similarly, the supply curve shows that at a price of $150, nation B is willing to export units of trade up to and including the 100 thousandth unit. This implies that B's cost of producing the 100 thousandth unit, and hence the lowest price at which B is willing to sell it, is $150. Thus, the vertical distance up to the supply curve shows B's cost for any given unit of trade.

With these principles in mind, consider the first unit traded between A and B. Nation A values this first unit at very close to $300, as reflected by the vertical intercept of $300 on the demand curve. Yet A only has to pay the equilibrium price of $150 to obtain the first unit, thus generating a gain from trade of close to $150 for that unit. On the other side, the cost of the first unit to B is very close to $50, as reflected by the vertical intercept of the supply curve. Yet B receives $150 when it exports the first unit, thus generating a gain from trade of close to $100 for that unit. Hence, for A and B together the gains from trade from the first unit traded is equal to $250, the vertical gap between the demand and supply curves. When the gains are computed similarly on all successive units traded, it can be seen that the total of the gains from trade at the equilibrium quantity of 100 thousand is equal to the area of the triangle *abc*. Computing the area of the triangle as one-half base times height, the resulting aggregate gains from trade in Figure 3.13 equal $12.5 million.

These gains provide a plausible explanation of the liberal peace hypothesis. Suppose that if war broke out between nations A and B, then

Table 3.2. *Taxonomy of goods with examples.*

	Excludable	Nonexcludable
Rival	Private good (e.g., cereal, medicine)	Common-resource good (e.g., fish in open waters, clean air)
Nonrival	Club good (e.g., proprietary Web site, satellite radio)	Public good (e.g., antimissile defense system, FM radio)

political and economic decisions would lead to the termination of trade between them. In Figure 3.13, trade quantity would go to zero. Unless some or all of this trade could be recovered elsewhere, A and B would lose gains equal to the trade triangle abc. Hence, the gains from trade that would be forgone raise the opportunity cost of war and thereby reduce the likelihood of war between A and B, everything else the same.

3.3. A Taxonomy of Goods

The supply and demand model is useful for understanding the market allocation of private goods like cereal. In economics terminology, however, not all goods are private. Goods can be classified as to whether they are rival or nonrival, and also as to whether they are excludable or nonexcludable. A good is rival if one person's consumption of a unit precludes another person's consumption of that same unit, and it is excludable if selected persons can be excluded from its consumption.

As summarized in Table 3.2, these characteristics combine to define four types of goods. (1) A private good is both rival and excludable. Cereal is a typical private good. One person's consumption of cereal necessarily means that the same cereal is unavailable to a second person; furthermore, suppliers can exclude those consumers who are not willing to pay the requisite price. (2) A public good is both nonrival and nonexcludable. A good example is an antimissile defense system. If one person enjoys the security of such a system, others in the same location can enjoy identical security at no added cost. Moreover, others cannot be excluded from that security, even if they contribute nothing to its cost. (3) A common-resource good is rival but nonexcludable. An example is fish in open waters. When fish are caught by one person, they are not available to be caught by other persons; other persons, however, cannot be excluded from attempting to catch those same fish. (4) A club good is nonrival but excludable. An example is a proprietary Web page that provides valuable data to subscribers. Subscribers can enjoy the use of the data simultaneously, but nonsubscribers are denied access.

The taxonomy in Table 3.2 assumes that the characteristics of rivalry and excludability are dichotomous, meaning that they are either present or absent. It is sometimes useful to assume instead that the characteristics can exist in different degrees. In this case, the types of goods would vary continuously across the two dimensions of rivalry and excludability.

It is important that the labels in Table 3.2 be correctly understood and applied. Private goods are not equivalent to privately provided goods, and public goods are not equivalent to publicly provided goods. Medicine is a private good, yet medicine is sometimes provided by the public sector. Going the other direction, FM radio broadcasts are public goods, but broadcasts are typically provided by the private sector. Thus, a good's type is determined by its characteristics, not by the economic sector through which it is provided or allocated.

That being said, it is true that private goods generally are more easily allocated through private-sector markets than are public goods. Because private goods are rival, additional consumption requires additional production and hence is costly. Because they are also excludable, additional consumption can be rationed by willingness to pay. Putting the two characteristics together, a private good can be allocated easily and efficiently by supply and demand forces, because consumers can be induced to pay for their own consumption and thereby allow producers to cover their costs. The same cannot be said for public goods. Because public goods are nonrival and nonexcludable, each consumer has the incentive to free ride, that is, to share in the consumption of the public good but not in its cost. In the absence of other institutional arrangements, such as tying radio broadcasts to advertisements, free riding by consumers leaves producers in the private sector with no incentive to supply the good.

Distinctions between private and public goods are important in many areas of conflict economics. A nation's deterrence of external enemies is often modeled as a public good: deterrence is nonrival because one person's security does not preclude other persons from enjoying the same security, and it is nonexcludable because individuals can enjoy the security regardless of whether they help cover the cost. In an alliance, two or more nations may find it in their interest to share the burden of defense when military goods used for deterrence purposes are nonrival. Peacekeeping operations can also have public goods characteristics. Establishing peace in a nation experiencing civil war might benefit several surrounding nations at the same time, regardless of whether they contribute to the peacekeeping operation. As a last example, consider resources like water and oil deposits that span national borders or ethnic communities. Such transboundary resources are clearly rival in consumption, but they are also nonexcludable because different groups have direct access to the same resource pool. Potentially violent disputes can arise between nations or groups over the division and optimal rate of depletion, due in large part to the nonexcludability of such common-resource goods.

3.4. Bibliographic Notes

Textbook presentations of the rational choice model, supply and demand, and the taxonomy of goods abound. In roughly ascending order of formalism, some better known texts include Frank (2008), Nicholson and Snyder (2008), Kreps (1990), and Mas-Colell et al. (1995). The utility functions reviewed in this chapter are called ordinal utility functions, because they preserve only the rank ordering of preferences. Some economic analysis, most particularly that involving risk and uncertainty, requires the assumption of cardinal utility, which preserves both the rank ordering and the intensity of preferences. For the extension of rational choice to situations involving chance, see Binmore's (2007) rigorous yet highly accessible treatment of expected utility theory. For references to some critical discussion pertaining to the rationality assumption, see the bibliographic notes for Chapter 1.

McGillivray and Morrissey (2000) review the theoretical and empirical literature on the fungibility of foreign aid. Various perspectives on the past and future of land mine control are available in a special issue of *Third World Quarterly* (Harpviken 2003) and in Chapter 10. Brauer (2007) reviews data and models on arms production and trade, including an overview of small arms and light weapons. Chapters 6 and 7 provide additional analyses and references for the liberal peace hypothesis.

4

Fundamentals of Game Theory

A strategic interaction wherein outcomes are systematically determined by the combination of players' actions is called a game. By this definition, poker and baseball are games, but so are wars and arms rivalries. Because outcomes in games are jointly determined, players' well-being depends not only on their own decisions but also on the decisions of others. This interdependence can greatly complicate any attempted rational choice by the players. It also makes game theory, the formal study of such strategic interaction, both challenging and fascinating.

4.1. Basic Concepts

Elements of a Game

Games consist of certain elements, the specifics of which distinguish the different games. The players may be individuals or groups, including nations. Explicit and/or implicit rules control the feasible actions, order of play, available information, and determination of outcomes. Preferences over outcomes in turn determine players' payoffs or utilities. In basic game theory, players are assumed to have common knowledge of the rationality of all players and of the elements of the game, including payoffs. When these assumptions hold, the game is said to be one of complete information.

To illustrate these elements, consider a simple game that we will refer to as the aggression game. The game involves two players called, generically, *A* and *B*. Player *A* moves first and can either *Aggress* against player *B* or *Refrain*. If *B* is aggressed against, then *B* can either *Retaliate* or *Appease*. For player *A*, assume that the most preferred outcome occurs when *A*'s aggression is followed by *B*'s appeasement; least preferred is aggression met with retaliation; intermediate is the status quo of no aggression. For player

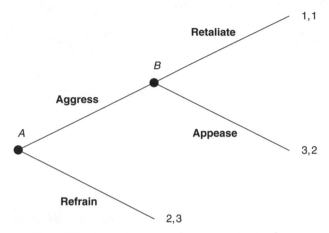

Figure 4.1. Aggression game shown in extensive form.

B, retaliation has a formidable cost. Hence, least preferred by *B* is a retaliatory response to aggression; most preferred is the status quo of no aggression; intermediate is a response of appeasement. Because *A* moves prior to *B*, the game is said to be sequential; because the prior move by *A* is known by *B*, the game involves what is called perfect information.

Extensive and Normal Forms

A game can be represented in either or both of two ways called the extensive form and the normal form. The preferred representation is largely a matter of convenience. As we will see, the extensive form is typically used when moves are sequential and the normal form is more often used when moves are simultaneous.

Figure 4.1 shows the extensive form for the aggression game. Appearing as a tree diagram, the extensive form gives special attention to the order of play and to the information available to the players. Points at which a player is obliged to make a choice are called decision nodes. Branches leading from the nodes represent the actions or moves available to a player. A play of the game generates a path through the tree diagram leading to a particular outcome and a pair of payoffs, with *A*'s payoff listed first. In Figure 4.1 the payoffs are assumed to be ordinal utilities, so that higher numbers indicate more preferred outcomes.

Game theory analyzes a game in terms of the strategies available to the players. A strategy specifies what action the player will take at each and every point at which the player is obliged to make a move. Hence, a

Player B

	Retaliate	Appease
Aggress	1,1	3,2
Refrain	2,3	2,3

Player A (Aggress / Refrain, left labels)

Figure 4.2. Aggression game shown in normal form.

strategy is a complete plan that in principle can be written down in advance and then executed as the play of the game unfolds. In the aggression game, the players' strategies are easily identified. Player A has two strategies *Aggress* and *Refrain*, and player B has two strategies *Retaliate* and *Appease*. Strategies in other games can be more numerous and also more complicated. A strategy profile is a listing of strategies, one for each player. In the aggression game there are four strategy pairs (with A's strategy first): (*Aggress,Retaliate*), (*Aggress,Appease*), (*Refrain,Retaliate*), and (*Refrain,Appease*). Because strategies are complete plans, a strategy profile determines a play of the game and hence a path leading to a particular outcome with payoffs. For example, in Figure 4.1 it can be seen that the strategy pair (*Aggress,Retaliate*) results in payoffs equal to 1 for each player. For the strategy pair (*Refrain,Retaliate*), the play of the game both begins and ends with A's move, resulting in payoffs of 2 for A and 3 for B. Note that B's specified strategy of *Retaliate* means that B will retaliate if the game reaches B's decision node, but the strategy profile determines whether that node will actually be reached during the play of the game.

This leads naturally to the second way that a game can be represented, namely, by its normal form, which gives emphasis to the available strategies and strategy profiles. As shown in Figure 4.2 for the aggression game, the normal form consists of a matrix of payoffs corresponding to the various strategy profiles. For example, if A's strategy *Aggress* in the first row is combined with B's strategy *Retaliate* in the first column, then the strategy profile (*Aggress,Retaliate*) is formed, resulting in the payoff pair (1,1) shown in the top left cell of the matrix and derived in the preceding paragraph. Other profiles and payoff pairs are generated similarly.

Solutions and Equilibriums

Given a game set forth in either extensive or normal form, we want to determine how the game will be played. Equivalently, we want to find the solution of the game expressed in the form of a strategy profile. Think of a solution as a way of playing the game that is compelling and hence is believable for the players and predictable by the theorist. Turning to the aggression game, are there any strategy profiles that qualify as a solution? We might attempt to answer the question by trial and error. For starters, could (*Aggress,Retaliate*) be a solution, that is, a compelling and hence believable way to play the game? The answer is no, shown as follows. If player *A* believed *B* was going to choose *Retaliate*, then *A*'s optimal strategy or best reply would be *Refrain* rather than *Aggress*, because her payoff would then be 2 compared to a lower payoff of 1 (see Figure 4.2). Hence, player *A* would not believe that the game will be played in accordance with the strategy pair (*Aggress,Retaliate*). Similarly, if *B* thought *A* was going to choose *Aggress*, then *B*'s best reply would be *Appease* rather than *Retaliate*, which would return for him a payoff of 2 rather than only 1. Hence, player *B* also would not believe that the game will be played according to the strategy pair (*Aggress,Retaliate*). In short, (*Aggress,Retaliate*) is not a compelling way to play the game and therefore cannot be a solution to the game. Similar reasoning shows that (*Refrain,Appease*) likewise cannot be a solution.

What emerges from this way of thinking is an important principle: if a strategy profile is a solution, then it must be the case that each player's strategy is a best reply to the strategies of the other players. This in turn leads to the concept of Nash equilibrium, defined as a strategy profile wherein each player's strategy is optimal given the equilibrium strategies of the other players. Equivalently, a Nash equilibrium is a strategy profile wherein no player has an incentive to change her or his strategy unilaterally. The original principle can now be restated as follows: if a strategy profile is a solution, then it must be a Nash equilibrium.

A consequence of the principle is that the search for a solution can be narrowed to a systematic identification of Nash equilibriums. The method of search follows from the definition of Nash equilibrium. To keep things simple, assume a two-person game represented in normal form. For each strategy of each player, identify the other player's best reply by underlining the highest payoff available to that player. A Nash equilibrium is then a pair of mutual best replies and is identified by a payoff pair in which both payoffs are underlined.

We can illustrate the method with the aggression game, repeated in normal form in Figure 4.3. We begin by finding player *A*'s best replies. Suppose *B* chooses *Retaliate*. Player *A*'s available payoffs appear in the first column of the payoff matrix and equal 1 if she plays *Aggress* and 2 if she plays *Refrain*. We underline the higher payoff of 2, thereby identifying *A*'s best reply as *Refrain*. Suppose instead that *B* chooses *Appease*. Now *A*'s

Player B

		Retaliate	Appease
Player A	Aggress	1,1	<u>3,2</u>
	Refrain	<u>2,3</u>	2,<u>3</u>

Figure 4.3. Aggression game with Nash equilibriums.

available payoffs appear in the second column and equal 3 if she plays *Aggress* and 2 if she plays *Refrain*. We underline the higher payoff of 3, thereby indicating *A*'s best reply as *Aggress*. We repeat the exercise to find *B*'s best replies. Suppose *A* chooses *Aggress*. Player *B*'s available payoffs are in the first row and equal 1 if he plays *Retaliate* and 2 if he plays *Appease*. We underline the higher payoff of 2, showing *B*'s best reply as *Appease*. Suppose instead that *A* chooses *Refrain*. Now *B*'s available payoffs are in the second row and both equal 3 regardless of whether he plays *Retaliate* or *Appease*. We underline the equal payoffs of 3, indicating that *Retaliate* and *Appease* are equally best replies for *B*.

Using this method, Nash equilibriums are shown by strategy pairs for which both players' payoffs are underlined in the corresponding payoff pair. As seen in Figure 4.3, the aggression game includes two Nash equilibriums (*Refrain,Retaliate*) and (*Aggress,Appease*). According to the Nash equilibrium principle, if a solution exists, it must be one of these two strategy pairs. But which one? In the case of the aggression game, we can push the analysis farther by either of two solution techniques, called iterated dominance and backward induction.

To understand iterated dominance, we need several definitions and another basic principle. When comparing a player's strategies, we say that one strategy strictly dominates another if the first strategy earns a payoff that is strictly higher regardless of what strategy the other player might choose. Hence, one strategy strictly dominates another if it is "always better." Similarly, we say that one strategy weakly dominates another if the first strategy earns a payoff that is (1) at least as high regardless of what strategy the other player might choose and (2) strictly higher for at least one strategy that the other player might choose. Hence, one strategy weakly dominates another if it is "always at least as good and sometimes better." If a single strategy dominates every other strategy available to a player, then it is called a dominant strategy for that player.

Building on these definitions, the dominance principle states that a rational player will not choose a dominated strategy. When the rationality of the players is common knowledge, the dominance principle can be used to eliminate dominated strategies from consideration in the search for a solution. In some games, a dominant strategy exists for each player, meaning that all other strategies can be eliminated. The game is then said to be solved by strict or weak dominance, and the profile consisting of each player's dominant strategy is called a dominant-strategy equilibrium. The best known example of a game solved by strict dominance is the prisoner's dilemma, which we will take up in section 4.2. Unfortunately, most games cannot be solved by either strict or weak dominance. Many games, however, do yield a solution by the repeated application of the dominance principle in a technique known as iterated dominance.

Iterated dominance can be used as follows to solve the aggression game in Figure 4.3. Notice that neither of *A*'s strategies initially dominates the other: *A*'s best reply is *Refrain* if *B* chooses *Retaliate*, but it is *Aggress* if *B* chooses *Appease*. On the other hand, player *B*'s strategy *Appease* weakly dominates *Retaliate*: *B*'s payoff for *Appease* is the same as for *Retaliate* if *A* chooses *Refrain*, and it is strictly higher if *A* chooses *Aggress*. By the dominance principle, player *B* will not choose *Retaliate*, so we can eliminate *Retaliate* from consideration and count on *B* to play *Appease*. But if it is known that *B* will *Appease*, player *A*'s *Aggress* now strictly dominates *Refrain*: *A* will earn a payoff of 3 by aggressing but only 2 by refraining. Thus, applying the dominance principle for a second time, player *A* will not choose *Refrain*. Successively eliminating the strategies *Retaliate* and *Refrain* leaves the strategy pair (*Aggress,Appease*), which is one of the two Nash equilibriums and what we take to be the solution to the game.

The same solution can be reached by the technique of backward induction. The method is built on the assumption that rational players are forward looking, so that in a sequential game they will choose their moves in anticipation of other players' optimal reactions. Accordingly, a sequential game of perfect information can be solved by determining players' optimal moves from back to front, that is, by beginning with the last move of the game and working backward to the first move. We illustrate the method with the aggression game, repeated in extensive form in Figure 4.4. The last decision point of the game belongs to player *B*, who, if given the move, would optimally choose *Appease* for a payoff of 2 rather than *Retaliate* with a payoff of 1. We indicate *B*'s optimal action by darkening the branch for *Appease*. Next we back up to the preceding move (here the first move of the game), which belongs to player *A*. If *A* chooses *Aggress*, she can anticipate that *B* will

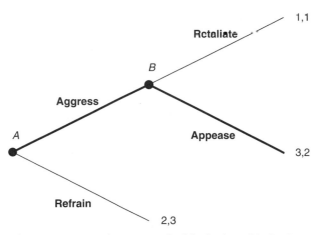

Figure 4.4. Aggression game solved by backward induction.

optimally play *Appease*, thereby returning to *A* a payoff of 3. If *A* chooses *Refrain*, she knows the game ends with a payoff of 2 for her. Thus, her optimal choice is *Aggress*, which we indicate by darkening the branch for that action. From the darkened actions we form the players' optimal strategies, yielding the strategy pair (*Aggress,Appease*), which we recognize as one of the two Nash equilibriums and again take as the solution of the game. In formal terms, the solution (*Aggress,Appease*) obtained by backward induction is known as a subgame perfect equilibrium; more intuitively, it is sometimes called a rollback equilibrium (see Dixit and Skeath 2004).

A side benefit of the backward induction technique is that it helps expose why the other Nash equilibrium of (*Refrain,Retaliate*) does not qualify as a solution to the aggression game. Think of *B*'s equilibrium strategy in this case as a threat made by *B* to retaliate if *A* aggresses against him. If *A* were to believe the threat, then *A*'s optimal action would be *Refrain*, which explains why (*Refrain,Retaliate*) counts as a Nash equilibrium. Under the assumptions of the game, however, Player *A* would not find the threat of retaliation to be credible. If *B* threatens to retaliate but *A* aggresses anyway, then as seen already, it is in *B*'s interest to appease, and *A* knows this. Thus, *A* will not believe that *B* will play *Retaliate*, and for that reason (*Refrain,Retaliate*) fails as a solution to the game.

4.2. Chicken and Prisoner's Dilemma Games

In this section we introduce two of the best known games, chicken and the prisoner's dilemma. These games are especially useful in conflict economics because they help explain why tensions between cooperation and conflict are prevalent in social interactions and particularly in international relations. They also allow us to illustrate and elaborate on some of the concepts introduced to this point.

Chicken

The generic game of chicken can arise in many contexts, but it takes its name from a supposed encounter between two teenage rivals who drive their cars toward each other on a collision course. The one who swerves first is a "chicken" and loses in the eyes of peers, while the one who steers straight is the winner. If both swerve, they share the shame; if both steer straight, they suffer the worst outcome, which is death. As one might imagine, the game has no satisfactory solution.

In what follows, we recast the game as a strategic interaction between nations *A* and *B* who are to send forces into a hostile territory, perhaps for peacekeeping purposes. The mission will be most successful if one country sends a military unit with heavy arms and the other contributes a more mobile unit with light arms. The success of the mission will be reduced if both send a heavy-arms unit and doubtful if both send a light-arms unit. The nations share in the realized benefits of the mission, but they bear individually their own unit's cost, which by assumption is lower for light arms. Each country must decide whether to send a heavy-arms or a light-arms unit.

Initially assume that *A* and *B* choose their respective deployments simultaneously. The result is a game of chicken, the normal form for which is shown with ordinal payoffs in Figure 4.5. Notice that there are two Nash equilibriums (*Light,Heavy*) and (*Heavy,Light*). Notice also that the solution methods of the preceding section do not help distinguish between the two equilibriums: neither player has a dominated strategy, and backward

		Country *B*	
		Heavy Arms	Light Arms
Country *A*	Heavy Arms	3,3	2,4
	Light Arms	4,2	1,1

Figure 4.5. Chicken game with simultaneous moves.

induction is of no use when the moves are simultaneous. Of the two equilibriums, country A prefers (*Light,Heavy*) because it allows A to enjoy the benefits of a successful mission with the lower cost of a light-arms unit. Unfortunately for the mission, country B prefers the second equilibrium (*Heavy,Light*) for like reason. The two nations thus face a tension between cooperation and conflict. They are pulled together by their shared interest in a successful mission, but they are pushed apart by their private interest in a low economic cost. Without something more, like an enforceable prior agreement, the simultaneous-move game of chicken admits no compelling way to play the game and hence no solution.

Consider an alternative protocol whereby the game is played sequentially with country A choosing first. Figure 4.6 shows the game's extensive form and its solution by backward induction. In the sequential game, country B has two decision nodes: the upper node is reached if A chooses *Heavy*, and the lower is reached if A chooses *Light*. If given the move, B will optimally choose *Light* at the upper node and *Heavy* at the lower node, as shown by the respective darkened branches. Backing up to A's decision node, if A chooses *Heavy*, then A can anticipate that B will play *Light*, thereby returning a payoff of 2 to A. By similar reasoning, if A chooses *Light*, then A can anticipate a higher payoff of 4. Thus A's optimal choice is *Light*, as indicated by its darkened branch. From the three darkened branches, we see that A's optimal strategy is *Light*, and B's optimal strategy is to choose the opposite of A's action. The outcome, therefore, is that A deploys a light-arms unit with a payoff of 4, and B deploys a heavy-arms

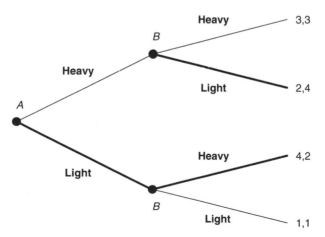

Figure 4.6. Chicken game with sequential moves.

unit with a payoff of 2. Notice that the tension between cooperation and conflict is resolved in favor of country *A*, which secures its preferred outcome. Hence, the sequential game of chicken is said to have a first-mover advantage. By moving first, country *A* is able to exploit its position in such a way that *B*'s own interest leads it to choose the action preferred by *A*. In some games the advantage goes to the second mover, who is able to exploit information revealed by the other player's prior move. In other games the order of play provides no advantage to either player, as we will see in the next subsection.

Prisoner's Dilemma

Like chicken, the prisoner's dilemma is a generic game that arises in many contexts. In the original scenario, two suspects in a crime are interrogated in separate rooms. If one of them confesses and the other does not, the first gets a light sentence of 1 year and the other gets a hard 10 years. If both confess, each gets a reduced sentence of 5 years. If neither confesses, they each get a 2-year sentence on a related but lesser crime. The dilemma is that while it is in their joint interest to stay quiet, self-interest drives them both to confess.

Here we present the prisoner's dilemma in the context of an arms rivalry between two countries *A* and *B*, where each country's national security is determined by its relative armaments. Each country simultaneously chooses either a *Low* or *High* level of arms, thus resulting in one of four possible outcomes. Assume that a country is best off when it has military superiority, with its own arms at a high level and its rival's at a low level. Second best for a country is an outcome of military balance of low arms and hence low economic costs. Less desirable is a military balance with high arms and thus high costs. Worst for a country is a position of military insecurity with low arms facing the rival's higher arms. Under these assumptions, the arms rivalry generates a prisoner's dilemma game, the normal form for which is shown in Figure 4.7 with ordinal payoffs. As mentioned in section 4.1, the game is solved by strict dominance. *High* is a strictly dominant strategy for *A*: if *B* chooses *Low*, then *A*'s best reply is to choose *High* so as to achieve military superiority; if *B* chooses *High*, *A*'s best reply is again *High* so as to reach military parity. By the same logic, *High* is also strictly dominant for *B*. Thus the solution is (*High,High*), which is a unique Nash equilibrium as shown in Figure 4.7.

To appreciate why this solution is remarkable, we begin with some additional terminology. An outcome is Pareto inefficient if there exists an

Country B

Low Armaments   High Armaments

	Low Armaments	High Armaments
Low Armaments	3,3	1,4̲
High Armaments	4̲,1	2̲,2̲

Country A (label between the two rows on the left)

Figure 4.7. Prisoner's dilemma game with simultaneous moves.

alternative outcome that would make at least one player better off and no player worse off. If no such alternative exists, then the outcome is said to be Pareto efficient. Now return to Figure 4.7. Instead of both choosing their dominant strategy of *High*, if both countries were to choose *Low*, they could continue enjoying the same military parity but at a lower economic cost to each. In this way both countries could be better off, thus rendering the solution outcome Pareto inefficient. Here again we see a tension between cooperation and conflict. The benefits of mutual restraint draw the countries toward low armaments, but the lure of military superiority pulls them even more strongly toward high armaments. Moreover, unlike the game of chicken, a switch in protocol changes little. If the game is played sequentially, backward induction shows that there is no first- or second-mover advantage, and the outcome will still be high armaments by both countries. Hence, whether the decisions are made simultaneously or sequentially, the predicted outcome is Pareto inefficient.

In response to the inefficiency of the prisoner's dilemma outcome, suppose the two rivals were to enter an arms control agreement that stipulated mutually low armaments. Their choices would then be to *Cooperate* (by abiding by the agreement with low arms) or to *Defect* (by cheating on the agreement with high arms). A little reflection shows that the rivals would still find themselves in a prisoner's dilemma, each with a dominant strategy to *Defect*. Game theoretic considerations would therefore predict that the agreement would fail.

4.3. Repeated Prisoner's Dilemma

Does game theoretic analysis of the prisoner's dilemma mean there is no prospect for cooperation between the rivals, despite the inefficiency of the outcome? This question is important and worth addressing more generally. Assume two players choose simultaneously between *Cooperate* and *Defect* in a prisoner's dilemma environment. Mutual cooperation promises

Player B

	Cooperate	Defect
Cooperate	R,R	S,T̲
Defect	T̲,S	P̲,P̲

Player A — Cooperate (top row), Defect (bottom row)

Figure 4.8. Stage game for repeated prisoner's dilemma game (adapted from Axelrod 1984, p. 8).

gains to both, but self-interest favors mutual defection. The question is this: In the absence of some kind of external enforcement, does standard game theory offer any reason to believe that cooperation might emerge and be sustained? The answer is yes, if the prisoner's dilemma game is repeated by the two players an indefinite or infinite number of times. The basic intuition is that in a repeated game, a player can be punished for defecting by the other player's choosing to defect in one or more subsequent rounds. If that punishment is anticipated and sufficiently costly, then it can be rational to cooperate throughout the repeated game. Without getting too formal, let's see if we can sharpen this intuition.

Suppose players A and B participate in a repeated prisoner's dilemma. Figure 4.8 presents the normal form using more general notation due to Axelrod (1984). In the present context, the figure shows what is known as the stage game, meaning the game that is played in each round of the repeated game. The payoffs in the stage game can be remembered as follows: T is the temptation to defect, R is the reward for mutual cooperation, P is the penalty for mutual defection, and S is the sucker's payoff. For the game to qualify as a prisoner's dilemma, assume that $T > R > P > S$. Assume also that the payoffs are cardinal, meaning that their magnitudes as well as rank ordering are meaningful. For simplicity, we can think of the payoffs as denominated in dollars. At the completion of each round, the game continues to the next round with known probability π and terminates with probability $(1 - \pi)$. Hence, the length of the game is indefinite but is known by the players to be subject to the laws of probability.

The impetus for cooperation within the repeated game is the threat that a player's defection will be punished. Suppose after a number of rounds of mutual cooperation, player A throws in a defection. How might player B punish that defection? Player B could defect in the next round and then forgive *A* by returning to cooperation in the round after that. More severely, *B* could defect in each of the next two rounds and then forgive *A* by returning to cooperation. Extending the logic, it is easy to see that the severest punishment available to *B* is to defect in every subsequent round and hence never forgive *A*. The strategy that threatens this severest punishment is called the grim-trigger strategy, or more simply *Unforgiving*: cooperate until the other player defects, and then always defect thereafter. If any strategies exist whereby player *B* can induce *A* to cooperate, *Unforgiving* must be among them. By the symmetry of the game, the same logic applies to *A*'s inducing *B* to cooperate. We can now rephrase our earlier question by asking whether the strategy pair (*Unforgiving,Unforgiving*) is a Nash equilibrium. If the answer is yes, then there is reason to believe that cooperation can emerge and be sustained; otherwise, basic game theory must predict that rational players will defect in a repeated game, just as in a one-shot game.

To determine whether (*Unforgiving,Unforgiving*) is a Nash equilibrium, let's focus on player *A* and ask whether *Unforgiving* is a best reply to *B*'s *Unforgiving*. If *A* plays *Unforgiving* (as does *B*), then she (like *B*) never defects, and in every round she (like *B*) receives the reward *R* for mutual cooperation. Alternatively, suppose *A* defects in some round *t*. Because that would elicit *B*'s defection in every subsequent round, *A* should also defect in every subsequent round so as to avoid the sucker's payoff *S* in those rounds. If *A* defects in round *t* and every round thereafter, then *A* will receive the temptation payoff *T* in round *t* and the penalty for mutual defection *P* in every round thereafter. Comparing these payoffs to those she would receive by playing *Unforgiving*, in the single round *t* she gains $(T-R)$, but in every round thereafter she loses $(R-P)$. If the single period's gain is outweighed by the string of subsequent losses, then defection does not pay, and *A*'s *Unforgiving* is a best reply to *B*'s *Unforgiving*. By symmetry, *B*'s *Unforgiving* is likewise a best reply. Thus, (*Unforgiving,Unforgiving*) is a Nash equilibrium, and the answer to our earlier question is a qualified affirmative: if the string of losses outweighs the gain, then cooperation can emerge and be sustained in the repeated game.

This is an important result because it says that cooperation can be mutually rational in long-term interactions characterized by prisoner's dilemma incentives. To this result we must add several points, however. First, in the formal mathematics of the preceding argument, the losses in subsequent rounds are systematically discounted because they are realized only if the game continues and because they occur later in time relative to the single-period gain. Holding constant the payoffs *T*, *R*, and *P*, the higher the continuation probability π and the lower the interest rate, the more heavily the future losses are weighted, and hence the greater is the prospect for cooperation. Second, while (*Unforgiving,Unforgiving*) can be a Nash equilibrium, it is by no means a unique equilibrium. A particularly well-known alternative strategy in the repeated prisoner's dilemma is *Tit-For-Tat* (*TFT*), whereby a player cooperates in the first round and then matches the other player's preceding move in each round thereafter. Using an argument similar to that noted earlier, it can be shown that (*TFT,TFT*) can be a Nash equilibrium with mutual cooperation in every round. Going to the opposite extreme, however, it can also be shown that both players' defecting in every round is also a Nash equilibrium, resulting in a decidedly Pareto inefficient outcome. Lastly, cooperation can emerge under standard assumptions only if the number of rounds is infinite or indefinite. In a game of known length, there is no incentive to cooperate in the end round and consequently, by backward induction, in any other round. Hence, for a finitely repeated game, mutual defection in all rounds is the predicted outcome.

4.4. Bibliographic Notes

This chapter is intended as a brief introduction to basic game theory, and as such there is much that is not covered. If we were to extend the introduction, we would want to include most particularly coverage of expected utility, mixed strategies, bargaining, incomplete information, and evolutionary games. Fortunately, there exist many fine texts that are rigorous and yet accessible. Among our favorites are Dixit and Nalebuff (1991), Gardner (2003), Dixit and Skeath (2004), and Binmore (2007), and, at a higher level, Kreps (1990) and Mas-Colell et al. (1995).

Because game theory's early impetus came largely from the Cold War, it is unsurprising that applications abound in conflict economics. For a single seminal contribution we would cite Schelling's (1960) wide-ranging analysis of rational behavior in situations that mix elements of conflict and common interest. For useful reviews of the application of game theory, see O'Neill (1994) on international relations and war, and Sandler and Arce (2007) on terrorism.

A Bargaining Model of Conflict

Economics involves the study of choices under conditions of scarcity. Whereas traditional economics assumes that choices are from among peaceful alternatives, conflict economics recognizes that some alternatives are violent or potentially violent. In this chapter we continue the move from traditional economics to conflict economics by sketching a simple economic model of conflict. The graphical model presented here is due originally to Hirshleifer (1995, pp. 172–175); more formal versions are available in Skaperdas (2006) and in Appendix B. Because the model is broadly consistent with what is known in political science as the bargaining (or rationalist) theory of war (Fearon 1995), we refer to it hereafter as Hirshleifer's bargaining model. Although by no means complete, the model provides a simple but effective framework for thinking systematically about the elements of conflict, some of the prominent explanations for war, and the possible effects of third-party intervention.

5.1. Elements of Conflict

Suppose that a disputed resource is to be divided between two players A and B. The players might be nation-states disputing territory, a government and a rebel group clashing over natural resources, or a government and a terrorist organization competing for control of a population. The players begin by diverting secure resources into arms, and then they divide the disputed resource either by fighting or by peaceful settlement. For simplicity, assume that each player chooses a level of arms that is the same whether fighting or settlement is anticipated. If the players fight, a portion of the disputed resource is destroyed, with the surviving portion divided between them based on their comparative arms and military technologies.

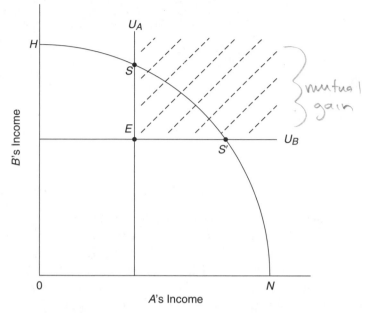

Figure 5.1. Bargaining model with peaceful settlement (adapted from Hirshleifer 1995, p. 172).

If they settle, the full amount of the disputed resource is divided by agreement, and the agreement is enforced by the threat embodied in the arms. Note here that the economic incentive to settle originates in the desire to avoid the resource destruction that accompanies fighting. On completion of either fighting or settlement, the players generate incomes from their final resources, which consist of their secure resources net of the diversion to arms plus their share of the disputed resource net of any destruction.

The choice between fighting and settlement rests on three elements: the expected income distributions based on fighting, the potential income distributions based on peaceful settlement, and the interpersonal preferences of the players. The attitudes of the players toward one another are reflected by their preferences over income distributions. These preferences may be benevolent, malevolent, or egoistic, depending on whether a player considers the other's income to be a good, a bad, or neither (called a neuter). Peaceful settlement occurs if there exists one or more distributions by settlement that would leave at least one player better off and neither player worse off than would be expected if they were to fight.

The elements of the model are illustrated in Figure 5.1 with a case of peaceful settlement. Assume that the players in the figure have complete information about armaments, conflict technology, and productive capabilities. This means that each player holds the same expectation about the outcome of any fight and resulting income distribution, shown by the conflict (or disagreement) point *E*. If the resource is divided peacefully, then alternative income distributions are feasible. These potential distributions are shown by the settlement-opportunity curve, which is labeled *HN*. Both players are assumed to be strict egoists, as indicated by their respective indifference curves U_A and U_B passing through point *E*. Player *A* cares only about her own income; thus her indifference curves are vertical, and she prefers all distributions to the right of *E*. For the same reason, player *B*'s indifference curves are horizontal, and he prefers all distributions above *E*. The highlighted area above and to the right of *E* is the region of mutual gain and includes distributions that are Pareto preferred to *E*, that is, distributions that make at least one player better off and neither player worse off relative to *E*. Because the settlement-opportunity curve intersects the region of mutual gain, the model predicts peaceful settlement over violence, resulting in a final outcome somewhere between points *S* and *S'* along the settlement-opportunity curve.

5.2. Sources of Violent Conflict

Inconsistent Expectations

Various elements of the situation depicted in Figure 5.1 combine to generate a peaceful settlement. To see how fighting might arise instead, assume now that the players' expectations are inconsistent. In particular, suppose in Figure 5.2 that player *A* expects the outcome of fighting to be income distribution E_A located toward the lower right, while player *B* expects it to be E_B toward the upper left. The region of mutual gain now lies entirely outside the settlement-opportunity curve *HN*. Because of the players' divergent expectations, the settlement-opportunity curve fails to intersect the region of mutual gain, and the predicted outcome is fighting.

Divergent expectations in this model imply that the players have incomplete information about various factors that determine the outcome of fighting, such as the other's capabilities, costs, strategies, or tactics. Figures 5.1 and 5.2 together suggest that an exchange of relevant

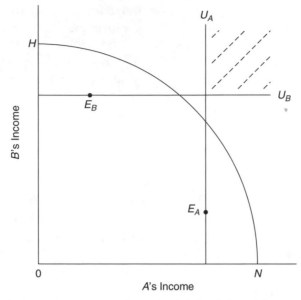

Figure 5.2. Inconsistent expectations with fighting (adapted from Hirshleifer 1995, p. 173).

private information between the players could generate a peaceful settlement that would be preferred to fighting. However, because expected outcomes determine which settlements are acceptable, the players have an incentive to withhold, exaggerate, or misrepresent certain information in order to attain a settlement more to their own advantage. This means that private information, even if accurate, tends to lack credibility when it is provided by the players. In this way, the exchange of information that might close divergent expectations is problematic (Fearon 1995).

Commitment Problems

A commitment problem exists when one player cannot trust the other because the latter has an incentive to renege after an agreement is reached. The essence of the problem is captured by the simplified game in Figure 5.3, which is part of a larger game wherein player B has proposed a specific settlement. Player A can either *Settle*, meaning agree to the peaceful settlement, or *Fight*. If A chooses *Settle*, then B can either *Abide* or *Renege*. Payoffs appear at the ends of the game-tree branches, with A's payoff listed first. As shown, both players are better off by acting in accordance with the

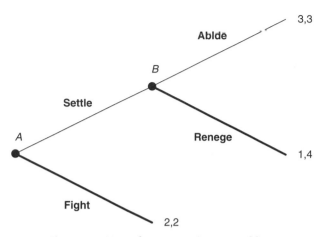

Figure 5.3. Two-player commitment problem.

peaceful settlement than by fighting, but given the settlement, *B* is better off by reneging than by abiding. Knowing that *B* is better off reneging, *A* mistrusts *B* and so chooses *Fight*. The predicted outcome is fighting with payoffs (2,2), despite its Pareto inefficiency when compared to the superior settlement with payoffs (3,3). To see how such commitment problems can lead to fighting, we look at three cases that are prominent in bargaining theory (Fearon 1995, Powell 2006).

Indivisibilities
Partial or complete indivisibility of a disputed issue is sometimes believed to be an important source of violence in conflicts over territory or political control (see Goddard 2006 and Toft 2006). Suppose two players dispute control of a sacred site that both players perceive to be completely indivisible. An example is shown in Figure 5.4, where each player is assumed to obtain income only when the site is completely held. If player *A* controls the site, the outcome is at point *N*; if *B* controls the site, the outcome is at point *H*. Thus the settlement opportunities frontier is represented entirely by the two points *H* and *N*. The expected outcome of fighting is shown by point *E*, which is determined by multiplying each player's probability of winning times her or his income from controlling that portion of the site not destroyed by fighting. Since the region of mutual gain includes neither settlement point *H* nor *N*, fighting is the predicted outcome.

Powell (2006) notes, however, that there are ways to peacefully distribute the disputed resource such that each player's expected payoff is

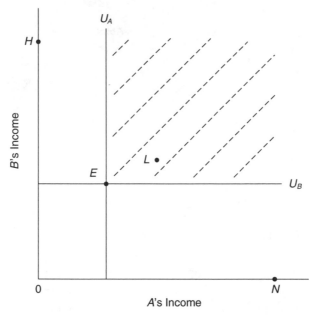

Figure 5.4. Commitment problem and indivisibilities.

greater under a settlement than under fighting. To see this, suppose each player has a 50 percent chance of winning control of the site through fighting, but each would suffer costs because of destruction. A lottery (e.g., a coin flip) that peacefully distributes the disputed item to each player with the same 50 percent probability would be preferred by both players because it avoids the costs of fighting. This is shown in Figure 5.4 by point *L*, which lies along a straight line (not shown) between *H* and *N*. Because costs of destruction are avoided under the lottery, point *L* lies within the region of mutual gain and is strictly preferred by each player to point *E*. Powell points out, however, that there is a commitment problem associated with the lottery. After the lottery, the disputed resource is distributed to the winning player, thus placing the outcome at either point *H* or *N*. But the loser has an incentive to renege on the lottery and initiate war, because the expected income from fighting at *E* is greater than the zero income assigned by the lottery.

Preemptive War

Consider next the case of preemptive war, which can arise from the existence of a first-strike advantage. Assume that the players have complete information and thus correctly anticipate the offensive advantage. In

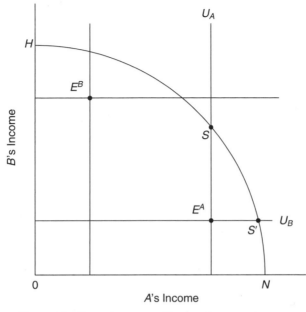

Figure 5.5. Commitment problem and preemptive war.

Figure 5.5, both players expect fighting to result in income distribution E^A if player A attacks first and in distribution E^B if player B attacks first. Suppose that the players bargain relative to E^A, the expected distribution if A attacks first. Any agreement by B to a settlement between S and S' is not credible, because B will have the incentive to renege, seize the first-strike advantage, and thereby shift the expected outcome to E^B. Knowing this, player A will be inclined to launch her own preemptive strike. By the same argument, any agreement by A relative to E^B is not credible, thereby leading B to strike. Because neither player can credibly commit to a mutually advantageous settlement, fighting is the predicted outcome.

Preventive War

To understand preventive war as a third case, the bargaining model must be extended to allow for dynamic considerations across time. Suppose the model consists of two periods. In period 1, the players choose levels of arms that result in conflict point E and settlement-opportunity curve HN. As seen in Figure 5.6, settlements between S and S' offer mutual gains relative to fighting. However, suppose it is known that a potential change in military technology exists that, if realized, would shift power toward player B in period 2. Assume that the shift in power can be prevented by

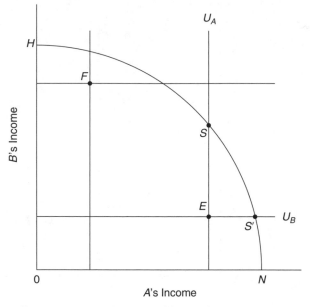

Figure 5.6. Commitment problem and preventive war.

fighting in period 1 but not by settlement. If the potential shift in power is sufficiently large, then a commitment problem arises, and fighting in period 1 is predicted.

To see the commitment problem most simply, assume in Figure 5.6 that arms levels (but not arms productivities) remain fixed, so that the change in technology would shift the conflict point northwest to point F in period 2 but would leave the settlement opportunity curve unchanged. In this case, an agreement by B in period 1 to a settlement between S and S' would not be credible. This is because such an agreement would leave B with a clear incentive in period 2 to threaten a fight and thereby secure a more advantageous settlement somewhere to the northeast of conflict point F. Knowing this, player A will weigh the prospective loss of income in period 2 against the cost of fighting in period 1. If the prospective shift in power is sufficiently large (as it is in Figure 5.6), player A will refuse settlement in period 1 and instead will lock in the distribution at point E by fighting.

Malevolent Preferences

As another source of violence, suppose that both players are highly malevolent. This means that they are willing to sacrifice large amounts of

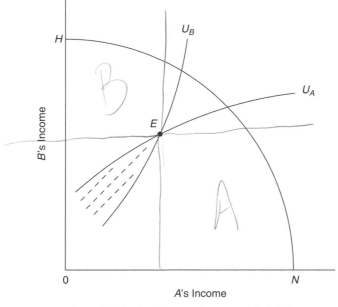

Figure 5.7. Malevolent preferences with fighting.

their own income in order to reduce the other's income. In Figure 5.7 the mutual malevolence of the players is shown by the positively sloped indifference curves passing through the conflict point *E*. Player *A* wants more income for herself and less for *B*; thus she prefers distributions down and to the right of *E*. Likewise, player *B* wants more income for himself and less for *A*; thus he prefers distributions up and to the left of *E*. In the figure, the region of mutual gain forms to the southwest of *E* and is nowhere intersected by the settlement-opportunity curve. This implies that the players would prefer to reduce each other's income further, but they can destroy resources only by fighting, not by settlement. Thus, to injure each other, the players can do no better than fight, and so fight they do.

Lesser levels of malevolence can leave open the possibility of peaceful settlement. This is shown in Figure 5.8, where the positive slopes of the indifference curves indicate mutual malevolence but nonetheless generate a region of mutual gain intersected by the settlement-opportunity curve. Notice, however, that the set of acceptable settlements *SS′* is diminished relative to the case with egoistic preferences in Figure 5.1. The general lesson is that malevolence reduces and possibly eliminates the range of settlements to which the players might agree.

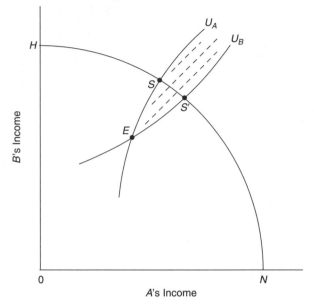

Figure 5.8. Malevolent preferences with peaceful settlement (adapted from Hirshleifer 1995, p. 173).

Political Bias

To this point we have assumed that players *A* and *B* are unitary actors who distribute a disputed resource by costly fighting or peaceful settlement. It is recognized in the social science literature, however, that a critical leader who substantially affects decisions to fight or settle can have different incentives relative to the group for whom the leader acts. Tarar (2006), for example, adapts Fearon's (1995) bargaining model of war to account for a critical leader's incentive to initiate war as a diversion from domestic problems. Also within a bargaining model, Jackson and Morelli (2007) consider a critical leader's "political bias," which encompasses anything that might cause the leader to have different incentives for war or peace relative to the group as a whole.

Here we relax the unitary actor assumption in Hirshleifer's model to illustrate how incentives facing a critical leader can be a distinct source of violence within the bargaining theory of war. For simplicity, suppose that only one of the players, say *B*, is subject to political bias. Assume also that each player chooses a level of arms that is unchanged whether fighting or settlement is anticipated and that any settlement achieved is enforced by those arms. Let *b* and $\hat{b}$ represent the proportion of *B*'s income controlled

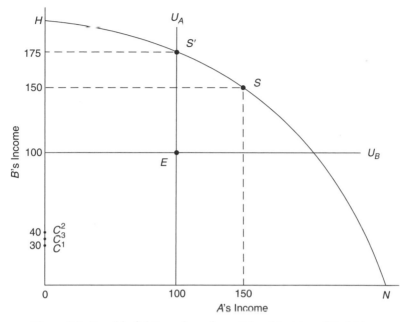

Figure 5.9. Possible fighting when player B is subject to political bias.

by the critical leader under peaceful settlement and fighting, respectively. For example, if $b = 0.2$ and $\hat{b} = 0.3$, then the critical leader in B controls 20 percent of B's income under peace but 30 percent of the income under fighting. Following Jackson and Morelli (2007, p. 1357), let $\hat{B} = \hat{b}/b$ represent the political bias of player B's critical leader. When $\hat{B} > 1$, the critical leader is biased in favor of fighting. For example, the critical leader might gain power or status with fighting that allows the leader to control a greater share of B's income than with settlement. Alternatively, a critical leader perpetrating atrocities during a war might expect retribution under settlement, causing the leader to control a smaller share of B's income under peace relative to fighting. Political bias does not necessarily favor fighting. When $\hat{B} < 1$, the pivotal leader controls a smaller share of income under fighting than under settlement. This might arise, for example, when peace confers popularity on the critical leader. When $\hat{B} = 1$, the leader's incentives between fighting and settlement match those of the broader group.

The essential trade-off for a critical leader with a political bias in favor of fighting is between controlling a larger share of less income by fighting versus a smaller share of more income by settling. To see how fighting might arise owing to political bias, begin by assuming in Figure 5.9 that

$b = 0.2$ and $\hat{b} = 0.3$ and that the critical leader controls the decision to fight or to settle. For players A and B as unitary actors, the outcome of fighting at E returns an expected income of 100 to each player. By avoiding the destructiveness of fighting, peaceful settlement at (say) point S promises each player an income of 150. Clearly, settlement at S is better for each player relative to fighting. In this particular case, the critical leader of B is indifferent between fighting and peaceful settlement at S: as shown in the figure, the leader will achieve the same income of 30 at point C^1 under fighting ($0.3 \times 100 = 30$) or peace ($0.2 \times 150 = 30$). Starting from point C^1, however, suppose that the proportion of B's income from fighting controlled by the critical leader rises from $\hat{b} = 0.3$ to $\hat{b} = 0.4$, other things constant. Now the critical leader for B will expect to gain more at C^2 from fighting ($0.4 \times 100 = 40$) than at C^1 from settlement ($0.2 \times 150 = 30$). Since the critical leader controls the decision to fight or to settle, fighting is the predicted outcome over settlement at S.

In a bargaining context, player A could attempt to appease the critical leader in B by offering a more generous settlement, such as point S' in Figure 5.9. As drawn, point S' reflects the maximum that A would be willing to offer the critical leader of B, because A's expected income from fighting would just equal her income from settlement at S'. Nevertheless, such a settlement offer would not be enough to prevent fighting. Under settlement at S', the critical leader of B would achieve income shown by point C^3 ($0.2 \times 175 = 35$), which is less than the leader's expected income of 40 at C^2 from fighting. Hence, the critical leader would still have an incentive to initiate a fight.

5.3. Third-Party Intervention

We have employed Hirshleifer's bargaining model to illuminate the elements of conflict and to identify several sources of violence. By extension, the model can also be used to suggest how third-party intervention might moderate violent conflict. Several of the various possibilities are shown in Figures 5.10 through 5.12. In each figure we assume for simplicity that the players' arms levels are unchanged by third-party intervention.

Consider first the possibility of economic intervention. In Figure 5.10, assume that a first-strike advantage exists such that the expected outcome is E^A if player A attacks and E^B if player B attacks. Consequently, the highlighted region of mutual gain lies outside of the settlement-opportunity curve, setting up the likelihood of preemptive war. Suppose, however, that a third party offers economic inducements to both players

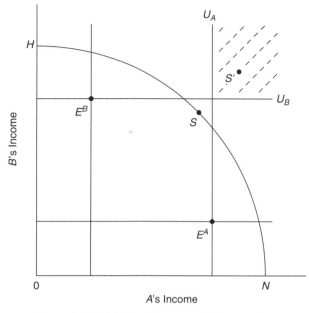

Figure 5.10. Third-party economic intervention.

contingent on peaceful settlement. If the inducements are sufficiently large and are tied to suitable settlements, then distributions within the region of mutual gain are feasible and settlement is expected. For example, conditioned on settlement at point S, the third party could offer subsidies to the players that would yield a final distribution at point S'.

As alternatives to economic intervention, a third party might provide diplomatic mediation (an example of peacemaking) or deploy military forces (an example of peace enforcement). In Figure 5.11, assume that A expects the outcome of fighting to be E_A while B expects it to be E_B. Since the highlighted region of mutual gain lies outside of the settlement-opportunity curve, fighting is the predicted outcome. Suppose, however, that a third party facilitates the credible exchange of private information between the players. If the expected outcomes of fighting are brought sufficiently close, then peaceful settlement becomes feasible. For example, if mediation shifts expectations to points $\tilde{E}_A$ and $\tilde{E}_B$, then in this case peaceful settlement between points S and S' along the settlement-opportunity curve is made possible. Alternatively, suppose that a third party undertakes military efforts to terminate violence between the players. In particular, assume that a third party deploys military forces against both A and B, thus eroding their expected returns from fighting. In this case, the expected

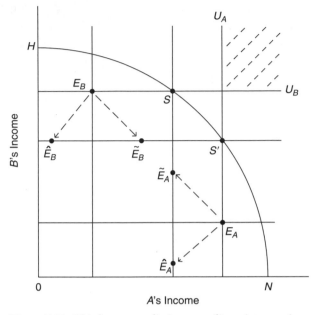

Figure 5.11. Third-party mediation or military intervention.

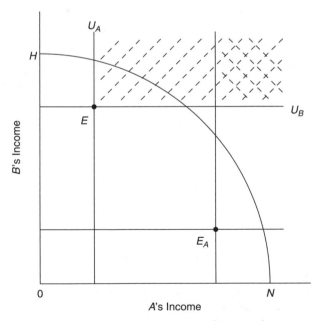

Figure 5.12. Third-party intervention favoring player *A*.

outcomes from fighting shift southwest to $\hat{E}_A$ and $\hat{E}_B$ in Figure 5.11, and peaceful settlement between S and S' is again made possible.

Figures 5.10 and 5.11 show how third-party intervention can ameliorate violence. If an intervention favors one side, however, it can leave the prospect for peaceful settlement unchanged or even worsened. For example, in Figure 5.12 assume that both players initially expect an outcome of fighting at point E, thus forming a region of mutual gain intersected by the settlement-opportunity curve. Now suppose that a third party intervenes privately to the advantage of player A, such that A expects the fighting outcome to be E_A while B continues to expect E. This means that the region of mutual gain, shown by the cross-hatched area, is reduced in size and now lies outside the settlement-opportunity curve. In this case, third-party intervention reduces the prospect for settlement.

5.4. Bibliographic Notes

The connection between conflict and bargaining was made by Schelling (1960), who famously wrote, "To study the strategy of conflict is to take the view that most conflict situations are essentially *bargaining* situations" (p. 5). The bargaining model sketched in this chapter is a modification of one first outlined by Hirshleifer (1985; 1987, ch. 10) and extended in Hirshleifer (1995) and Hirshleifer, Glazer, and Hirshleifer (2005). Early predecessors include Bush's (1972) model of anarchy and Wittman's (1979) model of war termination. Later models that are both more complete and more formal than Hirshleifer's model include Skaperdas (2006) and Garfinkel and Skaperdas (2007).

Whereas we assume that the contested prize is a resource, Hirshleifer (1995) leaves the nature of the prize unspecified. How the contested prize is specified constitutes a major distinction among formal models of conflict. In particular, the object up for grabs can be defined alternatively as a resource (Hirshleifer 1991, Grossman and Kim 1995, Anderton, Anderton, and Carter 1999), a production good (Rider 1999, Hausken 2004), a consumption good (Bush 1972, Bush and Mayer 1974), or an export or import (Anderton and Carter 2008b).

Various sources of violent conflict are explored individually in this chapter, but wars can have multiple causes or antecedents (Vasquez 2000, Levy 2008). Despite complexities, several sources of violence could be modeled together in the Hirshleifer framework. Other potential sources of violence not explored in this chapter include players' concerns for reputation (Schelling 1966, Walter 2006a, Crescenzi, Kathman, and Long

2007), risk-seeking preferences and increasing returns to production (Skaperdas 2006), and an intertemporal incentive to weaken or eliminate a rival (Garfinkel and Skaperdas 2000a, 2007).

As noted in the chapter's opening, Hirshleifer's model is broadly consistent with the bargaining theory of war in the political science literature. For literature reviews, see Powell (2002) and Reiter (2003). Particularly instructive are the costly lottery models of war found in Fearon (1995) and Powell (2006). For a game-theoretic discussion of commitment problems, see chapter 10 of Dixit and Skeath (2004). For formal conflict-settlement protocols, see Isard and Smith (1982), Raiffa (1982), Brams and Taylor (1996), and Garfinkel and Skaperdas (2007, pp. 667–682). Models of third-party intervention include Amegashie and Kutsoati (2007) and Chang, Potter, and Sanders (2007).

6

Conflict between States*

For millennia, philosophers and sages have pondered the origins and horrors of war. Despite this long history of inquiry, it is only in the last century that scholars from political science, economics, and other disciplines have attempted to use the quantitative methods of social science to study the causes and effects of war. Building on the early work of Lewis Richardson, Pitirim Sorokin, and Quincy Wright, the social scientific study of war was well established by the mid-1960s around a community of scholars associated with the Correlates of War Project, the Peace Science Society (originally, Peace Research Society), the *Journal of Conflict Resolution*, and the like. Since then, a wealth of social scientific studies of war has appeared in journals and books across the various disciplines (Singer 2000, Anderton and Carter 2007). In this chapter we focus on armed conflict between states, before we turn to civil war in Chapter 7.

6.1. The Conflict Cycle

Conflicts typically pass through phases, as shown by Lund's (1996) life-cycle diagram in Figure 6.1, which plots the level of conflict between parties across time. The conflict in question may be interstate as covered in this chapter, intrastate as in Chapter 7, or extra-state as in Chapter 8. The bell-shaped curve represents the course of a typical conflict as hostility rises and falls over time. The vertical axis marks levels of conflict beginning with durable peace and rising successively to stable peace, unstable peace, crisis,

* The introductory paragraph, sections 6.1 and 6.2, and parts of section 6.4 of this chapter are adapted from Charles H. Anderton and John R. Carter, "A Survey of Peace Economics," published in *Handbook of Defense Economics*, volume 2, edited by Todd Sandler and Keith Hartley, pp. 1211–1258, Copyright © Elsevier 2007. We gratefully acknowledge Elsevier's permission to republish material from the article.

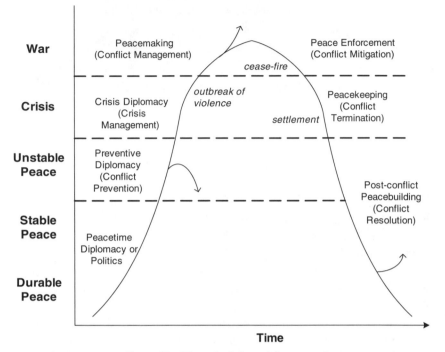

Figure 6.1. Lund's conflict life cycle (adapted from Lund 1996, p. 386).

and war. Around the outside of the curve are terms used for third-party interventions at various stages of a conflict. The "P series" (preventive diplomacy, peacemaking, etc.) is typically used in discussions associated with the United Nations, and the "C series" (conflict prevention, conflict management, etc.) is used in the scholarly literature (Lund 1996, p. 385). The arrows along the curve show that wars can be prevented, can escalate, or can recur.

Here and in Chapter 7 we focus on the upper portion of the conflict cycle corresponding to crises and wars. Among the empirical aspects of crises and wars are four that we highlight: frequency, seriousness, onset, and termination. The frequency of interstate crises and wars refers to the number of conflicts per time period. The seriousness of conflict includes duration (represented by the width of the upper portion of the bell), severity (casualties), and intensity (casualties per unit time). Moving initially upward along the conflict-cycle curve, we would like to know the risk factors for the onset of crises and wars. Moving down the curve to the right, we are interested in elements that contribute to war termination.

6.2. Patterns of Armed Interstate Conflict

Prominent Datasets

Figure 6.2 summarizes five well-known interstate conflict datasets. The first is the Correlates of War (COW) Project's data for interstate wars. The second and third datasets are provided jointly by the Uppsala Conflict Data Program (UCDP) and the International Peace Research Institute, Oslo (PRIO) for interstate wars and other interstate armed conflicts. The fourth is COW's dataset for militarized interstate disputes (MIDs). The fifth is the

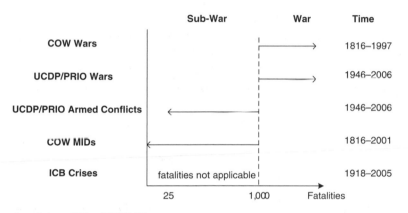

Correlates of War (COW) Wars:
Interstate war – combat between states involving a minimum of 1,000 battle deaths (military only) for the whole war among all states involved (Sarkees 2000).

Uppsala Conflict Data Program/International Peace Research Institute, Oslo (UCDP/PRIO) Wars:
Interstate war – combat between states leading to a minimum of 1,000 battle-related deaths (military and civilian) per year among all states involved (Gleditsch et al. 2002, UCDP/PRIO Codebook Version 4–2006).

Uppsala Conflict Data Program/International Peace Research Institute, Oslo (UCDP/PRIO) Armed Conflicts:
Armed conflict – Apply UCDP/PRIO's interstate war definition, but with battle-related deaths (military and civilian) of between 25 and 999 (Gleditsch et al. 2002, UCDP/PRIO Codebook Version 4–2006).

COW Militarized Interstate Disputes (MIDs):
Militarized interstate dispute – united historical case in which the "threat, display or use of military force short of war by one member state is explicitly directed towards the government, official representatives, official forces, property, or territory of another state" (Jones, Bremer, and Singer 1996, p. 168).

International Crisis Behavior (ICB) Crises:
Interstate crisis – a state's foreign policy leaders perceive a threat to basic values, a finite time for response, and a heightened probability of military hostilities (International Crisis Behavior Project at www.cidcm.umd.edu/icb).

Figure 6.2. Selected interstate conflict datasets.

International Crisis Behavior (ICB) Project's dataset on interstate crises. As shown in the upper portion of the figure, both COW and UCDP/PRIO recognize fatalities of 1,000 as a threshold for interstate war. For interstate conflicts short of war, COW counts fatalities from zero to 999, UCDP/PRIO covers fatalities between 25 and 999, and ICB does not apply any fatalities criterion. The time periods vary among the datasets: 1816–1997 for COW Wars, 1946–2006 for UCDP/PRIO Wars and Armed Conflicts, 1816–2001 for COW MIDs, and 1918–2005 for ICB Crises.

Further points of contrast among the datasets are discovered in the definitions in the lower portion of Figure 6.2. Notice that the datasets vary according to whether fatalities are counted per year or in total and whether those fatalities include both military and civilian deaths. Differences in definitions and other coding practices are important because they can lead to differences in the classification of specific conflicts. For example, the conflict between Chad and Libya in 1987 over the Aozou Strip is counted as an interstate war by UCDP/PRIO but not by COW. Important differences also exist between ICB and COW categorizations of sub-wars. One key difference is that classification as a COW MID requires a threat, display, or use of military force, whereas classification as an ICB crisis does not. Another is that an ICB crisis depends on what a state's leaders perceive or intend, whereas a COW MID can reflect decisions of subordinate personnel (e.g., an accidental or unauthorized threat, display, or use of force). These differences in classification result in substantial differences in coverage. For the period 1918–92, Hewitt (2003) identified 756 crisis dyads from ICB and 2,155 dispute dyads from COW. Of these, 501 conflicts were common to both datasets. At the same time, however, 255 (34%) of the crisis dyads did not show up as disputes, and 1,654 (77%) of the disputes did not count as crises.

Measures of Interstate Conflict

In what follows, we use data for MIDs and interstate wars to highlight the frequency and other empirical aspects of interstate conflict associated with the upper portion of the conflict life cycle. Before doing so, we need to emphasize two points about MIDs. First, according to COW definitions, a MID is not a war. The threat, display, and use of military force represent three sub-war categories in the MID definition. When a MID reaches a point where military combat is sufficiently sustained that it will lead to at least 1,000 total battle deaths, then COW reclassifies the MID as an interstate war (Jones, Bremer, and Singer 1996, p. 168). Second, some scholars depart from COW definitions by treating the *use* of military force between states as interstate war even though battle deaths are fewer than the 1,000 threshold. For example, the 1995 border conflict between Ecuador and Peru (known as the Cenepa War) totaled fewer than 1,000 battle deaths, but it is characterized as a war in some scholarly publications. Hence, MIDs involving the use of military force might be viewed as wars even though this is not COW's practice.

Figure 6.3 shows the number of new MIDs, called MID onsets, that occurred in the international system during five-year periods from 1816 through 2000. Figure 6.3 also shows the number of MID onsets that involved the use of military force (labeled MIDs-Use-Force) and the number of MID onsets that eventually rose to the level of interstate war (labeled MIDs-to-War). On the horizontal axis are indicated certain time periods identified as important by historians of international relations (Gochman and Maoz 1990, p. 198). Three facts stand out in the time series. First, the twentieth century witnessed considerably more MID onsets than did the nineteenth century. There were 2,297 MID onsets between 1816 and 2000, of which 1,986 (87%) occurred in the twentieth century (1900– 99). Second, a high percentage of MIDs involved the use of military force, although this varies substantially by historical period. For the entire period 1816–2000, 1,645 MID onsets (72%) involved military force. During the Bismarkian era (1871–90), 36 of 85 MID onsets (42%) involved military force, whereas 904 of 1,173 MID onsets (77%) involved force during the Cold War (1946–89). Third, the percentage of MIDs that crossed COW's threshold for war is very small. Of the 2,297 MIDs that arose in the period 1816–2000, only 106 (4.6%) escalated to war.

Table 6.1 presents various measures of the seriousness of interstate wars, as distinct from MIDS, from 1816 to 2006. The table reveals that the average duration of interstate war was highest during the Interwar and World War II era (1919–45) followed by the Cold War era (1946–89). The severity in terms of deaths per war was greatest during the Interwar and World War II era followed by the Age of Imperialism (1891–1918). These two periods also had the highest average intensity, with the more severe being the Age of Imperialism.

6.3. Hirshleifer's Bargaining Model and Interstate War

Hirshleifer's bargaining model of conflict, introduced in Chapter 5, provides a useful framework for thinking about various aspects of interstate war. Recall in the model that a disputed resource is to be divided between two players *A* and *B*, here nation-states assumed to be unitary actors with

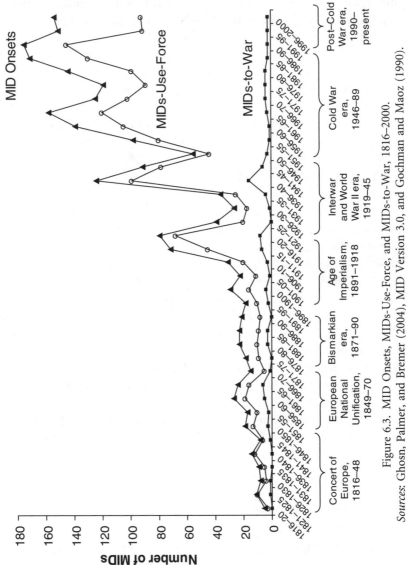

Figure 6.3. MID Onsets, MIDs-Use-Force, and MIDs-to-War, 1816–2000.

Sources: Ghosn, Palmer, and Bremer (2004), MID Version 3.0, and Gochman and Maoz (1990).

Table 6.1. *Interstate war duration, severity, and intensity, 1816–2006.*

Historical Period	Interstate War Onsets	Average Duration (days per war)	Average Severity (deaths per war)	Average Intensity (deaths per day)
Concert of Europe (1816–48)	5	350.0	32,762	93.6
European National Unification (1849–70)	15	392.3	59,301	151.1
Bismarkian era (1871–90)	6	406.0	53,055	130.7
Age of Imperialism (1891–1918)	14	265.7	638,075	2,401.5
Interwar and WW II era (1919–45)	16	557.0	1,132,556	2,033.3
Cold War era (1946–89)	22	490.0	150,333	306.8
Post–Cold War era (1990–2006)	3	395.3	26,390	66.8
1816–2006	81	428.0	392,742	917.6

Note: Franco-Prussian War ends in 1871.
Sources: Sarkees (2000), COW War Data Version 3.0 for 1820–1989 data; Uppsala Conflict Data Program (UCDP) and International Peace Research Institute, Oslo (PRIO) Armed Conflict Dataset v4–2007, Gleditsch et al. (2002), International Peace Research Institute, Oslo (PRIO) Battle Deaths Dataset Version 2.0, and Lacina and Gleditsch (2005) for 1990–2006 data.

egoistic preferences. The players divert secure resources into armaments and then divide the disputed resource through war or settlement. For simplicity it is assumed that each player's armaments are the same whether war or settlement is anticipated. If the players go to war, a portion of the disputed resource is destroyed, with the surviving portion divided between the players based on their comparative arms and military technologies. If they settle, the full amount of the disputed resource is divided by agreement, with the agreement enforced by the threat of war. After war or settlement, the players generate incomes from their final resources, which consist of their secure resources net of arms plus their share of the disputed resource net of any destruction. Settlement occurs if at least one player is better off and neither is worse off than would be expected under war. We highlight three implications that follow from the model.

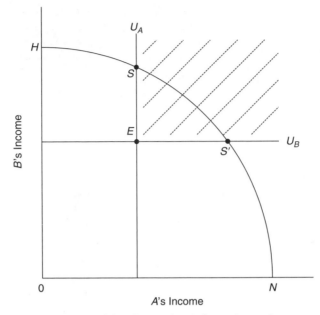

Figure 6.4. Bargaining model with complete information and no commitment problems (adapted from Hirshleifer 1995, p. 172).

First, given complete information and the absence of commitment problems, peaceful settlement rather than war is predicted. In Figure 6.4, suppose that if war occurs, both players expect the distribution of income to occur at point E. If the disputed resource is divided peacefully, alternative income distributions are possible, as shown by the settlement opportunity curve HN. Because potential settlements between points S and S' along the opportunity curve offer gains to both players relative to point E, peaceful settlement is predicted. The intuition is straightforward: the avoidance of the destructive costs of war provides a peace dividend that can be translated into mutual gains, thus leading the players to settle.

Second, again given complete information and the absence of commitment problems, relative power and the costs of war will influence the terms of settlement but not its occurrence. This follows immediately as a corollary of the first implication. If in Figure 6.4 there occurs a change in relative power or costs, a new conflict point and settlement-opportunity curve will be generated. However, as long as war remains destructive and hence costly, the new conflict point will lie inside the new opportunity curve. Thus, while the range of mutually advantageous settlements will be different, the prediction nonetheless will be for settlement rather than war.

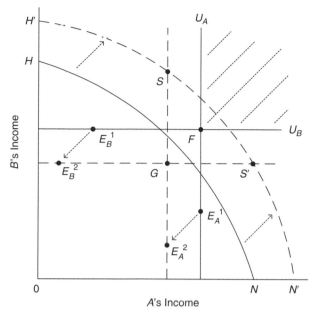

Figure 6.5. Bargaining model with incomplete information and increased cost of war.

Third, given incomplete information or potential commitment problems, relative power and the costs of war will influence not just the terms of any settlement but also whether the predicted outcome will be settlement or war. Here we illustrate the proposition for an increase in cost when there is incomplete information. Other more intricate cases are possible involving relative power and potential commitment problems.

In Figure 6.5, suppose both players have common knowledge of the destructiveness of war but incomplete information about their relative powers. Contrast now two scenarios. In the first, player A expects the outcome of war to be at point E_A^1, while player B expects it to be at E_B^1. As a consequence, the highlighted region of mutual gain forms to the northeast of point F. Because this region lies entirely outside of the settlement-opportunity curve HN, war is the predicted outcome. In the second scenario, suppose that the destructiveness and hence the cost of war is greater. The higher cost has two effects in Figure 6.5. First, increased destructiveness decreases postwar incomes and thus moves the respective conflict points inward to points like E_A^2 and E_B^2. Second, because of the decreased payoffs to war, players divert fewer secure resources into armaments; this in turn translates into larger postsettlement incomes, thus moving the settlement-opportunity curve outward to a curve like $H'N'$. The combined effect of the higher cost of war is a much-expanded region of mutual gain that forms to the northeast of point G. Because in this scenario the opportunity curve intersects the region of mutual gain, a peaceful outcome is predicted somewhere along $H'N'$ between points S and S'. Thus, in the presence of incomplete information, a higher cost of war can make peaceful settlement more likely.

6.4. Selected Empirical Studies of Interstate Conflict

Risk Factors for Interstate Armed Conflict

A vast empirical literature on the determinants of interstate armed conflict has appeared in recent decades, pushed by continued advancements in data, computing power, and statistical methods. The objective of most studies is to estimate the likelihood of armed conflict by applying regression techniques to pooled time-series data for countries (called monads) or for country-pairs (called dyads). Depending on the particular hypotheses, the studies typically focus on one or two explanatory variables, while including other possible factors for control purposes. Based on Hirshleifer's bargaining model, factors that foster incomplete information and commitment problems can be expected to increase the risk of armed conflict. Also, to the extent that incomplete information and potential commitment problems characterize the international system, variables that affect relative power and the costs of war should be relevant. Here we sample the risk-factor literature by briefly surveying a few studies that focus on territory, economic interdependence, and economic development. Along the way we make note of important political and military capability variables that are also considered.

Territory
Throughout history, issues of territory have played a prominent role in interstate conflict. Contemporary examples of territorial conflict include the Spratly Islands (involving China, the Philippines, Vietnam, Taiwan, Malaysia, and Brunei), the Golan Heights (Israel and Syria), and Kashmir (India and Pakistan). Disputes can be over land borders (e.g., Ecuador and Peru), maritime boundaries (e.g., Australia and East Timor), or access to resources like oil and minerals (e.g., Chad and Libya over uranium deposits in the Aozou Strip). Under the broad heading of territory we

include not only issues of boundaries and natural resources but also geographic considerations of proximity and contiguity.

As noted by Fearon (1995), the control of territory often has high strategic and/or economic advantage that translates into future military power. For this reason, bargaining concessions involving territory can cause an anticipated shift in relative power, giving the recipient state an incentive to renege on an agreement at a future date by exploiting its strengthened position. Consequently, a territorial dispute can generate a serious commitment problem, possibly leading to preventive war. In this way, the risk of armed conflict can be expected to be higher for territorial disputes than for nonterritorial disputes, other things equal. Proximity and contiguity can likewise increase the risk of armed conflict. States that are closer to each other have an easier time projecting military power against each other. Thus, as will be explored more fully in Chapter 9, the closer two countries are to each other geographically, the lower is the cost of their fighting one another, and hence the greater is the risk of armed conflict between them. Furthermore, proximity can increase the ability of a state to surprise its rival with a devastating first strike. Thus, states that are closer to one another, and especially those that are contiguous, are more likely to face the sort of commitment problem that favors preemptive war. As a practical matter, contiguous countries might be more apt to find themselves in disputes because of the frequency and multiplicity of their interactions (Bremer 2000). At the same time, proximity and contiguity can facilitate bilateral trade, which might reduce the risk of conflict, as suggested by the liberal peace hypothesis introduced in Chapter 3 and discussed further in the next subsection.

According to Hensel (2000, p. 78), a "substantial body of empirical evidence . . . finds a close relationship between conflict behavior and such geographic factors as contiguity and territorial issues." Senese's (2005) study of the risks of MID onset and escalation to war provides a good example of evidence supportive of Hensel's statement. The sample spans the period 1919–95 and includes almost a half million observations, where an observation is a dyad-year, meaning a pair of countries in a single year. Each observation is coded as to whether the dyad experienced a MID onset in that year; each MID onset in turn is coded as to whether the dispute escalated to war. Thus, there are two dependent variables, one indicating MID onset and the other war onset. The key risk assessment variables include an indicator for whether countries within a dyad were contiguous, another indicator for whether a territorial disagreement existed between them, and the interaction of the two indicators. Control variables used by

Senese include measures of alliance, democracy, major power status, economic development, and relative capability.

Senese's (2005, p. 777) statistical results show that both contiguity and territorial disagreement between states increase the risk of MID onset. The probability of a MID onset during a given year is estimated to increase from 0.001 for a noncontiguous dyad with no territorial disagreement to 0.038 for a contiguous dyad with territorial disagreement. The results pertaining to war onset are similar for territory, but not for contiguity. Senese finds clearly that a territorial dispute increases the risk that a MID will escalate to war. In particular, the estimated impact of a territorial dispute increases the probability of war onset from 0.030 to 0.282 for noncontiguous dyads and from 0.020 to 0.094 for contiguous dyads. Surprisingly, contiguity is estimated to decrease the probability of MIDs' escalating to war. According to Senese, a territorial MID without a shared border might imply a greater difficulty of resolving such a dispute by a means short of war. Another possibility is that the effect of contiguity might be underestimated owing to the omission of a dyadic trade variable, which could be positively correlated with contiguity but negatively correlated with armed conflict.

Economic Interdependence

In Chapter 3 we introduced the liberal peace hypothesis, according to which trade partners are less likely to engage in armed conflict against each other, other things equal. One rationale for the hypothesis is that trading nations face higher opportunity costs of war because of the economic gains they stand to forgo when war disrupts trade between them. Other rationales have been proposed, including reduction in misinformation and promotion of shared values or of trust between trading partners (Gartzke, Li, and Boehmer 2001, Reed 2003, Bearce and Omori 2005). Evidence relevant to the liberal peace hypothesis in the context of interstate conflict is provided by Russett and Oneal (2001) and Martin, Mayer, and Thoenig (2008). The studies are similar inasmuch as both find that bilateral trade openness reduces the likelihood of armed conflict between trade partners, everything else the same. The studies differ, however, in their conclusions about the effect of multilateral trade openness on the risk of conflict.

Russett and Oneal (2001) test the liberal peace hypothesis for a large sample of about 40,000 dyad-years. Their sample spans most years between 1886 and 1992 but is restricted to what Russett and Oneal term politically relevant dyads, which are dyads that were contiguous or contained at least one major power. Conflict is measured by a variable indicating whether the two countries in a dyad were involved in a militarized interstate dispute (MID) during the given year. For each country in a dyad, bilateral economic interdependence is gauged by how much the country traded with its partner relative to its GDP. The country in the dyad with the lower trade dependence is considered the weak link, so its dependence is treated as determinant of the likelihood of militarized disputes. Based on the liberal peace hypothesis, Russett and Oneal expect that bilateral interdependence lowers the risk of a militarized dispute. Russett and Oneal (2001, p. 137) note that if countries in a dyad also engage in multilateral trade, then bilateral disputes can disrupt trade with third countries, further raising the opportunity cost of bilateral conflict. Thus, Russett and Oneal hypothesize that multilateral trade openness, measured by a country's total trade relative to its GDP, also reduces the risk of interstate conflict. For control purposes, Russett and Oneal include variables for contiguity, distance between the countries, minor power status, shared alliances, shared intergovernmental organizations, democracy, and relative power.

Based on their statistical analysis, Russett and Oneal conclude that interstate trade has an important effect in reducing the risk of armed conflict. In their central results, Russett and Oneal (2001, p. 171) estimate the probability of MID involvement to be about 0.03 for the typical dyad-year. From this baseline they calculate that if bilateral trade dependence increases by one standard deviation above the sample mean, the risk of MID involvement falls to 0.017, or by 43 percent. Russett and Oneal (2001, p. 148) also report that when both trade dependence and multilateral trade openness are considered, each makes a substantial and independent contribution to reducing the risk of a MID. In response to certain methodological challenges, Oneal and Russett (2003a, 2003b) report additional estimates for the pacific effect of trade based on alternative approaches. These estimates of the risk reduction due to trade tend to lie in the range of 20 to 40 percent, and they rise to about 60 percent when the conflict variable is changed from MID involvement to MID onset with fatalities. Although we focus here on economic interdependence, Russett and Oneal also report empirical evidence of the pacific effects of democracy and intergovernmental organizations. Hence, Russett and Oneal (2001, p. 29) interpret their results as strongly supportive of a Kantian vision wherein peace stands on the three-part foundation of economic interdependence, democracy, and international law and organization.

To test the pacific effect of trade, Martin et al. (2008) begin with a bargaining model of war with asymmetric information. They then introduce a trade model that allows for differentiated products and also multiple trade partners with varying distances among them. From the combined models the authors derive their first hypothesis, which states that, because of the opportunity cost of forgone gains, when two countries trade more, they are less likely to fight each other. Martin, Mayer, and Thoenig go on to consider the effects of multilateral trade openness on the risk of bilateral conflict, and on this issue their theory is intriguing. If bilateral conflict does not disrupt trade with third parties too much, then a country with high multilateral trade openness may have a relatively low opportunity cost of bilateral conflict. The intuition for this result is that a country with high multilateral trade openness will have ample opportunity to offset forgone bilateral gains by trading elsewhere, thus lowering the opportunity cost of bilateral conflict. Hence, Martin, Mayer, and Thoenig's second hypothesis is that an increase in multilateral trade openness increases the risk of bilateral conflict.

Martin, Mayer, and Thoenig test their hypotheses for a sample of more than 500,000 observations, where each observation is a dyad-year. The sample spans the years between 1950 and 2000 and includes all dyads for which data are available. Conflict is measured by a variable indicating whether the two countries in a dyad were involved in a MID during the given year that involved the display of force or the use of force, or that crossed the threshold into war. For each dyad, bilateral trade openness is measured by the arithmetic average of each country's bilateral imports relative to its GDP. To measure multilateral trade openness, the authors use the arithmetic average of total imports of the two countries in the dyad, excluding their bilateral imports, divided by their GDPs. Control variables include contiguity, distance between the countries, number of peaceful years since the last MID, similarity of language, shared military alliance, UN voting correlation, and democracy.

Based on their statistical analysis, Martin, Mayer, and Thoenig conclude that the risk of bilateral interstate conflict falls with greater bilateral trade openness but rises with greater multilateral trade openness. For dyads with a bilateral distance of less than 1,000 km, the average risk of interstate conflict is 0.045 in 2000. From this baseline, Martin, Mayer, and Thoenig find that if bilateral trade openness declined to the level that prevailed in 1970, the risk of interstate conflict would rise to 0.048. For multilateral trade openness, a return to the lower level that prevailed in 1970 would reduce the risk of interstate conflict to 0.034. On net, Martin, Mayer, and Thoenig suggest that the increase in bilateral and multilateral trade openness that occurred between 1970 and 2000 increased the risk of interstate conflict for proximate countries from 0.037 to 0.045. The authors also report that the bilateral and multilateral trade effects on interstate conflict are much smaller for less proximate countries.

Note that Russett and Oneal (2001) and Martin et al. (2008) find that bilateral trade openness reduces the risk of interstate conflict, but they reach opposite conclusions on the effects of multilateral trade openness. Possible explanations of the discrepancy between the two studies include their use of different statistical methods, different samples (politically relevant dyads vs. all dyads), different sample periods (1886–1992 vs. 1950–2000), and different measures of conflict (MIDs vs. higher-level MIDs) and of bilateral and multilateral trade openness (weak link vs. arithmetic average). Discrepant results in social scientific studies of conflict are, of course, quite common. One of the benefits of cumulative social scientific inquiry is that both common and discrepant results emerge. The former tend to increase confidence in the results, whereas the latter tend to spur new research designed to better understand phenomena.

Economic Development

In Book V, Chapter 1 of the *Wealth of Nations*, Adam Smith (1776) provided a remarkable account of the effect of economic development on interstate conflict. Smith considered four levels of economic development: hunting, pastoral, agricultural, and manufacturing. According to Smith, the least developed (hunting) and most developed (manufacturing) societies would be unlikely to initiate war because of high opportunity costs. In hunter societies, armies would be limited in scale because if people spent time away from hunting and gathering, they would substantially reduce their means of livelihood. In developed societies, soldiers would have to be drawn away from manufacturing, leading to a significant loss in output. For moderately developed pastoral and agricultural societies, however, Smith believed that the opportunity cost of war was relatively low. Shepherds could bring their herds with them to war and maintain them during periods between battles. In agricultural societies, once the seeds were planted, younger men could participate in wars with little loss in output because crop maintenance could be left to women, children, and older men. Smith's ideas implied an inverted U-shaped relationship between economic development and the risk of war onset.

Most modern statistical studies assume a linear or logarithmic relationship between development and interstate armed conflict (see, e.g., East and Gregg 1967, Hegre 2000, Senese 2005). An exception is Boehmer and Sobek (2005, p. 5), who hypothesize an inverted-U relationship between development and armed conflict because the "changing orientation of economies from agricultural and extractive activities eventually to service-based economies alters the cost-benefit calculations concerning territorial acquisition." Less developed countries lack the wherewithal to project military power, and more advanced service-oriented countries have less to gain from territorial pursuits. In the middle are moderately developed countries that are most prone to armed conflict.

To test their hypothesis, Boehmer and Sobek construct a sample of over 5,000 observations spanning the period from 1870 to 1992, where each observation is a monad-year, meaning a single country in a single year. For each observation, they record whether the country initiated a new MID, was involved in a new MID over territory, or participated in a new MID with fatalities. The first two of these dependent variables measure the onset of interstate conflict, and the third measures the seriousness of conflict. Energy consumption per capita is used to measure a state's level of economic development. To permit a nonlinear effect, both the log and the log-squared of per capita consumption are included in the regression analysis. Control variables include economic openness, population growth and density, democracy, and military capability.

Boehmer and Sobek's statistical results indicate that economic development affects all three measures of interstate conflict in an inverted-U fashion. For example, they find that as the level of development increases from its minimum to its maximum sample value, the estimated probability of MID onset in a given year rises from 0.0014 to 0.0275 before falling to 0.0088. Similarly, they estimate that the probability of a state's involvement in a new MID with fatalities is 0.0003 for less developed states and 0.0002 for highly developed states, but 0.0026 for moderately developed states. Based on their analysis, Boehmer and Sobek project that moderately developed countries are most at risk for interstate armed conflict (e.g., China, India, Iran, Pakistan, and Nigeria), while in the future the risk will rise with continued development by poorer states (e.g., Liberia, Sudan, and the Democratic Republic of Congo).

Conflict Termination

Duration

Hirshleifer's simple bargaining model of conflict introduced in Chapter 5 and reviewed earlier is essentially static and for that reason can say little about strategic interaction once war begins. More formal models, however, allow for multiple periods and hence the possibility of intrawar bargaining and eventual war termination (see, e.g., Filson and Werner 2002, Slantchev

2003, Powell 2004, and Smith and Stam 2004). Absent commitment problems, incomplete information can generate inconsistent expectations and the initiation of war. As war proceeds, the adversaries update their expectations based on information revealed through battlefield outcomes, offers and counteroffers, and continued willingness to fight. This process continues until expectations converge sufficiently to permit mutually advantageous settlement. The challenge presented to social scientists when testing these models is that expectations and the private information on which they rest are unobservable.

Slantchev (2004) addresses this challenge by postulating that initial military parity implies relatively high uncertainty over who will win; this uncertainty in turn provides the incentive to delay settlement in order to gain or transmit information that will be advantageous in further bargaining. The hypothesis that follows is that the closer to parity is the observed initial relative capability, the longer is the expected duration of war, other things equal. Slantchev tests this hypothesis based on a sample of 104 interstate wars that occurred between 1816 and 1991. His dependent variable is war duration measured in months, and with military parity as his key explanatory variable, he includes a number of control variables such as terrain, contiguity, and democracy. His central finding is that military parity increases war duration, as predicted. For example, at the 12-month mark, the estimated probability that war will continue is less than 10 percent if the war began with military preponderance but more than 40 percent if it began with military parity (Slantchev 2004, p. 821). Expected duration is also increased when terrain is difficult, the adversary states are noncontiguous, the initiator is democratic, or more than two countries are involved.

Third-Party Intervention

Much like the literature on the risk factors for war, empirical research on third-party intervention has grown enormously. Hirshleifer's bargaining model in Chapter 5 shows clearly that intervention can promote peace if third parties succeed in coordinating expectations or resolving commitment problems. Numerous questions then arise that can be addressed by empirical analysis. Most fundamentally, how successful are third-party interventions at resolving conflict? But also, where, when, how, and by whom is intervention most successful?

Frazier and Dixon (2006) illustrate how such questions can be addressed using large-sample regression analysis. To gauge the successfulness of intervention, they begin with a sample of more than 2,200 dyads of countries involved in MIDs between 1946 and 2000. For each dyad they indicate whether or not the MID reached a negotiated settlement, thereby generating the dependent variable. At the same time, independent variables are constructed to indicate the presence or absence of various mediation methods (e.g., diplomatic approaches, legal processes, or military involvement) and mediator identities (including states, coalitions, or intergovernmental organizations [IGOs]). Also included in their analysis are control variables for dispute duration and for the presence of a major power country in the dyad.

Frazier and Dixon's (2006, p. 398) fundamental result is that "the presence of a third-party intermediary's efforts tend to substantially improve the probability that disputes are settled by negotiated means." In particular, they estimate that the probability of negotiated settlement roughly quadruples from a baseline of 0.100 to a new level of 0.397 when an intermediary is present. In their more detailed analysis, they find that the likelihood of negotiated settlement is most responsive to intermediary military intervention and IGO involvement. Consistent with other research, they also find that negotiated settlement is less likely when the dispute is short-lived or the dyad includes a major power.

Economic Costs of World War I

In Chapter 1, we identified three economic costs of conflict: diversion of resources, destruction of resources, and disruption of economic activities. In Chapter 2, we showed how the three types of costs can be presented in the context of a production possibilities model. Diversion of resources because of conflict implies fewer alternative goods, such as food and clothing, along a production possibilities frontier (PPF). Destruction of resources causes the PPF to shift in, implying diminished production possibilities over all goods. Disruption of economic activity, such as the loss of trade, leads to further decreases in national income and consumer well-being.

In Figure 6.6 we illustrate these categories of cost by summarizing the estimated economic costs of World War I that were due to diversion of resources, destruction of property, loss of human life, and disruption of trade. Estimates of the first two costs, resource diversion and property loss, are based on figures originally provided by Bogart (1919). We assume his estimates are denominated in 1918 dollars and then deflate them to 1913 using the consumer price index. The resource diversion costs of $123 billion include expenditures by belligerent and neutral governments for military personnel and equipment in excess of expenditures that would have been made without the war. Property losses of $22 billion include the costs of destroyed or disabled factories, farms, and merchant ships.

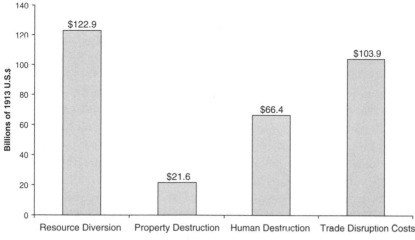

Figure 6.6. Diversion, destruction, and disruption costs of World War I.
Sources: Bogart (1919), Glick and Taylor (2008).

Estimates of the costs of human loss and trade disruption come from Glick and Taylor (2008). They impute the human cost of war by applying the prevailing average real wage to each life lost and half this wage to each person wounded in war. They also impute as income lost the value of trade forgone during the war. Because the costs of human loss and trade disruption were experienced both during and after the war, Glick and Taylor convert the flow of costs into one-time costs using standard amortization methods. Their final estimates of the economic costs of human loss and trade disruption associated with World War I are respectively $66 billion and $104 billion in 1913 dollars.

When the costs of resource diversion, property destruction, human loss, and trade disruption are combined, the estimated economic costs of World War I total $315 billion in 1913 prices. To appreciate the magnitude of such costs, consider that the world GDP in 1913, as reported by Glick and Taylor, equaled $204 billion. Thus, according to the estimates in Figure 6.6, the economic costs of World War I totaled more than one-and-a-half times the *world's* 1913 GDP, a truly staggering cost indeed.

6.5. Bibliographic Notes

The social scientific study of interstate armed conflict was inspired by Sorokin (1937), Wright (1942), Richardson (1960a, 1960b), and, according to Singer (2000, p. 5), the Polish economist de Bloch (1899). Isard

(2000) and Singer (2000) describe the emergence in the 1950s and 1960s of a critical mass of scholars devoted to the scientific study of war, which led to the establishment of the Center for Research on Conflict Resolution at the University of Michigan in 1957 and the Peace Science Society (International) in the early 1960s.

Economic choice perspectives of war are significant in the early literature of conflict economics. Schelling's (1960, 1966) classic works treated conflict initiation, management, and termination as a process of expectations formation among players within a mixed-motive bargaining game. Isard (1969) and Isard and Smith (1982) utilized oligopoly principles to develop numerous theoretical procedures for preventing, shortening, or terminating conflict. Raiffa (1982) presented practical procedures for managing business conflicts, with obvious parallels to interstate conflicts. Boulding (1962) explored a number of ways in which conflicts end. Wittman (1979) presented necessary conditions for war termination, while Cross (1977) emphasized the role of learning in conflict bargaining. Each of these contributions by economists treated the onset, duration, and termination of conflict as the result of players' rational cost-benefit calculations in the context of changing circumstances and information. For reviews of the thought of early (pre–World War II) economists on war, see Coulomb (1998), the edited volume of Goodwin (1991), and the special issue of *Defence and Peace Economics* (Brauer 2003).

The rational cost-benefit approach to war is not without controversy, as suggested by the extensive discussions of the approach among social scientists. For elaboration and critique of the rational choice approach to war, see Bueno de Mesquita (1981) and Singer (2000). To sample the debate on the rationality assumption in conflict studies, see Brown et al. (2000), Quackenbush (2004), and Vahabi (2004).

Geller and Singer (1998) provide an extensive summary of risk factors for interstate armed conflict based on approximately 500 statistical studies and numerous theoretical perspectives. Vasquez's (2000) edited volume reviews what social scientists have learned about the determinants of interstate war and highlights important issues for future research. A special issue of *Conflict Management and Peace Science* (Kadera and Mitchell 2005) offers spirited discussion and debate on statistical methods used in conflict research.

Rasler and Thompson (2006) provide a valuable summary of the empirical literature on territoriality and interstate armed conflict. Their own empirical investigation finds that contested territory and contiguity in the context of strategic rivalry is a particularly potent combination for the risk of militarized disputes and their escalation to war between states.

Vigorous research and debate continues on the effects of economic interdependence on interstate conflict. For various theoretical and empirical perspectives, see the edited volumes of Mansfield and Pollins (2003) and Schneider, Barbieri, and Gleditsch (2003), the special issue of *Journal of Peace Research* (Schneider and Barbieri 1999), and Polachek and Seiglie's (2007) extensive overview.

For additional empirical studies of war duration and termination, see Bennett and Stam (1996) and Ramsay (2008). See Schrodt and Gerner (2004), Beardsley, Quinn, Biswas, and Wilkenfeld (2006), and a special issue of *International Interactions* (Feng and Kugler 2006) for additional empirical studies of third-party mediation of interstate conflicts. See Wall, Stark, and Standifer (2001) for a review of the quantitative literature on mediation.

Comprehensive studies on economic diversion, destruction, and disruption from interstate war are surprisingly rare. For additional studies on the economic costs of interstate war, see Harris (1997) on the Iran-Iraq war of 1980–88, Broadberry and Harrison (2005) on World War I, and Harrison (2000) on World War II. For studies of the effects of interstate conflicts on economic growth and global financial markets, see Koubi (2005) and Schneider and Troeger (2006), respectively.

Civil War and Genocide

As documented in Chapter 1, wars within states have become far more numerous than wars between states, especially in recent decades. Over the period 1990–2006, for example, the Uppsala Conflict Data Program/Peace Research Institute, Oslo identified 23 war onsets within states compared to three between states. In this chapter we present theoretical and empirical perspectives on the onset, termination, and consequences of violent intrastate conflicts, particularly civil wars and genocides.

7.1. Definitions

For the purposes of this chapter, we draw on Marshall, Gurr, and Harff (2001, p. 5) and Sambanis (2002, p. 218) to define civil war as violent conflict within a country between a government and one or more internal opposition groups, with sizeable fatalities on each side. Scholars differ over the level of violence that qualifies as a civil war, but for coding purposes a fatality threshold of 1,000 is sometimes used. To distinguish it from a massacre, a civil war must entail sizeable fatalities on both sides. The Correlates of War Project, for example, requires that the stronger side's fatalities be least 5 percent of the weaker side's fatalities to qualify as a civil war (Henderson and Singer 2000, pp. 284–285).

An internal opposition group is generally identified by political, ethnic, religious, or cultural characteristics, and its objective might be to overthrow the government, seize power in a particular region, secede, or obtain major changes in its political, economic, or social status (Marshall, Gurr, and Harff 2001, p. 5). When an opposition group is significantly outnumbered, it often resorts to guerrilla warfare, whereby small bands of mobile forces attack larger government forces at times and locations advantageous to the rebels. Guerrillas also typically control territory from which they cultivate popular support, recruit members, and coordinate operations. An armed uprising against a government is referred to as an insurgency, an insurrection, or a rebellion, and the sudden violent over-throw of a government is known as a revolution (Sandler and Hartley 1995, pp. 306–307). When the opposition group in a revolution is itself part of the government, the conflict is known as a coup d'état. An inter-communal war within a state occurs among opposing ethnic, religious, or cultural groups, none of which is the state. Violence within a communal group is referred to as factional or intracommunal conflict.

An important form of conflict often associated with civil war is geno-cide. Here we draw on Harff (2003, p. 58), Fein (1993, p. 24), and the United Nations Genocide Convention to define genocide as an authority group's sustained purposeful implementation or facilitation of policies designed to destroy, in whole or in part, a national, ethnic, racial, or religious group. Politicide pertains when the victimized group is identified by its political opposition to the dominant party rather than by other communal characteristics. Genocides and politicides are not accidental outcomes but are purposeful actions carried out with the explicit or tacit support of an authority group (Harff 2003, p. 58).

7.2. Patterns of Armed Civil Conflict and Genocide

Prominent Datasets

Figure 7.1 summarizes eight intrastate conflict datasets. The first two cover civil wars and sub-war civil conflicts and are jointly provided by the Uppsala Conflict Data Program (UCDP) and the International Peace Research Institute, Oslo (PRIO). The third covers intrastate wars identified by the Correlates of War (COW) Project. The fourth distinguishes between revo-lutionary and ethnic wars and is furnished by the Political Instability Task Force (PITF), and the fifth and sixth identify civil wars as defined by James Fearon and David Laitin and by Nicholas Sambanis. The next dataset, from the Minorities at Risk (MAR) Project, provides information on civil, intercommunal, and factional conflicts. The final source is the Political Instability Task Force (PITF) dataset for genocides and politicides.

Major distinctions among the datasets, along with the years covered, are summarized at the top of Figure 7.1, with additional details provided at the bottom. Notice that different types of intrastate conflicts are distinguished, including civil wars, sub-war civil conflicts, revolutionary and ethnic conflicts, intercommunal conflicts, intracommunal (factional) strife, and

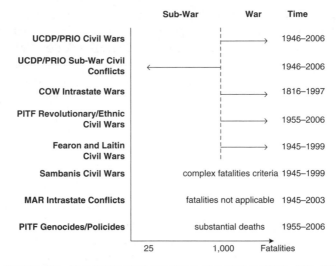

Uppsala Conflict Data Program/International Peace Research Institute, Oslo (UCDP/PRIO) Armed Conflict Dataset – Civil Wars:
Combat between a state and one or more internal opposition groups leading to a minimum of 1,000 battle-related deaths (military and civilian) per year among the parties involved (Gleditsch et al. 2002, UCDP/PRIO Codebook version 4–2006).

Uppsala Conflict Data Program/International Peace Research Institute, Oslo (UCDP/PRIO) Armed Conflict Dataset – Sub-War Civil Wars:
Apply UCDP/PRIO's civil war definition, but with battle-related deaths (military and civilian) between 25 and 999 (Gleditsch et al. 2002, UCDP/PRIO Codebook version 4–2006).

Correlates of War (COW) Intrastate Wars:
Combat between the central government and one or more intrastate groups (excluding massacres) leading to 1,000 battle deaths (military fatalities only) for the whole war. Data for intercommunal wars (between two or more groups, none of which is the state) is under development (Sarkees 2000).

Political Instability Task Force (PITF) Revolutionary/Ethnic Civil Wars:
Conflict between a government and a politically organized group or communal minority leading to a minimum of 1,000 direct conflict-related deaths (military and civilian) for the whole war among the parties involved. In addition, each party mobilizes at least 1,000 people in the conflict and there must be at least one year when the annual conflict-related deaths exceed 100 (Marshall et al. 2001, p. 5).

Fearon and Laitin Civil Wars:
Conflict between agents of a state and non-state groups, with at least 1,000 fatalities for the whole war, a yearly average of at least 100 fatalities, and at least 100 killed on both sides (including civilians killed by rebels) (Fearon and Laitin 2003, p. 76).

Sambanis Civil Wars:
Conflict between a government and one or more internal insurgent organizations, characterized by a high level of initial violence (at least 500 deaths caused by conflict in the first year, or 1,000 cumulative deaths in the initial three-year period) as well as sustained violence (no three-year period with fewer than 500 deaths caused by conflict) and substantial resistance by the weaker party (Sambanis 2004b, pp. 829–830).

Minorities at Risk (MAR) Intrastate Conflicts:
Three types of intrastate conflict are considered: conflict within a communal group (factional, or intracommunal conflict), between communal groups (intercommunal conflict), and between one or more communal groups and a regime (civil conflict). Conflict severity ranges from acts of harassment and sporadic violence to protracted warfare (Minorities at Risk Project 2005).

Political Instability Task Force (PITF) Genocides/Politicides:
"The promotion, execution, and/or implied consent of sustained policies by governing elites or their agents – or in the case of civil war, either of the contending authorities – that result in the deaths of a substantial portion of a communal group or politicized non-communal group" (Marshall et al. 2001, p. 12).

Figure 7.1. Selected intrastate conflict datasets.

genocides and politicides. UCDP/PRIO, COW, PITF, and Fearon and Laitin recognize conflicts as war only if they have fatalities numbering at least 1,000. UCDP/PRIO also provides data on conflicts short of war with fatalities between 25 and 999. The other data sources in Figure 7.1 have either complex fatality criteria (e.g., Sambanis) or no specific fatality criteria (e.g., MAR, PITF Genocides/Politicides). Whether and how fatalities are counted (e.g., military only vs. military plus civilian, per war vs. per year) differ across datasets.

Measures of Armed Civil Conflicts

We use UCDP/PRIO's Armed Conflict Dataset to highlight various characteristics of civil wars and sub-wars. Here we emphasize three points about the dataset. First, according to UCDP/PRIO, a civil conflict involves violence between a central government and one or more intrastate groups. Hence, conflicts within a state between two or more groups, none of which is the state, are excluded from the UCDP/PRIO dataset. Second, when battle-related (military and civilian) deaths number between 25 and 999 per year, the civil conflict is classified as a sub-war; when those deaths reach 1,000 per year, it is a civil war. Some scholars depart from UCDP/ PRIO definitions by treating an intrastate conflict as a civil war even though battle-related deaths are fewer than the 1,000 per year threshold. For example, in Sambanis's dataset, the threshold for civil war is substantially lower than 1,000 fatalities per year (see Figure 7.1). Third, there can be more than one civil conflict within a state in a given year. This occurs, for example, when a state fights against one group over one incompatibility (e.g., territory) and against another group over another incompatibility (e.g., government control).

Figure 7.2 shows the stock of armed civil conflicts per year in the world from 1946 to 2006. From the early 1950s through the early 1990s, the number of both civil wars and sub-wars increased substantially, although the increase was by no means uniform. In 1950, for example, there were five civil wars and six sub-wars; by 1992 these counts had risen to 17 and 32, respectively. Collier et al. (2003, pp. 94–95) hypothesize that the risk of civil war in many poor countries was suppressed by colonialism in the 1950s but then rose with decolonization by Britain and France, particularly in Africa in the early 1960s. Immediately after the end of the Cold War in 1989, there was a noticeable increase in civil conflicts, followed by a substantial decline in the mid-1990s. Collier et al. (2003, pp. 95–96) conjecture that Russian decolonization in the early 1990s may have

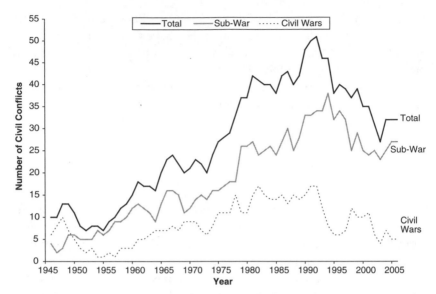

Figure 7.2. Stock of armed civil conflicts, 1946–2006.
Sources: Uppsala Conflict Data Program (UCDP), International Peace Research
Institute, Oslo (PRIO), and Gleditsch et al. (2002).

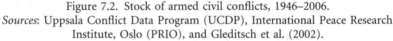

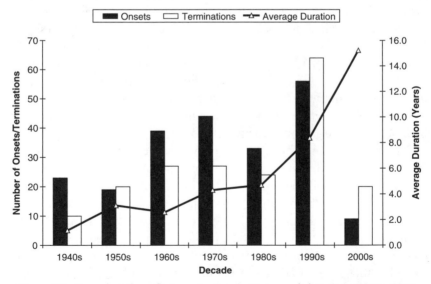

Figure 7.3. Armed civil conflict onsets, terminations, and durations, 1940s–2000s.
Note: The average duration is for civil conflicts terminated in the decade shown.
Because the temporal domain of the data source is 1946–2004, intrastate conflicts
initiated prior to 1946 or initiated/ongoing after 2004 are excluded.
Sources: Derived from Gleditsch et al. (2002) and Gates and Strand (2006).

increased the risk of civil conflict, but then unprecedented levels of peace-keeping operations became possible in the post Cold War era, leading to a surge of intrastate peace settlements in the mid-1990s. In the average year during the full period 1946–2006, 31.2 percent of armed civil conflicts qualified as civil war. In the period 2000–2006, however, this percentage dropped to 21.4 percent. Hence, the data suggest that civil wars more recently have become a smaller proportion of total violent civil conflicts.

Figure 7.3 shows the number of armed civil conflict onsets and terminations by decade (measured on the left axis) and the average duration of civil conflicts by decade (measured on the right axis). Note that the 1960s, 1970s, and 1980s experienced more civil conflict onsets than terminations, whereas the 1990s and 2000s show more terminations than onsets. These patterns of civil conflict inflows and outflows in the international system are consistent with the rising and then declining stock of armed civil conflicts observed in Figure 7.2. A conspicuous feature of Figure 7.3 is the relatively high duration of civil conflicts, especially in recent decades. Recall from Chapter 6 (see Table 6.1) that the average duration of wars between states over the period 1816–2006 was 1.2 years. Figure 7.3 shows that by the 2000s, the average duration of civil conflicts had reached a

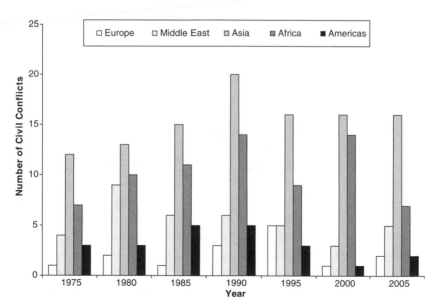

Figure 7.4. Stock of armed civil conflicts by region, 1975–2005.
Sources: Uppsala Conflict Data Program (UCDP), International Peace Research Institute, Oslo (PRIO), and Gleditsch et al. (2002).

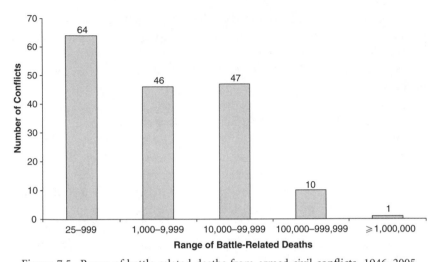

Figure 7.5. Range of battle-related deaths from armed civil conflicts, 1946–2005.
Notes: The figure was constructed by averaging the low and high fatality estimates
for each civil conflict for each year, cumulating the average yearly fatalities
for each civil conflict, and then assigning each conflict to one of the five size
categories. When high fatality estimates were missing, low fatality estimates were
used alone. Because UCDP/PRIO requires 1,000 fatalities per year for a civil
conflict to be categorized as a war, there are some civil conflicts represented
in the figure with cumulative fatalities of 1,000 or more that did not qualify
as civil wars in some (or all) years. Thirty-one of the civil conflicts in the figure
were ongoing as of 2005 and thus might move into higher cumulative fatality
categories in the future.
Sources: International Peace Research Institute, Oslo (PRIO) and Lacina
and Gleditsch (2005).

staggering 15.2 years. For the full period 1946–2004, the average duration
of civil conflicts was 8.1 years.

Figure 7.4 presents the geographic distribution of armed civil conflicts
around the world from 1975 to 2005. As seen, civil conflicts have been
heavily concentrated in Asia and Africa. This may be due to the large
number of countries in these regions and/or to regional characteristics that
influence the onset, duration, and termination of civil conflicts.

In Figure 7.5 we show the range of cumulative battle-related deaths from
armed civil conflicts over the period 1946–2005. More than one-third of
these civil conflicts had cumulative battle-related deaths above 10,000, and
6.5 percent of the civil conflicts reached cumulative fatalities of 100,000 or
more. In the case of China, 1946–49, cumulative battle-related fatalities
totaled 1.2 million.

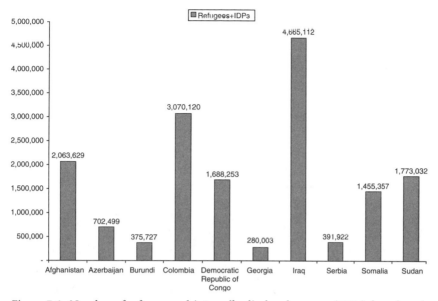

Figure 7.6. Number of refugees and internally displaced persons (IDPs) for selected
countries of origin, provisional data, end of year 2007.
Source: United Nations High Commissioner for Refugees (UNHCR) at
www.unhcr.org/statistics.html.

In addition to deaths and injuries, another important consequence of
intrastate conflicts is the rise of refugees and internally displaced persons
(IDPs). Refugees are "people who are outside their countries because of a
well-founded fear of persecution based on their race, religion, nationality,
political opinion or membership in a particular social group, and who
cannot or do not want to return home" (United Nations High Commissioner for Refugees 2006a, p. 6). IDPs are "civilians, mostly women and
children, who have been forced to abandon their homes because of conflict
or persecution" but continue to reside in their own countries (United
Nations High Commissioner for Refugees 2006b, pp. 5–6). Displaced
populations can arise for different reasons, but intrastate conflicts constitute a major cause (Weiner 1996). In Figure 7.6 we show the total
number of refugees and IDPs in 2007 for ten countries. The first nine of
these countries have a recent history of violent civil conflict, while the
tenth country, Sudan, experienced genocide. The magnitude of displaced
persons is striking. In Afghanistan the number of displaced persons
exceeds two million, and in Colombia and Iraq the number exceeds three
million and four million, respectively.

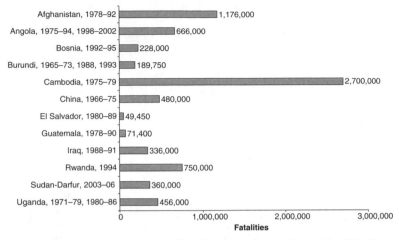

Figure 7.7. Estimated fatalities for selected genocides and politicides, 1965–2006.

Notes: The fatality data for Cambodia and Rwanda are from Harff (2003). A fatality estimate for each of the other cases is constructed from the PITF dataset by taking the midpoint of the death magnitude range for each case for each year and summing over the years. The Iraq 1988–91 figure of 336,000 is substantially greater than in other sources. Harff (2003, p. 60), for example, reports a fatality figure of 180,000.

Sources: Political Instability Task Force (PITF) Dataset on Genocides and Politicides at http://globalpolicy.gmu.edu/pitf/pitfpset.htm, Marshall et al. (2001), and Harff (2003).

Genocides and Politicides

History documents horrific cases of genocide and politicide with extraordinary fatalities, including Nazi Germany (11.4 million) and Japan (10 million) during World War II, the Soviet Union from 1920 to 1953 (20 million), and China during the 1958–1962 Great Leap Forward (30 million) (Simons 2006, p. 30). In Figure 7.7 we present fatality estimates for a selection of more recent intrastate genocides and politicides. As shown, the Afghan and Cambodian cases reached 1.2 million and 2.7 million fatalities, respectively. Notice that some genocides/politicides occur over long periods (e.g., Afghanistan and El Salvador), others are relatively brief and intense (e.g., Rwanda), and still others occur intermittently (e.g., Burundi). The civil war and genocide literatures have tended to be distinct and separate, but research is beginning to explore relationships between them (e.g., Bartrop 2002, Krain 1997). Such research is important because Harff (2003, p. 57) notes that "almost all genocides of the last half-century occurred during or in the immediate aftermath of internal wars, revolutions, and regime collapse."

7.3. Theoretical Perspectives on Civil War

Motives and Conditions for Civil Strife

Greed and Grievance Motives

Scholars often refer to a "greed or grievance" dichotomy to categorize possible motives for civil war. Some rebel leaders may be motivated by greed aimed at profits from control of natural resources (e.g., oil, diamonds, precious metals, timber), illegal activities (e.g., narcotics trafficking, protection rackets), or taxation. Other rebel leaders may be motivated by grievances stemming from the state's past or present mistreatment of a communal group. The notion that civil strife may be motivated by greed is associated with the research of economists Paul Collier and Anke Hoeffler, who maintain that a high level of natural resources within a state elevates the risk of civil war onset (Collier and Hoeffler 2004). Grievance explanations of civil strife are common in political science and social psychology, where various in-group versus out-group behaviors are believed to control the risk of violence. For example, a group with sufficient power within a state may close off political, economic, or social opportunities to others for a variety of reasons, including ideological commitment, exploitation of power, or perceived threats. When structures of closure fall on an identifiable ethnic, religious, cultural, or political group, and one or more catalytic events occur (e.g., an extreme episode of deprivation), conditions are ripe for civil unrest (Gurr 1968, Tellis, Szayna, and Winnefeld 1997, pp. 86–96.).

Weak State Conditions

For some scholars, a state's capacity to respond to a rebel movement is a crucial ingredient in the onset and duration of civil violence. In "weak state" explanations of civil strife, the state lacks the ability to forestall rebellion with force or through accommodation of the rebel organization's demands. Ballentine and Sherman (2003a, p. 9) note that the "defining condition of a weak or failing state is subject to competing definitions among scholars, [but] such states are minimally characterized by a loss of legitimacy and a loss of governing effectiveness in all or significant parts of their territory."

One important variable in weak state explanations of civil strife is the political system, often measured by a state's level of autocracy or democracy or by its transition from one political system to another. Intermediate and transitioning regimes have a relatively low political capacity to forestall unrest: they tend to practice some degree of grievance-generating repression, while also permitting enough openness that aggrieved groups can effectively organize and initiate civil protest (Hegre, Ellingsen, Gates, and Gleditsch 2001, p. 33). Furthermore, such regimes tend to experience relatively severe infighting and corruption, which can facilitate loss of government legitimacy, in-group versus out-group closure, and reduction in government resources available to address grievances. Autocracies and mature democracies, on the other hand, are believed to have a relatively high capacity to forestall rebellion: autocracies tend to use force to preclude rebellion, while mature democracies tend to encourage nonviolent reforms to address communal grievances. Hence, an inverted-U relationship between level of democracy and risk of civil war onset has been posited, and there is some empirical evidence to that effect (Hegre et al. 2001, Mousseau 2001).

A state's economic capacity for dealing with rebellion can also affect the onset and duration of civil war. States that are relatively poor tend to be at greater risk of civil war onset and long duration (Collier, Hoeffler, and Söderbom 2004, Sambanis 2004a). One possible explanation for the correlation between poverty and civil war is that rebel recruitment is relatively easy when legal income-earning opportunities are paltry. Another possibility is that poverty generates grievances when it is concentrated on a particular communal group. The weak state explanation for the correlation between poverty and civil war, however, is that poor states do not have the economic means to gather intelligence about an incipient rebel movement, respond with financial incentives to the demands of rebels, or put down a rebellion with force (Tellis et al. 1997, p. 104, Herbst 2004, p. 361).

Opportunistic Rebel Leaders and the Business of Rebellion

One or a few leaders are necessary to form a rebel group capable of engaging the military forces of a state (Roemer 1985, Grossman 1995, pp. 195–196). A rebel leader's role in establishing a rebel group is similar in many respects to an entrepreneur's role in starting a new business. A rebel leader, like a business entrepreneur, typically has a high personal stake in the venture and is willing to accept a high level of personal risk to promote the organization's goals (Clapham 1988). The crucial difference between business and rebel entrepreneurs, of course, is that rebel activities are generally illegal and violent. Hence, the rebel leader and other rebel personnel face risk of incarceration or death.

For a rebel group to form and survive, it must overcome four significant hurdles. First, financial resources are needed to recruit and train members, purchase weapons and supplies, and conduct military operations. Second, a command and control infrastructure must be established to govern rebel military operations and interactions with the government, population, and other groups (e.g., mediators, media, and nongovernment organizations). This too requires financial resources but also geographic conditions conducive to rebel group viability, such as mountains or jungles that allow rebels to hide. Third, rebel leaders must manage the morale and cohesiveness of the rebel group so as to minimize the risk that disenchanted members will provide information to the government or form an opposing faction. Fourth, a rebel organization may have to overcome a free-rider problem associated with recruitment. Even a person who is sympathetic to a rebel cause might abstain from joining a rebellion because of the risk of arrest or injury and the negligible impact of his or her individual participation. Collier (2000a, p. 100) maintains, however, that when a rebellion is motivated by material gains to the rebels, the free-rider problem can be eliminated if the gains are distributed exclusively to those who participate.

In their research on civil war duration, Collier et al. (2004) distinguish between "rebellion as investment" and "rebellion as business." Under rebellion as investment, the political, economic, or social payoff to rebellion is contingent on rebel victory. Hence, the rebel group invests in rebellion and experiences net losses each period until victory is achieved. If the investment in rebellion is "successful," the payoffs outweigh the costs in the long run. Under rebellion as business, rebel leaders are motivated to achieve positive net revenues each period. While investment-oriented rebellions could be motivated by grievance and business-oriented rebellions by greed, Collier et al. (2004, pp. 255–256) caution that there is no necessary correlation along these lines.

A Net Revenue Model of Rebellion

Economically Viable Rebellion

We assume that the economic viability of a rebel organization is a necessary condition for sustained armed conflict. This is analogous to the economic principle that both for-profit and nonprofit enterprises must generate sufficient revenues to cover long-run costs if they are to survive. Let the size of a rebellion be denoted by r, perhaps measured by the number of rebel attacks or the amount of territory controlled. Revenues for the rebel organization might include income from natural resources, voluntary or coerced material support from the surrounding population, and financial support from foreign governments, criminal syndicates, or diaspora. Costs to the rebel organization include various labor and capital costs, including the opportunity cost of any political, economic, or social access that is forgone once the rebellion is underway.

The revenues and costs of rebellion, R and C, are shown as functions of r in panel (a) of Figure 7.8. The positive vertical intercept on the cost curve allows for fixed costs, such as those associated with the startup of the rebel organization. As customary, we assume that revenues increase with r at a diminishing rate while costs increase at an increasing rate. For some forms of intrastate conflict, revenue and cost curves with alternative shapes might be applicable. In panel (b), net revenue or profit, $R–C$, is constructed by subtracting costs from revenues at each level of r in panel (a). In the case shown here, there exists a range of rebel activities between r_0 and r_1 where the rebel group is economically viable.

Implicit in Figure 7.8 is a fixed level of government resistance, meaning that the positions of the revenue, cost, and net revenue curves are dependent on government actions. For example, if the government exerts greater effort to cut off financial support to the rebel group, the revenue function would rotate downward, other things equal. Similarly, if the government improves legal employment prospects for potential rebels, it would be more costly for the rebel group to recruit labor, causing the cost curve to rotate upward, everything else the same.

To introduce preferences, assume that rebel utility is a function of net revenue and grievance, where grievance is satisfied by increases in rebel activity over a relevant range. If the rebel group desires both net revenue and the satisfaction of grievances, then indifference curves will slope downward, yielding an optimal level of rebellion like r^* in panel (b). Alternatively, if the group is motivated purely by greed, the indifference curves will be horizontal, leading to a profit-maximizing level of rebellion at r_p. At the other extreme, if the group is motivated purely by grievance, then indifference curves will be vertical, leading to a maximum economically viable rebellion at r_1.

Changes in Revenues and Costs of Rebellion
The net revenue model in Figure 7.8 lends itself to several comparative-static predictions. First, if grievance is weighted more heavily in the utility function relative to greed, the indifference curves will be steeper, and hence the optimal rebellion r^* will tend to increase. Second, if the revenue function rotates upward (thus raising marginal revenue), or the cost function rotates downward (thus lowering marginal cost), then the optimal rebellion will increase for both the pure greed and the pure grievance

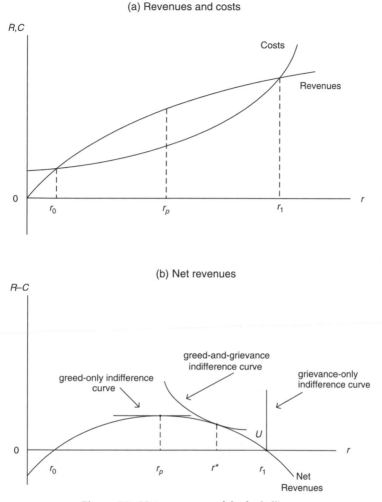

Figure 7.8. Net revenue model of rebellion.

cases. Examples of increases in marginal revenue would be higher prices for opium harvested by rebels or easier market access for conflict diamonds. Examples of decreases in marginal cost would include higher unemployment among potential recruits, lower market wages, greater use of child soldiers, and easier access to small arms and light weapons. Third, if the cost curve is shifted upward sufficiently, then rebellion at any level will be economically unviable. An example here would be political, economic, or social reforms that reduce closure against a previously disadvantaged group and thereby increase the fixed opportunity cost of rebellion.

7.4. Selected Empirical Studies of Civil War and Genocide

Risk Factors for Civil War and Genocide

Greed, Grievance, and Weak States

Empirical research on the determinants of civil war onset is extensive and growing. Particularly influential studies in this area are by economists Collier and Hoeffler (2004) and political scientists Fearon and Laitin (2003). Both studies can be interpreted as testing two broad hypotheses of the net revenue model in Figure 7.8. Other things equal, the model predicts that rebel activity will increase (1) if grievance increases relative to greed, hence steepening the indifference curves, or (2) if marginal revenues increase or marginal costs decrease, thus shifting the net revenue curve to the right. While the two studies differ in method and detail, together they reach the same basic conclusion. Collier and Hoeffler (2004, pp. 587–588) find "that a model that focuses on the opportunities for rebellion performs well, whereas objective indicators of grievance add little explanatory power." Fearon and Laitin (2003, p. 76) elaborate, "Our data show that measures of cultural diversity and grievances fail to postdict civil war onset, while measures of conditions that favor insurgency do fairly well. Surely ethnic antagonisms, national sentiments, and grievances often motivate rebels and their supporters. But such broad factors are too common to distinguish the cases where civil war breaks out."

Both studies use regression analysis to estimate the probability of civil war onset based on large samples encompassing 161 countries. The samples differ, however, in the years covered and in their definitions of civil war. Collier and Hoeffler's dataset spans the period 1960–99 and includes 79 wars, which are counted as such only if they caused at least 1,000 battle-related deaths per year. Fearon and Laitin's sample is larger, spanning 1945–99 and including 127 wars, which are required to have averaged at least 100 battle-related deaths per year and totaled at least 1,000 deaths over the course of the conflict. Proxies for grievance, including measures of ethnic and religious diversity, political repression, and income inequality, are generally found to be statistically insignificant. In contrast, a number of variables gauging conditions favorable to rebellion are significant and substantively important. In particular, the regression estimates indicate that the risk of civil war is higher when income and growth are lower, when exports of oil and other primary commodities are higher, when population is larger, and when terrain is more mountainous. Wars are also more likely when a state is new, has experienced recent instability or civil war, or is an inconsistent mix of autocracy and democracy.

While the two studies agree that the onset of civil war is determined primarily by nongrievance factors, they disagree in their interpretations of why particular factors operate as they do. For example, whereas Collier and Hoeffler see low per capita income as evidence of low opportunity costs for rebels, Fearon and Laitin treat it as an indicator of weak military and police capabilities of the state. Similarly, in Collier and Hoeffler exports of primary commodities represent sources of rebel revenues, but in Fearon and Laitin high oil exports are thought to matter because they correlate with weak state institutions. Differences like these motivate continued research on civil war onset, including both large-sample econometric tests and more detailed cases studies.

Economic Interdependence

According to the liberal peace hypothesis, salient trade makes war less likely, everything else the same. Evidence relevant to the hypothesis is provided in the context of civil war by Barbieri and Reuveny (2005) and Bussmann and Schneider (2007). The two studies are similar inasmuch as both estimate the risk of onset by including measures of economic openness along with key control variables from Collier and Hoeffler (2004) and Fearon and Laitin (2003). Barbieri and Reuveny begin with Fearon and Laitin's full sample but, owing to missing data, pare it down to a shorter period (1970–99) and 74 wars. Relative to Barbieri and Reuveny, Bussmann and Schneider substantially increase the number of observations by using a longer period (1950–2000) and, more important, by including armed conflicts with as few as 25 battle-related deaths per year. From these different samples, the authors obtain qualitatively different results. Barbieri and Reuveny find that trade openness has a negative but small and statistically insignificant effect on war onset. In contrast, Bussmann and Schneider report a negative effect that is both substantial and statistically significant, leading to the conclusion that "in the long term an open economy is related to less conflict" (p. 94).

It is worth noting that if the liberal peace hypothesis is true, then both of these studies may underestimate the total impact of openness on civil war onset. As shown in Chapter 2, trade generates gains (and hence opportunity costs if disrupted) in two distinct ways: trade increases utility when consumption is shifted toward more preferred goods, and trade increases income when production is shifted toward areas of comparative advantage. Both Barbieri and Reuveny (2005) and Bussmann and Schneider (2007) include per capita income as one of the key control variables in their regressions. This means that the regression coefficient on openness can capture only the direct effect of trade on civil war onset, not the indirect effect that would also operate through increased income. In this regard, it is interesting that Bussmann and Schneider report in an appendix to their paper that the openness coefficient increases in size and significance when per capita income is omitted from their model.

Genocide and Politicide

A major step toward understanding the risk of genocide and politicide is provided by Harff (2003). As documented by Harff, almost all modern genocide and politicide occurs in conjunction with or immediately after a civil conflict or a regime collapse. The reverse is not true, however, in that most conflicts do not involve purposeful mass killing. Harff therefore frames the research question as follows: given the existence of internal conflict or regime change, what factors predispose authorities to resort to mass elimination? Her sample consists of 126 countries, all of which experienced internal war or regime change sometime during the period 1955–97, but only 35 of which experienced genocide or politicide. Harff applies regression analysis to determine the risk of genocide or politicide based on an array of factors culled from the literature on political repression. She finds that six factors have important and statistically significant effects. Given internal conflict or regime change, the risk of genocide or politicide is higher when the severity of political upheaval is greater, when there is a history of prior mass killing, when the ruling elite holds an exclusionary ideology, when the regime is autocratic, when the ruling elite is from an ethnic minority, or when a country is less open to economic trade. From a baseline probability of about 3 percent, Harff calculates that any one of these six factors increases the risk of genocide or politicide by somewhere between two and six percentage points. The cumulative effect of the factors is huge: if all six factors occur together, then the probability of genocide or politicide rises to 90 percent. Also interesting, Harff finds that other anticipated factors, including active discrimination against minorities, high infant mortality, and sparse international political linkages, do not have a significant impact on genocide and politicide risk, conditioned again on the presence of internal conflict.

Conflict Termination

Duration

Large-scale analysis of civil war duration is difficult in part because sample construction requires investigators to date not only a war's onset but also its termination. Thus, it can be anticipated that samples and results might vary across studies of duration. Seminal papers include Collier et al. (2004) and Fearon (2004), which can be thought of as companion pieces to the onset articles reviewed earlier.

Fearon's (2004) paper is particularly noteworthy, not only for what it has to say about civil war duration but also as an illustration of the interplay between theory and observation that characterizes social science. Fearon begins by taking a broad look at the data. For his sample of 128 civil wars, Fearon finds that the median duration is 7.1 years, but a quarter of the wars ended within two years, while another quarter lasted 12 years or more, and a tenth survived for at least 20 years. This moves Fearon to ask in the paper's title, "Why do some civil wars last so much longer than others?" When he looks at the data more closely, several empirical regularities emerge that potentially point toward an answer. Coups and popular revolutions, civil wars in Eastern Europe and the former Soviet Union, and anticolonial wars have tended to be shorter. In contrast, "sons-of-the-soil" wars, wherein ethnic minorities resist majority encroachment into a country's peripheral regions, and wars that involve valuable contraband like diamonds and drugs have tended to be longer.

Fearon (2004) then offers a theoretical explanation for these observed differences among civil war types. The technology of coups and popular revolutions imply a first-mover advantage and generate what Fearon aptly terms a "tipping process," wherein either the government or the rebel force collapses quickly and decisively. Peripheral wars, in contrast, rarely threaten the government's continuance and hence tend to rely more on settlement. For wars of this sort, Fearon offers a sequential two-person game in which fluctuations in government strength create a commitment problem that can prevent settlement under plausible circumstances. In particular, the higher the net revenue of either side during the war, the less likely is settlement and hence the longer is the expected duration of war. For example, the greater the returns to rebels, the greater their demands in a prospective settlement, but also the more tempted the government is to renege in the future, thus making the realization of a settlement less likely. In this way, the model helps to explain the longer duration of sons-of-the-soil wars, which have high political or economic stakes, and wars that involve the control of contraband or natural resources.

Third-Party Intervention

In Chapter 5 we used Hirshleifer's bargaining model to show that third-party intervention can have a pacific effect if it coordinates expectations, reduces commitment problems, or ameliorates animosity. On the other hand, it can leave the prospect for peaceful settlement unchanged or even worsened if the intervention favors one side.

A large-sample study that is particularly cognizant of the complexity of the intervention issue is Regan and Aydin (2006). The authors estimate expected civil war duration based on a large sample comprising 153 conflicts and more than 1,400 interventions over the period 1945–99. Among the controls are factors drawn from Collier et al. (2004) and Fearon (2004), including dichotomous variables indicating the involvement of contraband or ethnic differences in the conflict. In order to get at their core question, the authors code the data to distinguish among military, economic, and diplomatic interventions, and for the latter they also record at what point in a war an intervention occurs. Most diplomatic interventions involve mediation voluntarily accepted by both sides. Third parties transfer "information about relative capabilities, prospects for victory or defeat, possible concessions, reservation points, and other bits of vital information that antagonists cannot credibly convey" and might also offer guarantees and incentives (Regan and Aydin 2006, p. 741). Hence, diplomatic mediation is predicted to have a pacific effect. The same prediction cannot be made for military and economic interventions, however, because they can be one sided.

Regan and Aydin's (2006) empirical results are broadly consistent with the logic of Hirshleifer's bargaining model. Their central finding is that diplomatic interventions have a large impact on shortening expected duration. Diplomatic efforts, especially those that occur in the middle stages of a conflict, decrease expected duration by well over half. In contrast, military interventions have a small and statistically insignificant effect, whereas economic interventions show a substantial and significant positive effect, meaning that they tend to prolong the course of a war. When a conflict includes both diplomatic and economic interventions, the pacific effect of diplomacy dominates, such that expected duration is still shortened considerably. Regan and Aydin (2006, p. 754) conclude that "interventions that have an explicit focus of conflict management are more likely to be effective at stopping the violence than those that focus on manipulating the structural conditions, such as relative capabilities."

Economic Consequences

Civil War and Economic Growth

As we have previously noted, three economic costs of war can be identified: resources are diverted to conflict activities, causing alternative production to be forgone; resources are destroyed, so that both current and future production is sacrificed; and ordinary production and exchange is disrupted, meaning that otherwise gainful activity is rendered uneconomical. One way to gauge these costs at an aggregate level is to examine their impact on economic growth. Because of the multiplicity of intrastate conflicts, large-sample studies have yielded good estimates of the effect of civil war on growth.

Murdoch and Sandler's (2004) study is distinguished because it estimates the short- and long-run effects due not only to a country's own war but also to a war in a nearby country. Consider two countries A and B located close to each other. Country A's growth can fall because of the various costs of conflict if a war occurs in its own territory. Country A's growth can also suffer if a civil war in B disrupts economic activity between the two countries or heightens uncertainty in the region. To allow for both possible effects, Murdoch and Sandler add indicators of own civil war and nearby civil war to an otherwise standard model of country-level growth. They then estimate the model using regression analysis for a large sample of countries over the period 1961–95. Long-run growth is measured as the change in the logarithm of per capita income over the full thirty-five-year period; short-run growth is measured as the same over a five-year period. For the long-run case, Murdoch and Sandler estimate that own-country civil war will reduce thirty-five-year growth from a sample mean of 0.55 to 0.39, or by about 30 percent, while nearby-country civil war will reduce it to 0.50, or by about 10 percent. Hence, the long-term impact of civil war is substantial, with the effect of a nearby civil war being about one-third that of a homeland war. For the short-run case, own-country civil war is estimated to reduce five-year growth from a sample mean of 0.06 to 0.01, or by about 85 percent, while nearby civil war will reduce it to 0.05, or by about 20 percent. Notice that the percentage reductions are greater in the short run than in the long run. Murdoch and Sandler interpret this as meaning that countries in the longer run are able to recover from past civil wars, those both at home and in neighbor countries.

Microlevel Costs

As in Murdoch and Sandler (2004), macrolevel studies use variation across countries to estimate the effects of conflict on aggregate measures of economic activity. In contrast, microlevel studies employ variation across individuals and communities to estimate more direct effects on variables like personal income, health, and education.

An excellent example of microlevel research is Deininger's (2003) study of civil strife in Uganda. He bases his empirical analysis on survey data covering approximately 10,000 Ugandan households spread across 1,000 communities over the period 1992–99. Included in the comparatively rich dataset are respondents' answers to the question, "Has your production of crops/cattle or livestock rearing/trading activities been harmed by civil strife over the last 12 months?" Also included is information about stocks of physical assets and receipt of income from non-farm non-livestock enterprises. Based on this and other information, Deininger is able to test two hypotheses regarding the consequences of civil conflict. During violent civil conflict, destruction or seizure of assets is made more likely, and access to markets is rendered more vulnerable and costly. Hence, it can be expected that civil strife will cause households (1) to reduce private investment and (2) to concentrate their economic activities more in subsistence farming and herding. Both hypotheses are strongly supported by Deininger's large-sample regression analysis. Controlling for demographics, education, and location, Deininger finds that civil strife reduces the likelihood by about 14 percentage points that a household will accumulate assets. Further, civil strife decreases the probability by about 10 percentage points that a household will establish or expand a non-farm non-livestock enterprise, and it increases the likelihood by about 2 percentage points that such an enterprise will be abandoned. In this way, the adverse effects on aggregate growth found by Murdoch and Sandler (2004) are traced by Deininger (2003) to the retrenchment of economic activity at the level of individual households.

7.5. Bibliographic Notes

Theoretical and empirical perspectives on violent civil conflicts are the focus of the literature reviews of Sambanis (2002, 2004a, 2004c) and Collier and Hoeffler (2007a), edited books of Berdal and Malone (2000), Ballentine and Sherman (2003b), Collier et al. (2003), Nafziger and Auvinen (2003), and Collier and Sambanis (2005, vols. 1 and 2), and special issues of *Defence and Peace Economics* (Sandler and Hegre 2002), *Economics of Governance* (Cusack, Glazer, and Konrad 2006), *Growth and Change* (Pickles 2000), *Journal of International Development* (Addison and Murshed 2003), *Journal of Peace Research* (Murshed 2002, Hegre 2004,

Brunborg and Urdal 2005), and *Journal of Conflict Resolution* (Collier and Sambanis 2002, Ron 2005). Connections between civil wars and refugees are explored in special issues of *International Migration Review* (Center for Migration Studies 2001) and *Conflict Management and Peace Science* (Gibney 2007). The *Journal of Genocide Research* and *Genocide Studies and Prevention* provide peer-reviewed articles on genocide, primarily from the disciplines of history, political science, psychology, and sociology. The Institute for the Study of Genocide/International Association of Genocide Scholars offers a list of books and reports about genocide at its Web site.

In addition to the topics of civil war onset, duration, and economic consequences emphasized in this chapter, numerous other facets of civil wars have been studied by social scientists; these include severity (Lacina 2006), recurrence (Walter 2004, DeRouen and Bercovitch 2008), contagion (Fox 2004, Buhaug and Gleditsch 2008), threshold effects (Kuran 1989), postwar partition or secession (Sambanis 2000, Tir 2005), child soldiers (Singer 2005, Wessells 2006), intentional violence against civilians (Valentino, Huth, and Balch-Lindsay 2004, Eck and Hultman 2007), and peacekeeping (Crawford and Kuperman 2006, Doyle and Sambanis 2006).

8

Terrorism*

As described in Chapter 1, international terrorism is a significant form of extra-state conflict, while domestic terrorism is a frequent mode of intrastate conflict. In this chapter we present data on worldwide patterns in international and domestic terrorism incidents, casualties, targets, and tactics. We then apply principles of economic choice and game theory to terrorists' resource allocation decisions and governments' counterterrorism efforts. Selected empirical studies of the risks and economic effects of terrorism are also summarized.

8.1. Defining Terrorism

There is disagreement among scholars regarding the distinction between terrorism and other forms of violence, such as armed robbery or nation-state warfare (Hoffman 1998, ch. 1). For the purposes of this chapter, we adopt Enders and Sandler's (2006a, p. 3) definition of terrorism as "the premeditated use or threat to use violence by individuals or subnational groups in order to obtain a political or social objective through the intimidation of a large audience beyond that of the immediate victims." By this definition, terrorism is fundamentally political or social in the sense that terrorists desire to "change the system," something that is not a priority for criminals (Hoffman 1998, p. 42). The political or social goals of terrorists coupled with their desire to intimidate a large audience lead

* Sections 8.1, 8.3, and 8.4 of this chapter are adapted from the *Journal of Economic Education*, "Applying Intermediate Microeconomics to Terrorism," Charles H. Anderton and John R. Carter, volume 37, issue 4, pp. 442–458, 2006. Reprinted with the kind permission of the Helen Dwight Reid Educational Foundation. Published by Heldref Publications, 1319 18th Street, NW, Washington, DC 20036–1802. www.heldref.org. Copyright © 2006.

terrorists to operate outside the usual rules of warfare. Hence, terrorist incidents often involve hostage taking of diplomats, execution of kidnapped military officers, and attacks against civilians (Hoffman 1998, pp. 34–35). Some terrorism scholars also distinguish between international and domestic terrorism, where the former involves "the interests and/or nationals of more than one country," while the latter is "perpetrated within the boundaries of a given nation by nationals from that nation" (LaFree et al. 2006, pp. 5 and 22).

8.2. Patterns of Terrorism

Prominent Datasets

Table 8.1 summarizes six terrorism datasets. The first is International Terrorism: Attributes of Terrorist Events (ITERATE), which provides data on terrorist incidents that transcend national boundaries. The second through fourth datasets encompass both international and domestic terrorism incidents and are provided by the Global Terrorism Database (GTD), the National Counterterrorism Center's Worldwide Incidents Tracking System (WITS), and the RAND Worldwide Terrorism Incident Database (RWTID). The next dataset, Terrorism in Western Europe: Events Data (TWEED), provides information on domestic terrorist incidents for various countries in Western Europe. The final source is the American Terrorism Study (ATS), which provides demographic and legal information for almost 500 terrorists indicted in the United States. Major distinctions among the datasets over types of incidents and years covered are summarized in the top of Table 8.1, with additional details about terrorism definitions and variables shown at the bottom.

Measures of Terrorism

We draw on two major datasets in our empirical overview of terrorism: the Global Terrorism Database (GTD) and International Terrorism: Attributes of Terrorist Events (ITERATE). GTD provides data on international and domestic terrorism combined from 1970–92 and 1994–2004. ITERATE uses print media to construct a database of terrorist incidents that transcend national boundaries from 1968 forward. Figure 8.1 shows the time paths for terrorist incidents worldwide based on GTD and ITERATE. Three observations follow. First, there are major differences in the number of incidents between GTD and ITERATE, mainly because the former

Table 8.1. *Selected terrorism datasets.*

Dataset	Type	Time Period
International Terrorism: Attributes of Terrorist Events (ITERATE)	International/transnational	1968–2007
Global Terrorism Database (GTD)	International and domestic	1970–92 and 1994–2004
National Counterterrorism Center's (NCTC) Worldwide Incidents Tracking System (WITS)	International and domestic	2004–2007
RAND Worldwide Terrorism Incident Database (RWTID)	International and domestic	1968–2008
Terrorism in Western Europe: Events Data (TWEED)	Domestic	1950–2004
American Terrorism Study (ATS)	Individual terrorists	1980–2002

International Terrorism: Attributes of Terrorist Events (ITERATE):
International/transnational terrorism is "the use, or threat of use, of anxiety-inducing, extra-normal violence for political purposes by any individual or group, whether acting for or in opposition to established governmental authority, when such action is intended to influence the attitudes and behavior of a target group wider than the immediate victim and when, through the nationality or foreign ties of its perpetrators, its location, the nature of its institutional or human victims, or the mechanics of its resolution, its ramifications transcend national boundaries" (Mickolus, Sandler, Murdock, and Flemming 2003, p. 2). The dataset covers international terrorism, in which perpetrators are controlled by a sovereign state, and transnational terrorism, in which perpetrators are non-state actors. Variables include date, location, and type of attack; perpetrator and victim characteristics; and damage.

Global Terrorism Database (GTD):
An incident is included if it is intentional, violent, perpetrated by subnational actors without state support, and meets two of the following three criteria: (1) has a political, economic, religious, or social objective, (2) is intended to coerce, intimidate, or express a message to people beyond the immediate victims, and (3) is outside the parameters of international humanitarian law, particularly regarding the targeting of noncombatants (LaFree and Dugan 2007b, Appendix A). Variables include date, location, and type of attack; perpetrator and victim characteristics; and damage. Data for 1993 are missing. GTD does not currently distinguish international and domestic terrorist incidents within the dataset.

National Counterterrorism Center's (NCTC) Worldwide Incidents Tracking System (WITS):
Terrorism is the "premeditated, politically motivated violence perpetrated against noncombatant targets by subnational groups or clandestine agents" (National Counterterrorism Center 2008, p. 2). Variables include date, location, and type of attack; perpetrator and victim characteristics; and damage. Prior to 2004, the US State Department provided data on terrorist incidents as part of its annual report, *Patterns of Global Terrorism*. Since 2004, the State Department reports have been titled *Country Reports on Terrorism* and data on terrorist incidents have been drawn from WITS. WITS does not currently distinguish international and domestic terrorist incidents within the dataset.

RAND Worldwide Terrorism Incident Database (RWTID):
Terrorism is "violence calculated to create an atmosphere of fear and alarm to coerce others into actions they would not otherwise undertake, or refrain from actions they desired to take." For

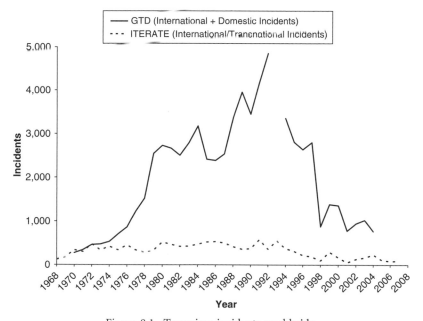

Figure 8.1. Terrorism incidents worldwide.
Note: GTD data for 1993 are missing.
Sources: LaFree and Dugan (2006, 2007a) and International Terrorism: Attributes of
Terrorist Events (ITERATE).

includes both international and domestic incidents, while the latter
excludes domestic incidents. Second, contrary to popular impression, no
upward trends are evident in terrorist incidents for either the GTD or
ITERATE series across the full time period shown. Third, although there

Foot note continued for Table 8.1.
international terrorism, "perpetrators go abroad to strike their targets, select domestic targets
associated with a foreign state, or create an international incident by attacking airline passengers
or equipment." Domestic terrorism is "perpetrated by local nationals against a purely domestic
target." (See www.rand.org/ise/projects/terrorismdatabase.) Variables include date, location, and
type of attack; perpetrator and victim characteristics; and damage. International and domestic
terrorist incidents are distinguished in the dataset. Domestic terrorism data begin in 1998.

Terrorism in Western Europe: Events Data (TWEED):
Terrorism is an act that inflicts (or intends to inflict) personal or material injury with the
intention of directing demands to or raising attention from others beyond the immediate victims
(Engene 2006, p. 5). Variables include date and location of attacks and perpetrator information
for 18 Western European countries.

American Terrorism Study (ATS):
Contains data on almost 500 terrorists indicted in the United States. Variables include
information on individual demographics; the terrorist group that an individual belongs to; and
prosecution, defense, and sentencing.

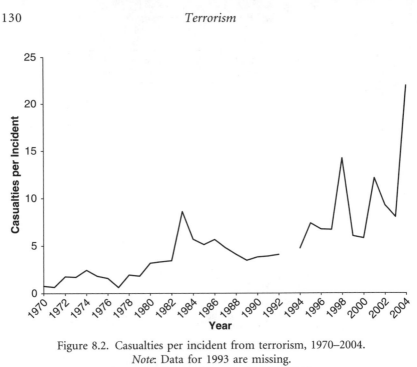

Figure 8.2. Casualties per incident from terrorism, 1970–2004.
Note: Data for 1993 are missing.
Sources: LaFree and Dugan (2006, 2007a).

are significant variations across GTD and ITERATE in definitions, coding rules, and incidents tracked, the large gap between the two series suggest that in recent decades domestic terrorism incidents worldwide have been much more numerous than international incidents (perhaps 8–10 times so). This observation was borne out in data provided by the Terrorism Knowledge Base, which was available online to the public but has been suspended owing to a lack of funding (Houghton 2008).

Figure 8.2 shows casualties (deaths plus injured) per incident caused by international and domestic terrorism worldwide based on GTD data. In contrast to Figure 8.1, an upward trend is evident in recent years for casualties per incident, suggesting that terrorism is increasing in serious-ness. Particularly noticeable are the higher casualty rates since the end of the Cold War in 1989. This is consistent with the analysis of ITERATE data by Enders and Sandler (2000), who estimate that international incidents during the period 1991–96 were 17 percentage points more likely to result in casualties than those in the preceding two decades. They and other analysts attribute the increased deadliness to the growth in religiously motivated acts of terrorism (Hoffman 1998, ch. 4, Enders and Sandler 2000, pp. 329–330, Juergensmeyer 2000; but see also Cavanaugh 2004).

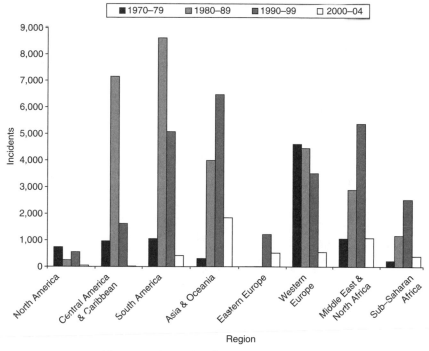

Figure 8.3. Terrorism by region, 1970–2004.
Note: Data for 1993 are missing.
Sources: LaFree and Dugan (2006, 2007a).

In Figure 8.3 we shift attention to the geographic location of terrorist attacks from 1970 to 2004 based on GTD data. The figure indicates that all regions of the world are impacted by terrorism. The figure also shows the emergence of terrorism in Eastern Europe, the substantial decline of terrorism in the Americas, and the preponderance of terrorist incidents in the early 2000s in Asia and Oceania and the Middle East and North Africa relative to the other regions shown.

Figure 8.4 turns attention to terrorists' modes of attack during the period 1970–2004. Using GTD data, we group terrorist incidents into bombings, assassinations, hostage incidents (hijackings plus kidnappings), and armed intrusions. We also include an "other" category for incidents such as sabotage, arson, basic assault, maiming, and attacks involving chemical, biological, radiological, or nuclear (CBRN) materials. Figure 8.4 shows that bombings and armed intrusions are the most frequent modes of attack, presumably because they are technically simple and difficult to prevent. Terrorists' desire for media attention has led to growing concern

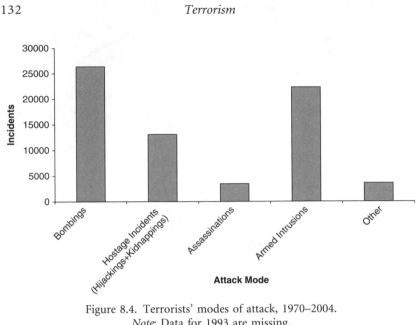

Figure 8.4. Terrorists' modes of attack, 1970–2004.
Note: Data for 1993 are missing.
Sources: LaFree and Dugan (2006, 2007a).

that organizations like al Qaeda will attempt to acquire and use weapons of mass destruction. A terrorist organization could spread deadly biological agents, create an explosion at a nuclear power reactor, or disperse radioactive materials using a radiological dispersion device (RDD) known as a dirty bomb. It is not beyond the realm of possibility that a terrorist organization could acquire an atomic bomb, but use of biological, chemical, or radiological weapons is more likely because they involve less of a technical challenge (Howard and Forest 2008).

8.3. A Rational Choice Model of Terrorism

Basic Model

The rational choice model introduced in Chapter 3 can be easily adapted to study some of the basic choices faced by terrorists. These choices might pertain to levels of terrorist activity or to specific targets for attack. Beginning from an initial optimum, various aspects of terrorist activity and counterterrorism policy can be explored by changing the parameters of the model, most specifically income, prices, and preferences.

To understand decisions about levels of terrorism, in Figure 8.5 we assume that a terrorist organization allocates income I between terrorist

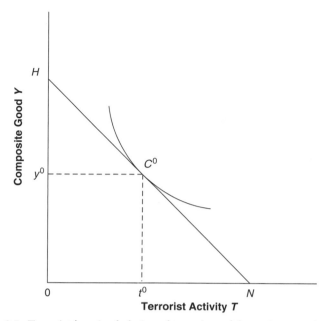

Figure 8.5. Terrorists' optimal choice of terrorist activity and composite good.

activity T and composite good Y, where T is measured in some standardized unit, and Y is real (inflation-adjusted) expenditures on all other goods such as food, clothing, and shelter. The terrorists' budget constraint HN then satisfies the equation $P_T t + P_Y y = I$, where P_T is the price or per-unit cost of carrying out terrorist activities and P_Y is the price of the composite good. Preferences over T and Y are represented by indifference curves in the usual manner. Negatively sloped indifference curves indicate that terrorists are willing to give up some of the composite good to obtain more terrorist activity. Steeper indifference curves would indicate a greater willingness to engage in terrorism, while more curvature would imply a lower degree of substitutability between T and Y. Assuming rationality, the optimum occurs at point C^0, where the marginal rate of substitution between T and Y is just equal to the relative price of terrorism P_T/P_Y.

To understand decisions about targets, we could alternatively assume that terrorists allocate an exogenous amount of resources R between two targets T_1 and T_2, which for example might be civilian and government targets, respectively. In this case, the budget equation would become $P_1 t_1 + P_2 t_2 = R$, where P_1 and P_2 are the prices or per-unit costs of carrying out the two types of missions. Indifference curves would show preferences

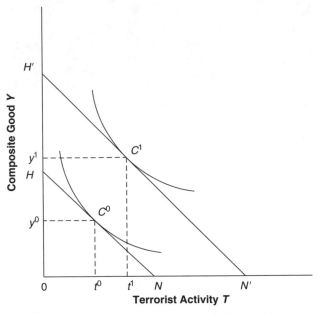

Figure 8.6. Changes in terrorists' budget constraint.

over competing targets and hence the subjective value of one target in terms of another.

Terrorist Access to Income

Terrorist groups depend on financial resources to carry out terrorist activities, so they obviously seek to maintain or increase their income. In Figure 8.6, assume that a terrorist group secures new financial resources, perhaps as a response by sympathizers to a publicized hijacking or hostage incident. This shifts out the group's budget constraint from HN to $H'N'$, which allows the group to increase its terrorist activity as well as consume more of the composite good. As part of counterterrorism policy, governments on the reverse side attempt to reduce resources available to terrorists by freezing financial assets and disrupting the flow of funds behind terrorist activities. For example, the US Patriot Act of 2001 expanded the power of federal authorities to issue new rules and regulations to restrain money laundering. Such counterterrorism income policies shift the terrorists' budget constraint from $H'N'$ back toward HN, thereby reducing the level of terrorist activity. If terrorism is sensitive to income, income policies can be effective. Moreover, if current terrorist activities enhance future terrorist fund-raising, as suggested earlier, then income policies that forestall current activity might also reduce future terrorism.

Terrorist Response to Price Changes

In addition to income policies, governments try to thwart terrorism with what can be thought of as price policies. For example, defense of potential targets, military strikes against training centers, capture of terrorist leaders, and infiltration of terrorist groups all increase the price or unit cost of terrorism P_T. Following Frey and Luechinger (2003), we refer to such actions that raise the cost of terrorism as deterrence, although Schelling (1966) uses the term more narrowly to mean threats of retaliation designed to alter preferences. In contrast to deterrence, Frey and Luechinger argue in favor of a policy of benevolence to reduce terrorism (see, also, Frey 2004). Benevolence policy raises the opportunity cost of terrorist activities, not by increasing the price of terrorism directly, but by reducing the price of the composite good. Examples include subsidized consumption goods or, as suggested by Frey and Luechinger, increased access to normal political processes.

In Figure 8.7 we contrast deterrence and benevolence price policies aimed at reducing terrorism. Assume that the initial budget constraint is HN, leading the terrorist group to choose a level of terrorist activity equal to t^0. In panel (a), a deterrence policy increases the price of terrorism P_T by raising the expected cost of terrorist activity, causing the budget constraint to rotate inward along the horizontal axis to HN'. The increased opportunity cost of terrorism is reflected in the steeper slope of the budget line. Consistent with the law of demand, terrorist activity falls to some lower level t^1. In panel (b), a benevolence policy also raises the opportunity cost of terrorism, but it does so by increasing terrorist access to other goods by lowering P_Y, the price of the composite good. Beginning from HN, benevolence policy rotates the budget line upward along the vertical axis to $H'N$. Again, the steeper budget line reflects the higher opportunity cost of terrorism. Under the price-reducing benevolence policy shown in panel (b), terrorists choose a reduced level of terrorism equal to t^1. However, as shown in panel (c), it is entirely possible for the decrease in P_Y instead to *increase* the level of terrorism. For the same benevolence policy but different preferences, terrorists in this case choose an increased level of terrorism equal to t^1.

The rational choice model thus shows an important contrast between deterrence and benevolence price policies. To the extent that deterrence

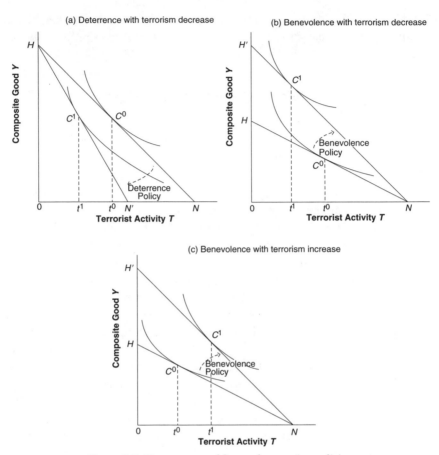

Figure 8.7. Deterrence and benevolence price policies.

effectively raises the price or per-unit cost of terrorism, the level of terrorist activity can be expected to decrease, based on the law of demand. On the other hand, if benevolence policy succeeds in lowering the price of the composite good, the effect on the level of terrorism is theoretically ambiguous (see Anderton and Carter 2005).

Terrorist Substitution Possibilities

An important general issue raised by terrorism-thwarting price policies is the potential for terrorists to substitute into other activities. For example, the question raised by consideration of benevolence policy is whether terrorism will rise or fall in response to a lower price of the composite good. A similar question arises when considering whether greater protection of government targets will cause terrorist attacks against civilians to rise or to fall. The scope of terrorist substitution possibilities is extensive. For example, terrorists can substitute between terrorism and ordinary goods, across target classes, across countries, among weapons technologies, and across time (Sandler 2003, pp. 794–796).

The rational choice model introduced in Chapter 3 can provide useful insights about the substitution behavior of terrorists. Recall that when the price of a good rises, the demands for that good and for related goods are affected in two distinct ways. First, the price rise makes the good relatively more expensive, thus creating an incentive to cut consumption of that good and to increase consumption of other goods. This is called the substitution effect, and the incentive to substitute away from the now more expensive good in favor of other goods is called the substitution principle. Second, the price rise of a good causes real income or purchasing power to decrease, normally creating an incentive to cut back on the consumption of that good and of other goods. This is called the income effect. Putting the substitution and income effects together, the consumption of the good whose price has risen can be expected to decrease, as asserted by the law of demand. If the related goods are close substitutes, so that the substitution effect is large relative to the income effect, then the consumption of the related goods will increase.

An excellent illustration of these insights involves the placement of metal detectors in airports around the world in 1973, which immediately raised the price or cost of hijackings to terrorists. As reviewed here, rational choice theory predicts that the incidence of hijackings would fall relative to other terrorist activities. This is just what is observed in data collected by Mickolus (1980) for the period 1968–77 and shown in Table 8.2. Beginning in 1973, hijackings declined both in absolute number and as a percentage of international terrorist incidents. Subsequent research by Enders and Sandler (1993, 1995), however, shows that airport metal detectors had the unintended consequence of significantly increasing hostage incidents and assassinations. Other terrorist substitutions across targets have been reported. For example, greater defense of airlines and political figures by Israel in the early 1970s may have contributed to the seizure of 11 Israeli athletes by Palestinian terrorists at the 1972 Olympic Games in Munich. Fuad al-Shamali, one of the architects of the incident, described his substitution possibilities as follows: "We have to kill their most important and most famous people. Since we cannot come

Table 8.2. *International terrorist hijackings, 1968–1977.*

Year	Total International Incidents	Hijackings	Hijackings as Percent of Total
1968	123	3	2.4
1969	179	12	6.7
1970	344	22	6.4
1971	301	10	3.3
1972	480	15	3.1
1973	340	6	1.8
1974	425	7	1.6
1975	342	2	0.6
1976	455	6	1.3
1977	340	6	1.8
Mean		8.9	2.9

Note: Metal detectors placed in airports in 1973.
Source: Mickolus (1980).

close to their statesmen, we have to kill artists and sportsmen" (Hoffman 1998, p. 71). In a similar vein, prior to September 11, 2001 (hereafter 9/11), Enders and Sandler (2000, p. 330) cautioned that terrorist substitution possibilities raise the risk to civilians: "If a government responds by tightening security at official sites (e.g., embassies and government buildings) as is currently being done by the United States, its civilian targets (e.g., hotels, marketplaces, parks) will become *relatively* less secure and [more] attractive."

Preference Policies

Although economists typically take preferences as given, attention to questions of how terrorist preferences are formed and modified might prove to be particularly valuable. We can think of counterterrorist preference policies in broad terms as a form of advertising. In Figure 8.5, the goal of such advertising would be to render the indifference curves as horizontal lines, so that potential terrorists would place no subjective value on terrorist activities. Because terrorist preferences appear to be formed within a complex web of cultural, historical, political, and economic factors, the advertising could take on many guises.

For example, governments are aware of regions of the world where terrorists reside and where the potential for terrorist recruiting is high. Some of these regions face a relatively high risk of natural disasters such as earthquakes or hurricanes. Extranormal publicity of natural disaster relief by the United States in these regions might affect preference formation at the margin. For example, following the severe earthquake in Pakistan in October 2005, US military personnel delivered tons of relief supplies to Pakistani victims. According to Pervez Hoodbhoy, a political commentator and professor of physics in Pakistan, "The [US] Chinook helicopters are usually used to bomb al Qaeda but now they are being used to save people's lives so they have become birds of peace, and that . . . so changes the view of America in Pakistan" (ABC News 2005).

Unfortunately, there are also examples of what can be thought of as negative advertising from the counterterrorism perspective. Consider the abuse of Iraqi prisoners by US military personnel in 2004. Images of abused prisoners were shown around the world in media outlets such as CNN and Aljazeera. It is likely that the degrading images of Iraqi prisoners hardened the preferences of terrorists against the United States. They may have also created terrorist preferences among some individuals who previously were at least neutral toward terrorist activities. The obvious implication is that counterterrorist policy must guard against catalytic events like the prisoner abuse scandal.

Terrorists also carry out advertising campaigns by portraying the evils of the enemy and attempting to convince people about the rightness of their cause. Hence, governments and terrorist organizations are engaged in an advertising war for the hearts and minds of people in strategic locales such as Iraq, Afghanistan, Pakistan, and Saudi Arabia. In this advertising game, each side tries to gain market share by affecting what people know, or think they know, about themselves, governments, and terrorists. Such strategic interdependence between terrorists and governments, and among governments as they attempt to counter terrorism, implies that game theory can be a useful supplement to the rational choice model in the study of terrorism.

8.4. Game Theoretic Perspectives of Terrorism

Hostage Game between a Government and Terrorists

Here is a puzzle to be explained. Governments often pledge never to give in to terrorists' demands when hostages are taken. Yet despite these

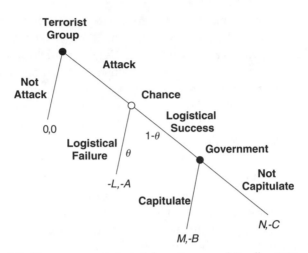

Figure 8.8. Hostage game (adapted from Lapan and Sandler 1988, p. 17).

pledges, governments sometimes deal with terrorists for the release of hostages. For example, in 1986 media reported that the Reagan administration had broken from its nonnegotiation policy by exchanging arms for hostages held in Lebanon (Lapan and Sandler 1988, p. 16). So why do governments so often pledge, and why do they sometimes deal? We address these questions using a simplified version of a hostage game originally due to Lapan and Sandler (1988). At the center of the game is a commitment problem, which as we have seen is characteristic of many conflict situations.

In Figure 8.8, terrorists begin a one-shot sequential hostage game by choosing whether to attack or not attack. If the terrorists do not attack, the status quo obtains with both players receiving a payoff of 0. If the terrorists do attack, they either fail or succeed in capturing hostages, with the probability of logistical failure equal to θ. If they fail to capture hostages, both the terrorists and the government suffer losses relative to the status quo, with respective payoffs of $-L < 0$ and $-A < 0$. If the terrorists succeed in taking hostages, the government must decide whether to capitulate or not capitulate to the terrorists' demands. If the government gives in, the terrorists receive a payoff of $M > 0$ and the government suffers a loss equal to $-B < -A$. If the government does not give in, the terrorist organization obtains payoff $N < M$, where N can be negative or positive, and the government endures a loss equal to $-C < -B$.

The game is solved by backward induction under the assumption that the players maximize their expected payoffs. Working backward, if the terrorists attack and achieve logistical success, the government will reluctantly but rationally capitulate, thereby suffering a loss of $-B$ rather than sacrificing the hostages at a greater loss of $-C$. Deducing that the government will capitulate, the terrorists then infer that if they attack, their payoff will be $-L$ with probability θ or M with probability $1-\theta$. Thus, if they attack, their expected payoff Z will be $Z=\theta(-L)+(1-\theta)M$, compared to their sure payoff of 0 if they do not attack. With a little algebra, it is easily shown that $Z>0$ and hence they will attack if $\theta < M/(M-(-L))$. Thus, knowing that the government will capitulate, the terrorists will attack as long as the probability of logistical failure is not too high.

It is obvious to both players that the terrorists' payoff to a successful attack is lower if the government refuses to give in to terrorists' demands. Thus, it is understandable that the government might hope to discourage attack by pledging beforehand that it will not negotiate with terrorists. What is critical, however, is whether the pledge is credible. As we will shortly show in a more formal way, if the pledge is credible and hence believed by the terrorists, then it will indeed lower the terrorists' expected payoff from attack. If, on the other hand, the pledge is not credible and hence not believed, then there is no change in incentives, and the one-shot game predicts that the government will capitulate if hostages are taken. Thus sometimes governments renege on their pledges because the pledges are not credible in the first place.

So what makes for a credible commitment to not capitulate? For a pledge to be credible, it must be coupled with some prior action that either eliminates the capitulation option or alters the payoffs so that capitulation is more costly to the government than noncapitulation would be. One example might be a constitutional rule against capitulation in a nation with a strong constitutional tradition. Another might be a reputation for noncapitulation earned in the past that would be damaged by capitulation in the present. Of course, this latter example suggests that the hostage game can be enriched if extended to a multiperiod framework, as found in Lapan and Sandler's (1988) more complete model.

We conclude by emphasizing that, from the government's perspective, solving the commitment problem is not equivalent to solving the hostage threat. Suppose that the government somehow achieves a credible prior commitment of no capitulation. Returning to Figure 8.8, in this case the terrorists will anticipate that if they attack, the government will not capitulate, so their payoff will be $-L$ with probability θ, or N with probability $1-\theta$. Thus, if they attack, their expected payoff Z will be $Z=\theta(-L)+(1-\theta)N$, which again is compared to a sure payoff of 0 if they do not attack. If N is negative, meaning that the terrorists take a loss when the government stands firm, then obviously Z will also be negative, and the terrorists will not attack. In this case the credible prior commitment has served the government's interest well. But suppose alternatively that N is positive, as it might be if the terrorists gain stature based on media coverage of their successful hostage taking. Then the same algebra shows that $Z > 0$, and the terrorists will attack if $\theta < N/(N - (-L))$. This means that if likelihood of logistical failure is sufficiently low, then the terrorists will still attack. If the attack succeeds in taking hostages, and if the commitment is truly credible as assumed, then the government will not capitulate, and presumably the hostages will be lost. In this case the government will be left with an outcome worse than if there had been no prior commitment and the government had been free to save the hostages by capitulating. This helps make clear why high-profile hostage incidents are so difficult for governments. It also indicates why it is in the interest of governments to expend resources up front to make the capture of hostages less likely.

Counterterrorism Games between Governments

The hostage game in the last section investigates strategic interdependence between a government and a terrorist organization. Here we consider strategic interdependence between governments themselves as they attempt to counter terrorism. Government efforts to counter terrorism can be broadly classified as either offensive or defensive. Offensive counterterrorism includes infiltration of terrorist groups and attacks against the terrorists' training centers, bases, resources, and leaders. Defensive counterterrorism includes screening devices and barriers in airports and buildings; risk-reducing protocols for diplomats, businesspeople, military personnel, and tourists; and security alerts for private citizens and civil authorities. Although counterterrorism actions cannot always be neatly classified as offensive or defensive, the distinction is useful because of the different incentives faced by nations as they attempt to counter terrorism.

Consider, for example, offensive counterterrorism efforts against a geographically dispersed organization like al Qaeda. The security benefits of a degraded al Qaeda network are nonrival, because they can be enjoyed by other nations at zero added cost, and nonexcludable, because they can be enjoyed by other nations even if they do not contribute to the efforts. Hence, a degraded al Qaeda organization is a public good for at-risk nations. According to public goods theory, these nations have an incentive to free ride on one another's efforts, which can lead to underprovision of offensive counterterrorism worldwide.

This naturally suggests modeling governments' offensive counterterrorism efforts as a prisoner's dilemma game (see, e.g., Lee 1988, Sandler 2003). Assume in the effort to degrade an international terrorist organization, nations A and B simultaneously choose between two levels of offensive effort *High* and *Low*. To introduce numerical payoffs, suppose that security benefits and resource costs are calibrated such that the strategy pair (Low_A, Low_B) returns 0 to each nation. Suppose further that when either nation raises its effort to *High*, costs increase by 12 for that nation alone, and security benefits increase by 10 for *each* nation.

The result is the prisoner's dilemma payoff matrix shown in Figure 8.9 (a). To understand the payoffs, suppose B chooses *High*. If A also chooses *High*, then A enjoys an increased security benefit of $10 + 10 = 20$ but incurs an increased cost of 12, for a payoff of $20 - 12 = 8$; alternatively, if A free rides and chooses *Low*, then A receives an added benefit of 10 with 0 added cost, resulting in a higher payoff of 10; thus, A's best reply is *Low*. Suppose instead that B chooses *Low*. If A chooses *High*, then A receives an added benefit of 10 but an added cost of 12, for a payoff of -2; if A chooses *Low*, then A receives 0 added benefit and incurs 0 added cost, yielding a higher payoff of 0; thus, again A's best reply is *Low*. Hence, A's dominant strategy is a *Low* effort. The game is symmetric and the result is the unique but Pareto inefficient Nash equilibrium (Low_A, Low_B).

The prisoner's dilemma provides an explanation for the low levels of offensive counterterrorism effort prior to 9/11 (Cauley and Sandler 1988). However, the also familiar assurance and chicken games might be more useful in characterizing offensive counterterrorism since 9/11. To illustrate the assurance game, assume that strategy pair (Low_A, Low_B) returns 0 to each nation as in the prisoner's dilemma. Continue also to assume that when either nation increases its effort to *High*, an increased resource cost of 12 is incurred by that nation alone. Now assume there exist what can be thought of as increasing marginal returns to security from offensive counterterrorism efforts. If one nation increases its effort to *High*, an added security benefit of 4 is generated for each nation, and if a second nation does the same, a further security benefit of 16 is generated for each nation.

The result is the assurance game of Figure 8.9(b), wherein a *High* effort is optimal only when matched by the other nation. Suppose B chooses *High*. If A also chooses *High*, then A receives an increased benefit of $4 + 16 = 20$ and incurs an increased cost of 12, for a payoff of 8; if A

(a) Prisoner's dilemma

		Player B	
		High Offense	Low Offense
	High Offense	8,8	-2,<u>10</u>
Player A	Low Offense	<u>10</u>,-2	<u>0</u>,<u>0</u>

(b) Assurance

		Player B	
		High Offense	Low Offense
	High Offense	<u>8</u>,<u>8</u>	−8,4
Player A	Low Offense	4,-8	<u>0</u>,<u>0</u>

(c) Chicken

		Player B	
		High Offense	Low Offense
	High Offense	8,8	<u>4</u>,<u>16</u>
Player A	Low Offense	<u>16</u>,<u>4</u>	0,0

Figure 8.9. Offensive counterterrorism games between governments.

chooses *Low*, then *A* has an increased benefit of 4 and 0 added cost, for a lower payoff of 4; thus, *A*'s best reply is *High*. Suppose instead that *B* chooses *Low*. If *A* chooses *High*, then *A* receives an added benefit of 4 and an added cost of 12, for a payoff of −8; if *A* chooses *Low*, then *A* has 0 added benefit and cost, for a higher payoff of 0; thus *A*'s best reply is *Low*. Note that *A*'s best reply depends on the strategy choice of *B*, who faces symmetric incentives. In Figure 8.9(b) there are two pure-strategy Nash equilibriums ($High_A$, $High_B$) and (Low_A, Low_B), where the former is Pareto superior to the latter. If free riding is the essence of the prisoner's dilemma, then "I'll try only if you help" is the intuition of the assurance game. Sandler and Enders (2004, pp. 310–311) suggest that the assurance game characterizes the coalition forged by the United States and the United Kingdom after 9/11.

There is, however, the suspicion that if the United States had anticipated itself to be a coalition of one, it still would have raised its offensive counterterrorism effort. This leads to consideration of the chicken game. Continue to assume that strategy pair (Low_A, Low_B) returns 0 to each nation and that when either nation increases its effort to *High*, an increased resource cost of 12 is incurred by that nation alone. Now assume there exist what might be thought of as diminishing marginal returns to security from offensive counterterrorism efforts. If one nation increases its effort to *High*, an added security benefit of 16 accrues to both nations, and if a second nation does the same, a further security benefit of 4 results.

The result is the chicken game of Figure 8.9(c), wherein a *High* effort is optimal for a nation only when the other nation chooses *Low*. To follow the payoffs, assume *B* chooses *High*. If *A* also chooses *High*, then *A* receives an increased security benefit of $16 + 4 = 20$ and incurs an increased cost of 12, for a payoff of 8; if *A* chooses *Low*, then *A* receives an increased benefit of 16 and incurs 0 added cost, for a higher payoff of 16; thus, *A*'s best reply is *Low*. Suppose instead that *B* chooses *Low*. If *A* chooses *High*, then *A* receives an added security benefit of 16 and incurs an added cost of 12, for a payoff of 4; if *A* chooses *Low*, then *A* has 0 added benefit and cost, for a lower payoff of 0; thus, *A*'s best reply is *High*. As in the assurance game, *A*'s best reply depends on the strategy choice of *B*. Two pure-strategy Nash equilibriums arise in Figure 8.9(c), in this case (Low_A, $High_B$) and ($High_A$, Low_B), which are both Pareto efficient. Nation *A* prefers the first equilibrium, wherein *B* contributes the greater effort and *A* free rides, whereas *B* prefers the second. The essence of this game is that each nation believes "something serious must be done" to counter terrorism, but each prefers that the other take the lead.

The prisoner's dilemma, assurance, and chicken games as presented here are distinguished by the size of security benefits relative to resource costs. Clearly, other games are plausible. For example, if security benefits are sufficiently high, then both nations can have a dominant strategy of *High* counterterrorism effort. To move away from symmetric games, if the security benefits vary between nations, one nation can have a dominant strategy of *High* while the other has a dominant strategy of *Low*. Another well-known game is battle-of-the-sexes, where each player is better off when both pick the same action rather than different actions. The game has two pure-strategy Nash equilibriums, but *A* prefers one equilibrium and *B* the other. Battle-of-the-sexes could be applicable when, for example, one nation prefers a preemptive war strategy whereas the other nation prefers sanctions and diplomacy.

In the offensive counterterrorism games just discussed, counterterrorism effort by one nation creates a *positive* security externality for other nations. In defensive counterterrorism games, however, counterterrorism effort by one nation can create a *negative* security externality for other nations. For example, greater defensive barriers in the United States could cause terrorists to strike at less protected countries, as implied by the substitution principle. If nations ignore the negative security externalities of terrorism defense, the allocation of terrorism defense worldwide can be Pareto inefficient. Numerous defensive counterterrorism games are possible depending on how security externalities and resource costs are structured in the game (Arce and Sandler 2005).

8.5. Selected Empirical Studies of Terrorism

Risk Factors for Terrorism

Conventional Terrorism
Prominent explanations for terrorism include economic distress, political repression, and cultural and religious differences. A growing literature seeks to sort through the competing explanations by means of systematic empirical observation. This literature is still in its early stages of development and faces serious conceptual and methodological challenges. Terrorism is a tactic that can serve different strategic ends; hence, the motives for terrorism are likely to be diverse and complex. Here we briefly sample two studies of terrorism risk factors that together suggest the diversity of methods and results that characterizes this developing literature.

One of the best-known studies is Krueger and Malečková's (2003) article entitled "Education, Poverty and Terrorism: Is There a Causal Connection?" Using US State Department data, Krueger and Malečková construct a dependent variable equal to the total number of significant international incidents *originating* from each of 148 countries during the full period 1997–2002. Notice here that countries are linked to incidents based on the origins of the terrorist perpetrators. To test whether economic distress breeds terrorism, the authors include country-level measures of per capita income and illiteracy as explanatory variables. Also included are measures of a country's civil liberties and religious makeup, along with population as a control variable. The resulting cross-country regression analysis indicates that neither low income nor illiteracy has a significant impact on the number of terrorist incidents originating from a given country. In contrast, the analysis suggests that politics and religion both matter. Other things equal, countries with fewer civil liberties are more likely to spawn international terrorists. The same is true for countries with larger populations in one of the major religions, Christianity, Hinduism, or Islam. Based on this and other evidence, Krueger and Malečková (2003, p. 118) conclude that international terrorism is best understood "as a response to political conditions and long-standing feelings of indignity and frustration that have little to do with economics."

In his article entitled "Does Democracy Promote or Reduce Transnational Terrorist Incidents?" Li (2005) moves the primary focus from economics to politics and extends the methodological approach from cross-country to panel analysis. Li looks at 112 countries spanning the period from 1975 to 1997, yielding a sample of about 2,000 country-year observations. Based on ITERATE data, he constructs a dependent variable equal to the number of international incidents *initiated* within a country in a given year. Notice that, in contrast to Krueger and Malečková (2003), incidents are linked to countries based on the locations of attacks rather than the origins of perpetrators. Given his large sample, Li is able to include a rich array of explanatory variables. The paper's central issue involves the effect of democracy on terrorism. Briefly stated, democracy might diminish terrorism by providing a peaceful alternative to violence, or it might facilitate terrorism by limiting a country's counterterrorism efforts, or it might do both. To allow for both possible effects, Li introduces two measures of democracy: the first indicates the level of electoral participation and is expected to have a negative effect; the second indexes the institutional constraints on the chief executive and is predicted to have a positive effect. Among the various control variables are per capita income and a composite index of government capability (including economic and military power). Li's primary result is that both measures of democracy are statistically significant, with participation reducing terrorist attacks and executive constraints increasing them, as predicted. Higher per capita income is associated with fewer terrorist attacks within a country, which contrasts with Krueger and Malečková's (2003) result that income does not systematically affect attacks originating from a country. Contrary to Li's expectation, government capability has a positive effect on terrorism. This might mean that countries with large, powerful governments present high-value, high-profile targets, as conjectured by Li; alternatively, it might reflect the comparative advantages of terrorism under conditions of highly asymmetric power.

Weapons of Mass Destruction

Compared to conventional terrorist incidents, chemical, biological, radiological, and nuclear (CBRN) attacks hold the potential for massive casualties or untold long-term economic costs. Thus, whereas Krueger and Malečková (2003), Li (2005), and others look at terrorist attacks in general, Ivanova and Sandler (2007) focus specifically on incidents wherein "CBRN substances are sought after, acquired, or used for a terrorist attack" (p. 276). To explore possible risk factors for target countries, they construct a panel of 126 nations with annual observations between 1988 and 2003. The dependent variable is the number of CBRN incidents in a given country-year and is derived from the Monterey WMD Terrorism Database, maintained by the James Martin Center for Nonproliferation Studies at the Monterey Institute of International Studies. Ivanova and Sandler find that the expected number of incidents in a country is positively related to the country's per capita income, level of democracy, degree of corruption, and number of incidents in the preceding year. They conclude that rich liberal democracies are high-risk targets, more so if there is a history of prior incidents, and that such nations must be particularly vigilant in guarding CBRN materials and know-how against illicit acquisition. It is worth noting that with regard to the relationship between terrorism and income of the target country, Li's (2005) and Ivanova and Sandler's (2007) results point in opposite directions. This suggests that the literature on terrorism risk factors remains in its early stages of development with much yet to be learned.

Suicide Attacks

Based on information drawn from the Global Terrorism Database (GTD), suicide missions constitute an increasingly frequent mode of terrorist attack. Over the period from 1998 to 2004, the GTD reports that international and domestic suicide attacks more than tripled, from 25 to 88. Nevertheless, suicide attacks account for a relatively low percentage of total terrorist incidents. According to GTD data, the total number of terrorist incidents between 1998 and 2004 exceeded 7,000, of which only about 5 percent were suicide missions. If this percentage seems low, it is because it contrasts sharply with the corresponding figure for associated casualties. During the 1998–2004 period, the total number of persons killed or injured from terrorism exceeded 70,000, of which more than 20 percent were due to suicide attacks. From 2001 to 2004, suicide attacks were about 8 percent of all terrorist incidents, but they were associated with more than

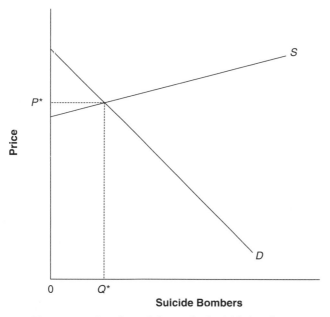

Figure 8.10. Supply and demand of suicide bombers.

30 percent of terrorism casualties. A good summary statistic, therefore, is that in recent years suicide attacks worldwide account for close to one-third of all casualties caused by terrorism.

Iannaccone (2006), in his paper titled "The Market for Martyrs," suggests that a useful approach for studying suicide terrorism is to think in terms of the supply and demand for suicide bombers. We take up his suggestion explicitly in Figure 8.10, treating as price the explicit or implicit compensation received by the bombers. On the supply side of the market are the individuals who execute the suicide missions. Iannaccone argues that, given appropriate incentives, a supply of would-be bombers will always exist. After all, many soldiers in wars past have undertaken missions despite knowing that they faced near certain death. On the other side of the market are the terrorist organizations, whose demand for bombers is derived from the demand for terrorist activity in general and for suicide bombing in particular. In very broad terms, the demand for bombers will depend on the value of the missions and the efficiency or productivity of the bombers. For Iannaccone, this is the crucial side of the market: because supply can be taken as given, it is the level of demand that will primarily determine whether there exists an active market for bombers. From an economic standpoint, it is also the more interesting side: terrorist organizations must somehow overcome serious free-rider problems when they recruit and train their operators and guard against defection.

Consistent with Iannaccone's general approach, Berman and Laitin (2008) derive two demand-side hypotheses from a formal model of club goods. The first hypothesis is that suicide bombing is more likely to be used by terrorist organizations that are part of a radical religious sect. The logic relies on Iannaccone's insight that terrorist organizations necessarily face a free-rider problem among those who support the terrorist agenda. It happens that religious sects are already particularly adept at overcoming free-rider problems among their members by providing spiritual and material goods that are excludable to nonmembers. Moreover, the sects maintain strict prohibitions that have the dual effects of screening out those who are less committed and increasing the participation of the more committed (see also Iannaccone 1992 and Iannaccone and Berman 2006). In terms of the model in Figure 8.10, association with a religious sect is expected to raise the loyalty and hence productivity of persons recruited for suicide missions, thereby increasing demand. A second hypothesis derived by Berman and Laitin is based on the distinction between soft targets and hard targets. Hard targets are those that are more heavily defended and therefore carry a higher risk of capture. Terrorist organizations are apt to be particularly sensitive to this risk, because capture can result in information breaches that threaten the survival of the organization or its leaders. When a suicide bomb is successfully detonated, a high-quality operator is lost, but at the same time the risk of capture is eliminated. The hypothesis is then that suicide bombs are more likely to be used when targets are harder. In Figure 8.10, this means that the hardening of targets raises the demand for suicide bombing relative to other modes of attack, thereby increasing the demand for suicide bombers.

Berman and Laitin provide empirical support for both hypotheses, drawing from multiple datasets on suicide terrorism spanning roughly from 1981 to 2003. Regarding the link between suicide attacks and religious sects, Berman and Laitin identify seven terrorist organizations that undertook at least one suicide attack in Israel or Lebanon. Three of those are radical Islamic organizations – Hamas, Hezbollah, and the Palestinian Islamic Jihad (PIJ). Of these three, Hamas and Hezbollah are classified as *strong* religious organizations based on their provision of various educational, medical, and welfare services. Because the social services are excludable, they can be used along with spiritual goods to support practices that screen out less committed individuals. The remaining four organizations are secular. The suicide data show that the religious organizations, and particularly the strong religious organizations, were more effective in terms of both the number and the lethality of attacks. On average, the three religious organizations carried out 48.0 suicide attacks with 9.5 fatalities per attack, compared to 10.3 attacks and 2.6 fatalities per attack for the secular groups. Berman and Laitin also use a subset of their database to look at the proportion of terrorist attacks that involve suicide bombs. Consistent with the hypothesis, they find that religious organizations are more likely to choose suicide bombing as a mode of attack. For the two Islamic organizations (Hamas and the PIJ, with Hezbollah unavailable), the proportion of attacks that were suicidal is 0.35, compared to 0.10 for the secular organizations.

On the hypothesis linking suicide attacks and the hardness of targets, Berman and Laitin provide two supporting observations. The first is that suicide attacks are seldom directed at persons whose religion is the same as that of the bombers. In their full suicide dataset, Berman and Laitin find that only about one in eight victims is of the same religion as the attacker. The explanation here is that when targets are coreligionists, the attackers tend to speak and appear much like the victims, making apprehension less likely. Thus coreligionists are softer targets against which other modes of attack are more effective. In contrast, when targets are of a different religion, the attackers are more easily profiled, making capture more probable. In this case the targets are harder, and suicide bombing is more likely to be the favored tactic. Berman and Laitin's second observation pertains to the comparatively greater incidence of suicide attacks on Israeli targets inside the 1949 armistice line than in the West Bank and Gaza. Terrorist attacks inside the Green Line between September 2000 and July 2003 resulted in 511 fatalities, of which 78 percent were due to suicide bombs. In contrast, similar attacks in the West Bank and Gaza resulted in 341 fatalities, of which only 2 percent were from suicide bombs. Again, this pattern is consistent with the hard target hypothesis. Because of the large Palestinian population and the favorable terrain, Israeli targets in the West Bank and Gaza are softer and hence more suitable for shootings and roadside bombs. Inside the Green Line, the targets are more heavily defended and profiling is easier, so the targets are much harder and thus favor suicide attacks.

Berman and Laitin (2008) derive their hypotheses from what they describe as a club good model, and they conduct their empirical tests primarily using data from the Israeli-Palestinian conflict. As they acknowledge, it remains to be seen whether the model can be extended to nonreligious-based clubs and confronted with data from conflicts in which religious differences are less salient.

Economic Consequences

Terrorism and Trade

One of the expected costs of conflict is the disruption of ordinary economic activities. Because terrorist attacks raise the costs of transacting, terrorism is expected to decrease the extent of mutually advantageous trade. Whether this effect extends to international trade is the question addressed empirically by Nitsch and Schumacher (2004). The authors begin with what is known as a gravity model, which postulates that trade between two countries is an increasing function of their incomes and populations and a decreasing function of the distance between them. To these standard trade variables they add a terrorism measure equal to the product of the number of international terrorist attacks in each of the two trading countries. The analysis involves approximately 200 countries over the time span 1968–79, resulting in a pooled time-series sample of about 6,000 observations, where each observation is a dyad-year. Nitsch and Schumacher find that the effect of terrorism on trade is statistically significant and economically important. In particular, they estimate that if the number of attacks in a country in a given year increases by 10 percent, then that country's trade with each trading partner will decrease during that year by about 0.4 percent. They also provide evidence that the effect of the attack will spill over to subsequent years.

Terrorism and Economic Growth

Violent conflict can depress a country's economic growth to the extent that it disrupts economic activity and destroys and diverts resources. Blomberg, Hess, and Orphanides (2004) provide a careful study of the growth effects of external conflict (including interstate war), internal conflict (including civil war and genocide), and international terrorist attacks, with particular emphasis on the latter. They base their analysis on a standard country-level growth model, wherein annual growth in per capita income is a function of lagged per capita income, investment as a share of GDP, and trade openness. To this baseline model the authors add explanatory variables that indicate the presence or absence of each of the three forms of violent conflict. Their sample involves a panel of 177 countries from 1968 to 2000, yielding approximately 4,000 country-year observations. An important feature of their regression analysis is the inclusion of what are called fixed effects, which control for unobserved influences that are specific to particular years or countries.

The authors' central finding is that all three forms of conflict have a statistically significant negative impact on economic growth. For terrorism, they estimate that the presence of an attack reduces growth by about 0.5 percentage points in that same year, with larger effects found for external and internal conflict. To better understand the mechanism by which terrorism affects growth, Blomberg, Hess, and Orphanides extend their analysis to consider how terrorism influences the composition of a country's economic activity. Interestingly, they find that a terrorist attack tends to decrease the investment rate by about 0.4 percentage points while increasing the government spending rate by the same amount. Notice that this means that a terrorist event can have a further indirect effect by crowding out investment, which in turn impacts negatively on subsequent economic growth.

8.6. Bibliographic Notes

For early applications of rational choice modeling to terrorism, see Landes (1978) on hijackings and Sandler, Tschirhart, and Cauley (1983) on hostage negotiations. The simple two-good choice model of terrorism sketched earlier draws from Frey and Luechinger (2003) and Anderton and Carter (2005, 2006). Note that the model treats terrorism as a consumption rather than a production activity. An alternative approach uses household production theory (Becker 1976) to model terrorist activities as inputs to the production of basic commodities like political instability (see, e.g., Enders, Sandler, and Cauley 1990, Enders and Sandler 1993). The Enders and Sandler (1993) article is also noteworthy for its treatment of some terrorist activities as substitutes and others as complements. See Sandler (2003), Sandler and Siqueira (2006), and Sandler and Arce (2007) for various game theoretic models of terrorism and counterterrorism, and Enders (2007) for a survey of data and statistical approaches. Enders and Sandler (2006a) provide an accessible and comprehensive book on the social scientific study of terrorism.

One of the limitations of the rational choice model is that preferences are typically taken as given. The origin of terrorist preferences and how preferences might be redirected are important issues. Scholars from a variety of disciplines have delved into why terrorists exist and how they are motivated. See, for example, Hoffman (1998) (political science), Lewis (2003) (history), and the edited volume of Victoroff (2006) (social psychology). An interesting analysis of preference formation is Arce and Sandler's (2003) evolutionary game model, which shows how moderates within a society adopt extremist preferences in order to fit within an extremist group. Crenshaw (2007) provides a valuable review of a number of books on suicide terrorism.

A wide range of studies on the economic, political, and psychological consequences of and risk factors for terrorism can be found in the special issues of *Defence Economics* (Sandler 1992), *Journal of Monetary Economics* (King and Plosser 2004), *Journal of Conflict Resolution* (Rosendorff and Sandler 2005), *Public Choice* (Rowley 2006), *Conflict Management and Peace Science* (Lai 2007), and *Risk Analysis* (Bier and Winterfeldt 2007), and in the edited books of Silke (2004), Richardson, Gordon, and Moore (2005, 2007), Brück (2006), and Schmid, Jongman, and Price (2008).

9

Geography and Technology of Conflict*

Geography and weapons technology form an important context in which interstate, intrastate, and extra-state conflicts occur. In this chapter we explore how geography and weapons technology affect the territory controlled by armed rivals and the risk of violence between them. We begin with Boulding's (1962) spatial model of intergroup rivalry, which highlights geographical and technological dimensions of conflict such as spheres of influence, offensive and defensive technologies, and strategic depth. We then summarize O'Sullivan's (1991) three-dimensional extension of Boulding's model. We turn to the Lanchester (1916) model of war attrition to illustrate how combinations of geography and weapons technologies create incentives for nations or groups to go on the offensive, or stay on the defensive, in violent encounters. We also present Alesina and Spolaore's (2003) theory of the number and size of nations in the international system. Selected empirical studies related to the geography and technology of conflict are summarized.

9.1. Boulding's Model of Spatial Conflict

Basic Model

In his classic work *Conflict and Defense: A General Theory*, Boulding (1962) modeled conflict over territory among states or non-state groups by adapting prior economic theory on spatial competition. The basic model is

---

* Parts of sections 9.3 and 9.5 of this chapter are adapted from Charles H. Anderton and John R. Carter, "A Survey of Peace Economics," published in *Handbook of Defense Economics*, volume 2, edited by Todd Sandler and Keith Hartley, pp. 1211–1258, Copyright © Elsevier 2007. We gratefully acknowledge Elsevier's permission to republish material from the article.

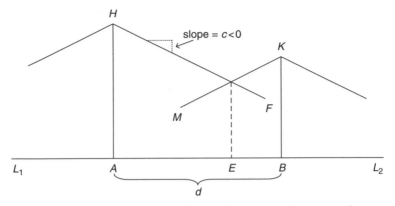

Figure 9.1. Boulding's basic model of spatial conflict (with military strength measured vertically) (adapted from Boulding 1962, p. 230).

shown in Figure 9.1, where two players A and B have home bases located at points A and B in a geographic space represented by line L_1L_2. A player's home base might be its capital if the player is a state, or a jungle or mountainous hideout if the player is a rebel or terrorist organization. In a battlefield context, the home base might be the location of a military's primary command, control, communications, computer, and information (C^4I) infrastructure, which represents the central nervous system of the military organization. The parameter d measures the distance between the players' home bases. Measured vertically in the figure is the military strength that a player can project when it concentrates its power at a given point in geographic space. By assumption, each player's strength is at a maximum at the player's home base, from which it falls off in either direction. The relevant portions of A's and B's power projection curves are labeled HF and KM, respectively, in the figure. The negative slope of a player's power projection line measures what Boulding called the loss-of-strength gradient, which is the rate at which a player's military strength decreases as the player moves away from its home base. According to Boulding (1962, p. 231), "The law of diminishing strength ... may be phrased as *the further, the weaker;* that is, the further from home any nation has to operate, the longer will be its lines of communication, and the less strength it can put in the field." In Figure 9.1, rivals A and B are equally strong at location E, which is called the boundary of equal strength. At points to the left of E, player A is stronger and thus can defeat B, while to the right of E, player B is stronger and can defeat A. Thus, A's sphere of influence lies to the left of E, and B's lies to the right.

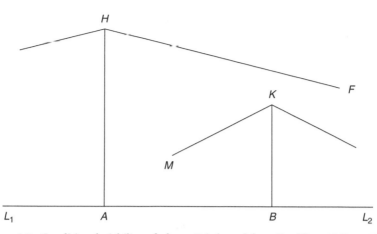

Figure 9.2. Conditional viability of player B (adapted from Boulding 1962, p. 232).

Boulding was particularly interested in the geographic and technological conditions under which one player can conquer another. In Figure 9.1, neither player can conquer the other because each is the stronger of the two at its own home base. Specifically, the height of A's power projection line is greater than the height of B's at location A, which implies that B cannot conquer A. Likewise, B's strength is greater than A's at location B, indicating that A cannot conquer B. Because each player is stronger at its own home base than its rival, both players are said to be unconditionally viable. This is not true in Figure 9.2, where player B is weaker at its home base than player A. In this case, B can be conquered by A and thus is said to be conditionally viable, meaning that its survival is dependent on whether A chooses to attack its home base.

Assume that A's and B's power projection curves are linear with the same common slope c. Then the condition for unconditional viability of both players is

$$\frac{AH - BK}{d} > c \text{ and } \frac{BK - AH}{d} > c, \tag{9.1}$$

where the first and second parts of the condition imply A's and B's unconditional viability, respectively (Boulding 1962, p. 232). Note that c is negative because it measures the loss-of-strength gradient. Hence, (9.1) implies that at least one of the two players will be unconditionally viable, because if $AH - BK$ is negative or zero, then $BK - AH$ is positive or zero, and vice versa. More important, the condition shows that both players will tend to be unconditionally viable when military strength falls steeply with distance (so that *c* is highly negative), the players' home-base strengths are roughly equal (so that the difference between *AH* and *BK* is close to zero), and substantial distance separates the rivals (so that *d* is large).

Applications

Defensive and Offensive Military Innovations

Boulding (1962, pp. 258–259) used his model to distinguish between defensive and offensive weapons technologies. Defensive weapons held by *A* inhibit *B*'s ability to attack *A*, without directly increasing *A*'s ability to attack *B*. For example, concrete barriers around US embassies diminish the ability of terrorists to attack the embassies, but the barriers do not directly increase the United States' ability to attack terrorists. Offensive weapons held by *A* increase *A*'s ability to attack *B*, but they do not directly inhibit *B*'s ability to attack *A*. For example, Hezbollah can use missiles to attack Israel, but the missiles do little to thwart Israel's ability to attack Hezbollah in southern Lebanon. The distinction between defensive and offensive weapons is not precise, however, because most weapons can be used for either defensive or offensive purposes. Moreover, weapons may be used offensively in a particular battle, whereas the battle may be part of a broader strategy designed to achieve a strong defensive posture. Despite these difficulties, Boulding maintained that the distinction between defensive and offensive weapons is important for understanding the risk and nature of intergroup violence.

An example of a defensive weapons innovation was the use of soccer stadiums by UN peacekeeping forces to defend Tutsi civilians against Hutu extremists during the 1994 Rwandan genocide. As documented in Chapter 7, the Rwandan genocide claimed some 750,000 lives as the Hutu-led government attempted to "cleanse" the country of Tutsis and moderate Hutus. Prior to the genocide, UN peacekeepers attempted to provide security to vulnerable civilians in the Rwandan capital of Kigali under the auspices of the United Nations Assistance Mission in Rwanda. The UN force had little capacity to control territory because it was significantly outnumbered by Hutu extremists.

Figure 9.3 depicts the strong position of the Hutus relative to the UN forces in Kigali. The initial Hutu and UN home strengths are *AH* and *BK*, and the respective power projection lines are *HF* and *KM*. The figure implies that the UN forces were only conditionally viable, meaning that the Hutus could carry out ethnic cleansing virtually anywhere in Kigali. If more UN peacekeepers were brought to Kigali, the strength of the UN

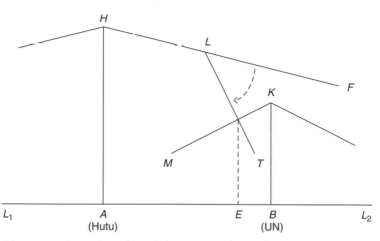

Figure 9.3. Protection of Tutsis in soccer stadiums during 1994 Rwandan genocide.

might have risen to the point where UN forces would have been unconditionally viable over a relatively large area. This could have allowed the UN to sequester a significant amount of territory to serve as a safe haven for vulnerable Tutsi, possibly moving Hutu extremists to consider a negotiated settlement. Such troops, however, were never supplied (Dallaire 2004).

Given limited forces, UN commander Roméo Dallaire developed a plan to protect civilians in soccer stadiums. At the Amahoro Stadium in Kigali, for example, Dallaire was able to defend about 10,000 civilians with just a few dozen UN troops. The stadium had high concrete walls and was surrounded by large open areas, making it highly defendable. Placement of UN troops on the walls of a soccer stadium did not enhance the UN's ability to attack the Hutus, but it did severely diminish Hutu ability to attack UN forces and Tutsis inside the stadium. In Figure 9.3, the defensive innovation is depicted by the redirection of the Hutu power projection line from *HF* to *HLT*. Near the stadium, Hutu ability to thwart UN troops and attack Tutsis was significantly diminished. In this way, the UN was able to achieve a small niche of unconditional viability using its defensive innovation.

In Boulding's model, a defensive innovation by player *A* causes the power projection line of *B* to rotate downward in some fashion. In contrast, an offensive innovation by *A* rotates its own power projection line upward, as shown in Figure 9.4. Assume that *A* and *B* initially have a boundary of equal strength at *E* based on power projection lines *HF* and *KM*. Suppose that *A* implements improved communications or weapons technologies, so that a given amount of military forces can be more effectively projected over

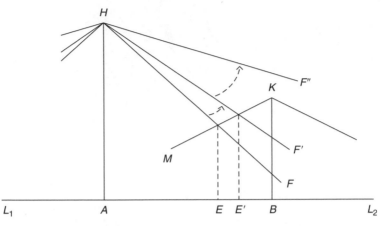

Figure 9.4. Offensive technological innovation by player *A*.

distance. *A*'s power projection line rotates upward to *HF*, pushing the boundary of equal strength to *E*′ and increasing *A*'s sphere of influence. If *A*'s offensive innovations are large enough, *A*'s power projection line could reach *HF*″, thus jeopardizing *B*'s viability.

Figure 9.4 depicts, in a simplified way, Germany's (player *A*) deployment of blitzkrieg technologies and tactics against France (player *B*) in 1940. The German blitzkrieg encompassed improved military communications and weapons technologies such as decentralized command and maneuverable and speedy mechanized infantry, tanks, and artillery. Under the blitzkrieg, Germany was able to project power over distance with extraordinary effectiveness, thus rendering France and other European nations only conditionally viable.

Figures 9.3 and 9.4 suggest that armed rivals will be motivated to integrate new technologies into their military organizations, even if their intentions are not aggressive. Failure to do so could cause a player to lose control of territory or become vulnerable to conquest because of technological breakthroughs adopted by a rival. As Buzan (1987, p. 109) notes, "States . . . face the constant worry that their rivals will gain a military advantage by being the first to adopt a decisive technological breakthrough. Such conditions create relentless pressure on states to lead, or at least to keep up with, the pace of change by continuously modernizing their armed forces."

Military Bases
Figure 9.5 illustrates how a player can reverse its loss of strength in a particular area by utilizing a secondary center of home strength such as a

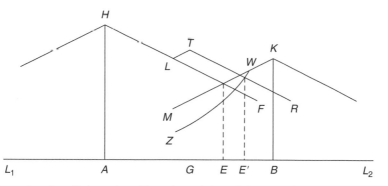

Figure 9.5. Installation of a military base (adapted from Boulding 1962, p. 262).

military base (Boulding 1962, pp. 262–263). Assume that players *A* and *B* initially have a boundary of equal strength at *E* based on power projection lines *HF* and *KM*. Suppose now that *A* establishes a military base at location *G*. The base provides additional communications and logistics support for *A*, allowing it to partially offset the loss of strength over distance. Thus, *A*'s power projection line becomes *HLTR*, which is above what it would have been had there been no military base. *A*'s base might also diminish *B*'s ability to project power over space, because *B* must exert extra effort to navigate around or through that location. Assuming *B*'s power projection line is now *KWZ*, a new boundary of equal strength emerges at *E'*, constituting an increase in *A*'s sphere of influence.

This illustrates the offensive and defensive nature of military bases (Boulding 1962, p. 263). On the one hand, *A*'s military base diminishes *B*'s power projection line, suggesting that *A* will view the base as defensive. On the other hand, the increase in *A*'s power projection line and the rightward movement of the boundary of equal strength suggest that *B* will view the base as offensive. During the 1962 Cuban Missile Crisis, for example, the United States viewed the Soviet attempt to place nuclear missiles on the island of Cuba as offensive, whereas Cuba and the Soviet Union viewed the base as defensive.

Figure 9.5 can also be used to highlight the strategic significance of high ground among armed rivals. In the 1967 Six-Day War, Israel captured the Golan Heights, a strategically important piece of geography in the border area between Israel and Syria. This action is easily translated in terms of Figure 9.5, with Israel as player *A*, Syria as player *B*, and the Golan Heights as location *G*. Control of the Golan Heights elevates Israel's power projection line from *HF* to *HLTR*, while Syria's power projection line is

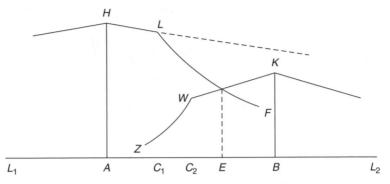

Figure 9.6. Effect of a buffer zone (adapted from Boulding 1962, p. 263).

diminished from *KM* to *KWZ*. The defensive/offensive nature of a prominent piece of geography is apparent in the Israel-Syria rivalry. Israel views control of the Golan Heights as defensive, because it diminishes the ability of Syria or other groups to launch attacks into important agricultural and industrial locations in northern Israel. Syria views Israeli control of the Golan as offensive, due in part to the short distance (about 60 km) between elevated areas of the Golan Heights and Syria's capital, Damascus.

Buffer Zones and Peacekeeping Forces

Boulding (1962, p. 263) also used his model to illustrate the theory of the buffer state. Assume in Figure 9.6 that state *C*'s territory $C_1 C_2$ lies between the home bases of *A* and *B*, where the latter are rivals to each other but not to *C*. The presence of *C* between *A* and *B* causes the rivals' power projection lines to decline at a more rapid rate than otherwise, because the rivals must allocate extra effort to get around or through *C*'s territory. As a consequence, notice that *C*'s presence generates unconditional viability for player *B*. Without *C* as a buffer, *A*'s power projection line would decline at a constant rate, rendering *B* only conditionally viable.

Figure 9.6 provides a basic illustration of the role of peacekeeping operations (PKOs) in thwarting conflict between armed rivals. Although mandates vary widely among PKOs, many attempt to reduce the ability of rivals to project military force against each other, thus diminishing their power projection lines. For example, the United Nations Organization Mission in the Democratic Republic of the Congo (MONUC) was implemented in 1999 to diminish intrastate and interstate conflict associated with regime change and control of resources in the Democratic Republic of the Congo (DRC). MONUC used force to implement a

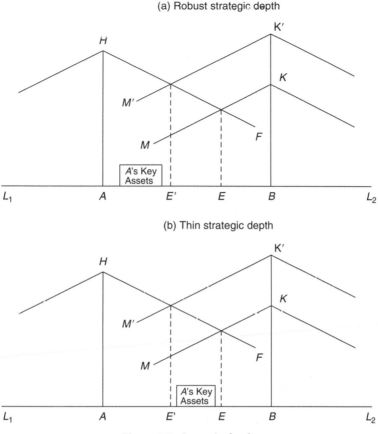

Figure 9.7. Strategic depth.

ceasefire agreement between combatants and then sought to facilitate disarmament and elections. Despite deployment of more than 16,000 personnel and an annual budget of $1.1 billion in 2007, the ability of MONUC to induce long-term peace in the DRC remains uncertain.

Strategic Depth

An oft-cited concept in the military history literature is that of strategic depth, which is a player's ability to absorb an attack while keeping its key industrial, agricultural, political, and security infrastructures unconditionally viable. Figure 9.7 illustrates the concept of strategic depth in the Boulding model. In panel (a), a boundary of equal strength initially exists at E. Assume that player B increases its home strength from BK to BK' and attacks A. The attack pushes the boundary of equal strength to E', but A's key assets (e.g., capital, industrial heartland, C^4I) remain unconditionally viable. Hence, *A* not only thwarts *B*'s further advance but also retains the assets necessary to build up its home base strength, counter *B*'s attack, and perhaps push the boundary of equal strength back toward *E*. In panel (a), *A*'s robust strategic depth allows it to trade space for time, meaning that it initially loses territory but then gains time to mobilize its key assets for a counterattack. In panel (b), however, player *A*'s strategic depth is seen to be thin. Player *B* increases its home strength from *BK* to *BK'* and invades *A*, but in this case *A*'s key assets near *E'* are vulnerable. Their conquest erodes *A*'s ability to provide strength over space, and in time its power projection line falls until *A* is ultimately rendered only conditionally viable.

A historical example of robust strategic depth was the Soviet Union's use of vast territory and forbidding climate to absorb Germany's attack in 1941. Although the Germans reached the suburbs of Moscow, it took them seven months to get there. This delay gave the Soviet's time to move key industrial assets east of the Ural Mountains. Moreover, consistent with the-further-the-weaker principle, the German troops became extended over a great distance during the onset of a brutal Soviet winter, severely compromising their supply lines and communications. The Soviet's ability to absorb an attack, resupply their defenders over a relatively short distance, and mount a robust counterattack rendered the German invasion a failure.

Contemporary examples of nations with thin strategic depth are Israel and its Arab neighbors. In the Israel-Syria rivalry, the Golan Heights is highly contentious because it borders key industrial and agricultural assets in northern Israel and is less than 60 kilometers from the Syrian capital, Damascus. To Israel's north, Beirut, Lebanon, is less than 100 kilometers away, and to the west, Amman, Jordan, is less than 40 kilometers. To the south, Israel shares borders with Jordan and Egypt. Thin strategic depth in the Arab-Israeli arena can make each state feel highly vulnerable to a quick attack from a rival, causing militaries in the region to be poised to strike quickly in the event of rising tensions. In Kemp and Harkavy's (1997, p. 165) words, "distances are very short in the core Middle Eastern zone of conflict, producing fast-moving wars with quick outcomes."

9.2. O'Sullivan's Three-Dimensional Model of Spatial Conflict

O'Sullivan (1991, pp. 80–85) provides an important three-dimensional extension of Boulding's spatial model of conflict, with applications to a rebel group's insurgency against a state. Implicit in Boulding's

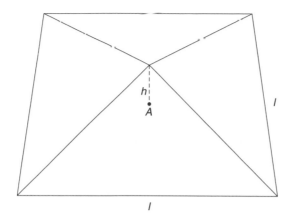

Figure 9.8. Pyramid model of spatial distribution of military power (adapted from O'Sullivan 1991, p. 81).

presentation of his basic model was the assumption that a player's power projection line depicts the maximum military strength that the player can concentrate at a particular location, effectively leaving no military strength available at other locations. O'Sullivan, however, assumes that a player can spread its military power over geographic space to control multiple areas at the same time. As a result, whether a player concentrates its military power in a small area or spreads it over a large area affects its loss-of-strength gradient, whereas in Boulding's model the gradient is exogenously fixed. O'Sullivan develops his model of spatial conflict in three dimensions based on the geometry of a square pyramid, to which we now turn.

Pyramid Model of the Distribution of Military Power

Following O'Sullivan (1991, pp. 80–81), player A's total military power M_A is represented by the volume of a square pyramid, with the base of the pyramid called the coverage area. The pyramid's volume M_A, height h, and base length l are related by the equation:

$$M_A = \frac{l^2 h}{3}. \tag{9.2}$$

Figure 9.8 provides a graphical interpretation of the spatial distribution of A's military power based on equation (9.2). The coverage area is shown by the square base of the pyramid with length l and area l^2. The vertical distance from any geographic location in the base up to the surface of the pyramid measures A's military strength at that point. By assumption, this strength is at its maximum and equal to h at the center of the base, which might be a key city or C^4I location. The decline in military strength with movements away from the center reflects the-further-the-weaker principle, which as in Boulding's model is due to difficulties in transportation and communication.

Equation (9.2) is helpful in thinking about how military power can be spread over alternative coverage areas. Assuming a fixed volume of military power, inspection of the equation reveals that if A increases its military strength h at the center, its coverage area l^2 will necessarily shrink. Going the other direction, if A increases its coverage area, its military strength at the center will necessarily decline. Thus, to increase its strength at the center without reducing its coverage area (or vice versa), A must increase its total military power M_A.

Extending these insights, it can be shown that the spatial distribution of military power over a square pyramid is governed by a proportionality principle as follows:

$$\frac{\Delta M_A}{M_A} = \frac{\Delta h}{h} + \frac{\Delta area}{area}, \tag{9.3}$$

where ΔM_A is the change in A's total volume of military power, Δh is the change in the pyramid's height, and $\Delta area$ is the change in the area of the pyramid's base. Equation (9.3) implies that for a given volume of military power $(\Delta M_A/M_A = 0)$, a 10 percent increase in central strength $(\Delta h/h = +0.10)$ implies a 10 percent decrease in the coverage area $(\Delta area/area = -0.10)$, and vice versa. More generally, a 10 percent change in the volume of military power implies a 10 percent change in strength at location A, or a 10 percent change in the coverage area, or some combination of changes adding up to 10 percent. The same proportionality principle applies to circular cones as well as to other pyramids and is independent of whether the apex of strength is directly above the center.

The logic of the proportionality principle is illustrated by the strategic difficulty faced in Iraq by coalition and Iraqi forces in 2006 and 2007. The circumstances included the extreme insecurity at the Baghdad center, the buildup of al Qaeda in Anbar Province and elsewhere, the inflow of weapons and fighters across Iraq's borders, and the relatively slow development of Iraqi military and police forces. As shown by the proportionality principle, a greater concentration of forces at the center to increase security there would worsen control in the peripheral areas, and vice versa.

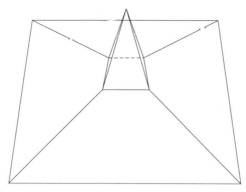

Figure 9.9. Rebel concentration of military power and conquest of the state (adapted from O'Sullivan 1991, p. 84).

Territorial Conflict

Assume that a territorial conflict arises between government forces A and a rebel group B. Following O'Sullivan (1991, pp. 81–84), their respective military powers M_A and M_B can be visualized as two square pyramids. Although the rebel group is comparatively weak, it nonetheless might be able to carve out an area in which it is unconditionally viable. Ordinarily it will do so by centering its power in the periphery of A's coverage area, where A's strength is more depleted, thus allowing B's pyramid to penetrate upward through A's. If the government spreads its military power in an attempt to increase control in the periphery, it reduces its strength at the center. B might then be tempted to try to take control of the state by concentrating its rebel forces at key location A. If the rebel group is strong enough, the result will be like that pictured in Figure 9.9, in which A's large pyramid is penetrated by B's narrow but tall pyramid. With control of key assets at the center, the rebel group might then be able to hinder the government's ability to redeploy forces back at the center. This illustrates the dilemma of government forces when facing an insurgency. If the government concentrates its forces to protect a key location, it is vulnerable to the rebel group's controlling some of the periphery of the state. If the government instead attempts to control a large area, it is vulnerable to a rebel group's concentration of forces at a key location.

O'Sullivan's three-dimensional model is applicable to the Taliban's unconditional viability in tribal areas of Pakistan. Following the September 11, 2001, terrorist attacks, the United States attacked Taliban forces in Afghanistan in retaliation for their support of al Qaeda. Although the

Taliban was initially decimated in Afghanistan, they were able to establish new command centers along the Pakistan-Afghan border. The Taliban's ability to carve out niches of unconditional viability along the Pakistan-Afghan border was due in part to the remote and mountainous terrain, to support for the Taliban among some tribal leaders, and to resistance in the Pakistani army to operations in the tribal areas. The relatively high degree of lawlessness in the tribal areas might also have facilitated the ability of a small number of Taliban to generate widespread extremism in the local population.

9.3. Schelling's Inherent Propensity toward Peace or War

According to the Nobel Prize–winning economist Thomas Schelling, certain configurations of geography, weapons technologies, and military organization can push adversaries toward either peace or war, independent of the rivals' preferences, perceptions, and goals (Schelling 1960, chs. 9 and 10, 1966, ch. 6; Schelling and Halperin 1961, chs. 1 and 2). In Schelling's (1966, p. 234) words, "There is, then, something that we might call the 'inherent propensity toward peace or war' embodied in the weaponry, the geography, and the military organization of the time." Here we develop Schelling's inherent propensity concepts using the Lanchester (1916) war model.

Basic Lanchester Model of War Attrition

Prior to war, suppose players A and B hold military stocks M_A^0 and M_B^0. The superscripts indicate that these are the players' initial, or time-zero, weapons holdings prior to the outbreak of war. Suppose now that A attacks B. The basic Lanchester model describes the attrition of the military stocks of the two sides with the following differential equations:

$$\dot{M}_A = -\beta_d M_B \tag{9.4}$$

$$\dot{M}_B = -\alpha_a M_A. \tag{9.5}$$

The $\dot{M}_A$ and $\dot{M}_B$ terms on the left side represent the rate of change of the players' military stocks during the war. For example, if time is measured in months and $\dot{M}_A = -100$ at a point during the war, A then would be losing weapons at a rate of 100 per month. The parameters α_a and β_d, called sometimes the attrition coefficients, describe the effectiveness of A's and

B's weapons in destroying the other player's weapons when *A* is the attacker and *B* the defender. Consistent with Schelling, we assume that the coefficients reflect the speed and accuracy of weapons, any geographic impediments or enhancements to fighting ability, and the effectiveness of military organization and training. The M_A and M_B terms represent the military stocks of the players at a point in time during the war. Because attrition causes these stocks to change over time, M_A and M_B are functions of time.

In the basic Lanchester model, the winner in a fight-to-the-finish war is determined when the opposing player's military stock is driven to zero. Given the prewar stocks M_A^0 and M_B^0, this means that when *A* initiates the war, equations (9.4) and (9.5) mathematically determine the winner in accordance with the well-known Lanchester square law (Taylor 1983, v. 1, pp. 72–74):

$$a_a(M_A^0)^2 > \beta_d(M_B^0)^2 \Rightarrow A \text{ wins}$$
$$a_a(M_A^0)^2 < \beta_d(M_B^0)^2 \Rightarrow B \text{ wins}. \tag{9.6}$$

For example, suppose *A* has 2,000 soldiers armed with assault rifles with effectiveness $a_a = 0.01$, and *B* has 1,000 soldiers with machine guns with effectiveness $\beta_d = 0.05$. Substituting the data into condition (9.6) yields the inequality $40,000 < 50,000$, implying that *B* will win the war even though *B* is outnumbered two-to-one. Condition (9.6) applies when *A* is the attacker and *B* the defender, which is indicated by the subscript *a* (for attacker) on *A*'s weapons effectiveness coefficient *a* and by the subscript *d* (for defender) on *B*'s weapons effectiveness coefficient β. If, instead, *B* attacks *A*, the coefficients would be a_d and β_a in equations (9.4) and (9.5) and condition (9.6).

Lanchester Attack/Defend Model

With a little work, we can use the Lanchester square law to formalize Schelling's notion of the inherent propensity for peace or war. Assuming that *A* is the attacker, solving the bottom half of (9.6) for M_B^0 defines the "*B* can defend" condition:

$$M_B^0 > (a_a/\beta_d)^{0.5} M_A^0 \Rightarrow B \text{ can defend}. \tag{9.7}$$

For given attack and defense effectiveness coefficients a_a and β_d, condition (9.7) shows the amount of military stock M_B^0 that *B* must have prior to war in order to successfully defend itself should *A* attack with military stock M_A^0. As an example, suppose $M_A^0 = 2,000$ weapons, $a_a = 0.01$, and

$\beta_d = 0.05$. Substituting the data into condition (9.7) indicates that B needs at least $M_B^0 = 895$ weapons to thwart A's attack. When the defend condition in (9.7) is not satisfied, then A can attack and eventually defeat B. Assuming that B is the attacker, similar methods give the "A can defend" condition:

$$M_A^0 > (\beta_a/a_d)^{0.5} M_B^0 \Rightarrow A \ can \ defend. \tag{9.8}$$

When (9.8) is not satisfied, B can attack and eventually defeat A. Conditions (9.7) and (9.8) highlight two elements that affect a player's ability to defend successfully in the event of war: (1) its own and its rival's military stocks prior to the war, and (2) its weapons' effectiveness, based on technology, geography, and military organization and training.

A graph of the defense and attack potentials of A and B is shown in Figure 9.10, where M_A is plotted on the horizontal axis and M_B on the vertical axis. Possible prewar military stocks M_A^0 and M_B^0 are represented by points in the graph, such as point q in panels (a) and (b). Based on condition (9.7), B's defend condition is plotted as a straight line with slope equal to $(a_a/\beta_d)^{0.5}$ and intercept equal to zero. At military stock points above and to the left of this line, B can successfully defend if A attacks; at points below and to the right, B cannot successfully defend and will eventually be defeated if A attacks. A's defend condition is plotted similarly from (9.8), with intercept equal to zero but with slope equal to $1/(\beta_a/a_d)^{0.5}$.

Figure 9.10(a) is drawn under the condition that the B defends line has a smaller slope than does the A defends line, thereby creating a zone of mutual defense. The condition that determines the existence of a mutual defense zone is

$$(a_a/\beta_d)^{0.5}(\beta_a/a_d)^{0.5} < 1. \tag{9.9a}$$

Condition (9.9a) tends to hold when geographic, technological, and military organization factors combine to cause low attack parameters a_a and β_a and high defense parameters a_d and β_d. Given an initial weapons stocks at point q in Figure 9.10(a), both sides can successfully defend, implying a relatively low risk of war. In Schelling's terminology, Figure 9.10(a) depicts an inherent propensity toward peace.

In Figure 9.10(b), the relative magnitudes of the parameters are reversed, creating a zone of mutual attack under the condition:

$$(a_a/\beta_d)^{0.5}(\beta_a/a_d)^{0.5} > 1. \tag{9.9b}$$

A problem arises at point q in Figure 9.10(b) because of the common knowledge that the first mover can successfully attack and eventually win.

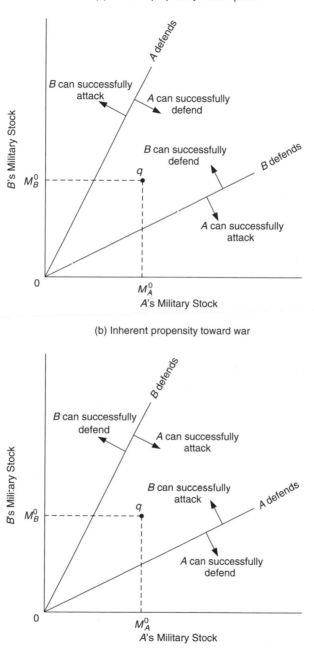

Figure 9.10. Lanchester attack/defend model.

Even rivals that fundamentally wish to avoid war may nevertheless be compelled by a first-mover advantage to attack before the rival does (Schelling 1966, ch. 6, Fischer 1984). In Schelling's terms, Figure 9.10(b) depicts an inherent propensity toward war.

Figure 9.10 highlights the importance of qualitative arms control. In Figure 9.10(b), reconfigurations of weapons technologies and military organization away from attack and toward defense, geographic repositioning of forces toward defensive postures, or placement of peacekeepers between the rivals could reduce relative attack effectiveness (lower β_a/a_d and a_a/β_d). Such qualitative arms control could change the rivalry from an inherent propensity toward war in Figure 9.10(b) to an inherent propensity toward peace in Figure 9.10(a).

Applications*

Egypt-Israel 1967 War

In the two decades leading up to their 1967 war, Egypt and Israel acquired substantial weapons stocks through arms imports and indigenous production. According to Mearsheimer (1985, p. 145), by the late spring of 1967 "the opposing forces were approximately equal in size." This approximate balance of forces could have implied an inherent propensity toward peace if the weapons technologies, geography, and military training of Egypt and Israel had given rise to a situation like that shown in Figure 9.10(a). A rough balance of forces at point q in Figure 9.10(a) would imply that both sides could successfully defend against an attack, thus enhancing the probability of peace, everything else the same. Some observers at the time believed this indeed was the case. For example, prior to the war, O'Balance (1964, p. 210) wrote, "It has long been the aim of the Western powers to keep an even balance of military power in the Middle East so that neither Israel nor any one of the Arab countries develops a dangerous overwhelming preponderance. As long as a fairly even state of parity exists, prospects of peace in that region are better as no one country becomes strong enough to quickly gulp up another."

Missing from the analysis, however, is consideration of geography and weapons technology, which likely placed Israel and Egypt at a point like q

---

* This application is adapted from Charles H. Anderton, "Toward a Mathematical Theory of the Offensive/Defensive Balance," published by Blackwell Publishers in *International Studies Quarterly*, volume 36, issue 1, pp. 75–100, 1992.

in Figure 9.10(b), where despite the balance of forces the propensity toward war was high. Consider the postwar explanation of Fischer (1984, p. 19), who wrote, "Both Israel and Egypt had vulnerable bomber fleets on open desert airfields. Each side knew that whoever initiated the first strike could easily bomb and destroy the hostile planes on the ground, thereby gaining air superiority." Fischer's analysis suggests that the attack effectiveness coefficients a_a and β_a were relatively large in the Egypt-Israel rivalry, because one plane in a surprise attack could destroy many vulnerable planes on the ground. Empirical evidence supports Fischer's contention. Epstein (1990, p. 45) reported that Israel's attack in 1967 caused Egypt to lose 20 aircraft for every Israeli aircraft lost. Also, the close proximity of the two countries enhanced the advantage of a surprise attack, further raising a_a and β_a. Prior to the outbreak of war, Aharon Yariv, head of Israeli intelligence, and General Yeshayahu Gavish, chief of the Israeli Southern Command, "believed that if Israel did not strike soon, the Egyptians might strike first, gaining the attendant benefits of delivering the first blow" (Betts 1982, p. 150).

Militarization of Space

The use of space for networked civilian communications, commercial navigation, weather forecasting, and verification of arms control treaties represents beneficial cooperation among nations. At the same time, however, space is increasingly used for military purposes. Growing reliance on military satellites and continuing research into antisatellite weapons (ASATs) raise concerns about a possible arms race in space. These concerns were magnified in January 2007 when China tested an ASAT by firing a ballistic missile 500 miles above the earth to destroy one of its aging weather satellites.

For centuries military strategists have emphasized the importance of controlling the high ground in war. Geographically, space represents the ultimate high ground, creating enormous incentives for states to control large regions of space. In the years ahead, territorial disputes in space might prove to be even more dangerous than the now-familiar earthly varieties. Particularly troublesome is the likelihood that the technologies involved in the militarization of space will carry inherent propensities toward war between states.

Suppose in some future scenario that two equally armed foes are extremely dependent on satellites to conduct military operations. These satellites are highly vulnerable. The players have launched their own satellites, so presumably they also have the capability of launching space vehicles to destroy their rival's military satellites. The development of laser technologies and legions of small killer satellites further increases the degree of vulnerability. Important here is the evident incentive to initiate a preemptive attack aimed at destroying a substantial portion of a rival's military satellites before the rival attempts to do the same. As Hardesty (2005, p. 49) observes, "Space-based weapons, like all space systems, are predictable and fragile, but they represent significant combat power if used before they are destroyed – leading to a strong incentive to use these weapons preemptively, to 'use them or lose them'." The scenario described might then be a point like q in Figure 9.10(b), where despite a balance of forces, the propensity toward war is high, and the need for arms control is urgent.

9.4. Number and Size of Nations

As shown in Figure 9.11, the number of nations in the international system has increased more than sevenfold since 1820. Furthermore, changes in the number of states appear to be associated at least in some instances with

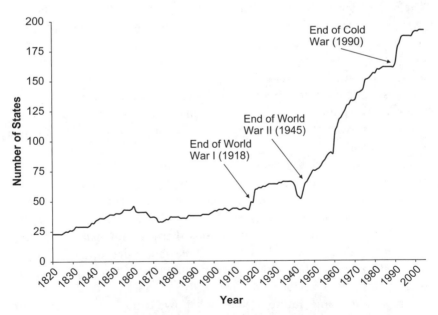

Figure 9.11. Number of states in the international system, 1820–2004.
Source: Correlates of War Project (2005), "State System Membership List, v2004.1." Online, http://correlatesofwar.org.

major events in international relations. Note, for example, the substantial increases in the number of states in the immediate years after World Wars I and II and the Cold War. Although the rise and fall of nations is not always associated with war or international tension, the threat or use of force to redraw borders is a major storyline in human history. In this section, we use the model of Alesina and Spolaore (2003) to explore determinants of the number and size of nations, with a particular emphasis on conflict and economic variables.

The Alesina-Spolaore Model

The fundamental principle of the Alesina-Spolaore model is that the number and size of states follow from a trade-off between the benefits and costs of increased size (Alesina and Spolaore 2003, pp. 3–6). On the benefit side, Alesina and Spolaore posit that per capita disposable income rises with size, because per capita taxes tend to fall as the cost of public goods is spread across a larger population. These lower costs and taxes derive from the nonrivalry property of public goods and also from likely scale economies in their provision. A prominent example is national defense, which because of its publicness can protect additional citizens at low or zero added cost. Other public goods for which per capita costs are likely to fall with increased size include monetary and judicial systems, law enforcement, and diplomatic embassies. Benefits of larger size can also arise for other reasons. To the extent that international trade is restricted, increased size generates higher per capita income owing to greater specialization and trade within a country. Also, larger states can use transfers and subsidies to provide what amounts to insurance against regional downturns and natural disasters. On the other side of the equation, Alesina and Spolaore argue that economic and political costs rise on a per capita basis as larger states encounter increased heterogeneity of preferences, languages, and cultures. Thus, as states grow larger, more individuals on average will be dissatisfied with their government's policies on matters of spending, taxation, redistribution, trade, foreign policy, language, race, religion, and so on.

In Figure 9.12 we offer a highly stylized graphical version of the Alesina-Spolaore model. In both panels of the figure, the horizontal axis measures the average size of states in terms of population. Assuming for simplicity that population and surface area are exactly correlated, the horizontal axis also measures the number of states, with the scale running from right to left. In panel (a), the vertical axis measures the total per capita benefits

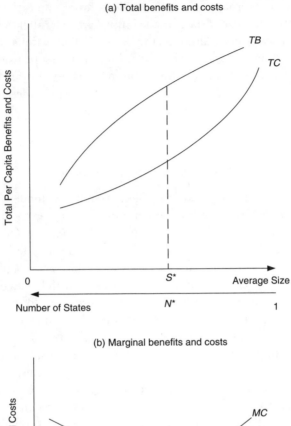

(a) Total benefits and costs

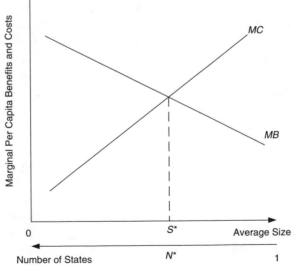

(b) Marginal benefits and costs

Figure 9.12. Determination of the number and average size of nations.

(*TB*) and costs (*TC*) associated with state size. As just posited, benefits increase with size owing to lower per capita taxes on public goods, wider internal specialization and trade, and more regional diversification, whereas costs increase with size owing to greater political heterogeneity. Panel (b) conveys the same information as panel (a) but does so in the more convenient form of marginal benefits (*MB*) and marginal costs (*MC*). For any given national size in panel (a), marginal benefit equals the corresponding slope of the total benefit curve; hence, marginal benefit measures the added benefit per additional unit of size. Geometrically this means that any basic change that rotates the total benefit curve upward in panel (a) will increase (i.e., shift upward) the marginal benefit curve in panel (b). Similarly, marginal cost equals the slope of the total cost curve and hence measures the added cost per added unit of size. Any change that rotates the total cost curve upward in panel (a) will increase (i.e., shift upward) the marginal cost curve in panel (b).

Net benefits in Figure 9.12 are maximized when the average state size is S^*, with a corresponding number of states N^*. The optimal or efficient size S^* is determined in panel (a), where the vertical distance between *TB* and *TC* is greatest, and it is found more conveniently in panel (b), where *MB* equals *MC*. For our purposes, it suffices to assume that the optimum also constitutes a long-run equilibrium. Thus we assume that incentives and processes exist that over the long run drive states to an average size that maximizes net benefits. This is a strong assumption about how incentives and processes actually combine to reshape national borders through both voluntary and coercive means. For more formal treatments that allow for a divergence between optimal and equilibrium size, see Alesina and Spolaore (1997, 2003).

Comparative-Static Analysis

Risk of International Conflict

When the risk of violent conflict rises in the international system, nations tend to increase their demand for military goods. Because national defense is a public good with scale economies, this means that the per capita benefits of national size will increase. In terms of Figure 9.12, increased risk of international violence will rotate the *TB* curve upward and thus cause the *MB* curve to shift upward. As a consequence, equilibrium size S^* will increase and the equilibrium number of states N^* will decrease. The opposite is predicted if the risk of violence decreases, perhaps because of reduced tensions or improved international law. As Alesina and Spolaore

(2003, pp. 95–96) explain, "In a more bellicose world, large countries have an advantage, but when the need to use military force is reduced internationally, defense becomes less important and smaller countries more safe." In this case, the *MB* curve shifts downward, leading to a decreased S^* and an increased N^*. As shown in Figure 9.11, the model's prediction of an increased number of small states is consistent with international trends following the end of the Cold War and the collapse of the Soviet Union.

Openness and Economic Integration
National size is advantageous when trade barriers exist, because specialization and trade can be extended when internal markets are larger. Thus, per capita incomes can be expected to be higher in larger countries, other things equal. Turning this reasoning around, if international trade is liberalized, the benefits of national size are reduced, as external markets are opened to smaller countries. According to Alesina and Spolaore (2003, p. 94), "As the world economy becomes more integrated, one of the benefits of large countries (the size of markets) vanishes. As a result the trade-off between size and heterogeneity shifts in favor of smaller and more homogeneous countries." In terms of Figure 9.12, trade liberalization can be expected to rotate the *TB* curve downward and thus shift the *MB* curve downward. Equilibrium size S^* will consequently decrease, and the equilibrium number of states N^* will increase. Inasmuch as the modern trend has been toward trade liberalization, the model's prediction is consistent with the rapid rise in the number of states since World War II shown in Figure 9.11.

Information Technologies and the Emergence of Trans-State Groups
The phenomenal growth of information technologies such as communication satellites, fiber optics, and microprocessors has spawned a worldwide information revolution. People around the globe can quickly and cheaply obtain information from a variety of nonprint outlets such as CNN and the internet, and they can communicate with one another in new ways via e-mail, blogs, and cell phones. This increased flow of information is likely to impact systematically the benefits and costs of national size. To the extent that the new technologies render people less dependent on state-provided information infrastructures, the benefits of national size are reduced. More important, wider information is likely to generate preferences that are more heterogeneous and hence higher costs associated with national size. If these conjectures are correct, in Figure 9.12 the increase in information shifts the *MB* curve downward and the *MC* curve

upward. As a consequence, equilibrium size S^* will decrease, and the equilibrium number of states N^* will increase.

The increase in N^* can be interpreted as a move toward increased political expression and statehood among people who learn of economic and political opportunities elsewhere and demand such opportunities for themselves. This construal is consistent with the emergence of new states in Eastern Europe at the end of the Cold War. Another interpretation might be the appearance of trans-state groups within and across nations. Trans-state groups are relatively large numbers of like-minded and connected people who view their "citizenship" as centered, not in a geographic location, but in a cause, interest, or philosophy that transcends the geographic location of a state. Transnational terrorist organizations and criminal syndicates are examples of trans-state groups that are in conflict with nations, but not all relations between trans-state groups and states are conflict prone. For example, some people serving in nongovernmental organizations or religious orders may view themselves as primarily inhabitants of their non-state organization.

9.5. Selected Empirical Studies

Determinants of Secession

Secession refers to a rearrangement of borders that is associated with a dispute between a state and an internal group and that results in the creation of a second state (see, e.g., Tir 2006, p. 310). By this definition, the dramatic rise in the number of states since World War II is largely the result of secessionist movements. In the broad terms of Alesina and Spolaore (2003), a demand for secession will arise when, owing to heterogeneity of preferences, the costs exceed the benefits of inclusion for the secessionist group. These preferences might be related to ethnic, religious, economic, or political issues. Following Boulding (1962) and O'Sullivan (1991), the secessionist demand is more likely to be manifested when the separatist group is able to carve out a region of unconditional viability against the state.

Empirical investigation of the determinants of secession generally follows one of two methodological lines. A substantial proportion of all intrastate conflicts are separatist in nature. Thus, one line of inquiry uses the country as the unit of observation and proceeds much like the study of risk factors for civil war reviewed in Chapter 7. At the same time, most separatist movements are associated with ethnic and religious identity. Hence, a second line of inquiry focuses on minority groups as the unit of observation. Representative of these respective approaches are Buhaug (2006) and Walter (2006b).

Based on the UCDP/PRIO dataset (Gleditsch et al. 2002), Buhaug (2006) reports that about one-third of all civil conflicts are aimed at securing territorial autonomy or secession, while the other two-thirds seek the more ambitious goal of governmental control. Because rebels' demands differ between these two types of civil conflict, Buhaug argues that the empirical determinants will vary systematically for secessions and revolutions. For example, drawing on both Boulding (1962) and Alesina and Spolaore (2003), he hypothesizes that larger countries, with their more distant territories and heterogeneous preferences, will be particularly likely to experience secessionist conflicts rather than revolutions, other things equal.

Buhaug tests his general thesis using a large sample of about 5,400 country-year observations spanning the period 1946–99 and including onsets of 80 secessionist conflicts and 123 governmental control conflicts. Among the various explanatory variables, he finds that country size is the single most important determinant of the likelihood of secessionist conflict, both absolutely and relative to the likelihood of governmental control conflict. Holding other factors constant, Buhaug estimates that a country in the 95th percentile for size is about 24 times more likely to experience a secessionist conflict in a given year than is a country in the 5th percentile. In contrast, country size has a much smaller and statistically insignificant effect on the likelihood of governmental control conflict. Other factors that are found to have comparatively large positive effects on the likelihood of secessionist conflict are the level of democracy and the extent of ethnic fractionalization in a country.

Shifting the focus from countries to groups, Walter (2006b) postulates that a minority group will challenge a state on issues of self-determination when the group believes that concessions can be won. To gauge the prospect of concessions, the group will look at not only current but also past and future conditions. If the state has some history of concessions to other groups, then the present group might anticipate that the state will be conciliatory to its own demands. However, this means also that if there exist other minority groups, the present group might expect the state to be less conciliatory in order to build a reputation of resoluteness. Because information is incomplete, miscalculation by a separatist group can lead to armed conflict.

Walter's sample consists of annual observations during the period 1940–2000 for 337 ethnic groups listed by the Minorities at Risk (MAR)

Project. To be listed, an ethnic group must reside in a country with a population of at least one half million, and it must be politically organized or experience discriminatory treatment. For any given group-year observation, Walter's dependent variable indicates whether the group acted violently for the first time in pursuit of "greater political autonomy, association with kin in neighboring states, and/or independence" (Walter 2006b, p. 130). Consistent with her conjectures, Walter finds that a minority group is about six times more likely to initiate violence if the government conceded autonomy or independence to one or more groups in the past; at the same time, the group is only one-third as likely to undertake violence when there are many other ethnic groups residing in the same country. Other factors showing a positive impact on the risk of violent challenge include political discrimination against the group, a loss of autonomy in the past, the absence of co-ethnics in neighboring countries that might offer a migration option, and geographic concentration of the group in a single region of the country.

Offense-Defense Theory and Evidence

Offense-defense theory (ODT) maintains that the character of international relations is influenced by the ease or difficulty of offensive relative to defensive military operations (Lynn-Jones 2004, p. xi). ODT has been applied to many aspects of international relations, including the risk of war, alliance formation, arms control, crisis behavior, size of states, and structure of the international system (Adams 2003/04, p. 46). ODT's central prediction is that war is more likely when offense has the advantage over defense in military operations (Van Evera 1999). Here we liken Schelling's concept of an inherent propensity toward peace or war with an offense-defense balance in favor of the defense and offense, respectively.

How the offense-defense balance (ODB) is defined will necessarily affect the explanatory scope claimed for ODT. Van Evera (1998) characterizes the ODB broadly to include military technology, geography, collective security systems, behavior of neutral states, and actors' perceptions. Given his broad definition, it is not surprising that he views ODT as an encompassing theory of war risk and other international relations phenomena. Indeed, Van Evera (1999, p. 190) claims that ODT should be viewed as the "master key to the causes of conflict." In contrast to Van Evera, Schelling (1966, p. 234) maintained that the elements that determine the inherent propensity toward peace or war "can hardly be

considered the exclusively determining factors in international conflict."
Schelling's more narrow approach suggests that the ODB is just one
among other factors purported to explain war risk and that the empirical
challenge is to determine the relative importance of the ODB.

An empirical test of ODT that is consistent with Schelling's more narrow approach is provided by Adams (2003/04), who defines the ODB
based on military technology alone. To apply the theory, Adams distinguishes among offense, defense, and deterrence, where the latter occurs
when a state prepares to use or shows an ability to use force against another
state's nonmilitary assets in order to discourage that state from initiating
or continuing an offensive operation (Adams 2003/04, p. 53). Based on a
review of the best technologies available since 1800, Adams determines
that offense was dominant during 1800–49 and 1934–45, defense was
dominant during 1850–1933, and deterrence was dominant in the nuclear
era beginning in 1946. Her central hypothesis is that attacks and conquests
would have been most frequent in the offense-dominant eras, less frequent
in the defense-dominant era, and rare in the deterrence-dominant era. To
test the hypothesis, she constructs a dataset on attacks and conquests by
great powers and nuclear states from 1800 to 1997. For each state and year,
Adams codes three dependent variables, indicating whether the state's
territory was conquered, whether the state attacked another great power,
and whether it attacked a non–great power. The key independent variable
is the offense-defense-deterrence balance, which is coded 0 in the deterrence-dominant era, 1 in the defense-dominant era, and 2 in the offense-
dominant eras. Additional variables include relative military capability,
number of years a state had been a great power or a nuclear state, and a
time trend.

Adams (2003/04, p. 76) finds strong support for her central hypothesis.
She estimates that attacks on other great powers were 12 times more
likely each year under offensive dominance (probability 0.156) than
under defensive dominance (probability 0.013) and that they were 13
times more likely each year under defensive dominance than under
deterrence dominance (probability 0.001). She also finds smaller but significant effects with the predicted pattern for conquests and attacks on
non–great powers. These results seem broadly supportive of the Lanchester
attack/defend model summarized earlier in Figure 9.10. When the
ODB favors the defense, Figure 9.10(a) pertains, and great power attacks
and conquests are relatively unlikely. When the ODB favors the offense,
Figure 9.10(b) obtains, and great power attacks and conquests are more
likely.

In addition to the results on the ODB, Adams (2003/04, p. 77) finds that the least capable great powers (those with capability indexes in the 10th percentile) were 2.5 times less likely to attack (probability 0.006) than were the most capable great powers (those in the 90th percentile, probability 0.015), and that they were 40 times more likely to be conquered (probabilities of 0.008 vs. 0.0002). In terms of the Lanchester model, these results on relative capability pertain to the position of the initial weapons point q in Figure 9.10. When a state's relative capability is sufficiently weak, the initial weapons point falls in a zone where its rival can attack and win. This condition can hold irrespective of the ODB. Hence, the ODB is just one element that affects the risk of attack in the Lanchester model; the relative capability of the rivals also matters as Adams shows.

Note that an intermediate conception of the ODB would incorporate geographic elements of war as implied by Schelling. In the Lanchester model, the presence of mobilization advantages tilts attack/defense possibilities toward the offense. One aspect of mobilization advantage is the geographic closeness of states, measured by proximity or contiguity. Empirical research has shown that proximity and contiguity are significant risk factors for interstate war (see, e.g., Russett and Oneal 2001, Senese 2005). In our view, this lends empirical support to the Lanchester exercises explored earlier and to the value of incorporating geography in the definition of the ODB.

9.6. Bibliographic Notes

In addition to Boulding's (1962) seminal work, other early perspectives on the geography of conflict are available from Wright (1942), Richardson (1960b), and Schelling (1960, 1966) and in a special issue of *Journal of Conflict Resolution* (Singer 1960). Along with statistical investigation of risk factors for violent conflict, social scientists now study the geographic spread of violence within and beyond the territories of conflicting states (Siverson and Starr 1990, Braithwaite 2006), within and beyond the borders of states experiencing civil war (Buhaug and Gleditsch 2008), and by terrorist organizations (Enders and Sandler 2006b). The International Peace Research Institute in Oslo's (PRIO) project, "Geographic Representation of War," provides numerous references to recent scholarship on the geography of civil conflict. A number of edited volumes consider the geography of conflict from various disciplinary perspectives (e.g., Cutter, Richardson, and Wilbanks 2003, Flint 2004, Kahler and Walter 2006, and Cox, Low, and Robinson 2008). New datasets on the geography of conflict have been developed, including Starr and Thomas's (2002) geographical information systems data on the nature of interstate borders and PRIO's datasets on petroleum and diamond resources, shared river basins, and length of international boundaries.

For additional perspectives on offense-defense theory, see the edited volumes of Brown, Coté, Lynn-Jones, and Miller (2004) and Gortzak, Haftel, and Sweeney (2005). The effects of weapons technologies on intergroup violence are also assessed in the military history literature (see, e.g., Rotte and Schmidt 2003) and in the nonprovocative defense literature (see, e.g., Fischer 1984, Wiseman 2002).

During much of the twentieth century, the Lanchester model consti-tuted the foundation of mathematical war modeling (Taylor 1983). Although Lanchester theory has been criticized by war modelers (e.g., Epstein 1985, Ancker 1995), it is still used in military service organizations to assess various dynamic aspects of war (Epstein 1985, p. 3) and in aca-demic articles on war risk and duration (Bellany 1999, Anderton and Carter 2007). Lanchester-type models have also been used to study, among other things, terrorist recruitment (Faria and Arce 2005), guerrilla warfare (Intriligator and Brito 1988), peacekeeping (Gaver and Jacobs 1997), primitive warfare among people groups (Beckerman 1991), historical battles (e.g., Weiss 1966, Hartley and Helmbold 1995, Lucas and Turkes 2003), and war among social animals and insects (e.g., Adams and Mes-terton-Gibbons 2003, Plowes and Adams 2005). For an extensive overview of quantitative methods of combat analysis, see Przemieniecki (2000).

Political economy models of the consolidation or fragmentation of states emphasize a variety of variables to explain the size and number of nations in the international system, including taxation (Buchanan and Faith 1987), wealth maximization (Wittman 2000), trade openness (Alesina, Spolaore, and Wacziarg 2000), citizens' policy preferences (Bolton and Roland 1997), states' ability to defend property (McGuire 2002), international conflict and the cost of defense (Alesina and Spolaore 2006), and civil conflict (Spolaore 2008a). Spolaore (2008b) offers a concise review of the literature. For a forum on fragmented states and trans-state groups, see Stanislawski (2008). The Federation of American Scientists provides an extensive list of para-state entities, many of which can be characterized as trans-state groups (www.fas.org/irp/world/para/index.html).

10

Arms Rivalry, Proliferation, and Arms Control*

Born in the tense early years of the Cold War, conflict economics has long been interested in arms rivalry, proliferation, and arms control. In this chapter we provide a summary of key principles and research results in this historically important branch of conflict economics. We begin with definitions followed by an empirical overview of military spending, weapons of mass destruction, and arms control treaties. We then return to the historical roots of conflict economics by sketching the seminal arms race models of Richardson and Intriligator and Brito. To these we add a rational choice model that highlights the interdependence of economics and security in issues of defense spending, arms rivalry, and arms control. Applications to historical and contemporary arms rivalries are presented, including possible proliferation of nuclear weapons to Iran, strategic implications of deployment of US antiballistic missile technology in Europe, and decay of the Soviet economy during the Cold War. We also briefly survey selected empirical studies, focusing on the structure of interstate arms rivalries, arms racing and the risk of war, and risk factors for nuclear weapons proliferation.

10.1. Definitions

An arms rivalry is a competitive increase in the weapons quantities or qualities of two or more parties. Arms rivalries are typically thought of as occurring between states, but they can also occur within states and can

---

* Sections 10.1, 10.3, and parts of 10.4 and 10.6 of this chapter are adapted from Charles H. Anderton and John R. Carter, "A Survey of Peace Economics," published in *Handbook of Defense Economics*, volume 2, edited by Todd Sandler and Keith Hartley, pp. 1211–1258, Copyright © Elsevier 2007. We gratefully acknowledge Elsevier's permission to republish material from the article.

involve transnational groups. Although the terms "arms rivalry" and "arms race" are often used interchangeably, an arms race is a special case of arms rivalry and is characterized by an unusually rapid rate of increase in weapons quantities or qualities. Proliferation is an increase in the number of parties obtaining weapons of mass destruction; it can grow out of an arms rivalry and can spawn new rivalries.

There are three major classes of weapons that states and non-state groups might acquire: major conventional weapons, such as tanks, destroyers, and fighter aircraft; small arms and light weapons, such as machine guns, assault rifles, and improvised explosive devices; and weapons of mass destruction, including nuclear, biological, chemical, and radiological weapons. Major conventional weapons are predominant in interstate wars, while small arms and light weapons are used extensively by non-state groups in intrastate and extra-state conflicts. Weapons of mass destruction can cause enormous casualties and destruction and can be developed directly or acquired through trade by states or by non-state groups (Anderton and Carter 2008a).

Based on Schelling and Halperin's (1961) classic text, arms control refers to all forms of military cooperation between potential adversaries designed to reduce (1) the risk of war, (2) the damage should war come, and (3) the economic and political costs of military preparation. This conception of arms control asserts a common interest between enemies, with the possibility of reciprocation and cooperation over military postures. The forms of cooperation might include changes in political or military communications, modes of force deployment, quantity or quality of weapons, and rates of weapons accumulation. Note that Schelling and Halperin's three goals of arms control are distinct, which raises the possibility of trade-offs among them.

10.2. Patterns of Arms Rivalry, Proliferation, and Arms Control

Arms Rivalry

Figure 10.1 summarizes the trend in worldwide real (inflation-adjusted) military spending from 1988 through 2007. The high spending level during the latter years of the Cold War is not surprising given the pervasive geopolitical significance of the US-Soviet rivalry at the time. The reductions in the late 1980s and early 1990s reflected a hoped-for peace dividend following the decline of the Cold War, while the increases in the 2000s

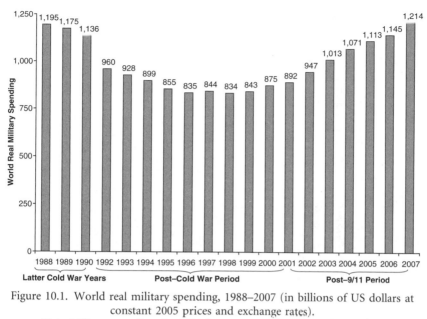

Figure 10.1. World real military spending, 1988–2007 (in billions of US dollars at constant 2005 prices and exchange rates).
Note: Military spending for 1991 is not reported owing to incomplete data for Eastern Europe.
Source: Data used with permission courtesy of Stockholm International Peace Research Institute (www.sipri.org).

correspond in part to the new challenges of terrorism faced by many nations. Notice in recent years that annual spending has been greater than one trillion dollars. To appreciate the economic enormity of such resource diversion, consider that world military spending of $1.1 trillion in 2005 easily exceeded Africa's total gross domestic product of $817 billion (International Monetary Fund 2007).

Figure 10.2 shows real military-spending patterns for selected years for four well-known interstate arms rivalries. We designate these cases as arms rivalries for three reasons. First, each shows a general increase in real military spending, a frequent proxy for armaments, over the periods specified. Second, according to Thompson (2001, p. 560), the actors in each dyad were involved in a strategic rivalry, whereby each regarded the other as a competitor, an enemy, and a source of threats that could become militarized. Third, Gibler, Rider, and Hutchison's (2005) review of historical accounts indicated that each rival pair in Figure 10.2 increased armaments or military personnel competitively for some of the years shown.

(a) India and Pakistan, 1980–83 (millions of constant 1989 US dollars)

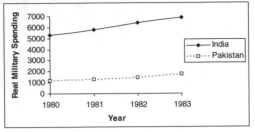

(b) Egypt and Israel, 1967–70 (millions of constant 1975 US dollars)

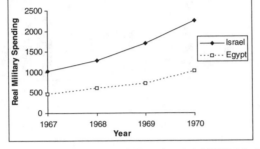

(c) Greece and Turkey, 1973–76 (millions of constant 1982 US dollars)

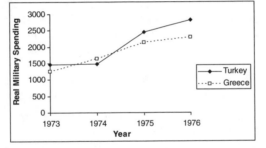

(d) United States and USSR, 1980–89 (billions of constant 1989 US dollars)

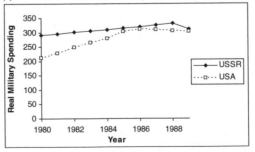

Figure 10.2. Real military-spending patterns in selected interstate arms rivalries.
Source: ACDA (1978, 1985, 1990).

But are the four cases in Figure 10.2 arms races? In our view, panels (a)–(c) suggest arms racing for the years shown, but panel (d) does not. In the first three panels, the average annual growth rates in real military spending were 9.1 percent for India and 15.6 percent for Pakistan, 30.2 percent for Israel and the same for Egypt, and 24.2 percent for Turkey and 22.0 percent for Greece. These growth rates represent unusually rapid increases in real military spending for the periods shown. Moreover, measuring military spending as a percentage of gross national product, each nation's defense burden rose between the first and last year: from 3.2 to 3.5 percent for India, 5.4 to 6.8 percent for Pakistan, 16.1 to 25.0 percent for Israel, 6.7 to 12.8 percent for Egypt, 3.9 to 6.0 percent for Turkey, and 4.0 to 6.7 percent for Greece (ACDA for various years).

The US-Soviet case in panel (d) does not depict arms racing in our view, even over the more limited period 1980–85. From 1980 to 1985, real military spending by the United States rose at an average annual rate of 7.4 percent, which we would count as unusually rapid. For the Soviet Union, however, real military spending grew at an average annual rate of only 1.6 percent over the same period.

Proliferation

Since the beginning of the Cold War, the spread of weapons of mass destruction (WMD) to states and non-state groups has received much attention by scholars and policy makers. At the time of this writing, there exist concerns about nuclear weapons programs in Iran and North Korea. There is also growing anxiety about the potential of terrorist organizations to acquire nuclear weapons (Allison 2004, Howard and Forest 2008). Even if a terrorist organization were unable to create a nuclear detonation, it could spread deadly radioactivity by causing an explosion at a nuclear power reactor or by using a radiological dispersion device known as a dirty bomb.

Nuclear weapons create enormous explosive yield through the fission of heavy atoms such as uranium or plutonium (for an atomic bomb) or the fusion of light atoms like hydrogen (for a hydrogen bomb). The atomic bomb dropped on Hiroshima in 1945 had an explosive force of 12 kilotons of TNT equivalent and resulted in approximately 140,000 deaths. Sixteen years later the Soviet Union tested a hydrogen bomb with an explosive yield of 50 megatons, about four thousand times more powerful than the bomb at Hiroshima (Perkins 1991, p. 23).

Biological weapons use microorganisms such as bacteria and viruses to kill or incapacitate humans, livestock, or crops. Diseases that might be unleashed by biological weapons include anthrax, cholera, plague, smallpox, botulism, and Ebola. The lethality of a biological attack can vary widely depending on dispersal methods, health responses, weather conditions, and contagiousness of the biological agent. In the fall of 2001, a number of anthrax-laced letters were mailed to various parties in the United States by an unknown perpetrator, leading to five deaths. In Japan in the early 1990s, the Aum Shinrikyo cult attempted a number of large-scale biological attacks in Tokyo using anthrax. The attacks failed because the cult mistakenly weaponized a nonvirulent form of anthrax. If not for Aum Shinrikyo's technical error, the number of casualties could have been substantial.

Chemical weapons use nonliving toxic chemicals to kill or incapacitate humans, livestock, or crops. Chemical weapons can be based on nerve agents such as tabun, sarin, or VX; blister agents such as sulphur mustard, nitrogen mustard, or lewisite; protein synthesis inhibitors such as ricin; or choking agents such as phosgene or chlorine. Iraq used tabun against Iranian forces during the 1980–88 war. Iraq also used nerve and blister agents to attack the Kurdish city of Halabja in 1988, with fatality estimates ranging from a few hundred to 7,000. In 1995, the Aum Shinrikyo cult unleashed sarin in the Tokyo subway, leading to 12 fatalities and more than 1,000 injuries.

Table 10.1 summarizes the estimated effects of large-scale WMD attacks on area and people based on hypothetical simulations reported in various studies. The first four rows compare the effects of nuclear, biological, and chemical weapons attacks. These studies reveal that biological weapons have the same or even greater potential to affect area and cause casualties than do nuclear weapons, while chemical weapons are less devastating. Of particular concern are the results of the studies on biological-line attacks summarized in the final two rows. In a line attack, a crop duster or ground vehicle with a specialized spray tank spreads a biological agent along a line so that prevailing winds disperse the agent over a population center. As Table 10.1 shows, a biological line attack has the potential to affect a vast area and cause hundreds of thousands of casualties.

In Figure 10.3 we show by decade the number of nations with nuclear weapons research programs and the number with actual nuclear weapons. In the 1940s, only the United States and the Soviet Union possessed nuclear weapons. By the 1960s, the nuclear group had grown to include the United Kingdom, France, and China. By the 1980s, India, Israel, and probably South Africa had joined the nuclear club. By the 2000s, South Africa had dismantled its nuclear program, but Pakistan and possibly North Korea had added weapons. The figure shows that more states have been suspected of nuclear weapons research than have developed actual weapons. Hence, it is

Table 10.1. *Estimated effects of large-scale weapons of mass destruction attacks.*

Selected Study	Weapon System	Area Affected (km^2)	Casualties
United Nations (1969)	1 mt nuclear	300	90% killed
	10 t biological	100k	50% ill; 25% killed
	15 t nerve agent	60	50% killed
Robinson, Hedén, and Schreeb (1973) – bomber attack	10 kt nuclear biological agent	30	
		0–50	
	VX nerve gas	0.75	
	5 t–6 t high explosive	0.22	
Fetter (1991) – missile attack on sparsely populated city	20 kt nuclear		40k killed; 40k injured
	30 kg anthrax spores		20k–80k killed
	300 kg sarin		200–3,000 killed
Office of Technology Assessment (1993) – missile attack on city with sparse-to-moderate population	12.5 kt nuclear	7.8	23k–80k killed
	30 kg anthrax spores	10	30k–100k killed
	300 kg sarin	0.22	60–200 killed
United Nations (1969) – line attack	biological agent at concentration of 10^{10} per gm along 100 km line	5k	50% killed
Office of Technology Assessment (1993) – line attack	100 kg anthrax spores	46 (clear day)	130k–460k killed
		140 (overcast)	420k–1.4m killed
		300 (clear night)	1m–3m killed

Sources: Studies shown in first column and Dando (1994, p. 5).

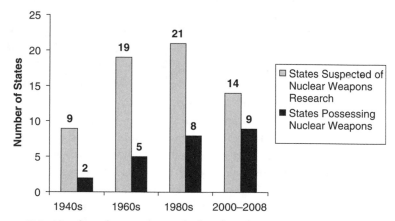

Figure 10.3. Number of states suspected of nuclear weapons research and possession. *Sources*: Singh and Way (2004) and James Martin Center for Nonproliferation Studies (http://cns.miis.edu/).

possible that far more states could have come to possess nuclear weapons than actually do. Still, the number of states possessing nuclear weapons has continued to rise over the decades from two in the 1940s to probably nine in recent years. For a range of views on the danger posed by nuclear proliferation, see Sagan and Waltz (2002) and Goldstein (2006).

Table 10.2 summarizes the status of WMD proliferation for selected states as of 2007. The first column of data shows that eight, and probably nine, states possess nuclear weapons, while Iran is believed by many analysts to be carrying out research consistent with nuclear weapons development. The next column shows the number of nuclear warheads in each nuclear state's arsenal. A wide range of nuclear warheads is reported for the United States and Russia, with the upper estimates encompassing thousands of warheads in reserve or awaiting dismantlement. The columns on biological and chemical weapons show the recent status of various nations' programs in these areas. The final column offers a brief summary of WMD delivery capabilities, including the range available to each nation. We qualify the data in Table 10.2 by acknowledging that there exists disagreement about the classification of states' WMD stocks and programs, particularly for biological and chemical weapons and for the number of North Korean nuclear warheads. The table reflects our conservative interpretation of information available in the sources indicated.

Arms Control

During and after the Cold War, the United States and Russia negotiated numerous arms control agreements to limit or reduce nuclear warheads, missiles, ballistic missile defenses, conventional forces, and other weapons technologies. Table 10.3 summarizes selected US-Russia arms control agreements. Note that some agreements, such as SALT I and SALT II, limited nuclear delivery systems (e.g., intercontinental ballistic missiles [ICBMs] and submarine-launched ballistic missiles [SLBMs]), but they put no brake on the number of nuclear warheads. Other treaties, such as START II and SORT, were designed to reduce the number of strategic warheads. The ABM Treaty limited each side's ability to defend itself in a nuclear attack, and START II reduced multiple independently targetable reentry vehicles (MIRVs), which allow one missile to carry multiple warheads.

The agreements shown in Table 10.3 represent traditional arms control, whereby detailed formal agreements are used by rivals to achieve one or more of Schelling and Halperin's arms control objectives. During the Cold War, arms control advocates viewed formal agreements to limit weapons

Table 10.2. *Proliferation of weapons of mass destruction for selected nations, 2007.*

Nation	Estimated Number of Warheads	Nuclear	Biological	Chemical	Delivery System Capability[a]
US	5,045–10,000[b]	Known weapons		Eliminating weapons	ICBM, SLBM, aircraft; range = 15,000 km
Russia	5,614–15,000[b]	Known weapons	Suspected research	Eliminating weapons	ICBM, SLBM, aircraft; range = 15,000 km
UK	160–195	Known weapons			SLBM; range > 7,400 km
France	348	Known weapons			SLBM, aircraft; range = 6,000 km
China	145–200	Known weapons			ICBM, SLBM, aircraft; range = 3,000 km
Israel	≤100	Known weapons	Suspected research	Suspected research	MRBM, IRBM, aircraft; range = 4,000 km[c]
India	50	Known weapons		Eliminating weapons	SRBM, MRBM, aircraft; range > 2,000 km
Pakistan	60	Known weapons			SRBM, MRBM, aircraft; range = 1,600 km
North Korea	0–6	Suspected weapons	Suspected weapons	Known weapons	SRBM, MRBM, ICBM; range = 1,300 km[d]
Iran		Suspected research			
Egypt				Suspected weapons	
Syria			Suspected research	Known weapons	
Libya				Eliminating weapons	

Notes: SRBM – Short-range ballistic missile (<1,000 km), MRBM – Medium-range ballistic missile (1,000–3,000 km), IRBM – Intermediate-range ballistic missile (3,000–5,500 km), ICBM – Intercontinental ballistic missile (>5,500 km), SLBM – Submarine-launched ballistic missile.

[a] The delivery system ranges reported are high-end estimates, which are not necessarily the maximum ranges attainable based on range-extension technologies such as lighter payloads or postboost vehicle enhancements (see National Air and Space Intelligence Center 2006).

[b] The first number is an estimate of operational nuclear warheads; the second number is an estimate of operational warheads plus warheads held in reserve or awaiting dismantlement.

[c] Stockholm International Peace Research Institute (2007, p. 548) reports that if Israel converted its Shavit space launch vehicle to a ballistic missile, a 775 kg payload could be delivered a distance of 4,000 km.

[d] The range estimate reported for North Korea is for the Nodong MRBM. As of 2007, many analysts do not believe that North Korea's Taepodong-2 ICBM is functional.

Sources: Stockholm International Peace Research Institute (2007) for nuclear warheads and delivery capability for the first nine countries listed. The remaining information is our interpretation of WMD country profiles provided by the James Martin Center for Nonproliferation Studies (http://cns.miis.edu/).

Table 10.3. *Selected US-Russia (USSR) arms control treaties.*

Arms Control Treaty	Summary Description
Strategic Arms Limitation Talks I (SALT I); entered into force: 1972	Limited the number of intercontinental and submarine-launched ballistic missiles and ballistic missile submarines. Included Anti-Ballistic Missile Treaty to limit strategic defensive systems.
Treaty on the Limitation of Anti-Ballistic Missile Systems (ABM Treaty); entered into force: 1972 US withdraws from treaty: 2002	Each side limited antiballistic missile (ABM) systems to two sites (national capital and around ICBM silos) separated by at least 1,300 km, with no more than 100 ABM interceptor missiles at each site.
Strategic Arms Limitation Talks II (SALT II); signed: 1979 (never entered into force) US announces nonabidance: 1986	Included the following limits on each side: 2,400 strategic nuclear delivery vehicles (ICBMs, SLBMs, and heavy bombers), 1,320 multiple independently targetable reentry vehicles (MIRVs), and no new construction of land-based ICBMs.
Intermediate-Range Nuclear Forces Treaty (INF Treaty); entered into force: 1988	Committed the parties to eliminate medium-to-intermediate-range (1,000–5,500 km) and short-range (500–1,000 km) missiles.
Conventional Forces in Europe Treaty (CFE Treaty); entered into force: 1992 Russia suspends participation: 2007	Established equal limitations on major conventional forces for NATO and Warsaw Pact states, including 20,000 battle tanks, 30,000 armored combat vehicles, 20,000 artillery pieces, 6,800 combat aircrafts, and 2,000 attack helicopters.
Strategic Arms Reduction Treaty II (START II); signed: 1993 Extension protocol signed: 1997 Russia withdraws from treaty: 2002	By the end of 2004, the parties were to reduce their total deployed strategic nuclear warheads to 3,800–4,250. By the end of 2007, each party's total number of deployed strategic nuclear warheads was to be no more than 3,000–3,500, and all MIRVs were to be eliminated from ICBMs.
Strategic Offensive Reductions Treaty (SORT) (Moscow Treaty); entered into force: 2003	By the end of 2012, each party is to limit the aggregate number of strategic nuclear warheads to 1,700–2,200.

Source: James Martin Center for Nonproliferation Studies (http://cns.miis.edu/).

as an essential element of foreign policy that reduced the risk of war and the costs of military preparation. Arms control opponents maintained that formal agreements were vulnerable to cheating, did little to dampen US-Soviet development of nuclear and conventional weapons capabilities, and did not stem superpower-related conflict in other parts of the world. Disagreements between arms control proponents and opponents sometimes led to political stalemates over arms control treaties. For example, in the United States the SALT II Treaty was signed by President Carter but was never ratified by the US Senate. President Carter declared that the United States would comply with the treaty as long as the USSR reciprocated. Soviet general secretary Brezhnev made a similar statement regarding Soviet compliance. In 1986, President Reagan announced that the United States would no longer abide by SALT II.

Traditional arms control was important during the Cold War, and it will probably retain some salience for the United States, Russia, and other states in the years ahead. For example, Levi and O'Hanlon (2005, pp. 124–126) maintain that the Conventional Forces in Europe Treaty could provide a model for controlling conventional weapons on the Korean Peninsula. In addition to traditional arms control approaches, many states involved in arms rivalries will utilize less formal approaches to arms control, such as unilateral reductions in weapons and confidence-building measures. All of that said, it is likely that efforts to stem the proliferation of weapons of mass destruction to new states and non-state groups will dominate the arms control agenda in the immediate decades ahead.

Table 10.4 summarizes selected nonproliferation treaties and programs designed to limit the spread of nuclear, biological, and chemical (NBC) weapons technologies and missile delivery systems around the world. The first three treaties in the table concern nonproliferation of nuclear weapons, while the next two target biological and chemical weapons proliferation. The Missile Technology Control Regime focuses on the proliferation of particularly fast means of delivery of WMD. The final two programs in the table aim at controlling WMD materials of former Soviet states and the illicit shipment of WMD materials by states or non-state organizations. These programs are noteworthy because of persistent reports about the loss or theft of weapons-grade nuclear materials from the former Soviet Union and the fear that these materials could end up in the hands of terrorists.

A fundamental difficulty associated with efforts to control the spread of NBC weapons is their dual-use nature. Nuclear facilities for enriching uranium and reprocessing plutonium for nuclear energy purposes can be converted to produce nuclear weapons-grade material. Virtually all of the

Table 10.4. *Selected nonproliferation treaties and programs.*

Nonproliferation Treaty or Program	Summary Description
Non-Proliferation Treaty (NPT); entered into force: 1970 Current membership: 188 states	The "five nuclear weapons states" (US, Russia, UK, France, and China) agree to not transfer nuclear weapons technologies to any other parties and to pursue negotiations in good faith toward general and complete disarmament. Nonnuclear weapons states agree to not receive nuclear weapons technologies from any transferor and to not manufacture nuclear weapons.
Comprehensive Test Ban Treaty (CTBT); opened for signature: 1996 Number of signatories: 176 states	Any nuclear weapon explosion for testing or peaceful purposes is prohibited.
Treaty of Tlatelolco; entered into force: 1969 Current signatories: 33 Latin American and Caribbean states	Prohibits testing, use, production, storage, or acquisition of nuclear weapons by the parties or on behalf of anyone else.
Biological and Toxin Weapons Convention (BTWC); entered into force: 1975 Number of signatories: 169 states	Parties agree to not develop, produce, stockpile, or acquire biological agents or toxins for hostile purposes or for armed conflict and to not assist a recipient in acquiring any of the agents, toxins, weapons, equipment, or means of delivery.
Chemical Weapons Convention (CWC); entered into force: 1997 Number of signatories: 186 states	Parties agree to not develop, produce, stockpile, or acquire chemical weapons, to not assist others in acquiring or using chemical weapons, and to not engage in military preparations for use of chemical weapons. Each party agrees to destroy all chemical weapons and chemical weapons production facilities it possesses.
Missile Technology Control Regime (MTCR); established: 1987 Number of members: 34 states	An informal association of states that follows guidelines to stem the proliferation of missiles, unmanned air vehicles, and related technologies.
Cooperative Threat Reduction Program (CTRP) (Nunn-Lugar Program); established: 1991	Provides funding and expertise to the new independent states of the former Soviet Union (e.g., Russia, Belarus, Ukraine, Kazakhstan) to dismantle WMD and to enhance the security of nuclear weapons and fissile materials associated with dismantlement.
Proliferation Security Initiative (PSI); established: 2003 Number of members: 15 states	Encourages states to develop a broad range of legal, diplomatic, economic, and military means to interdict threatening shipments of WMD and missile-related technologies via air, land, and sea.

Source: James Martin Center for Nonproliferation Studies (http://cns.miis.edu/).

technologies and many of the precursor materials necessary to produce biological and chemical weapons are used in the production of civilian goods. Hence, it is relatively easy for states to take first steps toward nuclear weapons under the guise of peaceful nuclear energy development and to hide production of biological and chemical weapons within civilian infrastructure. This suggests that robust inspection regimes are necessary to control WMD developments. Nevertheless, the ability of states or non-state groups to hide biological weapons development in small labs implies that traditional approaches to international inspection are unlikely to be effective in controlling such weapons (Levi and O'Hanlon 2005, p. 75).

Despite the emphasis of past and present arms control initiatives on WMD and major conventional weapons, most casualties in armed conflicts around the world are due to small arms and light weapons (SALW) such as assault rifles, machine guns, rocket-propelled grenades, and improvised explosive devices. Stemming the production and trade of SALW can be difficult because of the large number of producers and recyclers of such weapons, the potential for such activities to generate commercial profits, and the ability of suppliers to bypass government controls. Nevertheless, some preliminary efforts to monitor and control the flow of SALW are underway. Table 10.5 summarizes selected conventions and protocols designed to stem the trade in SALW. The table implies that SALW control is being promoted by a mixture of governmental and nongovernmental organizations, whereas traditional arms control and nonproliferation regimes tend to be initiated by states. Although most current approaches to SALW control are limited in scope to a single type of weapon (e.g., anti-personnel mines) or region (e.g., the Nairobi Protocol) and thus are vulnerable to the substitution principle, they have encouraged governments to alter their SALW production and trade policies.

10.3. The Richardson Arms Race Model

A common theoretical starting point for the study of arms rivalry is the one-play and repeated prisoners' dilemma games described already in Chapter 4. Here we move on to the well-known Richardson model, which has been used in a vast number of theoretical and empirical studies of arms rivalry.

In the context of growing tension between the United States and the Soviet Union in the 1950s, Richardson's (1939, 1960a) mathematical model of arms rivalry captured the imagination of a growing number of social scientists, particularly from political science. What was significant to this community of scholars was Richardson's conviction that arms rivalry,

Table 10.5. *Selected SALW control organizations and protocols.*

Organization or Protocol	Summary Description
United Nations Conference on the Illicit Trade in Small Arms and Light Weapons; established: 2001	Conference involved representatives from states, international organizations, and NGOs. States agreed to a Programme of Action whereby various steps would be undertaken to improve control of SALW trade.
Nairobi Protocol; entered into force: 2006 Signatories: 12 states	Commits states to concrete actions (e.g., mandatory gun registration and ban on civilian ownership of military assault rifles) to control small arms in the Horn of Africa and the African Great Lakes region.
Middle East North Africa Action Network on Small Arms; established: 2002	An association of NGOs from Iraq, Jordan, Lebanon, Palestine, North Sudan, Syria, and Yemen facilitating actions by communities, NGOs, and governments to lessen the demand for SALW.
Antipersonnel Mine-Ban Treaty (also known as the Ottawa Convention); entered into force: 1999 Signatories/ Accession: 156 states	Binds each party to not use, develop, produce, acquire, stockpile, or transfer antipersonnel mines; to destroy all antipersonnel mines it possesses within four years; and to clear all laid landmines under its jurisdiction within 10 years.
International Action Network on Small Arms (IANSA); established: 1998 Affiliates: 700+ NGOs	A global network of civil society organizations working through national and local legislation, regional agreements, public education, and research to stop the proliferation and misuse of small arms and light weapons.

Sources: James Martin Center for Nonproliferation Studies (http://cns.miis.edu/), International Campaign to Ban Landmines (www.icbl.org), International Action Network on Small Arms (www.iansa.org), Middle East North Africa Network on Small Arms (www.mena-small-arms.org).

the risk of war, and other international relations phenomena could be fruitfully studied with mathematics and statistics. Some consider Richardson's arms race model and statistical methods to be crude by today's standards, but his (and Quincy Wright's) vision of applying scientific methods to the study of war and peace became the wellspring for numerous organizations and journals devoted to quantitative research on conflict, including the Peace Science Society (International), Correlates of War Project, *Journal of Conflict Resolution*, *Journal of Peace Research*, and *Conflict Management and Peace Science*.

Richardson's Differential Equations

Let M_A and M_B be the military stocks of two rival players A and B, while $\dot{M}_A$ and $\dot{M}_B$ are the rates of change in military stock per unit of time. Richardson hypothesized that three factors would affect a player's military buildup: (1) the insecurity created by the rival's military stock, (2) the fatigue or expense of the player's own military stock, and (3) the grievances or ambitions of the player toward the rival. The three factors are embodied in the Richardson arms race model, which is characterized by the following differential equations:

$$\dot{M}_A = kM_B - aM_A + g \qquad (10.1)$$

$$\dot{M}_B = rM_A - \beta M_B + h. \qquad (10.2)$$

In equations (10.1) and (10.2), k and r are reaction parameters that reflect how sensitive or insecure each player is to the military stock of its rival, while a and β are fatigue parameters representing the economic or political costs of a player's own military stock. Parameters g and h are grievance or ambition terms, representing sources of hostility between the players, such as past conflicts or territorial disputes.

Reaction Functions and Equilibrium

In the Richardson model, A adjusts its military stock until the elements on the right side of the equality in equation (10.1) are such that $\dot{M}_A = 0$. Intuitively, $\dot{M}_A = 0$ means that A's desired change in military stock is zero. By the same reasoning, $\dot{M}_B = 0$ signifies that B does not want to change its own military stock. By setting $\dot{M}_A$ and $\dot{M}_B$ equal to zero in equations (10.1) and (10.2), the following reaction functions for A and B can be derived:

$$M_A = \left(\frac{k}{a}\right)M_B + \left(\frac{g}{a}\right) \qquad (10.3)$$

$$M_B = \left(\frac{r}{\beta}\right)M_A + \left(\frac{h}{\beta}\right). \qquad (10.4)$$

A reaction function shows the level of military stock that each player chooses in response to the level of military stock of its rival. Equilibrium military stocks (M_A^*, M_B^*) are then found by solving the two equations (10.3) and (10.4) simultaneously for M_A and M_B, yielding:

$$M_A^* = (kh + \beta g)/(a\beta - kr) \qquad\qquad (10.5)$$

$$M_B^* = (rg + ah)/(a\beta - kr). \qquad\qquad (10.6)$$

Arms Race Stability

Although Richardson did not formally study the relationship between arms rivalry and the risk of war, it is clear from his writings that he was particularly concerned about the risk of war associated with an unstable arms rivalry. Given an initial increase in military stocks above the equilibrium, a rivalry is said to be unstable if the players react by further building up their stocks, and it is said to be stable if they respond by reducing their stocks back toward the equilibrium levels. In the Richardson model, the arms rivalry equilibrium can be shown to be stable when $(k/a)(r/\beta) < 1$. Note that the stability condition is governed by the slope terms, k/a and r/β, of the reaction functions in equations (10.3) and (10.4). If each player is sufficiently insecure and hence sensitive to its rival's armaments, so that k and r are large, relative to the cost of building weapons, shown by a and β, then $(k/a)(r/\beta)$ will be greater than one, giving rise to an unstable arms rivalry. Under these conditions, an arms rivalry could become a true arms race, with accelerating armaments leading to growing fears and suspicions and an elevated risk of war (Richardson 1960a, p. 61). Hence, in Richardson's view, limiting weapons buildups in an unstable arms rivalry could contribute to all three of Schelling and Halperin's arms control objectives: reduced risk of war, less damage should war come, and lower costs of military preparations.

Numerical Examples

Assume the following symmetric values for the reaction, fatigue, and grievance parameters of the Richardson model: $k = r = 1$, $a = \beta = 2$, and $g = h = 10$. Based on equations (10.5) and (10.6), equilibrium military stocks are $(M_A^* = 10, M_B^* = 10)$. Figure 10.4(a) shows the determination of equilibrium graphically using the reaction functions of equations (10.3) and (10.4). Since $(k/a)(r/\beta) = 1/4 < 1$, the players are not overly sensitive to rival military stocks, and the equilibrium at point e is stable. Hence, an

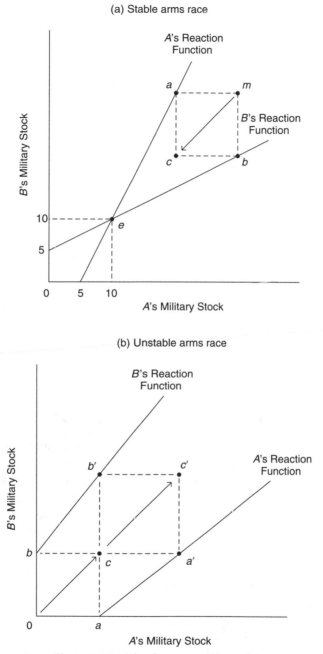

Figure 10.4. Richardson arms race model.

upward shift in military stocks to a point above the equilibrium, like m, causes military stocks to move back toward the equilibrium, as governed by the reaction functions. At point m, player A prefers to move to point a, and player B prefers to move to point b. Both moves taken together imply that the military stocks arrive at point c. From there the process repeats itself, and eventually, military stocks arrive back at equilibrium point e.

Assume now that $k = r = 4$, with all other parameter values remaining the same. Mathematically, equilibrium military stocks become negative, which is not meaningful in an armaments context. What is meaningful, however, is that the relatively large reaction coefficients cause the slope terms on the reaction functions in equations (10.3) and (10.4) to become large. Now each player reacts more strongly to the military stock of its rival. In Figure 10.4(b), the reaction functions imply an escalation of military stocks. Beginning from the origin of zero military stock for each player, A prefers to move to point a, and B prefers to move to point b. Both moves taken together imply that military stocks arrive at point c. In the next round, A increases its military stock to a', while B does the same to b', bringing the joint weapons point to c'. Note that the increases in military armaments in the second round are greater than in the first. Subsequent rounds will depict ever-increasing armaments for each side, reflecting a runaway arms race when $(k/a)(r/\beta) > 1$.

10.4. The Intriligator-Brito Model

Richardson focused on the accumulation of weapons in an arms rivalry under the assumption that the reaction, fatigue, and grievance parameters were constant. Hence, Richardson ignored strategic elements such as the deterrent or attack capability of accumulated weapons that might affect the degree of reactivity of each player to its rival. In an influential model developed in a Cold War context, Intriligator and Brito (I-B) focused on the deterrence and attack implications of two nations' missile stocks M_A and M_B. Here we present a simplified version of the I-B model drawing from Intriligator and Brito (1986) and Wolfson (1985).

Deterrence and Attack Conditions

Consider first how a nation can deter an attack by its rival. Suppose nation A's military planners are concerned that rival nation B might launch an all-out attack to destroy some or all of A's missile forces. In an all-out counterforce (military against military) attack by B, assume that $f_B M_R$ of A's missiles would be destroyed, where the parameter f_B is the number of A's missiles destroyed per counterforce missile launched by B. With any surviving missiles, A could then launch a countervalue (military against civilian) strike against B. Assume A believes there exists for B an unacceptable level of casualties denoted $\bar{C}_B$, such that if A credibly threatens that level of casualties in retaliation, then B will be deterred from initiating the attack. Let v_A be the number of casualties in B caused per countervalue missile fired by A in retaliation. Then the number of surviving missiles that A believes it needs to deter B is $\bar{C}_B/v_A$. Putting this together, if A's missile stock is at least equal to $f_B M_B$ (the number of its own missiles that would be destroyed by an attack) plus $\bar{C}_B/v_A$ (the number of missiles required to retaliate), then A believes it can successfully deter B from attacking. Applying similar logic to B's deterrence of A leads to the following deterrence conditions for nations A and B:

$$M_A \geq f_B M_B + \bar{C}_B/v_A \tag{10.7}$$

$$M_B \geq f_A M_A + \bar{C}_A/v_B. \tag{10.8}$$

Now consider how each nation can successfully attack its rival. Let $\hat{C}_A$ be the maximum casualties that A is willing to sustain if B retaliates to an attack by A, and let v_B be the number of casualties suffered by A per countervalue missile launched by B. In an all-out counterforce attack by A, $f_A M_A$ of B's missiles would be destroyed, leaving $M_B - f_A M_A$ missiles with which B could retaliate and thereby cause $(M_B - f_A M_A)v_B$ casualties in A. If such casualties are no more than $\hat{C}_A$, then A can successfully attack. Applying similar logic to B's attack potential leads to the following attack conditions for A and B:

$$(M_B - f_A M_A)v_B < \hat{C}_A \text{ or equivalently}$$
$$M_A \geq (M_B/f_A) - (\hat{C}_A/f_A v_B) \tag{10.9}$$

$$(M_A - f_B M_B)v_A \leq \hat{C}_B \text{ or equivalently}$$
$$M_B \geq (M_A/f_B) - (\hat{C}_B/f_B v_A). \tag{10.10}$$

Figure 10.5 shows graphically the deterrence and attack conditions (10.7)–(10.10) of the I-B model. It is important to understand that in the later writings of Intriligator and Brito conditions (10.7)–(10.10) do not model or specify the number of weapons that A and B will choose to accumulate. Rather, the conditions expose various strategic implications

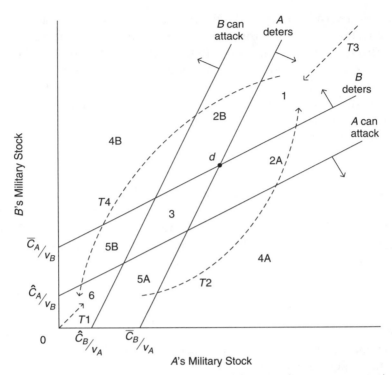

Figure 10.5. Intriligator-Brito model (adapted from Intriligator 1975, p. 349).

for alternative military stocks that A and B might accumulate. Combinations of M_A and M_B on or to the right of the "A deters" line (regions 1, 2A,
and 4A) are missile holdings for which A believes it can deter B, while
combinations on or above the "B deters" line (regions 1, 2B, and 4B) are
those for which B believes it can deter A. Formed at the upper right is an
area known as the cone of mutual deterrence (region 1), with d representing a point of minimum mutual deterrence. Combinations of M_A and
M_B on or to the right of the "A can attack" line (regions 4A, 5A, and 6)
imply that A can successfully attack B, while points on or above the "B can
attack" line (regions 4B, 5B, and 6) imply that B can successfully attack A.
In the region of jittery deterrence (region 3), A and B can neither attack
nor deter. Areas 5A, 5B, and 6 are regions of war initiation. In regions 5A
and 5B one side can attack and neither can deter. Region 6 is particularly
dangerous because it represents weapons holdings such that each side can
attack and neither can deter.

The I–B model can be used to explore the effects of increases or
decreases in weapons on the risk of war (Intriligator and Brito 1986).

Beginning from the origin in Figure 10.5, trajectory *T1* is an arms rivalry that moves the nations' weapons holdings into region 6. Because each nation can successfully attack and neither believes it can deter, each nation has an incentive to attack before its rival does, and the likelihood of war is high. Arms rivalry *T1* is consistent with Richardson's view that an arms rivalry increases the risk of war. But Richardson's view is not the only one that emerges in the I–B model. Suppose trajectory *T2* occurs, which according to Intriligator and Brito is roughly descriptive of the first few decades of the Cold War rivalry between the United States and the USSR. Trajectory *T2* pushes the weapons holdings into region 1, where each nation believes it can deter. An increase in weapons into region 1 thus lowers the risk of war, contrary to Richardson's view. At the same time, damage should war come and the cost of military preparation are both higher along *T2*, suggesting that trade-offs among the several goals of arms control exist for some trajectories.

The effects of arms reduction on the risk of war can also be considered in the I-B model. Trajectory *T3* moves the nations' weapons holdings further down in the cone of mutual deterrence, implying less damage should war come and lower costs of military preparation, but no increase in the risk of war. In this case, two of the three goals of arms control are promoted without attenuation of the third. Trajectory *T4* leads to a different result, however. A substantial reduction in weapons moves the nations' holdings into the dangerous region 6 where the risk of war is high. Note also that arms reduction trajectories *T3* and *T4* are implicitly assumed to be costless. In reality, destroying weapons and enforcing arms control treaties can be costly, which tends to reduce the peace dividend available from arms control. As just one example, according to the James Martin Center for Nonproliferation Studies, Japan estimates that the dismantlement and cleanup costs of removing the chemical weapons it left in China after World War II are in the neighborhood of $1.6 billion.

Applications

Iranian Nuclear Weapons Proliferation

At the time of this writing, numerous states have imposed economic sanctions against Iran because of its uranium enrichment and reprocessing programs. Currently, there is uncertainty about whether Iran will attempt to acquire nuclear weapons in the future. Here we restrict our attention to a potential nuclear rivalry between Israel and Iran, should the latter come

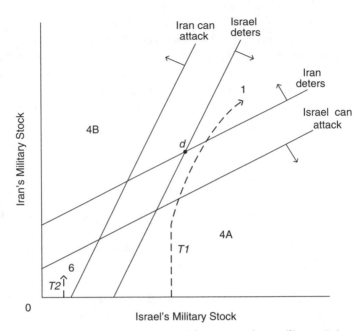

Figure 10.6. Iranian nuclear weapons proliferation in the Intriligator-Brito model.

to possess nuclear weapons. In Figure 10.6, Iranian acquisition of nuclear weapons is represented by an arms trajectory that emerges from the horizontal axis. Of the many possible proliferation trajectories that could occur, two are shown in the figure. Proliferation trajectory *T1* assumes that Israel is already well-stocked with nuclear weapons (see Table 10.2), that Iran begins to accumulate nuclear weapons, and that a nuclear arms rivalry occurs between Israel and Iran. It is conceivable that such an arms rivalry could move into a cone of mutual deterrence (region 1), but not before passing through region 4A where Israel can attack. Whereas trajectory *T1* is potentially dangerous, trajectory *T2* is particularly disconcerting. For this trajectory, the weapons holdings move into region 6, where each country can attack and believes it cannot deter. The I-B model by itself cannot determine whether trajectory *T1*, *T2*, or some other trajectory might better reflect the strategic implications of Iranian nuclear proliferation vis-à-vis Israel. It does indicate, however, that a move toward deployment of nuclear weapons by Iran has the potential to raise the risk of war between Iran and Israel.

Antiballistic Missile Technology in Europe
Although developed for a Cold War context, the I–B model can be used to explore numerous present and future scenarios where weapons

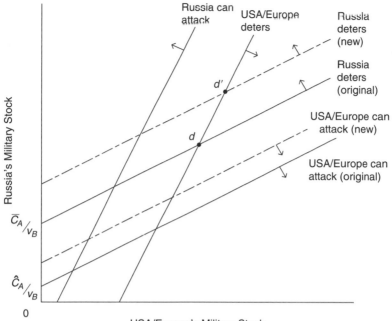

Russia can attack

USA/Europe deters

Russia deters (new)

Russia deters (original)

USA/Europe can attack (new)

USA/Europe can attack (original)

Russia's Military Stock

$\bar{C}_A/v_B$

$\hat{C}_A/v_B$

d'

d

0

USA/Europe's Military Stock

Figure 10.7. One-sided antiballistic missile defense in the Intriligator-Brito model.

effectiveness (f_i and v_i) or acceptable casualties ($\bar{C}_i$ and $\hat{C}_i$) change among arms rivals. For example, at the time of this writing the United States and some of its European allies are considering deployment of antiballistic missile (ABM) defense technology in Europe to protect cities against possible future missile threats from nations such as Iran. In 2007, Russia suspended its participation in the Conventional Forces in Europe Treaty in protest over the ABM deployment. Figure 10.7 provides possible insight into Russia's opposition to the ABM technology. Let nation A be the United States and its European allies and nation B be Russia. The deployment of an ABM system in Europe to protect cities from an accidental or purposeful missile strike from a third party also lowers the countervalue effectiveness v_B of Russia's missiles. This shifts the "Russia deters" and "USA/Europe can attack" lines upward in Figure 10.7, so that the USA/Europe's attack capability is expanded at the same time that Russia's deterrent capability is undermined. This prospective change in relative capabilities helps explain the strong opposition by Russia, which claims that deployment of ABM technologies in Europe would undermine regional stability.

Inherent Propensity toward War in the I-B Model

In Chapter 9 we explored Thomas Schelling's (1966, ch. 6) idea that certain configurations of military technology, geography, and military organization could imply a first-mover advantage in war. Such an "inherent propensity toward war," to use Schelling's phrase, is shown in the I-B model by region 6 of Figure 10.5, where each side can attack the other and neither can deter. A more pervasive form of incentive for mutual attack arises when the model's usual counterforce effectiveness assumptions are altered so that region 1, the cone of mutual deterrence, is eliminated.

To demonstrate this point, we rely on the fact that the cone exists only when the product of the counterforce effectiveness terms is less than one, that is, when $f_A f_B < 1$ (Wolfson 1987, p. 293). As a way of illustration, we begin with the usual assumption that the condition for the cone is satisfied. Suppose, for simplicity that f_A and f_B are both less than one. As indicated by equations (10.7) and (10.8), the slopes of the "A deters" and "B deters" lines in Figure 10.5 are $1/f_B$ and f_A, respectively. This means that when $f_B < 1$ and $f_A < 1$, the "A deters" line is steeper than the "B deters" line, so that a cone of mutual deterrence arises, as depicted by region 1 in Figure 10.5. Intuitively, when military technology is such that one missile in a counterforce attack destroys less than one rival missile, then attack effectiveness is relatively low and mutual deterrence is possible.

Now assume that attack effectiveness for each player is high so that the condition for the cone is not satisfied, that is, so that $f_A f_B > 1$. For example, suppose that f_A and f_B are each greater than one, such that one missile in a counterforce attack can destroy more than one rival missile. In this case the "A deters" line is flatter than the "B deters" line, and as a consequence no cone of mutual deterrence exists. This result of high attack effectiveness is depicted in Figure 10.8. With the disappearance of the cone, notice that region 6, the area of mutual attack, now occupies a substantial portion of the graph. Whereas the customary Figure 10.5 predicts that relatively high and roughly balanced missile stocks imply mutual deterrence and a low risk of war, Figure 10.8 suggests that such missile holdings can be associated with a dangerous inherent propensity toward war.

The possibility of an inherent propensity toward war in the context of weapons of mass destruction cannot be precluded. Based on MIRV technology, for example, one missile can contain multiple independently targetable warheads. The United States' MX missile, for example, can hold

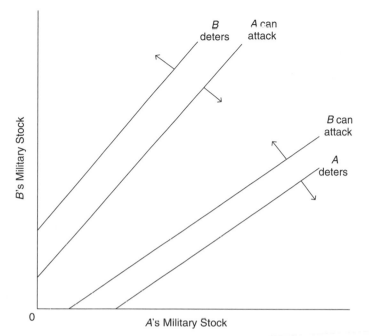

Figure 10.8. Inherent propensity toward war with high attack effectiveness.

up to 10 independently targetable warheads. Hence, it is technologically feasible for a missile to have a counterforce effectiveness term greater than one. Negotiated reductions in multiple warhead missiles by the United States and Russia have been partly motivated by concerns over the first-strike potential of such weapons. We saw in Chapter 9 how fleets of fast and deep-strike military aircraft may have contributed to an inherent propensity toward war between Egypt and Israel in 1967. Imagine a future nuclear weapons rivalry between Israel and Iran wherein aircraft are a primary delivery platform and each aircraft contains multiple warheads. In such a scenario, the risk of nuclear war could be unusually high. The militarization of space discussed in Chapter 9 also suggests the potential for "futuristic" technologies to generate an inherent propensity toward war. For example, suppose two nuclear rivals each deploy a sophisticated array of satellites designed to detect and target enemy missile sites and to shoot down incoming missiles with satellite-based laser technologies. If such technologies could be made effective against fast-moving missiles, it is reasonable to believe that the same technologies could be used to destroy the slow-moving satellites of a rival, thus conveying a first-mover advantage in war.

10.5. An Economic Choice Model of Arms Rivalry

Optimal Allocation of Resources to Military and Civilian Goods

We turn now to a rational choice model of arms rivalry due originally to Anderton (1990). As earlier, there exist two rivals A and B, who may be nations or non-state groups. Player A's choice problem is to allocate its resources between military output M_A and a composite civilian good Y_A so as to maximize utility, where utility is a function of A's composite good and level of security S_A. Because the two players are rivals, A's security can be written generally as $S_A(M_A, M_B)$, with the assumption that its security increases with its own military output M_A but decreases with its rival's output M_B. Player B faces an analogous choice problem.

In Figure 10.9 we depict A's choice problem in a four-quadrant diagram, where all variables are measured positively as distances from the origin. Quadrant II, at the upper left, shows A's production possibilities frontier (PPF) for alternative combinations of military and civilian outputs M_A and Y_A. Quadrant III simply plots a 45-degree line, which serves to project A's military output from quadrant II into quadrant IV. Quadrant IV graphs A's security function, which shows A's level of security for alternative stocks of military output, holding B's military output M_B constant. These three quadrants systematically join various levels of civilian output Y_A with corresponding levels of security S_A, thereby generating in quadrant I a civilian-security possibilities frontier (CSPF). Included also in quadrant I are A's indifference curves, representing A's utility function defined over alternative combinations of civilian output and security. Geometrically, A's choice problem is to choose a feasible combination of civilian output and military output (and hence security) so as to reach the highest indifference curve along the CSPF, taking as given the military output of player B.

To understand Figure 10.9, assume initially that the military output of rival B is M_B^0, thus generating the higher security line $S_A(M_A, M_B^0)$ shown in quadrant IV. This security line together with the PPF in quadrant II combine in quadrant I to generate the CSPF labeled HN. Given M_B^0, player A maximizes its utility at optimum C^0 by producing outputs M_A^0 and Y_A^0, thereby enjoying the security benefit S_A^0 of its military output and the consumption benefit of its composite good. Now suppose that player B increases its military output to M_B^1. Because B is a rival, player A suffers a decrease in security, other things equal, causing its security function to rotate downward to $S_A(M_A, M_B^1)$. Owing to the linkages in the model, the

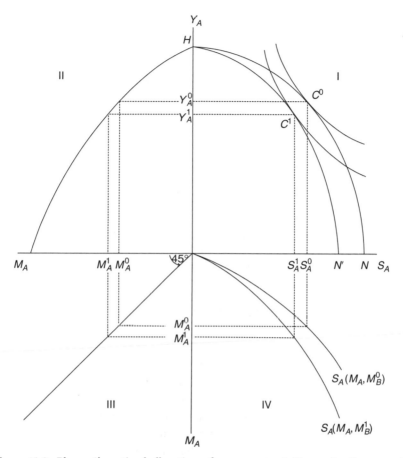

Figure 10.9. Player *A*'s optimal allocation of resources to civilian and military goods (adapted from Anderton 1990, p. 152).

CSPF in turn rotates downward to HN'. As a consequence, A is motivated to reallocate its resources until it achieves optimum C^1, with military output M_A^1, civilian good Y_A^1, and security S_A^1. Notice that player A reacts to B's increase in military output with an increase of its own, a point to which we will return.

Two broad themes emerge from Figure 10.9. First, economic and security variables are inextricably linked. The point at which a player operates on its production possibilities frontier in quadrant II is governed in part by security considerations. Moreover, the level of security a player is able to achieve is influenced by the economic capacity available to the player. Second, the figure reflects the multidisciplinary nature of modeling

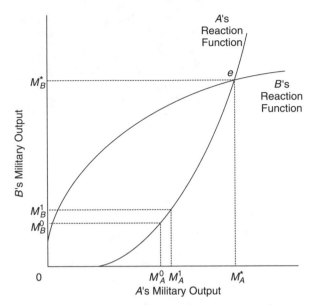

Figure 10.10. Arms rivalry equilibrium in the economic choice model.

a player's resource allocation decision. Quadrant II reflects the supply side of the model, a traditional domain of economics. Quadrant IV involves security issues, which are emphasized in international relations. The preferences of a group over Y and S in quadrant I are shaped by various people within the group and by the institutions that govern the group's collective actions. Hence, preference formation belongs in the domains of political science and public choice.

Reaction Functions and Arms Rivalry Equilibrium

As already noted, the rivalrous nature of A's and B's relationship induces player A to respond to increases in B's military output with increases of its own. This principle is formally represented in Figure 10.10 by A's reaction function, which shows A's optimal military output for any given military output by B. We have already derived two points on A's reaction function in Figure 10.9: if B produces M_B^0, A's best reply is M_A^0, and if B produces M_B^1, A's best reply is M_A^1. Additional points on A's reaction function are derived by repeating the exercise in Figure 10.9 for various other outputs by B. In an analogous manner, working again through a four-quadrant analysis generates B's reaction function, also shown in Figure 10.10.

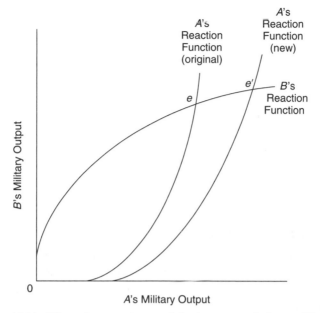

Figure 10.11. Effect of economic growth in A on arms rivalry equilibrium.

A Nash equilibrium exists when each rival's military output is a best reply to the other's. Geometrically, this means that an equilibrium is determined in Figure 10.10 at point e, where the two reaction functions intersect. Thus, in equilibrium, A chooses output M_A^*, which is a best reply to B's M_B^*, at the same time that B chooses M_B^*, which is a best reply to A's M_A^*. Because the reaction functions are generated from each player's four-quadrant model, the equilibrium in Figure 10.10 is equivalent to the simultaneous solution of the players' economic choice problems.

Applications

Economic Strength and Arms Rivalry Competitiveness

The position and curvature of a player's reaction function are determined by the several components of the economic choice model from which the reaction function is derived. One of these components is the production possibilities frontier, which reflects the economic capacity of a player to react to an arms rival by producing weapons of its own. In Figure 10.11 we show how the arms equilibrium moves from e to e' when player A experiences economic growth but player B's economy is unchanged. In A's four-quadrant model, economic growth pushes outward the PPF in quadrant II, thus expanding A's CSPF in quadrant I (not shown). Player A finds that economic growth allows it to expand its military and civilian production, holding B's military output constant. Hence, A's reaction function shifts outward, indicating an increased demand for military output. This shift sets off new rounds of action and reaction between A and B until a new equilibrium emerges at point e' in the figure. Note that A's military output increases substantially more than does B's, which is plausible because A's economic strength has expanded while B's is unchanged. As an illustration of the process depicted in Figure 10.11, some scholars maintain that economic stagnation in the Soviet Union during the 1980s made it increasingly difficult for the Soviets to maintain competitiveness in its Cold War rivalry with the United States (Wolfson 1985).

Arms Control

An arms rivalry generates a security dilemma, wherein each player's attempt to improve its security by increasing its own weapons causes the rival to respond by also increasing weapons, which in turn reduces the original player's security. This dilemma provides a basic rationale for arms control, namely, that a mutual reduction in weapons can save resources without sacrificing security.

We demonstrate this rationale for arms control with Figure 10.12, which is similar to Figure 10.10 but is more complete and thus more intricate. Recall in the earlier model that player A's utility is a function of its civilian output Y_A and its security S_A. With a little work, this function can be translated mathematically into a utility function defined in terms of both players' military outputs M_A and M_B. Without getting formal, the key is to recognize that A's PPF implicitly defines Y_A as a function of M_A, and its security function explicitly defines S_A as a function of M_A and M_B. Consequently, player A's PPF and security function can be substituted into its utility function, thereby resulting in a translated utility function written generally as $U_A(M_A, M_B)$. As usual, this utility function can be represented with indifference curves, but the behavior of the indifference curves needs some explanation.

Of A's many indifference curves in Figure 10.12, we have drawn just one, that being the curve passing through the Nash equilibrium point e. Because e lies on A's reaction function, we know that A's military output at that point is A's best output, given the corresponding military output of B. Player A could be equally satisfied with less military output, but only if A was compensated for its lost security by an appropriately reduced level of military output by B. Thus, A's indifference curve must fall off to the left of

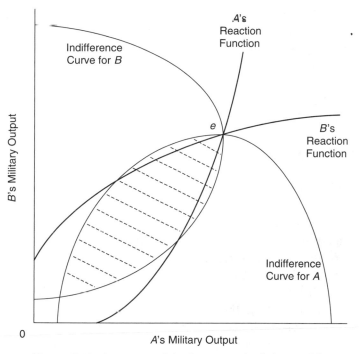

Figure 10.12. Arms control in the economic choice model.

e, as shown. Going the other direction, *A* could be equally satisfied with more military output, but only if *A* was compensated for its forgone civilian output, once again, by an appropriately reduced military output by *B*. Thus, *A*'s indifference curve must also fall off to the right of *e*. Repeating the logic for other points along *A*'s reaction function means that *A*'s indifference curves are positively sloped to the left of *A*'s reaction curve and negatively sloped to the right. Notice also that because unilateral reductions in *B*'s military output M_B leave player *A* better off, points on lower indifference curves are more preferred by *A*.

Similar reasoning applies to player *B*, whose original utility function can be translated into a function written generally as $U_B(M_B, M_A)$. The translated function can then be represented by indifference curves, one of which is drawn for *B* passing through point *e*. As shown, *B*'s indifference curves are negatively sloped above *B*'s reaction function and positively sloped below it, and points on indifference curves to the left are more preferred by *B*.

With the properties of *A*'s and *B*'s indifference curves in mind, we can illustrate the basic rationale for arms control using Figure 10.12. Notice that the two indifference curves drawn through equilibrium point *e* form a highlighted lens-shaped area. Points within the lens lie below *A*'s indifference curve through *e* and hence are preferred to *e* by *A*; they also lie to the left of *B*'s indifference curve through *e* and hence are preferred to *e* by *B*. Therefore, the lens-shaped area forms the region of mutual gain, wherein at least one player is better off and neither is worse off relative to the equilibrium *e*. This means in principle that the players should be able to negotiate an arms control agreement whereby they both benefit by reducing their weapons levels to some specified point within the lens. The immediate qualification to this statement, however, is that each player will have an incentive to cheat on the agreed arms control point by unilaterally increasing its weapons output toward its reaction function, thereby increasing its utility. This incentive explains why many arms control agreements contain formal inspection and verification protocols to guard against cheating.

Arms rivalry and arms control reflect Schelling's (1960, pp. 4–6) central thesis that conflict often involves mutual dependence alongside of opposition, and that for this reason many conflicts are essentially bargaining situations. In Figure 10.12 the players have an incentive to mutually reduce armaments, despite their hostility toward one another. By jointly reducing weapons outputs from point *e* into the region of mutual gain, the players can keep their security levels roughly the same while freeing up resources to produce civilian goods, thus increasing overall utility. Note that a mutual reduction supports Schelling and Halperin's second and third goals for arms control: since weapons stocks are lower, damage is decreased should war come, and the cost of military preparation is lowered. Figure 10.12 does not by itself address Schelling and Halperin's first arms control objective, namely, reduction in the risk of war. In Richardson's view, lower weapons stocks would reduce the risk of war. In the Intriligator-Brito model, however, if weapons stocks are so low that a region of mutual attack is reached, the risk of war could be high.

There are a number of important factors that might offset the resource savings generated by arms control. For example, inspection and verification procedures are not costless, and efforts to dismantle or destroy weapons can be quite costly, as the Cooperative Threat Reduction Program explicitly recognizes. Moreover, the substitution principle reminds us that efforts to restrain one form of activity can lead to substitutions into other activities. If the weapons class controlled in Figure 10.12 is, for example, long-range missiles (as in the SALT treaties), the players might expand their production of nuclear warheads. Alternatively, if missiles and warheads are controlled, the players might increase the quantity or technological sophistication of their conventional weapons. In intrastate arms rivalries, if rebel leaders lose access to land mines, they might recruit additional personnel and arm them with assault rifles (see Chapter 3). As Schelling and Halperin (1961, p. 120) noted: "[I]t is by no means obvious that arms control, even rather comprehensive arms control, would entail rapid and substantial reductions in military outlays . . . . It is quite possible that arms control would increase them." Surprisingly, there have been few formal empirical studies of the resource cost or the substitution possibilities associated with arms control agreements. One exception is Craft (2000), who finds empirical evidence that the Washington Naval Agreements of the 1920s between the United States, the United Kingdom, and Japan provided resource savings for a limited time period, followed by greater expenditures to promote new naval technologies.

10.6. Selected Empirical Studies

Structure of Arms Rivalries

A large number of studies have attempted to estimate Richardson-type arms models, but they have tended to yield reaction coefficients that are statistically insignificant, incorrectly signed, or exceedingly fragile. Reviewing the literature, Dunne and Smith (2007) argue that changing technologies and environments mean that the action-reaction relationships among arms rivals are probably too unstable to support the usual time-series analysis. They express optimism, however, that studies employing panel or cross-section methods might provide useful estimates of average interaction effects.

An example of such a study comes from Collier and Hoeffler (2007b), who estimate a military expenditures model based on a dataset spanning 161 countries over the period 1960 to 1999. Observations are country averages computed over five-year periods 1960–64, 1965–69, . . ., and 1995–99. The dependent variable is the logarithm of (average) defense burden, where defense burden is equal to military expenditure as a percentage of GDP. The key right-hand variable for our purposes is the lagged logarithm of a measure of the defense burden of neighboring countries. Other independent variables include measures for current interstate war, past interstate war, current civil war, risk of civil war, foreign aid, income, population, democracy, post–Cold War period, and Israel.

Collier and Hoeffler's (2007b) results are methodologically encouraging and substantively interesting. The estimated coefficients on the various control variables are as might be expected: war and the risk of war lower security and hence generate increased military spending; increased population tends to decrease the defense burden, suggesting economies of scale in the production of security (see Chapter 9); foreign aid increases military spending, reflecting the fungibility of foreign financial assistance (see Chapter 3); and defense burdens are lower in democracies and after the Cold War. On the issue of arms rivalry, Collier and Hoeffler estimate the reaction coefficient for neighbors' military spending to be 0.10. This means that if a country's neighbor increases military spending by 10 percent, then the country on average will react by increasing its own spending by one percent. This action and reaction between the country and its neighbor then sets up a multiplier effect that further increases spending in equilibrium. As one example, Collier and Hoeffler (2007b, p. 16) estimate that if the risk of civil war increases generally by 10 percentage points across a region, then each country within the region will increase military spending immediately by 7.3 percent and eventually by 8.1 percent after all actions and reactions are completed.

Arms Rivalry and the Risk of War

Based on studies of military expenditures prior to World Wars I and II, Richardson (1939, 1960a) believed that arms rivalries increased the risk of war. In the 1970s, introduction of the Intriligator-Brito model raised questions about the generality of Richardson's view. Recall that some arms rivalry trajectories (e.g., *T1* in Figure 10.5) are associated with a greater risk of war while others (e.g., *T2* in Figure 10.5) can be associated with a lower risk. Wallace (1979) was the first to empirically test the issue, and he found that arms rivalries between major powers had a strong positive effect on the escalation of militarized disputes to war. Diehl (1983) and others questioned Wallace's results in subsequent studies.

Building on this earlier literature, Sample (2002) investigates the effect of military buildups on the risk of war based on data for militarized interstate disputes (MIDs). Recall that a MID is a "threat, display or use of military force short of war by one member state ... explicitly directed towards the government, official representatives, official forces, property, or territory of another state" (Jones et al. 1996, p. 168). Sample's study spans the period 1816–1992 and covers 2,304 dispute dyads, of which 267 involved major states, 1,196 involved minor states, and 841 involved a major and a minor state. The dependent variable in her regression is an indicator for whether a MID escalated to war. Her key right-hand variable measures whether both nations in the dyad were involved in rapid military buildups. Other right-hand variables control for nuclear capability, the presence of a territorial dispute, contiguity, comparative military capabilities, and high defense burdens.

Sample's statistical results for her full sample show a significant positive relationship between military buildups and escalation to war. Disputes involving dyads with rapid buildups are estimated to be more than twice as likely to escalate to war, other things equal. Sample also finds that the presence of nuclear weapons lowers the risk of war by about half. When she estimates her model separately for the three types of dyads, she discovers that military buildups increase the risk of war for major power and minor power dyads but not for mixed (major-minor) dyads. If she further restricts her analysis to the post–World War II period, she can discern no significant effect of buildups on the risk of war, but the presence of nuclear weapons continues to reduce the risk of war for major and mixed dyads. According to Sample, rivals in mixed dyads react to each other's buildups differently relative to rivals in major and minor dyads, and countries in general have changed their perception of deterrence since the use of nuclear weapons in World War II.

Determinants of Nuclear Weapons Proliferation

While most analyses of nuclear weapons proliferation have been case studies, Singh and Way (2004) provide a large-sample investigation of risk factors based on the status of states' nuclear weapons research and development programs. They begin by defining four stages of nuclear weapons proliferation, ranging from no interest to serious exploration to program launch to weapons acquisition. For their sample of 154 countries over the period 1945–2000, 23 nations seriously explored nuclear weapons, 16 proceeded to launch programs, and 9 acquired nuclear weapons. Variables for the three active stages of nuclear weapons proliferation are coded for each country in each year and serve as dependent variables. Explanatory variables include income, industrial capacity, external security concerns, political organization, and trade policy. Singh and Way find that external security issues have a powerful effect on a state's interest in nuclear weapons. States that are involved in long-lived rivalries and frequent militarized interstate disputes are at substantially greater risk of moving toward nuclear weapons. Economic development generally has a positive effect on a state's interest in nuclear weapons, but the likelihood of proliferation actually drops off at higher income levels. Singh and Way also show that the more open a state is to trade, the lower the risk of nuclear weapons proliferation.

10.7. Bibliographic Notes

Accessible overviews of data on military expenditures worldwide are provided by Brzoska (1995) and Stockholm International Peace Research Institute (2007, ch. 8). Data and policy articles on WMD proliferation, bilateral and multilateral arms control treaties, and nonproliferation regimes are available from the James Martin Center for Nonproliferation Studies (http://cns.miis.edu/). The Norwegian Initiative on Small Arms Transfers (www.nisat.org) and the Graduate Institute of International Studies (Geneva) Small Arms Survey (www.smallarmssurvey.org) offer data and policy articles on the production and trade of small arms and light weapons (SALW). Brauer (2007) provides an excellent survey of data and models on the production and trade of MCW, SALW, and WMD.

Cirincione, Wolfsthal, and Rajkumar (2005) present an in-depth overview of nuclear, biological, and chemical weapons proliferation. Langford's (2004) analysis of biological, chemical, and radiological weapons materials and technologies can be helpful to health professionals, emergency responders, and the media. Guillemin (2005) provides a compact summary of the history of biological weapons and suggests ways to curtail their spread, while Schelling (2006) offers a fascinating interpretation of a "taboo" against the use of nuclear weapons that has emerged among states. The edited volumes of Banks and Castillo-Chavez (2003) and Davis and Schneider (2004) provide numerous articles on biological weapons proliferation and control. Allison (2004) and Howard and Forest (2008) explore the potential for terrorists' use of WMD.

Rapoport (1957) and Hess (1995) offer insightful overviews of Richardson's quantitative approach to war and peace. Boulding's (1962, ch. 2) important extension of the Richardson model generalizes action-reaction processes to numerous forms of hostility and friendliness, not just arms rivalry, and includes applications to states, non-state groups, and individuals. Isard (1988, ch. 2) and Sandler and Hartley (1995, pp. 82–89) review other extensions of the Richardson model.

Brito and Intriligator (1995) provide an accessible overview of the I-B strategic model of arms rivalry. Anderton (1992a) generalizes the I-B model to include alternative assumptions about attack capabilities and counterforce effectiveness. Wolfson (1985) combines the strategic components of the I-B model with resource scarcity inherent in an economic choice model, which he then applies to the United States' "arms race economic warfare" against the USSR during the Cold War.

McGuire (1965) offers an early economic choice model of arms rivalry that embeds strategic concerns of deterrence and attack in a rational choice framework. His theoretical applications are extensive and include explorations of Cournot-Nash equilibrium, the contract curve available under bilateral arms control, the Stackelberg solution available under unilateral arms control, survival-extinction solutions, and the effects of information (and secrecy) on arms rivalry and arms control. Brito (1972) provides the first dynamic optimization model of arms rivalry. Reviews of theoretical arms race models include Isard (1988), Brito and Intriligator (1995), and Sandler and Hartley (1995). Hammond (1993) provides a historical analysis of interstate arms races occurring over the 1840–1991 time period. Colaresi, Rasler, and Thompson (2007) examine more than 150 interstate strategic rivalries spanning the nineteenth and twentieth centuries and draw important lessons about conflict risk, arms racing, alliance behavior, and relative capability advantages.

The empirical literature on the structure of military buildups in interstate arms rivalries is vast; valuable literature reviews include Brauer (2002) and Dunne and Smith (2007). Geller and Singer (1998, pp. 79–81) and Gibler et al. (2005) provide concise overviews of empirical studies of the relationship between arms rivalry and interstate war. Singer (2007) provides a historical perspective and review of empirical evidence on nuclear proliferation.

Formal theoretical models of arms control inspection and verification are presented by Saaty (1968) and Brams (1985, ch. 4), while Rueckert (1998) provides a nonquantitative overview. Levi and O'Hanlon (2005) offer insightful analysis of past and future arms control and nonproliferation policies. Larsen (2005) provides a dictionary on arms control and disarmament, which includes an extensive bibliography and information on treaties, government and nongovernment organizations, weapons, journals, and Web sites.

11

Military Alliances

Agreements wherein parties pledge various forms of military cooperation are common in the international system and are often prominent in conflict settings. In 1949, for example, the United States, Canada, and numerous Western European states formed the North Atlantic Treaty Organization (NATO) to counter the threat of attack by the Soviet Union. In turn, the Soviet Union and various Central and Eastern European nations formed the Warsaw Pact in 1955 to counter threats from NATO. Since the end of the Cold War, the Warsaw Pact has dissolved while NATO has remained in force and expanded its membership. Article 5 of the NATO Charter specifies that an attack against any member state will be considered an attack against all member states. Following al Qaeda's attack against the United States on September 11, 2001, Article 5 was invoked for the first time. The United States and its NATO allies then cooperated in an invasion of Afghanistan to overthrow the Taliban, who had supported al Qaeda. US-led forces also cooperated militarily with the "Northern Alliance," an intrastate coalition of Afghan groups fighting against the Taliban. Meanwhile, various transnational terrorist groups and criminal syndicates have been reported to cooperate with al Qaeda in ways that appear to constitute non-state alliance behavior.

The scholarly literature on alliances is vast, encompassing both theoretical and empirical research, with extensive coverage of political and economic determinants and effects. In this chapter we focus primarily on economic aspects of military alliances. In particular, we consider alliance formation as an economic choice whereby a nation or non-state group can increase its security while reducing its cost or burden of defense. We begin with definitions followed by an overview of data on interstate alliances. We then use the economic choice model from Chapter 10 to explore the seminal contributions of Olson and Zeckhauser (1966) and of Sandler and his colleagues (Sandler and Cauley 1975, Sandler 1977, Murdoch and Sandler 1982) on the economic theory of alliances. We conclude with selected empirical studies pertaining to burden sharing within NATO and the effects of alliances on the risk of armed conflict.

11.1. Definitions

We define a military alliance as a cooperative security arrangement between two or more parties that conditions their involvement in military conflict. Such arrangements can include agreements that pertain to offensive action, defensive action, neutrality, consultation, and/or nonaggression (Leeds 2003, p. 429). Although the alliance literature focuses on cooperative security arrangements between states, the definition allows for non-state parties, such as rebel groups or transnational terrorist organizations. There is some disagreement over whether alliances must be based on formal written security arrangements. According to Walt (1987, p. 12), alliances can be formal treaties or informal arrangements. Olson and Zeckhauser (1966) suggest the possibility that "most alliances are never embodied in any formal agreement" (p. 273). Snyder (1997, p. 6) and Leeds, Ritter, Mitchell, and Long (2002, p. 239), however, distinguish between alliances and alignments, with the former based on formal written agreements and the latter regarded as tacit cooperation. Some might also question whether nonaggression pacts are alliances because they commit states to mutual nonaggression but entail no cooperation regarding conflict with third parties (Leeds 2005, p. 12).

Table 11.1 provides summary information for a selection of alliances. The top entries of the table show that the Cold War and World Wars I and II all involved rivalries between alliances. Hence, interstate alliances are a major element of actual and potential conflict in the international system. As suggested by the table's bottom entries, intrastate and non-state alliances are also significant and can be expected to grow in the decades ahead. The United States, for example, faces major security challenges from within by gang alliances and from abroad by transnational alliances of terrorist organizations and criminal syndicates. While factual details of non-interstate alliances are difficult to ascertain, some cases demonstrate formal coordination. For example, in January 2006 the two parties forming the Alliance of Revolutionary Forces of West Sudan issued the following joint statement: "The two movements have agreed to join and coordinate all political, military and social forces, their international relations and to double their combat capacity in a collective body under the name, the Alliance of Revolutionary Forces of West Sudan" (Online NewsHour 2006).

Table 11.1. *Selected military alliances.*

Name	Type	Members	Time Frame	Brief Summary
North Atlantic Treaty Organization (NATO)	Interstate	United States, Canada, various European states	1949–present	Formed to counter Soviet threat during the Cold War. Carries out peacekeeping, counterterrorism, and other security operations today.
Warsaw Pact	Interstate	Soviet Union and various Eastern European states	1955–91	Formed to counter NATO threat during the Cold War.
Triple Alliance	Interstate	Germany, Austria-Hungary, Italy	1882–1915 (periodic)	Formed to counter threat by France and other great powers.
Triple Entente	Interstate	France, Russia, United Kingdom	1907–17	Served as counterweight to Germany and the Triple Alliance.
Tripartite Axis Pact	Interstate	Germany, Italy, Japan (later other states became members)	1940–45 (Italy departs in 1943)	Opposed the Allies of WW II.
Allies of WW II	Interstate	Numerous states	1939–45	Opposed the Axis powers of WW II.
Alliance of Revolutionary Forces of West Sudan	Intrastate	Sudanese Liberation Army/ Movement (SLA/M), Justice and Equality Movement (JEM)	Formed in 2006	Fighting against the Sudanese government.

People Nation	Intrastate	Approximately two dozen US gangs operating in Chicago and other cities	Formed in the 1980s	Involved in highly organized violent criminal activities and turf wars against rival alliance known as Folk Nation.
World Islamic Front for Jihad against Jews and Crusaders	Non-state	al Qaeda and a number of other terrorist organizations	Formed in 1998	Goal is to establish a pan-Islamic Caliphate by killing Americans (military and civilian), overthrowing non-Islamic regimes in the Muslim world, and expelling non-Muslims from Muslim countries.
Golden Triangle Alliance (a.k.a. Juárez Cartel)	Non-state	Three illegal drug organizations located in Mexican states that border the United States	1990s into the mid-2000s	Goal is to conduct illegal narcotics trafficking from Mexico into the southwestern region of the United States.

Sources: Encyclopedia Britannica Online (www.britannica.com), Online NewsHour (2006), Florida Department of Corrections (2007), Federation of American Scientists (www.fas.org/irp/world/para/ladin.htm), and the US Drug Enforcement Agency (www.usdoj.gov/dea).

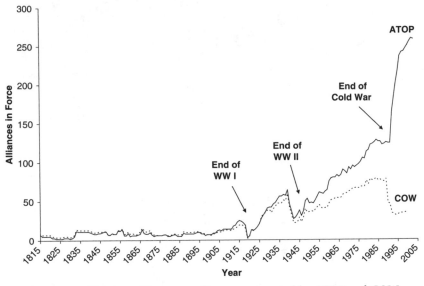

Figure 11.1. Number of interstate alliances as reported by ATOP and COW. *Sources*: Leeds et al. (2002) for ATOP and Gibler and Sarkees (2004) for COW version 3.03.

11.2. Patterns of Interstate Alliances

Figure 11.1 shows the number of interstate alliances in force by year based on data from the Alliance Treaty Obligations and Provisions (ATOP) Project and the Correlates of War (COW) Project. As indicated, many interstate alliances have existed over the past two centuries and particularly since World War I. The most striking aspect of the figure, however, is the close correspondence between ATOP and COW data on the number of alliances up to 1945, followed by a significant and growing divergence since then. Moreover, around the end of the Cold War COW shows a sudden decline in the number of alliances in force, while ATOP shows a dramatic increase. It is difficult to explain fully the divergence based on ATOP's and COW's coding rules, but part of the discrepancy apparently is due to differences in collection methods and in the classification of non-aggression pacts.

ATOP distinguishes five obligations that nations might have with an ally in the event of military conflict: to provide active military support to an attacked ally (a defense pact); to provide active military support to an ally under conditions wherein the ally is not attacked (an offense pact); to refrain from helping an ally's rival in a military conflict (a neutrality pact);

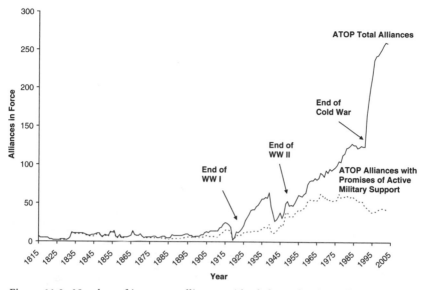

Figure 11.2. Number of interstate alliances with pledges of active military support. *Source:* Leeds et al. (2002).

to refrain from engaging in military conflict with an ally (a nonaggression pact); and to communicate with partners during crises that have the potential for military conflict (a consultation pact) (Leeds 2005). The five obligations detailed in the ATOP data are not mutually exclusive; hence, a single alliance agreement can contain more than one type of obligation.

Figures 11.2 through 11.4 provide some sense of the composition of interstate alliances over time. The first figure shows by year the number of alliances in force that contained promises of active military support. Active military alliances are those that contain defensive or offensive obligations or both, so that the allies are relying to some degree on one another's military capability. The number of active military alliances has increased since World War I but has declined as a proportion of total alliances since about 1960, thus implying that neutrality, nonaggression, and consultation pacts have become increasingly significant. Figure 11.3 reports by year the number of multilateral alliances, defined as those with three or more members. Since the end of World War II, multilateral alliances have generally increased in frequency but declined as a proportion of total alliances. Figure 11.4 shows the alliance commitments as of 2003 based on ATOP data for the seven major international powers as designated by COW. Based on these data, substantial differences are evident in the total number and composition of commitments among the major powers. For

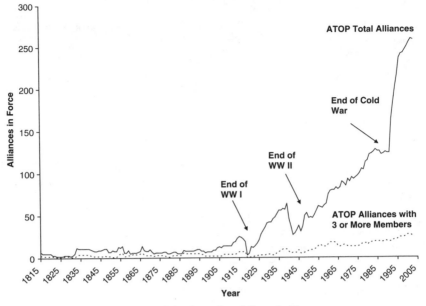

Figure 11.3. Number of multilateral alliances.
Source: Leeds et al. (2002).

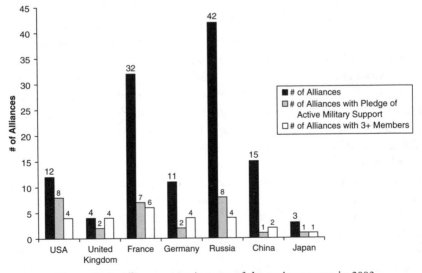

Figure 11.4. Alliance commitments of the major powers in 2003.
Source: Leeds et al. (2002).

example, Russia and France have substantially more commitments than each of the other major powers. Note also that the United States is the only major power for which more than half of its alliance commitments involve pledges of active military support.

11.3. Pure Public Good Model of Alliances

Public Goods and Alliances

Recall from Chapter 3 the distinction between private goods and public goods. A good is classified as private when its benefits are rival and excludable. For example, cereal is a private good because one person's consumption of cereal necessarily means that the same cereal cannot be consumed by others (rival); furthermore, the person possessing the cereal can withhold it from consumption by others (excludable). In contrast, the consumption benefits of a public good are nonrival and nonexcludable. For example, mosquito control is a public good for the residents of a neighborhood. One family's benefit in the form of reduced risk of disease does not preclude another family's consumption of that same benefit (nonrival); nor can the other family be denied that benefit depending on whether it contributes to the cost of the mosquito control (nonexcludable).

Olson and Zeckhauser's (1966) seminal economic model of alliances is built on the basic insight that "above all alliances produce public goods" (p. 272). The premier example of a collective benefit for alliance members is the deterrence of a common enemy. Suppose members of an alliance credibly commit to retaliate in force against any attack on one or more of its members. If the threat to retaliate successfully deters the enemy, then all members of the alliance benefit from increased security in a manner that is both nonrival and nonexcludable. Similarly, as seen in Chapter 8, offensive counterterrorism efforts can provide a public good for alliance members. To the extent that a terrorist organization is a common threat, degradation of the organization will benefit all members of the alliance, and no member can be excluded from the enhanced security.

A Diagrammatic Model

Optimization
In the model that follows, two players A and B form an alliance in the provision of a pure public good, which is a good that is perfectly nonrival and nonexcludable. For concreteness, the public good can be thought of as

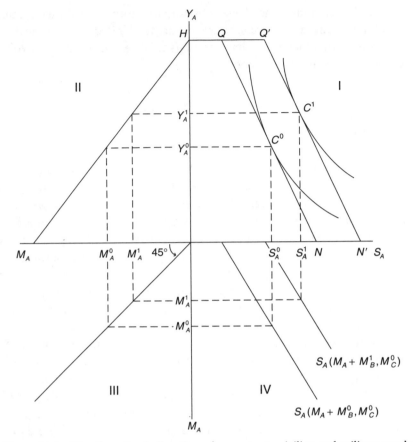

Figure 11.5. Ally A's optimal allocation of resources to civilian and military goods.

military strength aimed at deterring a common enemy C. The allies' respective military outputs M_A and M_B are equally effective against the enemy, and the deterrence produced by one ally spills over fully to the other. Hence, the allies share a common military strength M equal to the sum of their military outputs, or $M = M_A + M_B$. Security for each ally i ($i = A,B$) is a function of the strengths of the alliance and the enemy and can be written $S_i(M_A + M_B, M_C)$. The choice problem for each ally is to allocate resources between military output M_i and a composite civilian good Y_i so as to maximize utility, where utility $U_i(S_i, Y_i)$ is a function of security and the civilian good.

Figure 11.5 depicts the choice problem for ally A using a linear version of the four-quadrant diagram introduced in Chapter 10; a similar figure would apply for ally B. To review, quadrant II shows A's production possibilities frontiei (PPF) for alternative combinations of military and civilian outputs M_A and Y_A. Quadrant III uses a 45-degree line to project A's military output into quadrant IV, which shows A's security function given the military outputs of ally B and enemy C. These three quadrants systematically link various civilian outputs Y_A with corresponding levels of security S_A, thus generating the civilian-security possibilities frontier (CSPF) in quadrant I. The diagram is completed by adding A's indifference map to quadrant I. In geometric terms, A's choice problem is to choose a combination of civilian and military outputs (and hence security) so as to reach the highest indifference curve possible along the CSPF, taking as given the military outputs of B and C.

To see how the model works, suppose that the initial military outputs of ally B and enemy C are respectively M_B^0 and M_C^0, thus generating the lower security line $S_A(M_A + M_B^0, M_C^0)$ shown in quadrant IV. Notice that the intercept of the security line is not at the graph's origin. This is because even if ally A were to choose a military output equal to zero, it would still enjoy some positive level of security due to the deterrence spillover from its ally's military output M_B^0. The security line and PPF in quadrant II combine in quadrant I to generate the CSPF labeled HQN, which is shown with an initial horizontal stretch, again due to the spillover from B's military output. Given M_B^0 and M_C^0, ally A maximizes its utility at optimum C^0 by producing outputs Y_A^0 and M_A^0, thereby enabling ally A to enjoy the consumption benefit of the former and the security benefit S_A^0 of the latter.

Suppose now that ally B's military output increases to M_B^1, with the enemy's output held fixed at M_C^0. Because military strength in the alliance is a pure public good, ally A benefits from increased security, other things equal, causing its security line to shift rightward to $S_A(M_A + M_B^1, M_C^0)$. Because of the linkages in the model, the CSPF in turn shifts rightward to $HQ'N'$. This allows ally A to reallocate its resources until it achieves optimum C^1 with civilian good Y_A^1, military output M_A^1, and security S_A^1. Notice carefully what has happened. Given the increased output of its ally, A has been able to reduce its own military output, while at the same time enjoying not only more civilian good but also more security. The result is increased utility for A and thus a compelling incentive to free ride off the military output of its ally. This perhaps surprising result is quite general, relying only on the publicness of the alliance's military strength and the additional but reasonable assumption that the civilian good and security are both normal goods.

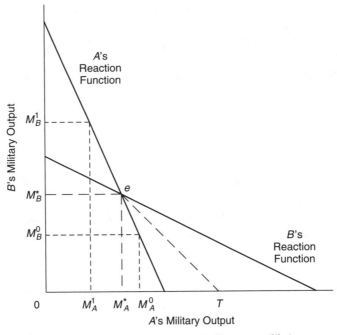

Figure 11.6. Reaction functions and alliance equilibrium.

Reaction Functions and Alliance Equilibrium

The pure public good model is completed by bringing the optimal behavior of ally A together with the optimal behavior of ally B to determine the equilibrium military outputs of the two allies. Notice that the preceding analysis already sketches how Figure 11.5 can be used to derive a reaction function for A. For example, if ally B chooses output M_B^0, A's best reply in Figure 11.5 is M_A^0, and if B chooses M_B^1, A's best reply is M_A^1. As seen in Figure 11.6, this generates two of the points along A's reaction function, which shows A's best reply for any given output by B. Similar four-quadrant analysis for ally B generates B's reaction function. Notice that the reaction functions are negatively sloped, reflecting the incentive of each ally to free ride off the military output of the other. A Nash equilibrium exists when each ally's output is a best reply to the other's. Hence, the equilibrium for the alliance is determined in Figure 11.6 at point e, where the two reaction functions intersect (for a similar diagram, see Sandler and Hartley 1999, p. 33). In equilibrium, A chooses output M_A^*, which is a best reply to B's M_B^*, while B chooses M_B^*, which is a best reply to A's M_A^*. The total alliance strength $M^* = M_A^* + M_B^*$ equals the distance OT, determined

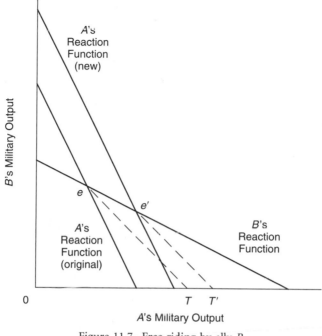

Figure 11.7. Free riding by ally B.

geometrically by the dashed line drawn from the equilibrium to the horizontal axis with a slope of −1 (Cornes and Sandler 1996).

Implications

Free Riding
The incentive to free ride identified earlier in the allies' reaction curves carries over to the comparative-statics of the full equilibrium model. Suppose, for example, that ally A perceives a new threat to its security, but ally B does not. A will tend to increase its demand for military goods, as shown by the rightward shift of its reaction function in Figure 11.7 (for a similar diagram, see Sandler and Hartley 2001, p. 874). A new alliance equilibrium emerges at point e', which entails increased military output by A but decreased output by B. Note that ally B clearly free rides on player A's increased output: despite B's own decrease in military output, B nonetheless is able to enjoy an increase in total defense from OT to OT' and therefore an increase in its own security.

Alliance Suboptimality
Alliance formation can improve each player's well-being relative to "going it alone" but still be inefficient in the sense that additional gains are

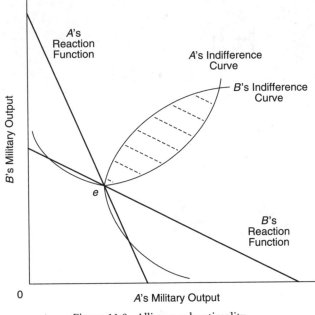

Figure 11.8. Alliance suboptimality.

available to the allies relative to the alliance equilibrium. We demonstrate this implication by supplementing the allies' reaction curves with their associated indifference curves, as shown in Figure 11.8 (for a similar diagram, see Sandler and Hartley 1995, p. 28). The logic of adding indifference curves is very similar to that used for the arms rivalry model in the preceding chapter. In brief, the PPFs and security functions are substituted into the respective allies' utility functions, resulting in translated utility functions defined in terms of both allies' military outputs M_A and M_B (along with the enemy's output M_C).

   The translated utility functions are represented by indifference curves in the usual manner. Of A's many indifference curves, in Figure 11.8 we have drawn just one, that being the curve passing through the equilibrium point e. Because e lies on A's reaction function, we know that A's military output at that point is optimal given the corresponding military output of B. Thus, A would be indifferent to a change in its own output only if the change was accompanied by a suitable change in B's output as well. In particular, A would be content with an increase in its own output only if it was compensated for the added cost by a higher level of security emanating from an increase in B's output. This means that A's indifference curve must turn upward to the right of *e*, as shown. In the other direction, *A* would be indifferent to a decrease in its own output only if it was compensated for its forgone security, once again, by higher security generated by an increase in *B*'s output. Thus, *A*'s indifference curve likewise must turn upward to the left of *e*. Repeating the same reasoning for other points along *A*'s reaction function means that *A*'s indifference curves are U-shaped around the reaction function. Also, because unilateral increases in *B*'s military output leave player *A* strictly better off, points on higher indifference curves are more preferred by *A*. For ally *B* we likewise show a single indifference curve passing through the equilibrium point *e*. Similar reasoning means that *B*'s indifference curves are U-shaped relative to the vertical axis, and points on indifference curves farther to the right are more preferred by *B*.

Notice now that the two indifference curves drawn through equilibrium point *e* form a highlighted lens-shaped area in Figure 11.8. Points within the lens lie above *A*'s indifference curve and hence are preferred to *e* by *A*; they also lie to the right of *B*'s indifference curve and hence are preferred to *e* by *B*. Thus, the lens-shaped area forms a region of mutual gain and thereby demonstrates the equilibrium *e* to be Pareto inefficient. In the absence of unspecified transaction costs, this means that both allies can benefit if they coordinate their military outputs to reach some specified point within the lens.

The source of the alliance's inefficiency is subtle but important. In the pure public good model, the players enjoy the defense benefits that spill over from their ally's military goods. Nevertheless, in their own utility functions they place no value on the defense benefits created for their ally from their own military goods. Hence, the players may form an alliance and enjoy security benefits from each other's military goods, but they make autonomous allocation choices that ignore the spillover benefits to their ally. This leads to underprovision of military goods for the alliance as a whole, a result echoed in the government counterterrorism games of Chapter 8. Elimination of the underprovision requires an alliance agreement that goes well beyond the sharing of the public good to include some form of centralized coordination of the allocation choices (see, e.g., Sandler and Hartley 1999, ch. 8).

Disproportionate Burden Sharing

Under certain assumptions, the pure public good model predicts that the wealthier ally will bear a disproportionately large defense burden, as measured by the ratio of its military goods to its aggregate output (Olson and Zeckhauser 1966, pp. 269–270; Sandler and Hartley 2001, p. 875). We

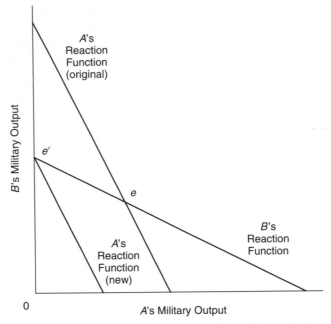

Figure 11.9. Disproportionate burden for wealthier ally *B*.

refer to this as the disproportionality hypothesis; in the alliance literature it is also known as the exploitation hypothesis. Note that the hypothesis does not say simply that the wealthier ally will produce more military goods than the poorer ally, but that the wealthier ally will allocate a greater proportion of its aggregate output to defense than the poorer ally. Figure 11.9 offers a stylized example of the disproportionality hypothesis. Assume that *A* and *B* are initially identical in every respect, including the same PPFs, security functions, and preferences, thus generating a symmetric equilibrium at point *e*. Assume now that *A*'s aggregate output, as modeled by the PPF in the four-quadrant diagram, falls until *A*'s reaction function just intersects the vertical intercept of *B*'s reaction function. In this corner solution at point *e'*, player *A* produces zero military goods, while *B* produces all of the alliance's output. This then is an extreme but clear example of the disproportionality hypothesis inasmuch as the wealthier ally *B* incurs a positive burden while *A* suffers no burden at all.

Optimal Alliance Size
Suppose an additional player joins the alliance of *A* and *B* arrayed against *C*, and the transaction costs of assimilating the new ally are zero. In the

pure public good model, the military output of the new ally will be a perfect substitute for the outputs of A and B. Hence, the addition of the ally will enable A and B to reduce their respective demands for military goods, increase civilian production, and enjoy greater security, everything else the same. Similar benefits would arise if even more players enter the alliance. Consequently, there is no reason in terms of benefits and costs to limit the number of allies. In practical terms, when the security benefits generated by military goods are purely public and the transaction costs of new allies are minimal, an alliance has the incentive to bring in as many new allies as possible. A contemporary example that may approximate a purely public defense good for many players is degradation of the al Qaeda terrorist organization. If al Qaeda is weakened, all potential targets of al Qaeda benefit at the same time, and they cannot be excluded from such benefits. The pure public good model suggests that states arrayed against al Qaeda should bring in as many allies as possible if the transaction costs of operating as an alliance are sufficiently low.

11.4. Joint Product Model of Alliances

Pure Public, Impure Public, and Private Goods

The key assumption in the model just discussed is that each ally's security is based exclusively on the sharing of a pure public good. The assumption is restrictive in at least two ways. First, it requires that security be derived from a pure public good, meaning a good that is both perfectly nonrival and perfectly nonexcludable. The prototypical example is deterrence based on strategic nuclear weapons: all allies can simultaneously enjoy the security benefit of a deterred adversary, and none of the allies can be excluded from that benefit. In practice, however, the public good shared by an alliance need not be pure; rather, it can be partially rival or partially excludable or both, in which case it is called an impure public good. An example of an impure public good is territorial defense based on conventional forces. Suppose that A is attacked by adversary C, leading ally B to send in military forces to help counter C's advance against A. Notice that the defense provided is partially rival: the forces committed by B are not available at the same time to counter an attack by C on B's territory. Sandler and Hartley (1995, p. 31) describe this as force thinning, whereby forces are spread along a border or across an area. The defense provided by B is also partially excludable: ally B can choose to hold back some of its forces to defend its own territory. Second, the model's key assumption is restrictive in that it requires security to be based solely on a public good. In fact, however, military activity can generate security derived from goods that are wholly private to the providing ally (Olson and Zeckhauser 1966, p. 272; van Ypersele de Strihou 1967). For example, many nations use military forces to stem civil unrest, protect coastlines, or defend against domestic terrorists. All or most of the benefits of such activity do not spill over to the security of allies.

Technology of Public Supply and the Joint Product Model

In a series of formal extensions, Sandler and his colleagues relaxed the restrictive pure public good assumption and in doing so developed what is known as the joint product model of alliances (Sandler and Cauley 1975, Sandler 1977, Murdoch and Sandler 1982). In this model, allies' military goods generate a variety of defense products that range from purely public (e.g., deterrence), to impurely public (e.g., damage limitation), to private (e.g., control of domestic terrorism). The extensions represent far more than minor adjustments to the pure public good model of alliances. Rather, they culminate in a general alliance model that includes the original pure public good model as a special case. In what follows, we highlight the main elements and key results of the joint product model. More formal and complete coverage is provided by Cornes and Sandler (1984) and Sandler and Hartley (2001).

Suppose that the military outputs of allies A and B generate shared security benefits, which may be either pure or impure, and possibly also defense benefits that are strictly private. Assuming symmetry in the technology of public supply, the security functions for A and B can be written:

$$S_A = S_A(M_A + \theta M_B, \delta M_A, M_C) \qquad (11.1a)$$

$$S_B = S_B(\theta M_A + M_B, \delta M_B, M_C), \qquad (11.1b)$$

where $0 < \theta \leq 1$ and $\delta \geq 0$. The θ term in either equation gauges the degree to which a player benefits from a spillover from the other ally's output. When θ equals one, the alliance's shared good is purely public; when θ is less than one, the shared good is impurely public. The δ term captures the extent to which a player's military output generates private benefits. If δ is zero at the same time that θ equals one, then the security functions are identical to those in the pure public good model.

In Figure 11.10 we show reaction functions for two alternative technologies of public supply, supposing for simplicity that the allies have identical PPFs, security functions, and preferences. In both cases we stipulate

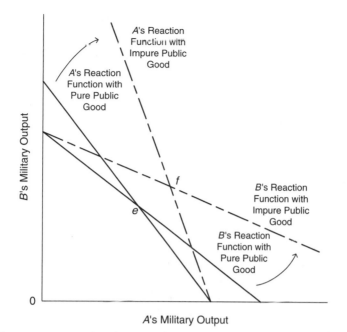

Figure 11.10. Reaction functions for a pure versus impure public good.

no private benefits, so $\delta = 0$. For the first case we assume that $\theta = 1$, meaning that the allies share a pure public good. The result is the set of solid-lined reaction functions, which are similar to those in Figure 11.6 and yield equilibrium military outputs at point e. For the second case we assume that $\theta < 1$, meaning that the spillover from each other's military output is less than complete, so that the allies share an impure public good. The result this time is the set of dashed reaction functions with equilibrium point f. Relative to the first case, notice that the reaction functions with an impure public good are rotated outward around a fixed intercept. Because the spillover is reduced, the incentive to free ride on an ally's output is reduced, causing the steepness of A's reaction curve to increase and B's to decrease. If as a third case we were to introduce private benefits with $\delta > 0$, we would expect shifts in the reaction functions (not shown), with equilibrium military outputs changing relative to cases of pure or impure public goods.

Implications

The joint product model modifies the predictions of the original pure public good model in important ways (see, e.g., Cornes and Sandler 1984,

Sandler and Hartley 2001). When military goods generate partially excludable and/or partially rival defense benefits among allies, then the allies must rely more on their own military outputs to achieve security. Under such conditions, it can generally be expected that the extent of free riding, the degree of suboptimality, the disproportionality of contributions, and the optimal number of allies will all be reduced relative to what is implied in the pure public good model. Recall in Figure 11.10 that A's reaction function is steeper when the alliance's public good is impure rather than when it is pure. Hence, a given increase in M_B will lead to a smaller decrease in M_A and hence less free riding. In the same way, diminished free riding is also implied by the flatter slope of B's reaction function. The presence of excludable private benefits further increases the allies' reliance on their own military outputs. With decreased incentives for free riding, disproportionate burdens on wealthier allies and under-provision of alliance defense are reduced. Moreover, the impurity of the public good that arises with force thinning causes the optimal size of the alliance to be finite. In the presence of force thinning, optimality requires that allies be added only to the point where the marginal security benefits created by additional military goods just equal the marginal costs caused by additional thinning (Sandler and Hartley 1995, p. 34).

11.5. Selected Empirical Studies

Burden Sharing within NATO

A key implication of the pure public good model is that larger allies will bear a disproportionate share of the alliance burden because of free riding by smaller allies. In their seminal paper, Olson and Zeckhauser (1966) operationalized the hypothesis as follows: "In an alliance, there will be a significant positive correlation between the size of a member's national income and the percentage of its national income spent on defense" (p. 274). They tested their hypothesis in a relatively simple manner using a cross section of 14 NATO allies in 1964. The test was based on the correlation between two rank orderings – one for income (measured by GNP), and the other for defense budget as a percentage of income. These rank orderings are replicated in the left half of Table 11.2. If the disproportionality hypothesis is correct, countries that rank higher in income should also tend to rank higher in defense spending as a percentage of income. That is what the data show, although the strength of the pattern is moderate. Of the top six allies in terms of income, four of them also rank

Table 11.2. *Burden sharing in NATO, 1964 and 1971.*

Country	1964 GNP Rank	1964 Defense Budget as Percent of GNP Rank	Country	1971 GNP Rank	1971 Defense Budget as Percent of GNP Rank
US	1	1	US	1	1
Germany	2	6	Germany	2	10
UK	3	3	France	3	6
France	4	4	UK	4	3
Italy	5	10	Italy	5	9
Canada	6	8	Canada	6	13
Netherlands	7	7	Netherlands	7	7 (tie)
Belgium	8	12	Belgium	8	12
Denmark	9	13	Denmark	9	11
Turkey	10	5	Turkey	10	4 (tie)
Norway	11	11	Norway	11	7 (tie)
Greece	12	9	Greece	12	4 (tie)
Portugal	13	2	Portugal	13	2
Luxembourg	14	14	Luxembourg	14	14
Correlation		0.490			0.165
p-value (one-tailed)		0.038			0.286

Sources: Olson and Zeckhauser (1966, p. 267) and International Institute for Strategic Studies (1974, p. 78).

among the top six in defense spending as a percentage of income. As reported by Olson and Zeckhauser, across all 14 allies the correlation between the two rank orderings equals 0.490 and is statistically significant. Olson and Zeckhauser (1966, p. 265) concluded that "large nations in NATO bear a disproportionate share of the burden of the common defense," thus supporting the public good model of alliances.

Subsequent researchers, however, discovered that the rank correlation between income and defense burden diminished and ceased to be statistically significant after the mid-to-late 1960s (Sandler and Forbes 1980, Oneal and Elrod 1989, Khanna and Sandler 1996, Sandler and Murdoch 2000). As an illustration, on the right side of Table 11.2 we replicate Olson and Zeckhauser's methodology for 1971. Notice that of the top six allies in terms of income, only three also rank among the top six in spending as a percentage of income. More formally, across all 14 countries, the rank correlation falls sharply to 0.165 and is now statistically insignificant.

As might be expected, a considerable body of research has followed since the weakened rank correlations were discovered. Within this literature there exists an interesting and lively debate about NATO behavior and the applicability of the disproportionality hypothesis. We highlight some of the methodological differences and interpretive disagreements by briefly reviewing two representative studies.

Sandler and Forbes (1980) maintain that the explanatory power of the pure public good model as it pertains to NATO has been diminished by changes in weapons technologies, strategic arms control, and especially NATO strategy. In the late 1960s, NATO shifted from a doctrine of mutually assured destruction, with its objective of pure nuclear deterrence, to one of flexible response, with its increased emphasis on protection and damage limitation. As a consequence, NATO relied more on conventional and tactical nuclear weapons and hence produced more private and impure public defense goods. Based on the joint product model, Sandler and Forbes (1980, p. 426) hypothesize that as a result of the change in NATO doctrine, free riding is reduced and defense burdens are shared more in accordance with the distribution of alliance benefits. To test their hypothesis, Sandler and Forbes compute the relative defense burden of each ally as the ratio of its own expenditures to the total expenditures for NATO. Also they estimate each ally's share of the alliance's total benefits, using national income, population, and exposed borders as benefit proxies. In general, they find that while the benefit shares were quite stable, the expenditure shares shifted in the expected direction during the 1970s. For example, while the United States' share of NATO benefits remained stable at roughly 41 percent between 1960 and 1975, its share of NATO expenditures over the same period dropped from 73 percent to 67 percent. Taking on larger relative burdens were the Europeans, whose aggregate expenditure share increased from 24 percent to 31 percent. Across all 14 allies, Sandler and Forbes find that the differences between relative defense burdens and those predicted based on benefit shares diminished over the same period. The general conclusion reached by Sandler and Forbes is that changes in NATO doctrine favor the applicability of the joint product model over the pure public good model.

In a pooled cross-sectional time-series analysis, Oneal and Diehl (1994) also appeal to the joint product model, postulating that defense burdens depend on the mix of pure public, impure public, and private goods produced by NATO members. Following Olson and Zeckhauser (1966), defense burden is measured by an ally's military spending as a proportion of its national income. The key independent variables are (1) national income as a share of NATO's total income, (2) military expenditures of contiguous allies as a share of NATO's total expenditures, and (3) involvements in non–Cold War militarized disputes. These three variables allow for the effects of the pure public good of deterrence, the impure public good of territorial defense, and any private benefits that arise from non-NATO conflicts, respectively. Also included are controls for Soviet military spending and for regional interdependence among the European allies. Estimation of the model for a sample of 15 allies over the period 1950–86 shows all coefficients to be statistically significant. The effect of spending by neighboring allies is unexpectedly negative, which Oneal and Diehl interpret as an indication of free riding. Also consistent with free riding is the positive coefficient on national income as a share of NATO income. Over the sample period 1950–86, larger allies in terms of national income bore larger defense burdens, thus supporting Olson and Zeckhauser's disproportionality hypothesis. Oneal and Diehl (1994) conclude that "NATO seems primarily to have supplied a relatively pure public good throughout this period" (p. 391).

Alliances and the Risk of Armed Conflict

A seemingly natural question to ask about alliances is whether they increase or decrease the likelihood of armed conflict. As argued by Leeds (2003), however, the question is poorly posed because alliance agreements can give rise to different obligations and hence have different effects. To see this, consider three players – potential challenger A, potential target B, and ally C. In a defensive pact between B and C, if A attacks B, then C is obligated to support B. In an offensive pact between A and C, if A attacks B, then C is obligated to support A. Lastly, in a neutrality pact between A and C, if A attacks B, then C is obligated not to intervene on B's behalf. Assuming that alliances are formal agreements with credible commitments, they provide public information about the likely conduct of an armed conflict and hence about its expected outcome. Under suitable circumstances, this means that the presence of an alliance can either decrease or increase the probability of armed conflict, depending on whether the obligations favor the target or the challenger. Based on these considerations, Leeds (2003, p. 431) puts forward three hypotheses: defensive pacts decrease the likelihood of armed conflict, offensive pacts increase the likelihood, and neutrality pacts increase the likelihood.

Leeds (2003) provides a direct test of her three hypotheses based on the ATOP database, which provides sufficient information to distinguish among defensive, offensive, and neutrality obligations. Besides being an important contribution to the alliance literature, Leeds's article has the bonus benefit for our purposes of illustrating the use of directed dyads. Consider any two countries, say Iran and Israel. This single dyad provides two directed dyads. In the context of Leeds's article, one directed dyad treats Iran as the potential challenger, that is, as the country that might initiate a militarized dispute against the potential target country, in this case Israel. The second directed dyad reverses the roles, with Israel as the potential challenger and Iran as the potential target.

By drawing on all politically relevant directed dyads for each year between 1816 and 1944, Leeds constructs a sample of almost 70,000 observations, where each observation is a dyad-year. With this sample she applies advanced regression analysis to estimate the probability that for a randomly selected directed dyad-year, the challenger will initiate a militarized interstate dispute (MID) against the target. The dependent variable equals one if a dispute is initiated and zero otherwise. The key right-hand variables indicate whether the target has a defensive ally, whether the challenger has an offensive ally, and whether the challenger benefits from a relevant neutrality pact. Control variables are included for joint democracy, contiguity, common foreign policy interests, shared alliances, and comparative strength. Leeds's (2003, pp. 435–436) empirical results strongly support all three hypotheses. The estimated coefficients on the key alliance variables are statistically significant and substantively important. Assume that all control variables are fixed at their sample means. Then, compared to a no-alliance baseline, the estimated probability that a challenger will initiate a dispute is 28 percent lower if the target has a defensive ally, 47 percent higher if the challenger has an offensive ally, and 57 percent higher if the challenger has a neutral ally.

11.6. Bibliographic Notes

Since the seminal contributions of Olson and Zeckhauser (1966, 1967), Sandler and Cauley (1975), Sandler (1977), and Murdoch and Sandler (1982), numerous extensions to the economic theory of alliances have appeared. These include models that incorporate action and reaction among allies and a rival (Niou and Tan 2005), alternative technologies of public supply (McGuire 1990, Conybeare, Murdoch, and Sandler 1994), and equilibrium concepts other than Nash (Sandler and Murdoch 1990).

The theory is applied and/or tested in studies of the Warsaw Pact, Triple Alliance, and Triple Entente (Conybeare et al. 1994), peacekeeping operations (Khanna, Sandler, and Shimizu 1998, Seiglie 2007, Solomon 2007), global strategic defense (McGuire 2004), peace as an international public good (Brauer and Roux 2000), arms trade control (Sandler 2000), and protection against national emergencies (Ihori 1999). Sandler and Hartley (2001) provide a thorough review of the theoretical and empirical literature on the economic theory of alliances.

The economic analysis of alliances includes the effects of economic factors on alliance behavior and the effects of alliances on economic outcomes. The former literature includes studies of the effects of trade on alliance burden sharing (Wong 1991), while the latter considers the effects of alliances on trade (Gowa and Mansfield 2004, Long and Leeds 2006), defense industrial policy (Hartley 2006), economic growth (Macnair, Murdoch, Pi, and Sandler 1995), and exchange-rate regimes (Li 2003).

Although we emphasize the economics of alliances in this chapter, political scientists have delved into other aspects of alliance behavior, including alliance formation causes (Siverson and Starr 1994), alliance duration (Bennett 1997), and ally reliability (Leeds and Anac 2005). Special issues of *International Interactions* (Krause and Sprecher 2004) and *Journal of Peace Research* (Sprecher and Krause 2006) offer excellent summaries of quantitative research on alliances from the perspective of political science.

For studies of alliances or alignments among terrorist organizations and criminal syndicates, see Picarelli (2006) on forms of crime-terrorism interconnection, Björnehed (2004) on narcotics trafficking and terrorism, Shelley (2006) on the smuggling of nuclear materials, and the edited volume of Holmes (2007) on terrorism and corruption.

Conflict Success Functions and the Theory
of Appropriation Possibilities

Standard economics treats individuals and groups (including nations) as enriching themselves through specialized production and trade. These are presented as peaceful activities because the resources used and the goods produced and traded are implicitly assumed to be secure from appropriation. We have seen in this book, however, that conflict over resources and goods abound. While previous chapters modeled conflict as a choice and considered the interdependence of economic and conflict variables, this chapter adds a new premise, namely, that appropriation stands coequal with production and trade as a fundamental category of economic activity. The chapter begins with an overview of the conflict success function, which is a key element of the theory of appropriation possibilities. We then present a model of conflict over a resource, which reveals, among other things, a paradox of power and incentives for peaceful settlement. The resource conflict model is then integrated with an Edgeworth box model of production and trade, showing how various economic variables are affected by appropriation possibilities.

12.1. Conflict Success Functions

A central building block for introducing appropriation possibilities into mainstream economic models is the conflict success function (CSF) (Hirshleifer 1995, Garfinkel and Skaperdas 2007). A CSF specifies how the weapons or fighting efforts of players combine to determine the distribution of a contested resource or good. Suppose, for example, that players A and B employ M_A and M_B units of military goods to determine the holdings of a resource such as land, oil, or water. Let p_A be A's conflict success in the resource dispute, with p_B the same for B. Conflict success might be measured by the proportion of the disputed resource controlled

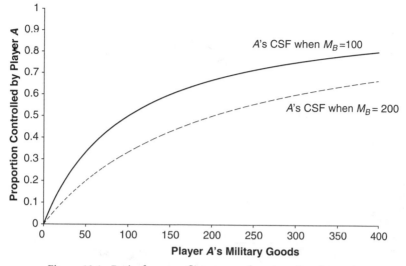

Figure 12.1. Ratio form conflict success functions for player A.

by a player or by the probability that a player controls the entire resource in a winner-take-all contest. The technology relating the military inputs M_A and M_B and the success outputs p_A and p_B is summarized by the CSF, which is assumed mathematically to take on either a ratio or logistic form.

According to the ratio form, the conflict successes of A and B are

$$p_A = \frac{(M_A)^m}{(M_A)^m + (ZM_B)^m}$$

$$\text{and} \quad p_B = \frac{(ZM_B)^m}{(M_A)^m + (ZM_B)^m}, \text{ with } m > 0, Z > 0. \tag{12.1}$$

Parameter m is a decisiveness coefficient that captures the degree to which greater military input translates into conflict success, while parameter Z represents the relative effectiveness of B's military goods. Figure 12.1 illustrates the ratio form CSF for player A when $m = Z = 1$, with A's military goods M_A measured horizontally and conflict success p_A vertically. Assume first that B's military goods are fixed at $M_B = 100$, which results in the solid curve in the figure. As seen, A's conflict success rises at a diminishing rate as M_A increases from zero along the horizontal axis. When A's military goods reach $M_A = 100$, A's conflict success p_A equals 0.5; for values of M_A above 100, A's conflict success is greater than 0.5. Suppose now that player B's military goods rise to $M_B = 200$. This causes A's conflict success function to rotate downward, as shown by the dashed curve in Figure 12.1. In this case, A does not reach a conflict success of 0.5 until M_A is 200.

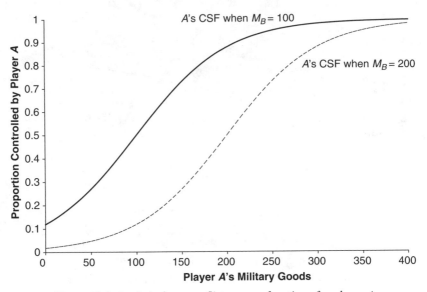

Figure 12.2. Logistic form conflict success functions for player A.

For the logistic form of the CSF, the conflict successes are

$$p_A = \frac{1}{1 + exp[m(ZM_B - M_A)]}$$

$$\text{and} \quad p_B = \frac{1}{1 + exp[m(M_A - ZM_B)]},$$

(12.2)

where the second term in each denominator represents the natural constant e raised to the power shown in brackets. Figure 12.2 illustrates the logistic form CSF for player A when $m = 0.02$ and $Z = 1$. The solid curve occurs when $M_B = 100$, while the dashed curve holds when $M_B = 200$.

The ratio and logistic forms differ in two major ways. First, under ratio technology, conflict success depends on the *ratio* of military goods M_A/M_B, whereas under logistic technology, conflict success depends on the *difference* in military goods $M_A - M_B$ (Hirshleifer 1995, p. 176, Garfinkel and Skaperdas 2007, pp. 655–656). Second, the vertical intercept is zero for the ratio CSF but positive for the logistic CSF. This means that under ratio technology, a player with zero military goods will have zero success, even if the opposing player has only a negligible amount of military goods. In contrast, under logistic conflict technology, a player with zero military goods will still experience some degree of conflict success. Hirshleifer (1995, p. 178) notes that in the context of military combat the ratio CSF would apply under the ideal conditions of a uniform battlefield, full information, and absence of fatigue, whereas the logistic CSF would be relevant when combat is subject to imperfect information or the presence of safe havens.

12.2. A Model of Appropriation Possibilities

Economists have begun to incorporate conflict over resources and goods into traditional models of economic activity. A common theme linking these models is that appropriation possibilities divert resources away from alternative economic activities such as production or consumption. Some models also consider destruction of assets and disruption of economic activities such as trade. Another theme linking economic models of conflict is the use of a conflict success function whereby appropriative outcomes are determined by competing military goods and conflict technology. We illustrate these themes by presenting a variation of a resource conflict model due originally to Skaperdas (2006, pp. 664–666).

Basic Model of Resource Conflict

Suppose players A and B dispute control of a fixed resource $\tilde{R}$. The players also have respective holdings of secure and undisputed resources, R_A and R_B. A and B are free to divert M_A and M_B units of their respective secure resources to produce military goods, which in turn can be used to fight over the disputed resource. For simplicity, we assume that each unit of resources diverted to conflict generates one unit of military goods. We assume for the same reason that fighting between A and B destroys a fixed proportion δ of the disputed resource, where $0 < \delta < 1$. Hence, $\tilde{R}(1 - \delta)$ is the amount of the disputed resource that would remain following a fight. Assuming a ratio CSF with a decisiveness coefficient of $m = 1$, the net resources NR_A and NR_B controlled by the players if fighting occurs will be

$$NR_A = (R_A - M_A) + \left(\frac{M_A}{M_A + ZM_B}\right)\tilde{R}(1 - \delta)$$

$$= \left[R_A + \left(\frac{M_A}{M_A + ZM_B}\right)\tilde{R}(1 - \delta)\right] - M_A \tag{12.3a}$$

$$NR_B = (R_B - M_B) + \left(\frac{ZM_B}{M_A + ZM_B}\right)\tilde{R}(1 - \delta)$$

$$= \left[R_B + \left(\frac{ZM_B}{M_A + ZM_B}\right)\tilde{R}(1 - \delta)\right] - M_B. \tag{12.3b}$$

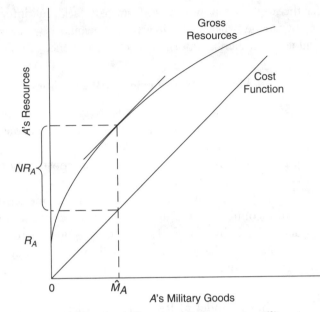

Figure 12.3. *A*'s optimal allocation of resources to military goods.

Equations (12.3a) and (12.3b) show that each player's amount of net resources is calculated as the secure resource holding minus the diversion of resources to military goods plus the portion of the remaining disputed resource claimed in the fight. We assume that the CSF determines the share of $\tilde{R}(1-\delta)$ seized, so that equations (12.3a) and (12.3b) show the net resources controlled by *A* and *B* with certainty. If we assume alternatively that the CSF determines the probability of capturing the resource in a winner-take-all contest, then NR_A and NR_B equal expected net resources of *A* and *B*.

Optimization Problem

We focus on player *A*'s optimization problem, with *B*'s being analogous. Player *A*'s objective is to choose M_A to maximize its net resources. The trade-off that *A* faces in (12.3a) is that, for any given M_B, more M_A will increase *A*'s share of the remaining disputed resource $\tilde{R}(1-\delta)$, but it will also divert additional resources away from *A*'s secure resource holding. Figure 12.3 shows *A*'s optimization problem graphically. The diversion of *A*'s resources to conflict, M_A, is measured horizontally, while the amount of resources is measured vertically. The gross resources schedule in Figure 12.3 reflects the square-bracketed term in equation (12.3a); it has an intercept equal to R_A and a positive but diminishing slope due to the CSF. The cost function in Figure 12.3 reflects the M_A term shown to the right of the brackets; it has an intercept of zero and a slope of one. Given M_B, A maximizes net resources in Figure 12.3 by allocating to military goods a level of resources $\hat{M}_A$, where the marginal amount of resources obtained in conflict equals the marginal cost of resources diverted to military goods. Geometrically, this occurs where the slope of the gross resources schedule is equal to the slope of the cost function. The vertical distance between the two functions at $\hat{M}_A$ measures the net resources controlled by A in the conflict.

Changes in the gross resources or cost schedules can be considered in Figure 12.3 in much the same way that changes in revenues and costs were discussed in the net revenue model of Chapter 7. For example, an increase in the amount of the disputed resource $\tilde{R}$ would lead to an upward rotation of the gross resources function in Figure 12.3, causing an increase in A's optimal level of military goods. Alternatively, an increase in A's secure resource holding R_A would shift A's gross resources schedule upward in a parallel fashion, leaving the optimal amount of military goods unchanged at $\hat{M}_A$ but increasing A's net resource holdings. On the cost side, suppose one unit of military goods could be acquired for less than one unit of resources. This would cause the cost function in Figure 12.3 to have a lower slope, leading to an increase in A's optimal resource diversion to military goods.

Reaction Functions and Equilibrium

The optimization problem just sketched gives rise to A's reaction function, which shows the level of military goods that A will choose given alternative levels of military goods for B. Algebraically, A's reaction function is derived by differentiating equation (12.3a) with respect to M_A, setting the derivative to zero, and then solving for M_A. B's reaction function is derived similarly using equation (12.3b). Assuming that each player's optimal resource diversion to military goods is less than its secure resource holding, the respective reaction functions of A and B are

$$M_A = \sqrt{ZM_B\tilde{R}(1-\delta)} - ZM_B \qquad (12.4a)$$

$$M_B = \frac{1}{Z}\left(\sqrt{ZM_A\tilde{R}(1-\delta)} - M_A\right). \qquad (12.4b)$$

Solving simultaneously the two reaction functions in equations (12.4a) and (12.4b) yields the equilibrium military goods M_A^* and M_B^*, where:

$$M_A^* = M_B^* = \frac{Z\tilde{R}(1-\delta)}{(1+Z)^2}.$$ (12.5)

Equation (12.5) shows that the players' equilibrium military goods depend positively on the amount of the disputed resource $\tilde{R}$, positively (negatively) on the relative effectiveness of B's military goods for $Z < 1$ (for $Z > 1$), and negatively on the destructiveness of war δ. Substituting M_A^* and M_B^* into the CSF and multiplying by $\tilde{R}(1-\delta)$ shows that the amounts of the remaining disputed resource seized in a fight, D_A^* and D_B^*, will be

$$D_A^* = \frac{\tilde{R}(1-\delta)}{1+Z}$$ (12.6a)

$$D_B^* = \frac{Z\tilde{R}(1-\delta)}{1+Z}.$$ (12.6b)

Similarly, substituting M_A^* and M_B^* back into equations (12.3a) and (12.3b), the final net resources controlled by the players in equilibrium after a fight can be shown to be

$$NR_A^* = R_A + \frac{\tilde{R}(1-\delta)}{(1+Z)^2}$$ (12.7a)

$$NR_B^* = R_B + \frac{Z^2\tilde{R}(1-\delta)}{(1+Z)^2}.$$ (12.7b)

Numerical Example

As a numerical example, suppose the amount of the disputed resource is $\tilde{R} = 200$, the secure resource holdings of A and B are $R_A = R_B = 100$, the relative military effectiveness parameter is $Z = 1$, and the destructiveness of conflict is $\delta = 0.2$. Based on equation (12.5), each player diverts 40 units of secure resources to military goods. If they fight over the disputed resource, 20 percent of the disputed resource is destroyed, leaving 160 resource units. Based on the CSF, the players' military capabilities imply that each claims 50 percent of the remaining disputed resource, or 80 resource units each. The net resources controlled by each player in equilibrium is then 140 units, made up of the 60 units of secure resources not diverted to military goods plus 80 units of the remaining disputed

Table 12.1. *Numerical example of resource conflict model.*

Parameters	
Secure resource holding of A	$R_A = 100$
Secure resource holding of B	$R_B = 100$
Amount of disputed resource	$\tilde{R} = 200$
Relative military effectiveness of B	$Z = 1$
Destructiveness of conflict	$\delta = 0.2$
Equilibrium values of the variables	
Military goods of A and B	$M_A^* = M_B^* = 40$
Remaining disputed resources controlled by A and B	$D_A^* = D_A^* = 80$
Final net resources controlled by A and B	$NR_A^* = NR_A^* = 140$

resource seized. This result is consistent with the equilibrium net resource values implied by equations (12.7a) and (12.7b). Table 12.1 summarizes the numerical example of the resource conflict model.

Paradox of Power and the Irrelevance of Initial Resource Holdings

One might think that in a conflict over resources or goods, the poorer side would be at a disadvantage relative to the wealthier side. In a number of economic models of conflict, however, scholars have found what Hirshleifer called the paradox of power (POP). In the strong form of the POP, the players end up with identical amounts of the disputed item $(D_A^*/D_B^* = 1)$ despite disparity of initial resource holdings (e.g., $R_A/R_B > 1$). In the weak form of the POP, the distribution of the disputed item is less dispersed than the initial distribution of resources (e.g., $1 < D_A^*/D_B^* < R_A/R_B$) (Hirshleifer 1995, p. 182).

In the resource conflict model developed here, a strong form of the POP is evident when $Z = 1$. Equations (12.6a) and (12.6b) imply that when $Z = 1$, each player ends up controlling the same amount of the disputed resource, regardless of initial holdings of secure resources. For example, if $\tilde{R} = 200$ and $\delta = 0.2$, in equilibrium each player will control 80 units of the remaining disputed resource, even if the secure resource holdings of A and B are unequal, say at $R_A = 100$ and $R_B = 50$. In this example we find that the disparity of initial resources in favor of A ($R_A/R_B = 2$) does not translate into a greater share of the disputed resource controlled by A in the conflict $(D_A^*/D_B^* = 1)$.

The paradox of power does not hold generally when $Z \neq 1$. For example, suppose the parameters are $\tilde{R} = 200$, $R_A = 100$, $R_B = 50$, and $\delta = 0.2$, but now $Z = 1/3$. Equations (12.6a) and (12.6b) imply that A will control 120 units and B 40 units of the remaining disputed resource. Hence, contrary to the POP, the disparity of initial resources in A's favor ($R_A/R_B = 2$) translates into an even greater disparity of the seized amounts of disputed resource in A's favor ($D_A^*/D_B^* = 3$). Inspection of equations (12.6a) and (12.6b) reveals that the paradox of power is a product of the irrelevance of initial resources in determining the final distribution of the disputed item. Note that R_A and R_B do not appear in the two equations. In the resource conflict model presented here, the distribution of the remaining disputed resource in equilibrium is governed exclusively by relative military effectiveness Z. Specifically, equations (12.6a) and (12.6b) imply that the ratio of the amounts of the remaining disputed item controlled by A and B is $1/Z$. Hence, when $Z = 1$, disparity of initial resources in favor of A ($R_A/R_B = 2$) corresponds to an equal distribution of the disputed resource ($D_A^*/D_B^* = 1$) because of the more general point that the final distribution is determined exclusively by the technology of conflict parameter Z.

Settlement Opportunities in the Resource Conflict Model

To this point we have assumed that the players fight to determine control of the disputed resource. Given the destructiveness of conflict, however, each player can potentially gain from nonviolent settlement of the dispute. This is shown in Figure 12.4 using a linear version of Hirshleifer's bargaining model from Chapter 5, together with the parameters and equilibrium values of the resource conflict example in Table 12.1.

The horizontal axis in Figure 12.4 measures A's net resources expected from fighting or settlement and the vertical axis does the same for B. If A and B fight, the net resources controlled by each player equal 140 units, as shown by point E in the figure and the last row of Table 12.1. If fighting is avoided, however, $\delta\tilde{R} = 40$ units of the disputed resource will not be destroyed, which is a surplus available to the players from peaceful settlement. Assume for simplicity that under peaceful settlement the players distribute the disputed resource according to what Garfinkel and Skaperdas (2007, p. 674) call the "split-the-surplus rule of division." Under this division rule, the surplus from peaceful settlement $\delta\tilde{R}$ is split evenly, while the remaining disputed resource $(1 - \delta)\tilde{R}$ is divided according to the players' military stocks and the conflict success function in equation

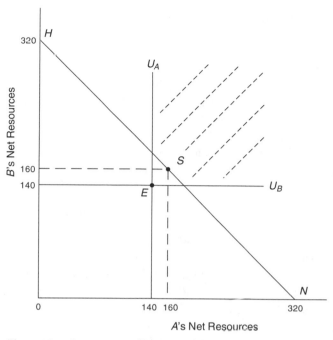

Figure 12.4. Resource conflict in Hirshleifer's bargaining model.

(12.1). Given the split-the-surplus division rule, each player's diversion of resources to military goods is the same whether they fight or settle (Skaperdas 2006, pp. 665–666). Based on Table 12.1 and the split-the-surplus division rule, each player will divert 40 units of secure resources to military goods under war or peace, but if war is avoided $\delta\tilde{R} = 40$ units of the disputed resource will not be destroyed. Hence, under peaceful settlement, 320 resource units will be available to the players, made up of 100 units of secure resources for each player, 200 units of disputed resources, less each player's diversion of 40 units of secure resources to military goods. Since 320 resource units are potentially available to the players' under peace, the settlement opportunity line *HN* in Figure 12.4 has intercept values of 320.

Players are assumed to be strict egoists as indicated by their respective indifference curves U_A and U_B passing through point *E*. Since the settlement opportunity line intersects the region of mutual gain, the model predicts peaceful settlement over violence. Given that the players are fully informed, equally capable ($M_A^* = M_B^* = 40$ and $Z = 1$), and adopt the split-the-surplus division rule, the players are predicted to reach a peaceful settlement whereby each obtains 160 units of net resources, as shown by point *S* in Figure 12.4.

12.3. Appropriation Possibilities in a Production/Exchange Economy

Virtually all textbook models of economic activity assume that resources and goods are secure against appropriation. Given perfectly secure property, an ideal economy emerges wherein costs from conflict are absent and specialized production and trade generate increases in consumption opportunities relative to autarky. In what follows we present a simple model of production and trade to illustrate how that ideal economy is reshaped by the introduction of appropriation possibilities.

Specialized Production and Trade under Secure Property

Production Possibilities and Autarky Equilibrium
We begin with the resource conflict model summarized in Table 12.1, where the amount of the disputed resource is $\tilde{R} = 200$ and the secure resource holdings of A and B are $R_A = R_B = 100$. Assume now that the entire disputed resource is split evenly between A and B and that all resource holdings and goods produced are perfectly secure. The secure resource holdings of A and B are now $R_A = R_B = 200$. Given the assumption of perfect security, there is no incentive to produce military goods because there is no ability to take property from others and thus no need to defend. Hence, the full amount of the players' resources ($R_A = R_B = 200$) is available for producing goods.

We assume that the players can use their resources to produce two goods X and Y. The production of each good is based on a production technology that specifies the number of units of resources required to produce one unit of a good. For example, let $a_X = 1$ and $a_Y = 2$ be player A's unit resource requirements. These coefficients imply that A needs one unit of resources to produce one unit of good X and two units of resources to produce one unit of good Y. Hence, if A allocated all 200 units of her resources to produce good X, she could produce 200 units of X. Alternatively, if A allocated all 200 units of resources to produce good Y, she could produce 100 units of Y. Of course, A might choose to produce some combination of both X and Y. For example, if A allocated half of her resources to the production of each good, she could produce $X_A = 100$ and $Y_A = 50$. For simplicity, assume player B's unit resource requirements are the reverse of A's, namely, $b_X = 2$ and $b_Y = 1$. Player B could allocate all 200 units of his resources to produce good X (giving $X_B = 100$) or good Y (giving $Y_B = 200$), or he might divide his resources between the two goods to produce, say, $X_B = 50$ and $Y_B = 100$. In

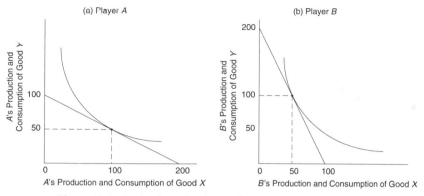

Figure 12.5. Optimal production and consumption in autarky.

general, player A's production possibilities are governed by the constraint equation $R_A = a_X X_A + a_Y Y_A$ and B's by $R_B = b_X X_B + b_Y Y_B$. Given the parameter values, player A's production possibilities frontier (PPF) is shown by the straight line in panel (a) of Figure 12.5, while B's is shown in panel (b).

The production possibilities frontiers in Figure 12.5 show possible production points for players A and B, but not the specific production points that they would choose. To know where A would like to operate on her PPF, we need to know A's preferences over X and Y, and likewise for B. For simplicity, assume that A and B have identical preferences represented by an equal weight Cobb-Douglas (CD) utility function $U = XY$. A convenient property of a CD utility function wherein each good is equally important is that a utility maximizer operating in autarky will allocate an equal amount of resources to each good. Hence, given $R_A = 200$, player A will maximize utility in autarky by allocating 100 units of resources to produce good X and 100 units of resources to produce good Y. With unit resource requirements $a_X = 1$, and $a_Y = 2$, this results in 100 units of good X, denoted $X_A^\wedge = 100$, and 50 units of good Y, denoted $Y_A^\wedge = 50$. Similarly for player B with $R_B = 200$, $b_X = 2$, and $b_Y = 1$, B will allocate 100 units of resources to the production of each good, leading to $X_B^\wedge = 50$ and $Y_B^\wedge = 100$. The determination of A's and B's optimal production and consumption in autarky are shown geometrically in Figure 12.5, where each player's indifference curve is tangent to her or his PPF.

Gains from Trade

Beginning from the autarky equilibrium in Figure 12.5, mutual gains are available to A and B from specialized production and trade. To

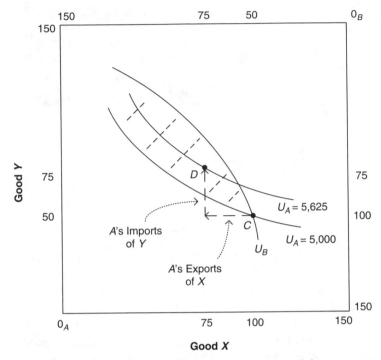

Figure 12.6. Gains from exchange in an Edgeworth box.

demonstrate this we rely on a graphical device known as the Edgeworth box. Figure 12.6 shows the box for the autarky equilibrium of Figure 12.5. The dimensions of the box reflect the total quantities of X and Y produced by A and B in autarky. Since $X_A^\wedge = 100$ and $X_B^\wedge = 50$ in Figure 12.5, the width of the box in Figure 12.6 is 150 units of X. Similarly, since $Y_A^\wedge = 50$ and $Y_B^\wedge = 100$ in Figure 12.5, the height of the box in Figure 12.6 is 150 units of Y. We measure A's autarky production and consumption of $X_A^\wedge = 100$ and $Y_A^\wedge = 50$ in the usual manner from the lower-left origin 0_A, leading to point C in the Edgeworth box. For B's autarky production and consumption of $X_B^\wedge = 50$ and $Y_B^\wedge = 100$, however, we measure left and down from the upper-right origin 0_B. Because of the way the box is constructed, this places B's autarky point also at C. In summary, the dimensions of the Edgeworth box in Figure 12.6 reflect the aggregate production of the two goods under autarky, while point C reflects the distribution of this total production between A and B.

Now consider A's and B's indifference curves passing through the autarky point C. From Figure 12.5, A's indifference curve at the optimum

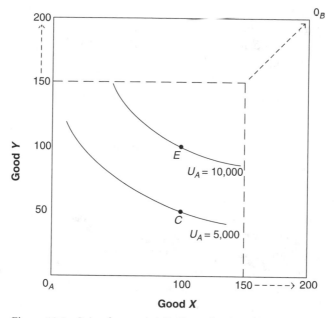

Figure 12.7. Gains from specialized production and exchange.

has a slope of $-1/2$ (equal to the slope of A's PPF) while B's has a slope of -2 (equal to the slope of B's PPF). In Figure 12.6, these divergent slopes are shown by the intersection of A's and B's indifference curves at point C. Since the indifference curves cross at point C, a region of mutual gain arises to the northwest of C. Hence, both players have an incentive to work out a trade that moves them into this region. For example, beginning from point C, if A were to export 25 units of X to B in exchange for 25 units of Y, the players' consumption bundles would be at point D. Both players would gain from this exchange. Player A's utility would rise from $U_A = X_A Y_A = 100 \cdot 50 = 5,000$ in autarky at point C to $U_A = X_A Y_A = 75 \cdot 75 = 5,625$ under trade at point D. Player B would experience the same increase in utility when moving his consumption bundle from C to D.

As noted in Chapter 2, there are generally two sources of increased wealth from trade: (1) gains from exchange and (2) gains from specialization. When moving from point C to D in Figure 12.6, we considered only gains from exchange. Specifically, we allowed the players to use exchange to redistribute their existing stocks of goods at point C so that each was better off, but we did not allow them to alter production to take advantage of gains from specialization. Figure 12.7 shows what happens when we do.

Since $a_X = 1$, $a_Y = 2$, $b_X = 2$, and $b_Y = 1$, player A is comparatively better at producing good X, and B is comparatively better at producing good Y. Given $R_A = 200$ and $R_B = 200$, if each player completely specializes in producing the comparative advantage good, then 200 units of each good will be produced. Figure 12.7 shows the substantial increase in the dimensions of the Edgeworth box under completely specialized production. The Edgeworth box under autarky is shown by the dashed box with dimensions $150X$ and $150Y$. Complete productive specialization expands the Edgeworth box by 50 units along each dimension to $200X$ and $200Y$, as shown by the solid-lined box. Beginning from complete specialization at the lower-right corner of the expanded box, suppose that A exports 100 units of X in exchange for 100 units of Y, with B the other side of the trade. The consumption bundles of A and B will now each be $X = 100$ and $Y = 100$, as shown by point E in Figure 12.7. Recall that player A's autarky consumption bundle was $X_A^\wedge = 100$ and $Y_A^\wedge = 50$, as shown by point C. At trade equilibrium point E, A's consumption of X remains at $X_A = 100$, but A's consumption of Y increases by 50 units to $Y_A = 100$. Hence, A's gains from trade are equal to 50 units of Y. Similarly, B's gains from trade are 50 units of X. The total gains from trade of $50Y$ and $50X$ are also reflected in the expansion of the Edgeworth box by these same amounts when moving from autarky to specialized production and trade. Note also that A's utility rises from $U_A = 100 \cdot 50 = 5{,}000$ in autarky to $U_A = 100 \cdot 100 = 10{,}000$ under specialized production and trade. Player B experiences the same increase in utility.

Insecure Resources and Dissipation of the Production/Exchange Economy

We now consider how conflict radically changes the idealized production/exchange economy of Figure 12.7 by reintroducing the numerical example of resource conflict from Table 12.1. In the example, the amount of disputed resource is $\tilde{R} = 200$, A and B have respective secure resource holdings $R_A = R_B = 100$, the destructiveness of conflict is $\delta = 0.2$, and the relative military effectiveness is $Z = 1$. Whether there is fighting or a split-the-surplus settlement, each player diverts 40 units of secure resources to military goods. Under fighting, each player controls 140 units of resources, made up of the 60 units of secure resources not diverted to military goods plus 80 units of the remaining disputed resource claimed in the fight. Under settlement, each player controls 160 units of resources, consisting of 60 units of secure resources not diverted to military goods plus 100 units of

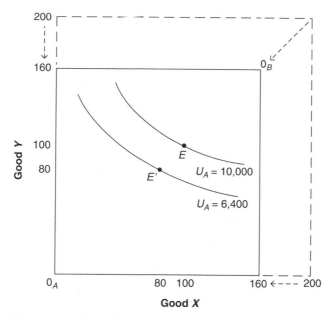

Figure 12.8. Effects of diversion of resources to military goods.

the disputed resource acquired in the settlement. For simplicity, we assume that potential gains from trade between A and B and war's diminution of such gains do not alter the parameters or equilibrium values of the resource conflict model in Table 12.1. This assumption allows us to illustrate, in the simplest way possible, how a resource conflict undermines the idealized production/exchange economy.

Diversion

We repeat the idealized production/exchange economy as the large dashed Edgeworth box in Figure 12.8 with dimensions $200X$ and $200Y$. For reference purposes, we show again A's indifference curve through consumption point E with utility level $U_A = 100 \cdot 100 = 10,000$. From the resource conflict model, assume that the players reach a settlement so that the destructiveness of conflict is avoided. Under settlement, each player allocates 40 units of secure resources to military goods and controls 160 units of resources on net. Since violence is avoided, we assume that the players are able to maintain a trading relationship. The diversion of resources to military goods, however, shrinks the dimensions of the Edgeworth box as shown in Figure 12.8. Because specialized production and trade continue under settlement, A produces $160X$ and B produces

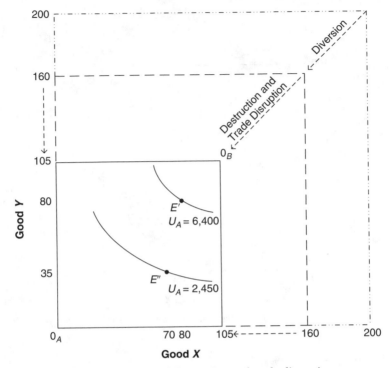

Figure 12.9. Effects of destruction and trade disruption.

160Y, causing the solid-lined box to emerge with A's origin remaining fixed but B's origin shifting inward. Suppose that A exports 80X in exchange for 80Y with B the other side of the trade. Thus, specialization and trade result in consumption bundles for both A and B at X = 80 and Y = 80, as shown by point E' in the reduced Edgeworth box. Note that diversion of resources to military goods causes the Edgeworth box to shrink by 40 units along each dimension, with the result that both players consume 20 fewer units of each good relative to what they would in the idealized economy with perfectly secure property. As shown in Figure 12.8, A's utility falls from $U_A = 10,000$ to $U_A = 80 \cdot 80 = 6,400$, and similarly for B.

Destruction and Disruption
Figure 12.9 shows the effects of resource destruction and trade disruption when violence erupts. We repeat the idealized production/exchange economy as the large dashed-and-dotted Edgeworth box with dimensions 200X and 200Y. Within the large box is the dashed Edgeworth box with dimensions 160X and 160Y, which recall results when the players each

divert 40 units of secure resources to military goods but reach a settlement. Suppose instead of settlement, the players fight over the disputed resource. We assume that the outbreak of violence not only destroys $\delta\tilde{R} = 40$ units of the disputed resource, but it also disrupts trade between A and B (Anderton and Carter 2003). For simplicity, assume that trade ceases altogether.

Under fighting, cessation of trade causes the players to operate in autarky, where each player in the end controls 140 units of resources. Given the equal weight Cobb-Douglas utility function $U = XY$, each player allocates half of its 140 resource units to the production of each good. Given $a_X = 1$, $a_Y = 2$, $b_X = 2$, and $b_Y = 1$, player A produces $X_A^\wedge = 70$ and $Y_A^\wedge = 35$, while B produces $X_B^\wedge = 35$ and $Y_B^\wedge = 70$. Hence, under fighting, the solid-lined Edgeworth box emerges with dimensions $105X$ and $105Y$. When moving from settlement to fighting, 55 units of each good are lost from the production/exchange economy: 20 units of each good are lost from resource destruction, and an additional 35 units of each good are lost from the termination of specialized production. Since trade has ceased, consumption occurs at production point E''. Comparing points E' (with settlement) and E'' (with fighting) reveals that player A's utility falls from $U_A = 80 \cdot 80 = 6{,}400$ to $U_A = 70 \cdot 35 = 2{,}450$. Note that the amount of goods available to the players in *total* under fighting ($105X$ and $105Y$) in Figure 12.9 is only slightly larger than the amount of goods consumed by *one* player ($100X$ and $100Y$) in the idealized Edgeworth box economy in Figure 12.7. Polachek (1994, p. 12) characterizes violent conflict as "trade gone awry," and so it is in Figure 12.9.

Appropriation Possibilities and Equilibrium in a Production/Exchange Economy

Figure 12.9 suggests that the textbook model of peaceful economic activity is but a special case of a more general model wherein appropriation possibilities both shape and are shaped by the traditional economic activities of production and trade. At one extreme of this general model, appropriation possibilities are ignored and the full potential of specialized production and trade is realized. This is the approach taken in standard economics texts. At the other extreme, gains from trade are ignored under actual or threatened violent conflict. Many theoretical models of conflict ignore potential gains from trade. Between these extremes lies a wide range of human behavior where specialized production and trade occur, but they are radically modified by appropriation possibilities. To show further the

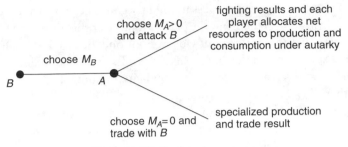

Figure 12.10. Predator/prey game.

interdependence of appropriation, production, and trade, and also to illustrate the emergence of equilibrium out of this interdependence, we conclude with a few numerical examples based on a model due originally to Anderton et al. (1999).

A Predator/Prey Model of Appropriation, Production, and Exchange

We begin again with the resource conflict example, where the amount of the disputed resource is $\tilde{R} = 200$, the secure resource holdings of A and B are $R_A = R_B = 100$, and the destructiveness of fighting is $\delta = 0.2$. Assume now that the disputed resource is split evenly between A and B such that $R_A = R_B = 200$. Unlike earlier, assume that player A's resource holding is secure but B's resource holding is vulnerable to attack by A. This assumption casts player A in the role of attacker or predator and player B as defender or prey. One possible outcome of the predator/prey relationship between A and B is that a fight will ensue over B's vulnerable resource holding. Another possibility is that A and B will avoid fighting and instead engage in specialized production and trade. For simplicity, assume that an attack by A against B's resources precludes the possibility of specialized production and trade. Moreover, suppose that a peaceful settlement of the predation is not possible, perhaps owing to a commitment problem.

Figure 12.10 provides a schematic of the predator/prey game. Player B moves first, diverting some of its resources to produce military goods M_B with which it defends its remaining vulnerable resources. Player A moves second, taking as given B's stock of military goods M_B. In particular, player A either diverts some of its resources into military goods ($M_A > 0$) and attacks B's remaining resources, or it produces no military goods ($M_A = 0$) and engages in specialized production and trade with B. The combined decisions of A and B result in either fighting or specialization and trade, as shown by the top and bottom branches of the game tree, respectively.

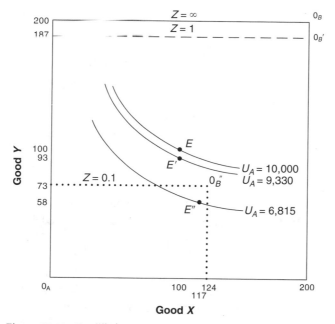

Figure 12.11. Equilibrium economies in the predator/prey game.

As the first mover, player B anticipates A's reaction and chooses a level of military goods that brings about the state of the world (fighting or specialization and trade) that yields B the higher utility. When profitable to do so, player B chooses a level of military goods that defends its resources to the point that A prefers to trade with rather than to attack B. When it is not profitable to induce trade, B chooses a level of military goods that minimizes its loss from A's attack. If fighting occurs, the ratio conflict success functions, $p_A = M_A/(M_A + ZM_B)$ and $p_B = ZM_B/(M_A + ZM_B)$, determine the proportion of B's surviving net resources $(R_B - M_B)(1 - \delta)$ claimed by A and B, respectively. Following the fight, the players use their respective net resource holdings in autarky to produce goods X and Y according to the unit resource requirements $a_X = 1$, $a_Y = 2$, $b_X = 2$, $b_Y = 1$. If trade occurs, A specializes in good X, B in good Y, and trade ensues.

Under these assumptions, what type of economy will emerge in equilibrium, and what will be its production, consumption, and utility characteristics? In the predator/prey game, the Z parameter in the conflict success functions reflects the security of B's resource holdings. Figure 12.11 illustrates the equilibrium economies that emerge for $Z = \infty$, $Z = 1$, and $Z = 0.1$. For $Z = \infty$, B's resources are perfectly secure, so neither player has an incentive to produce military goods. This generates the idealized

Edgeworth box economy with origins 0_A and 0_B, dimensions $200X$ and $200Y$, consumption bundles for each player of $X = 100$ and $Y = 100$ at point E, and utility for each player of $U = 100 \cdot 100 = 10,000$. For $Z = 1$, B's resources are moderately vulnerable to attack by A, and thus B has an incentive to defend them. It can be shown in the predator/prey game that the utility maximizing action by B when $Z = 1$ is to produce $M_B = 13.4$ units of military goods to induce A to trade rather than attack. This diversion of resources to defense alters the economy in numerous ways, as shown by the dashed Edgeworth box with origins 0_A and $0_B'$ in Figure 12.11. The new box has dimensions $200X$ and $186.6Y$, consumption bundles for each player of $X = 100$ and $Y = 93.3$ at point E', and utility for each player of $U = 100 \cdot 93.3 = 9,330$. The volume and terms of trade are also altered. In the idealized economy $100X$ is exchanged for $100Y$ at a terms of trade of one; for $Z = 1$, $100X$ is exchanged for $93.3Y$ at a terms of trade of 0.93.

When Z falls to 0.1, player B's resources are so vulnerable to attack by A that specialized production and trade are precluded altogether and fighting ensues. Specifically, when $Z = 0.1$, player B is unable to profitably induce player A to prefer to trade. The best that B can do is to defend itself with $M_B = 100$ units of military goods and fight it out with A. Player A's optimal allocation for military goods is $M_A = 18.3$. Following the fight, the players' net resource holdings are $NR_A = 233.4$ and $NR_B = 28.3$, which lead to autarky production and consumption bundles of $X_A^\wedge = 116.7$, $Y_A^\wedge = 58.4$, $X_B^\wedge = 7.1$, and $Y_B^\wedge = 14.2$. Hence, when $Z = 0.1$, the dotted Edgeworth box emerges in Figure 12.11, with origins 0_A and $0_B''$, dimensions $123.8X$ and $72.6Y$, autarky consumption bundles shown at E'', and much reduced utilities of $U_A = 116.7 \cdot 58.4 = 6,815$ for the predator and $U_B = 7.1 \cdot 14.2 = 101$ for the prey.

Discussion
The broad lesson of Figure 12.11 is that appropriation, production, and trade are indeed deeply intertwined: appropriation possibilities determine the security of property on which specialized production and trade depend, while at the same time the production and trade possibilities shape the incentives for appropriation. Modern physics provides an analogy to the interconnectedness of appropriation, production, and trade in the economic realm. In the physical universe, space, time, and matter are profoundly intertwined because matter alters space-time and space-time in turn alters the paths of matter. Hence, the fundamental categories of physical reality are understood integrally in the general theory of

relativity. In a similar manner, the interdependence of appropriation, production, and trade requires that appropriation join production and trade as a fundamental dimension of economic activity, and that economic outcomes be understood as arising from this economic triad.

12.4. Bibliographic Notes

Conflict success functions (CSFs) have been used in many areas of conflict analysis. See Garfinkel (1990) on arms racing, Nalebuff and Riley (1985) on wars of attrition, Garfinkel and Skaperdas (2000b) on conflict over the distribution of output, Usher (1989) and Collier (2000b) on civil conflict, Konrad and Skaperdas (1998) on extortion, and Anderson and Marcouiller (2005) on piracy. Ratio and logistic CSFs have been used to construct alternatives to the ethnolinguistic fractionalization index in empirical studies (Montalvo and Reynal-Querol 2005, Cederman and Girardin 2007). For general theoretical formulations of the CSF, see Dixit (1987), Skaperdas (1992), and Neary (1997). For an intuitive and graphical review of ratio and logistic CSFs, see Hirshleifer (1995). Skaperdas (1996) derives general and specific CSFs from easily interpretable axioms. A valuable review of theoretical properties of CSFs is provided by Garfinkel and Skaperdas (2007).

While previous chapters of this book emphasized the use of economic principles and variables in understanding conflict, this chapter added the theme that appropriation stands coequal with production and trade as a fundamental category of economic activity. This relatively new branch of conflict economics grows out of the seminal work of Bush (1972), Brito and Intriligator (1985), Hirshleifer (1988, 1991), Usher (1989), Garfinkel (1990), Skaperdas (1992), and Grossman and Kim (1995), who developed models of appropriation and production. Experimental tests of models with production and appropriation include Durham, Hirshleifer, and Smith (1998), Carter and Anderton (2001), and Duffy and Kim (2005). More recent work has introduced appropriation into models of exchange. See, for example, Anderton et al. (1999), Rider (1999, 2002), Skaperdas and Syropoulos (2002), Hausken (2004), Anderson and Marcouiller (2005), Garfinkel and Skaperdas (2007, pp. 682–690), and Anderton and Carter (2008b).

The results of conflict models are often surprising based on intuitions that tend to ignore appropriation possibilities. For example, in Hirshleifer's (1991) paradox of power model, agents with equal output productivities but unequal resource holdings can end up with an equal share of disputed output. Skaperdas (1992) and Skaperdas and Syropoulos (1997) find that the more productive player in a conflict model can receive a smaller share of disputed output, even when the players have equal resource endowments. In a model of trade and appropriation, Anderton (2003) finds that increases in the productivity of each player in its area of comparative advantage can cause aggregate output to fall.

APPENDIX A

Statistical Methods

Statistical analysis involves populations, samples, luck of the draw, and systematic inferences. This appendix provides an informal and somewhat intuitive introduction to the basic statistical methods used in conflict economics.

A.1. Populations and Samples

A population is just a collection of relevant objects. A simple example might be the citizens of a country. Associated with the citizens are variables that measure attributes like income, age, gender, political opinion, and so on. Thus, populations can be thought of as collections of values of various variables of interest. Summary measures of these population values are called parameters. Suppose the variable of interest is income. Then the parameters might include the mean μ and the standard deviation σ of income. The mean is just the arithmetic average of the citizens' incomes. The standard deviation measures dispersion and indicates how far the income values typically lie above or below the mean. Alternatively, suppose the variable of interest is citizens' political opinion. Then a key parameter might be the proportion π of citizens who oppose the current regime.

While the full population is of ultimate interest, researchers usually work with a subset of the population called a sample. To the extent that the sample is representative, it provides useful information about the larger population. Corresponding to population parameters are sample statistics. Just as parameters summarize the values in the population, statistics summarize the values in a sample. Thus, corresponding to the population mean μ, population standard deviation σ, and population proportion π are the sample mean $\bar{X}$, sample standard deviation S, and sample proportion *P*. From the observed sample statistics, researchers attempt to make reliable inferences about the unobserved population parameters. These inferences are based on the laws of probability, which provide the bridge between sample statistics and population parameters.

A.2. Probability and Sampling

Samples are subject to the luck of the draw, even when they are drawn carefully and expertly. Most samples will be broadly representative of the larger population from which they are drawn. But some samples will be misleading, and this is where the laws of probability play a role.

To continue the earlier example, suppose an investigator is interested in the proportion π of citizens who oppose the current regime. The investigator cannot afford to survey the full population of citizens, so she decides instead to take a random sample. For each person sampled, she asks, "Do you oppose the present regime?" and the answer comes back either Yes (denoted Y) or No (denoted N). Based on the proportion of citizens *P* in the sample who answer Yes, the investigator will make an inference about the population proportion π.

Assume that unknown to the investigator, the proportion is in fact 50 percent, so $\pi = 0.50$. To keep the example simple, assume further that the investigator plans to sample just four citizens. What samples might she happen to draw? One possible sample is NNNN, which means that each of the four citizens drawn answers in turn No. Because on each successive draw, a Yes and a No are equally likely (with $\pi = 0.50$), the probability of observing the sample NNNN is $(0.5)(0.5)(0.5)(0.5) = 0.0625$. Another possible sample is NNNY, meaning that the first three citizens answer No but the fourth answers Yes. By the same reasoning, the probability of this sample is also 0.0625. Indeed, because citizens' opinions are equally split, every sample consisting of a distinct arrangement of Y's and N's is equally likely with a probability of 0.0625.

In Table A.1, we list the arrangements and find that there are 16 possible samples in total. For each of these samples, we take note of the proportion *P* of citizens who answer Yes. For example, in the sample NNNN, no one answers Yes, so $P = 0.00$. There is only one such sample, and it has a probability of 0.0625. Thus, the probability of drawing a sample with $P = 0.00$ is 0.0625. In four samples (NNNY, NNYN, NYNN, and YNNN), exactly one person out of four answers Yes, so in these samples $P = 0.25$. Because there are four such samples, each with a probability of 0.0625, the probability of drawing a sample with $P = 0.25$ is $4(0.0625) = 0.25$. By

Table A.1. *Possible samples and the corresponding proportions answering Yes.*

Possible Samples	Proportion Yes	Possible Samples	Proportion Yes
NNNN	0.00	YNNN	0.25
NNNY	0.25	YNNY	0.50
NNYN	0.25	YNYN	0.50
NNYY	0.50	YNYY	0.75
NYNN	0.25	YYNN	0.50
NYNY	0.50	YYNY	0.75
NYYN	0.50	YYYN	0.75
NYYY	0.75	YYYY	1.00

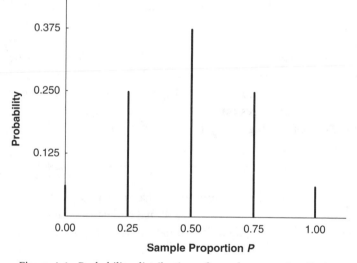

Figure A.1. Probability distribution of sample proportion P when $\pi = 0.50$ and sample size is four.

similar logic, we can also determine that the probabilities of drawing samples with $P = 0.50$, 0.75, and 1.00 are respectively 0.375, 0.25, and 0.0625. These computations generate the probability distribution of the sample proportion P, which is depicted in Figure A.1 and formalizes what we casually call the luck of the draw.

A.3. Expected Values and Unbiased Estimators

In conducting her research, the investigator would actually take only one sample. But for the moment, suppose instead that she were to draw many such samples. Given the full population of citizens with a proportion opposed $\pi = 0.50$, some samples would have comparatively few opposed ($P = 0.00$ or 0.25), some would be perfectly representative ($P = 0.50$), and some would have comparatively many opposed ($P = 0.75$ or 1.00). On average, by the luck of the draw, what proportion P would be expected? Thinking of probabilities as long-run relative frequencies, the probability distribution in Figure A.1 indicates that 6.25 percent of the samples would have $P = 0.00$, 25 percent would have $P = 0.25$, 37.5 percent would have $P = 0.50$, 25 percent would have $P = 0.75$, and 6.25 percent would have $P = 1.00$. Thus, the weighted average of P, called the expected value $E(P)$, can be computed by using the appropriate probabilities as weights such that $E(P) = 0.0625(0.00) + 0.25 (0.25) + 0.375(0.50) + 0.25(0.75) + 0.0625(1.00) = 0.50$. This says that if many samples were taken, then on average the sample proportion P would equal 0.50.

Notice that $E(P) = \pi$. As can be proven more generally, this is no coincidence. By the luck of the draw, the sample proportion P will be sometimes too low and sometimes too high, but on average it will equal the true population proportion π. Because there is no systematic tendency to either underestimate or overestimate, the statistic P is called an unbiased estimator of the corresponding population parameter π.

A.4. Statistical Inference

Continuing the example, suppose the investigator will take just one sample, and based on its proportion P, she will make a reasoned judgment about the true proportion π for the full population. In particular, suppose she will test the null hypothesis H_0 that $\pi = 0.50$ versus the one-sided alternative H_1 that $\pi > 0.50$. As careful as she might be, the conclusion of her test will nonetheless be subject to possible error. For example, even if the null hypothesis is true with $\pi = 0.50$, she could by chance get a sample with a high proportion of citizens opposed and on that basis incorrectly reject the null hypothesis. This means that, because sampling involves luck of the draw, she cannot avoid the risk of mistakenly rejecting the null hypothesis. She can, however, control the risk by appropriately choosing the standard of evidence that she will require. To see how this might work, consider two scenarios. In both scenarios we ask whether a sample proportion of $P = 0.75$ is sufficiently high for the investigator to reject H_0 in favor of H_1.

In the first scenario, assume the investigator is willing to run a risk as high as 40 percent for incorrectly rejecting H_0 and concluding in favor of H_1. In the language of statistical inference, this is equivalent to her choosing a significance level of 0.40 for the test. At this significance level, would she be willing to reject the null hypothesis on the basis of a sample proportion of $P = 0.75$? From Figure A.1, we know that if in truth $\pi = 0.50$, then there is a $25 + 6.25 = 31.25$ percent probability of getting a sample proportion as high (or higher) than 0.75, just by the luck of the draw. This probability of 31.25 percent is called the p-value for an observed sample proportion of 0.75; it measures the risk of incorrectly rejecting H_0 on the basis of a sample proportion of 0.75 or higher. Notice that the p-value of 31.25 percent (the risk of incorrectly rejecting H_0) is less than the investigator's chosen significance level of 40 percent (the amount of risk she is willing to bear). Thus, in this scenario, if the investigator were to draw a sample with $P = 0.75$, she would declare the result to be statistically significant, meaning that the evidence was sufficiently strong for her to reject H_0 in favor of the alternative H_1.

The significance level of 0.40, however, is exceedingly generous by common standards of scientific research, so consider a second scenario in which the test is more stringent. Assume instead that the investigator is willing to run a risk no higher that 10 percent for incorrectly rejecting H_0, such that the significance level is lowered to 0.10. The question again is whether a sample proportion of 0.75 would be sufficiently high for her to reject the null hypothesis. If in truth $\pi = 0.50$, the p-value is the same as earlier: the probability of incorrectly rejecting H_0 on the basis of a sample proportion of 0.75 or higher is 31.25 percent. But in this scenario, she is only willing to run a risk as high as 10 percent. Thus, if she were to draw a sample with $P = 0.75$, she would not consider the evidence to be sufficiently strong, and she would not reject H_0. In this scenario, how strong would the evidence have to be in order for her to conclude against the null hypothesis? Having chosen a significance level of 0.10, she would require a sample proportion of $P = 1.00$, which has a p-value of 0.0625, before she would be confident enough to reject H_0.

In summary, because sampling involves luck of the draw, statistical inference is necessarily subject to error. How strong the evidence must be before the null hypothesis can be rejected depends on how much risk of error the decision maker is willing to bear. Because errors can have costly consequences, in most scientific research the risk of falsely rejecting a null hypothesis is kept low by adopting a level of significance of 0.10, 0.05, or even 0.01.

A.5. Regression Analysis

Social scientists understand the world in terms of a complex web of relationships. These relationships are formalized by assuming that certain dependent variables of interest are functions of one or more independent variables. The primary method of estimating and testing these postulated relationships is called regression analysis. As in statistical analysis more generally, regression analysis is about populations, samples, and luck of the draw. We illustrate the method of regression analysis with a simple example.

Suppose for a population of countries we are interested in the relationship between democracy and military spending. In particular, suppose we want to test the conjecture that more democratic nations on average spend less on military activities. For our limited purposes here, we postulate two linear regression models:

$$E(\text{Military Spending}) = \beta_1 + \beta_2 \text{Democracy} \tag{A.1}$$

and

$$E(\text{Military Spending}) = \beta_1 + \beta_2 \text{Democracy} + \beta_3 \text{Income}. \tag{A.2}$$

Equation (A.1) is called a simple regression because it specifies expected military spending as a function of a single explanatory variable, here democracy. Equation (A.2) is an example of multiple regression because it includes two or more explanatory variables, here democracy and income. In this case income is used as a control variable that, as will be explained, allows for a better estimate of the effect of democracy, the variable of primary interest.

We estimate the two spending equations based on 2003 data for a sample of 40 European countries. Military spending and income are measured in millions of 2003 US dollars and are derived from the Stockholm International Peace Research Institute (2005). Democracy is measured by an index ranging from -10 (strongly autocratic) to $+10$ (strongly democratic) and is taken from Marshall and Jaggers (2007). The equations are estimated by a regression technique called ordinary least squares (OLS). In brief, OLS fits a line through the data by choosing estimates of β_1, β_2, and (in equation (A.2)) β_3 so as to minimize the sum of the squared differences between the actual and the estimated expenditures of the sample countries.

Table A.2. *Regression results for military spending as a function of democracy and income.*

	(A.1)	(A.2)
Intercept	1481.05	813.61
	(1456.30)	(709.91)
	[1.02]	[1.15]
Democracy	611.83	−83.90
	(253.10)	(86.73)
	[2.42]	[−0.97]
Income		0.02
		(0.00)
		[5.61]
No. of observations	40	40

Notes: See text for variable definitions and sources. Robust standard errors are shown in parentheses, while *t*-statistics are in brackets.

The regression results are shown in Table A.2. Consider first the substantial difference between the estimated values for β_2 in equations (A.1) and (A.2). In the first equation, the coefficient on democracy is 611.8, meaning that an increase of one point in a country's democracy index is estimated to *increase* that country's military spending by approximately 612 million dollars. In the second equation, however, the same coefficient is −83.9, meaning that a one-point increase in democracy is estimated to *decrease* spending by about 84 million dollars. The contrast between the two estimates illustrates the critical importance of including relevant control variables that might be correlated with the primary variable of interest. In the particular case here, more democratic countries tend to be more developed with higher levels of income, and countries with higher incomes tend to spend more on the military. When income is omitted from equation (A.1), its positive effect on spending is inadvertently picked up by the estimated coefficient for democracy. As a consequence, the OLS estimator for β_2 is biased upward if income is omitted.

Focus now on the more appropriately specified equation (A.2). Recall that the conjecture being tested is that more democratic countries on average will spend less on the military, holding constant other relevant factors like income. Formally, the null hypothesis is that democracy has no effect (H_0: $\beta_2 = 0$), which is tested against the one-sided alternative that the effect is negative (H_1: $\beta_2 < 0$). As already noted for equation (A.2), the estimated marginal effect of democracy is −83.9, thus suggesting that the conjecture is correct. But is the evidence sufficiently strong to reject the null hypothesis H_0 in favor of the conjecture H_1? In our earlier example of statistical inference dealing with public opinion, the strength of the evidence was gauged by the probability distribution of the sample statistic P. In regression analysis, the relevant statistic is known as the t-statistic, whose probability distribution is widely available in spreadsheet programs and statistical software.

The t-statistic is typically computed as the ratio of the estimated coefficient and its standard deviation, where the latter is commonly known as the standard error. For the democracy variable in equation (A.2), the estimated coefficient of -83.9 divided by its standard error of 86.7 (shown in parentheses) yields a t-statistic of -0.97 (shown in brackets). Suppose we choose for our standard of evidence a significance level of 0.05. Using the probability distribution of the t-statistic, it can be shown that the p-value associated with the observed statistic of -0.97 is approximately 0.17. Because the risk of incorrectly rejecting H_0 (equal to 17 percent) exceeds the risk we are willing to bear (equal to 5 percent), we cannot reject the null hypothesis. Thus, while the regression result in equation (A.2) is suggestive of a negative relationship between democracy and military spending, the evidence is not sufficiently strong to permit us with confidence to conclude in favor of the conjecture. Turning to the income variable, however, the t-statistic of 5.61 is quite large and yields a p-value of 0.00. As anticipated, therefore, income is shown to have a statistically significant positive effect on military spending.

A More Formal Bargaining Model of Conflict

In this appendix we present a linear mathematical version of Hirshleifer's bargaining model of conflict introduced in Chapter 5. We derive a peaceful settlement equilibrium and then show how fighting can emerge as the predicted outcome based on inconsistent expectations, pre-emption, or preventive war. Throughout the appendix we assume that each player is risk neutral and that an interior solution holds.

B.1. Basic Model of Resource Conflict

We begin with the resource conflict model of Chapter 12, which is a variation of a model due originally to Skaperdas (2006). Assume players A and B have respective holdings of secure and undisputed resources R_A and R_B, but they dispute control of a fixed resource $\tilde{R}$. The players divert M_A and M_B units of their respective secure resources to produce military goods, which in turn can be used to fight over the disputed resource. Each diverted unit generates one unit of military goods, and fighting destroys a fixed proportion δ of the disputed resource, where $0 < \delta < 1$.

Net Resource Functions under Fighting

Let p_A be A's conflict success in the resource dispute, with p_B the same for B. We assume conflict success is measured by the proportion of the disputed resource controlled by a player, although it could be interpreted as the probability that a player controls the entire resource in a winner-take-all contest. The technology relating the military inputs M_A and M_B and the conflict success proportions p_A and p_B is summarized by a ratio form conflict success function

$$p_A = \frac{M_A}{M_A + ZM_B} \quad \text{and} \quad p_B = \frac{ZM_B}{M_A + ZM_B}, \tag{B.1}$$

where the parameter $Z > 0$ represents the relative effectiveness of B's military goods. The net resources controlled by the players if fighting occurs, denoted as fighting net resources FNR_A and FNR_B, will be

$$FNR_A = R_A + \left(\frac{M_A}{M_A + ZM_B}\right)\tilde{R}(1 - \delta) - M_A \tag{B.2a}$$

$$FNR_B = R_B + \left(\frac{ZM_B}{M_A + ZM_B}\right)\tilde{R}(1 - \delta) - M_B. \tag{B.2b}$$

Reaction Functions and Fighting Equilibrium

Assume that players choose their respective military goods so as to maximize their net resource holdings under fighting, with their rival's military goods held fixed. For $i = A,B$ in equation (B.2), set the derivative of FNR_i with respect to M_i to zero and solve for M_i. This results in the following reaction functions for A and B:

$$M_A = \sqrt{ZM_B\tilde{R}(1 - \delta)} - ZM_B \tag{B.3a}$$

$$M_B = \frac{1}{Z}\left(\sqrt{ZM_A\tilde{R}(1 - \delta)} - M_A\right). \tag{B.3b}$$

Solving the two reaction functions simultaneously yields the equilibrium military goods M_A^* and M_B^*, where

$$M_A^* = M_B^* = \frac{Z\tilde{R}(1 - \delta)}{(1 + Z)^2}. \tag{B.4}$$

Substituting M_A^* and M_B^* into equations (B.2a) and (B.2b) gives the equilibrium fighting net resources FNR_A^* and FNR_B^*, where

$$FNR_A^* = R_A + \frac{\tilde{R}(1 - \delta)}{(1 + Z)^2} \tag{B.5a}$$

$$FNR_B^* = R_B + \frac{Z^2\tilde{R}(1 - \delta)}{(1 + Z)^2}. \tag{B.5b}$$

Net Resource Functions under Settlement

Given the destructiveness of conflict, both players can potentially gain from nonviolent settlement of the dispute. Let s_A be the proportion of the disputed resource received by A in the settlement, with s_B the same for B. Under settlement, assume that the players divide the disputed resource according to a split-the-surplus division rule (see Garfinkel and Skaperdas 2007, p. 674). According to this rule, the surplus from peaceful settlement $\delta \tilde{R}$ is split evenly, while the remaining disputed resource $(1 - \delta)\tilde{R}$ is divided according to the players' military goods and the ratio conflict success function in (B.1). This leads to the following peaceful settlement proportions:

$$s_A = \delta\left(\tfrac{1}{2}\right) + (1 - \delta)\left(\frac{M_A}{M_A + ZM_B}\right)$$

$$\text{and} \quad s_B = \delta\left(\tfrac{1}{2}\right) + (1 - \delta)\left(\frac{ZM_B}{M_A + ZM_B}\right). \tag{B.6}$$

The net resources under settlement, denoted as settlement net resources SNR_A and SNR_B, are then

$$SNR_A = R_A + \left[\delta\left(\tfrac{1}{2}\right) + (1 - \delta)\left(\frac{M_A}{M_A + ZM_B}\right)\right]\tilde{R} - M_A \tag{B.7a}$$

$$SNR_B = R_B + \left[\delta\left(\tfrac{1}{2}\right) + (1 - \delta)\left(\frac{ZM_B}{M_A + ZM_B}\right)\right]\tilde{R} - M_B. \tag{B.7b}$$

Reaction Functions and Settlement Equilibrium

Assume that the players choose their respective military goods so as to maximize their net resource holdings under settlement, with their rival's military goods held fixed. Since their net resource functions under settlement in (B.7) differ from their respective net resource functions under fighting in (B.2) by a fixed amount $\delta\left(\tfrac{1}{2}\right)\tilde{R}$, the same reaction functions and equilibrium military goods shown in (B.3) and (B.4) obtain here. Substituting M_A^* and M_B^* from (B.4) into equations (B.7a) and (B.7b) yields the equilibrium settlement net resources SNR_A^* and SNR_B^*, where

$$SNR_A^* = R_A + \frac{\tilde{R}(1 - \delta)}{(1 + Z)^2} + \delta\left(\tfrac{1}{2}\right)\tilde{R} \tag{B.8a}$$

$$SNR_B^* = R_B + \frac{Z^2 \tilde{R}(1-\delta)}{(1+Z)^2} + \delta\left(\tfrac{1}{2}\right)\tilde{R}. \tag{B.8b}$$

Since settlement avoids the destructiveness of war, net resources under settlement in (B.8) are greater than net resources under fighting in (B.5) for each player by the amount $\delta\left(\tfrac{1}{2}\right)\tilde{R}$. Hence, peaceful settlement is the predicted outcome of the resource conflict model.

B.2. Selected Sources of Violence

Inconsistent Expectations

As shown in Chapter 5, there are a number of reasons why violence might occur even though violence is destructive. One possibility is that the rivals have inconsistent expectations about how well they would do in a fight. For example, player A might have private information about the tactical potential of its military stock that would give an advantage to A during war. We assume that if A revealed this information to B prior to war, the advantage would disappear or the information would be deemed not credible by B. Let e represent A's advantage, which is perceived by A but not by B. For simplicity we introduce e as an additive exogenous term in player A's conflict success function, and we assume that e is not so large that A would perceive the proportion of conflict success to be greater than one. This leads to the following perceptions of conflict success under fighting:

$$p_A = \frac{M_A}{M_A + ZM_B} + e \quad \text{and} \quad p_B = \frac{ZM_B}{M_A + ZM_B}. \tag{B.9}$$

The net resource function of A under fighting will now be

$$FNR_A = R_A + \left(\frac{M_A}{M_A + ZM_B} + e\right)\tilde{R}(1-\delta) - M_A, \tag{B.10}$$

while B's perceived net resource function will continue to be given by equation (B.2b). Comparing the net resource functions in (B.10) and (B.2a) reveals that A's additional expectation of conflict success adds a fixed amount $e\tilde{R}(1-\delta)$ to A's net resource function. Hence, the same reaction function for A shown in (B.3a) and equilibrium military goods shown in (B.4) again hold. It follows that the equilibrium fighting net resources for A are

$$FNR_A^* = R_A + \frac{\tilde{R}(1-\delta)}{(1+Z)^2} + e\tilde{R}(1-\delta), \tag{B.11}$$

while *B*'s anticipated equilibrium fighting net resources continue to be given by equation (B.5b).

If instead of fighting the players peacefully settle under the split-the-surplus division rule shown in (B.6), the equilibrium net resources under settlement are given by (B.8). Inspection of (B.8a) and (B.11) shows that player *A* strictly prefers peaceful settlement to fighting when $\delta(\frac{1}{2})\tilde{R}>e\tilde{R}(1-\delta)$. Hence, the following relationship arises between the destructiveness of conflict δ and the degree of *A*'s additional conflict success *e*:

$$\delta \begin{matrix} > \\ < \end{matrix} \frac{e}{\frac{1}{2}+e} \qquad \begin{matrix} \Rightarrow \textit{settlement} \\ \Rightarrow \textit{war} \end{matrix} . \tag{B.12}$$

Condition (B.12) implies that for a given degree of additional conflict success *e*, a sufficiently high degree of conflict destructiveness δ will lead to peaceful settlement rather than to fighting. Alternatively, for a given degree of conflict destructiveness, a sufficiently high degree of additional conflict success will lead to fighting rather than to settlement.

Preemption

Preemptive war can arise from the existence of a first-strike advantage. Assume that players *A* and *B* have complete information and thus correctly anticipate the offensive advantage. Assume also that one of the players strikes first if fighting occurs. For simplicity we introduce a first-strike advantage into the model by adding an exogenous term *e* to the first-mover's conflict success function while subtracting the same value *e* from the second-mover's conflict success function. We assume that *e* is not so large that the proportion of conflict success under a first strike would be greater than one.

If player *A* strikes first, the following conflict success proportions apply under fighting:

$$p_A = \frac{M_A}{M_A + ZM_B} + e \quad \text{and} \quad p_B = \frac{ZM_B}{M_A + ZM_B} - e. \tag{B.13}$$

Alternatively, if *B* strikes first, the algebraic signs on *e* are reversed in (B.13). The net resource functions for *A* and *B* under fighting when *A* strikes first are

$$FNR_A = R_A + \left(\frac{M_A}{M_A + ZM_B} + e\right)\tilde{R}(1-\delta) - M_A \tag{B.14a}$$

$$FNR_B = R_B + \left(\frac{ZM_B}{M_A + ZM_B} - e\right)\tilde{R}(1-\delta) - M_B. \qquad \text{(B.14b)}$$

Alternatively, when B strikes first, the algebraic signs on e are reversed in equations (B.14a) and (B.14b). In either case, since a first-strike advantage adds or subtracts a fixed amount $e\tilde{R}(1-\delta)$ to a player's net resource function, the same reaction functions and equilibrium military goods shown in equations (B.3) and (B.4) obtain. It follows that the equilibrium net resources after A initiates an attack are

$$FNR_A^* = R_A + \frac{\tilde{R}(1-\delta)}{(1+Z)^2} + e\tilde{R}(1-\delta) \qquad \text{(B.15a)}$$

$$FNR_B^* = R_B + \frac{Z^2\tilde{R}(1-\delta)}{(1+Z)^2} - e\tilde{R}(1-\delta). \qquad \text{(B.15b)}$$

Alternatively, if B initiates an attack, the algebraic signs on e are reversed in equations (B.15a) and (B.15b).

When considering a first strike, players compare their net resources under settlement in equation (B.8) with their net resources if they attack first. Each player prefers peaceful settlement to fighting when $\delta\left(\frac{1}{2}\right)\tilde{R} > e\tilde{R}(1-\delta)$. Hence, the relationship between δ and e set forth in condition (B.12) holds here, with the proviso that e now represents the presence of a common first-strike advantage available to the first-mover rather than A's additional conflict success. Applying condition (B.12) to preemption implies that for a given degree of first-strike advantage e, a sufficiently high degree of conflict destructiveness δ will lead to peaceful settlement rather than to fighting. Alternatively, for a given degree of conflict destructiveness, a sufficiently high degree of first-strike advantage will lead to fighting rather than to settlement.

Preventive War

Assume that the players have complete information and no first-strike advantage exists. Suppose the model now consists of two periods and that constant flows of secure resources R_A and R_B and the disputed resource $\tilde{R}$ occur in each period. We assume for simplicity that military goods must be renewed completely each period and that there is zero discounting. In period 2, the players choose levels of arms that result in fighting or split-the-surplus settlement. Since fighting is destructive, both players prefer peaceful settlement to fighting in period 2. In period 1, suppose both players know that a potential change in military technology exists that, if realized, would shift power in favor of player B in period 2. Assume that the shift in power can be prevented by fighting in period 1 but not by settlement. If the potential shift in power is sufficiently large, then player A has an incentive to initiate a preventive war in period 1. To model the incentive, we represent a shift in power in favor of B (if it occurs) by a greater relative military effectiveness parameter in period 2, Z_2, than in period 1, Z_1. Because the power shift would favor player B, in both periods B prefers split-the-surplus settlement to fighting. Hence, whether fighting or settlement occurs in period 1 depends critically on player A.

Suppose that a split-the-surplus settlement occurs in period 1, so that power shifts in B's favor and a new split-the-surplus settlement occurs in period 2. In this case, the total net resources controlled by player A with settlement in both periods, denoted SNR_A^*, will be

$$SNR_A^* = \left[R_A + \frac{\tilde{R}(1-\delta)}{(1+Z_1)^2} + \delta\left(\tfrac{1}{2}\right)\tilde{R} \right] + \left[R_A + \frac{\tilde{R}(1-\delta)}{(1+Z_2)^2} + \delta\left(\tfrac{1}{2}\right)\tilde{R} \right]. \tag{B.16}$$

In equation (B.16), the two bracketed terms show the net resources controlled by A under settlement in periods 1 and 2, respectively.

Suppose instead of settling in both periods, player A initiates fighting in period 1 to prevent the power shift in favor of B in period 2. In this case, the total net resources controlled by player A with fighting in period 1 and settlement in period 2, denoted FNR_A^*, will be

$$FNR_A^* = \left[R_A + \frac{\tilde{R}(1-\delta)}{(1+Z_1)^2} \right] + \left[R_A + \frac{\tilde{R}(1-\delta)}{(1+Z_1)^2} + \delta\left(\tfrac{1}{2}\right)\tilde{R} \right]. \tag{B.17}$$

In equation (B.17), the first bracketed term shows the net resources controlled by A in period 1 under fighting, while the second shows the same in period 2 under settlement. Notice that fighting in period 1 means that B's relative military effectiveness does not change between periods 1 and 2.

Inspection of equations (B.17) and (B.16) shows that player A prefers preventive war rather than settlement when the first bracketed term in (B.17) is greater than the second bracketed term in (B.16), which occurs when $(1-\delta)/(1+Z_1)^2 > [(1-\delta)/(1+Z_2)^2] + 0.5\delta$. This implies the following relationship between the destructiveness of conflict δ and the relative effectiveness of B's military goods in periods 1 and 2, Z_1 and Z_2:

$$\delta \begin{array}{c} > \\ < \end{array} \frac{(1+Z_2)^2-(1+Z_1)^2}{(1+Z_2)^2-(1+Z_1)^2+0.5(1+Z_2)^2(1+Z_1)^2} \begin{array}{c} \Rightarrow settlement \\ \Rightarrow war. \end{array} \quad (\text{B}.18)$$

Note that the right side of the condition (B.18) is positive because $Z_2 > Z_1$. Treating the condition as an equality, it can be shown also that the derivative of δ with respect to Z_2 is positive. Hence, it follows that for given relative military effectiveness parameters Z_1 and Z_2, a sufficiently high degree of conflict destructiveness δ will lead to peaceful settlement rather than to preventive war. Alternatively, for a given degree of conflict destructiveness and relative military effectiveness in period 1, anticipation of a sufficiently high relative military effectiveness parameter in period 2 will lead to preventive war rather than to settlement.

References

ABC News (2005), "Will Aid Effort After Asia Quake Help U.S. Image?" http://abcnewsgo.com (downloaded 11/9/05).

ACDA (various years), *World Military Expenditures and Arms Transfers* (Washington, DC: U.S. Arms Control and Disarmament Agency).

Adams, Eldridge S. and Michael Mesterton-Gibbons (2003), "Lanchester's Attrition Models and Fights among Social Animals," *Behavioral Ecology*, 14(5), 719–723.

Adams, Karen R. (2003/04), "Attack and Conquer? International Anarchy and the Offense-Defense-Deterrence Balance," *International Security*, 28(3), 45–83.

Addison, Tony and S. Mansoob Murshed (eds.) (2003), "Special Issue: Explaining Violent Conflict: Going beyond Greed versus Grievance," *Journal of International Development*, 14(4), 391–524.

Alesina, Alberto and Enrico Spolaore (1997), "On the Number and Size of Nations," *The Quarterly Journal of Economics*, 112(4), 1027–1056.

(2003), *The Size of Nations* (Cambridge, MA: The MIT Press).

(2006), "Conflict, Defense Spending, and the Number of Nations," *European Economic Review*, 50(1), 91–120.

Alesina, Alberto, Enrico Spolaore, and Romain Wacziarg (2000), "Economic Integration and Political Disintegration," *American Economic Review*, 90(5), 1276–1296.

Allison, Graham (2004), *Nuclear Terrorism: The Ultimate Preventable Catastrophe* (New York: Times Books).

Amegashie, J. Atsu and Edward Kutsoati (2007), "(Non)intervention in Intra-state Conflicts," *European Journal of Political Economy*, 23(3), 754–767.

Ancker, C. J. Jr. (1995), "A Proposed Foundation for a Theory of Combat," in Jerome Bracken, Moshe Kress, and Richard E. Rosenthal (eds.), *Warfare Modeling* (Alexandria, VA: Military Operations Research Society), 165–197.

Anderson, James E. and Douglas Marcouiller (2005), "Anarchy and Autarky: Endogenous Predation as a Barrier to Trade," *International Economic Review*, 46(1), 189–213.

Anderton, Charles H. (1990), "Teaching Arms-Race Concepts in Intermediate Microeconomics," *Journal of Economic Education*, 21(2), 148–166.

(1992a), "A New Look at the Relationship among Arms Races, Disarmament, and the Probability of War," in Manas Chatterji and Linda R. Forcey (eds.), *Disarmament, Economic Conversion, and Management of Peace* (New York: Praeger), 75–87.

(1992b), "Toward a Mathematical Theory of the Offensive/Defensive Balance," *International Studies Quarterly*, 36(1), 75–100.

(2003), "Conflict and Trade in a Predator/Prey Economy," *Review of Development Economics*, 7(1), 15–29.

Anderton, Charles H. and John R. Carter (2003), "Does War Disrupt Trade?" in Gerald Schneider, Katherine Barbieri, and Nils Petter Gleditsch (eds.), *Globalization and Armed Conflict* (Boulder, CO: Rowman & Littlefield), 299–310.

(2005), "On Rational Choice Theory and the Study of Terrorism," *Defence and Peace Economics*, 16(4), 275–282.

(2006), "Applying Intermediate Microeconomics to Terrorism," *Journal of Economic Education*, 37(4), 442–458.

(2007), "A Survey of Peace Economics," in Todd Sandler and Keith Hartley (eds.), *Handbook of Defense Economics*, vol. 2 (New York: Elsevier), 1211–1258.

(2008a), "Arms Trade," in Steven Durlauf and Lawrence Blume (eds.), *The New Palgrave Dictionary of Economics*, 2nd ed. (New York: Palgrave Macmillan). The New Palgrave Dictionary of Economics Online, Palgrave Macmillan, 23 June 2008 (www.dictionaryofeconomics.com).

(2008b), "Vulnerable Trade: The Dark Side of an Edgeworth Box," *Journal of Economic Behavior & Organization*, 68(2), 422–432.

Anderton, Charles H., Roxane A. Anderton, and John R. Carter (1999), "Economic Activity in the Shadow of Conflict," *Economic Inquiry*, 37(1), 166–179.

Arce, Daniel G. and Todd Sandler (2003), "An Evolutionary Game Approach to Fundamentalism and Conflict," *Journal of Institutional and Theoretical Economics*, 159(1), 132–154.

(2005), "Counterterrorism: A Game-Theoretic Analysis," *Journal of Conflict Resolution*, 49(2), 183–200.

Aslam, Rabia (2007), "Measuring the Peace Dividend: Evidence from Developing Economies," *Defence and Peace Economics*, 18(1), 39–52.

Axelrod, Robert (1984), *The Evolution of Cooperation* (New York: Basic Books).

Ballentine, Karen and Jake Sherman (2003a), "Introduction," in Karen Ballentine and Jake Sherman (eds.), *The Political Economy of Armed Conflict* (Boulder, CO: Lynne Rienner), 1–15.

Ballentine, Karen and Jake Sherman (eds.) (2003b), *The Political Economy of Armed Conflict* (Boulder, CO: Lynne Rienner).

Banks, H. Thomas and Carlos Castillo-Chavez (eds.) (2003), *Bioterrorism: Mathematical Modeling Applications in Homeland Security*, SIAM Series Frontiers in Applied Mathematics, vol. 28 (Philadelphia: Society for Industrial and Applied Mathematics).

Barbieri, Katherine and Rafael Reuveny (2005), "Economic Globalization and Civil War," *The Journal of Politics*, 67(4), 1228–1247.

Bartrop, Paul (2002), "The Relationship between War and Genocide in the Twentieth Century: A Consideration," *Journal of Genocide Research*, 4(4), 519–532.

Bearce, David H. and Sawa Omori (2005), "How Do Commercial Institutions Promote Peace?" *Journal of Peace Research*, 42(6), 659–678.

Beardsley, Kyle C., David M. Quinn, Bidisha Biswas, and Jonathan Wilkenfeld (2006), "Mediation Style and Crisis Outcomes," *Journal of Conflict Resolution*, 50(1), 58–86.

Becker, Gary (1968), "Crime and Punishment: An Economic Approach," *Journal of Political Economy*, 76(2), 169–217.

(1976), *The Economic Approach to Human Behavior* (Chicago: University of Chicago Press).

Beckerman, Stephen (1991), "The Equations of War," *Current Anthropology*, 32(5), 636–640.

Bellany, Ian (1999), "Modeling War," *Journal of Peace Research*, 36(6), 729–739.

Bennett, D. Scott (1997), "Testing Alternative Models of Alliance Duration, 1816–1984," *American Journal of Political Science*, 41(3), 846–878.

Bennett, D. Scott and Allan C. Stam III (1996), "The Duration of Interstate Wars, 1816–1985," *American Political Science Review*, 90(2), 239–257.

Benoit, Emile (1973), *Defense and Economic Growth in Developing Countries* (Boston: D.C. Heath).

Berdal, Mats and David M. Malone (eds.) (2000), *Greed and Grievance: Economic Agendas in Civil Wars* (Boulder, CO: Lynne Rienner).

Berman, Eli and David D. Laitin (2008), "Religion, Terrorism and Public Goods: Testing the Club Model," *Journal of Public Economics*, 92(10/11), 1942–1967.

Betts, Richard K. (1982), *Conventional Deterrence: Predictive Uncertainty and Policy Confidence; Compound Deterrence vs. No-First-Use: What's Wrong is What's Right*. Brookings General Series Reprint 412 (Washington, DC: Brookings Institution).

Bier, Vicki M. and Detlof Von Winterfeldt (eds.) (2007), "Special Issue on Terrorism," *Risk Analysis*, 27(3), 503–787.

Binmore, Ken (2007), *Playing for Real: A Text on Game Theory* (New York: Oxford University Press).

Binmore, Ken and Larry Samuelson (1994), "An Economist's Perspective on the Evolution of Norms," *Journal of Institutional and Theoretical Economics*, 150(1), 45–63.

Björnehed, Emma (2004), "Narco-Terrorism: The Merger of the War on Drugs and the War on Terror," *Global Crime*, 6(3&4), 305–324.

Bloch, Jean De [1899] (1903), *The Future of War* (Boston: Ginn).

Blomberg, S. Brock, Gregory D. Hess, and Athanasios Orphanides (2004), "The Macroeconomic Consequences of Terrorism," *Journal of Monetary Economics*, 51 (5), 1007–1032.

Boehmer, Charles R. and David Sobek (2005), "Violent Adolescence: State Development and the Propensity for Militarized Interstate Conflict," *Journal of Peace Research*, 42(1), 5–26.

Bogart, Ernest L. (1919), *Direct and Indirect Costs of the Great World War* (New York: Oxford University Press).

Bolton, Patrick and Gerard Roland (1997), "The Breakup of Nations: A Political Economy Analysis," *The Quarterly Journal of Economics*, 112(4), 1057–1090.

Boulding, Kenneth E. (1962), *Conflict and Defense: A General Theory* (New York: Harper).

Braithwaite, Alex (2006), "The Geographic Spread of Militarized Disputes," *Journal of Peace Research*, 43(5), 507–522.

Brams, Steven J. (1985), *Superpower Games: Applying Game Theory to Superpower Conflict* (New Haven: Yale University Press).

Brams, Steven J. and Alan D. Taylor (1996), *Fair Division: From Cake-Cutting to Dispute Resolution* (New York: Cambridge University Press).

Brauer, Jurgen (2002), "Survey and Review of the Defense Economics Literature on Greece and Turkey: What Have We Learned?" *Defence and Peace Economics*, 13 (2), 85–107.

Brauer, Jurgen (ed.) (2003), "Special Issue: Economics of Conflict, War, and Peace in Historical Perspective," *Defence and Peace Economics*, 14(3), 151–236.

(2007), "Arms Industries, Arms Trade, and Developing Countries," in Todd Sandler and Keith Hartley (eds.), *Handbook of Defense Economics*, vol. 2 (New York: Elsevier), 973–1015.

Brauer, Jurgen and André Roux (2000), "Peace as an International Public Good: An Application to Southern Africa," *Defence and Peace Economics*, 11(6), 643–659.

Bremer, Stuart A. (2000), "Who Fights Whom, When, Where, and Why?" in John A. Vasquez (ed.), *What Do We Know About War?* (New York: Rowman & Littlefield), 23–36.

Brito, Dagobert L. (1972), "A Dynamic Model of an Armaments Race," *International Economic Review*, 13(2), 359–375.

Brito, Dagobert L. and Michael D. Intriligator (1985), "Conflict, War and Redistribution," *American Political Science Review*, 79(4), 943–957.

(1995), "Arms Races and Proliferation," in Keith Hartley and Todd Sandler (eds.), *Handbook of Defense Economics*, vol. 1 (New York: Elsevier), 109–164.

Broadberry, Stephen and Mark Harrison (eds.) (2005), *The Economics of World War I* (New York: Cambridge University Press).

Brown, Michael E., Owen R. Coté Jr., Sean M. Lynn-Jones, and Steven E. Miller (eds.) (2000), *Rational Choice and Security Studies: Stephen Walt and His Critics* (Cambridge, MA: MIT Press).

(eds.) (2004), *Offense, Defense, and War* (Cambridge, MA: The MIT Press).

Brück, Tilman (ed.) (2006), *The Economic Analysis of Terrorism* (New York: Routledge).

Brunborg, Helge and Henrik Urdal (eds.) (2005), "Special Issue on the Demography of Conflict and Violence," *Journal of Peace Research*, 42(4), 371–519.

Brzoska, Michael (1995), "World Military Expenditures," in Keith Hartley and Todd Sandler (eds.), *Handbook of Defense Economics*, vol. 1 (New York: Elsevier), 45–67.

Buchanan, James M., and Roger L. Faith (1987), "Secession and the Limits of Taxation: Towards a Theory of Internal Exit," *American Economic Review*, 77(5), 1023–1031.

Bueno de Mesquita, Bruce (1981), *The War Trap* (New Haven, CT: Yale University Press).

Buhaug, Halvard (2006), "Relative Capability and Rebel Objective in Civil War," *Journal of Peace Research*, 43(6), 691–708.

Buhaug, Halvard and Kristian Skrede Gleditsch (2008), "Contagion or Confusion? Why Conflicts Cluster in Space," *International Studies Quarterly*, 52(2), 215–233.

Bureau of Justice Statistics (2008), "Direct Expenditure by Level of Government, 1982–2005," available at http://www.ojp.usdoj.gov/bjs/glance/tables/expgovtab. htm (accessed September 24, 2008).

Bush, Winston C. (1972), "Individual Welfare in Anarchy," in Gordon Tullock (ed.), *Explorations in the Theory of Anarchy* (Blacksburg VA: Center for Study of Public Choice), 5–18.

Bush, Winston C. and Lawrence S. Mayer (1974), "Some Implications of Anarchy for the Distribution of Property," *Journal of Economic Theory*, 8(4), 401–412.

Bussmann, Margit and Gerald Schneider (2007), "When Globalization Discontent Turns Violent: Foreign Economic Liberalization and Internal War," *International Studies Quarterly*, 51(1), 79–97.

Buzan, Barry (1987), *An Introduction to Strategic Studies: Military Technology and International Relations* (London: Macmillan for International Institute for Strategic Studies).

Carter, John R. and Charles H. Anderton (2001), "An Experimental Test of a Predator-Prey Model of Appropriation," *Journal of Economic Behavior & Organization*, 45(1), 83–97.

Cauley, Jon and Todd Sandler (1988), "Fighting World War III: A Suggested Strategy," *Terrorism: An International Journal*, 11(3), 181–195.

Cavanaugh, William T. (2004), "Sins of Omission: What 'Religion and Violence' Arguments Ignore," *The Hedgehog Review*, 6(1), 34–50.

Cederman, Lars-Erik and Luc Girardin (2007), "Beyond Fractionalization: Mapping Ethnicity onto Nationalist Insurgencies," *American Political Science Review*, 101 (1), 173–185.

Center for Migration Studies (2001), "Special Issue: UNHCR at 50: Past, Present, and Future of Refugee Assistance," *International Migration Review*, 35(1), 1–384.

Central Intelligence Agency (2008), *The World Factbook 2008* (Washington, DC: Office of Public Affairs of the Central Intelligence Agency).

Cha, Victor D. and David C. Kang (2005), *Nuclear North Korea: A Debate on Engagement Strategies* (New York: Columbia University Press).

Chang, Yang-Ming, Joel Potter, and Shane Sanders (2007), "War and Peace: Third-Party Intervention in Conflict," *European Journal of Political Economy*, 23(4), 954–974.

Cirincione, Joseph, Jon Wolfsthal, and Miriam Rajkumar (2005), *Deadly Arsenals: Nuclear, Biological, and Chemical Threats*, 2nd ed. (Washington, DC: Carnegie Endowment for International Peace).

Clapham, Christopher (ed.) (1988), *African Guerrillas* (Oxford, UK: James Currey).

Colaresi, Michael P., Karen Rasler, and William R. Thompson (2007), *Strategic Rivalries in World Politics: Position, Space and Conflict Escalation* (New York: Cambridge University Press).

Collier, Paul (1999), "On the Economic Consequences of Civil War," *Oxford Economic Papers*, 51(1), 168–183.

(2000a), "Doing Well Out of War: An Economic Perspective," in Mats Berdal and David M. Malone (eds.), *Greed and Grievance: Economic Agendas in Civil Wars* (Boulder, CO: Lynne Rienner), 91–111.

(2000b), "Rebellion as a Quasi-Criminal Activity," *Journal of Conflict Resolution*, 44 (6), 839–853.

Collier, Paul and Anke Hoeffler (2004), "Greed and Grievance in Civil War," *Oxford Economic Papers*, 56(4), 563–595.

(2007a), "Civil War," in Todd Sandler and Keith Hartley (eds.), *Handbook of Defense Economics*, vol. 2 (New York: Elsevier), 711–739.

(2007b), "Unintended Consequences: Does Aid Promote Arms Races?" *Oxford Bulletin of Economics and Statistics*, 69(1), 1–27.

Collier, Paul and Nicholas Sambanis (eds.) (2002), "Special Issue: Understanding Civil War," *Journal of Conflict Resolution*, 46(1), 1–170.

Collier, Paul and Nicholas Sambanis (eds.) (2005), *Understanding Civil War: Evidence and Analysis*, vols. 1 and 2 (Washington, DC: The World Bank).

Collier, Paul, Anke Hoeffler, and Måns Söderbom (2004), "On the Duration of Civil War," *Journal of Peace Research*, 41(3), 253–273.

Collier, Paul, Lani Elliott, Håvard Hegre, Anke Hoeffler, Marta Reynal-Querol, and Nicholas Sambanis (2003), *Breaking the Conflict Trap: Civil War and Development Policy* (Washington, DC: The World Bank).

Conybeare, John A. C., James Murdoch, and Todd Sandler (1994), "Alternative Collective-Goods Models of Military Alliances: Theory and Empirics," *Economic Inquiry*, 32(4), 525–542.

Cornes, Richard and Todd Sandler (1984), "Easy Riders, Joint Production, and Public Goods," *Economic Journal*, 94(3), 580–598.

(1996), *The Theory of Externalities, Public Goods, and Club Goods*, 2nd ed. (New York: Cambridge University Press).

Coulomb, Fanny (1998), "Adam Smith: A Defence Economist," *Defence and Peace Economics*, 9(3), 299–316.

Cox, Kevin R., Murray Low, and Jennifer Robinson (eds.) (2008), *The SAGE Handbook of Political Geography* (London: Sage Publications).

Craft, Cassady B. (2000), "An Analysis of the Washington Naval Agreements and the Economic Provisions of Arms Control Theory," *Defence and Peace Economics*, 11 (2), 127–148.

Crawford, Timothy W. and Alan J. Kuperman (eds.) (2006), *Gambling on Humanitarian Intervention: Moral Hazard, Rebellion and Civil War* (New York: Routledge).

Crenshaw, Martha (2007), "Explaining Suicide Terrorism: A Review Essay," *Security Studies*, 16(1), 133–162.

Crescenzi, Mark J. C., Jacob D. Kathman, and Stephen B. Long (2007), "Reputation, History, and War," *Journal of Peace Research*, 44(6), 651–667.

Cross, John G. (1977), "Negotiation as a Learning Process," *Journal of Conflict Resolution*, 21(4), 581–606.

Cusack, Thomas, Amihai Glazer, and Kai A. Konrad (eds.) (2006), "Special Issue on Social Conflict," *Economics of Governance*, 7(1), 1–107.

Cutter, Susan L., Douglas B. Richardson, and Thomas J. Wilbanks (eds.) (2003), *The Geographical Dimensions of Terrorism* (New York: Routledge).

Dallaire, Roméo (2004), *Shake Hands with the Devil: The Failure of Humanity in Rwanda* (New York: Carroll & Graf).

Dando, Malcolm (1994), *Biological Warfare in the 21st Century* (London: Brassey's).

Davis, Jim A. and Barry R. Schneider (eds.) (2004), *The Gathering Biological Warfare Storm* (London: Praeger).

Deger, Saadet and Somnath Sen (1995), "Military Expenditure and Developing Countries," in Keith Hartley and Todd Sandler (eds.), *Handbook of Defense Economics*, vol. 1 (New York: Elsevier), 275–307.

Deininger, Klaus (2003), "Causes and Consequences of Civil Strife: Micro-level Evidence from Uganda," *Oxford Economic Papers*, 55(4), 579–606.

DeRouen, Karl R. Jr. and Jacob Bercovitch (2008), "Enduring Internal Rivalries: A New Framework for the Study of Civil War," *Journal of Peace Research*, 45(1), 55–74.

Diehl, Paul F. (1983), "Arms Races and Escalation: A Closer Look," *Journal of Peace Research*, 20(3), 205–212.

Dixit, Avinash (1987), "Strategic Behavior in Contests," *American Economic Review*, 77 (5), 891–898.

Dixit, Avinash and Barry J. Nalebuff (1991), *Thinking Strategically: The Competitive Edge in Business, Politics, and Everyday Life* (New York: W. W. Norton).

Dixit, Avinash and Susan Skeath (2004), *Games of Strategy*, 2nd ed. (New York: W.W. Norton).

Doyle, Michael W. and Nicholas Sambanis (2006), *Making War and Building Peace* (Princeton, NJ: Princeton University Press).

Duffy, John and Minseong Kim (2005), "Anarchy in the Laboratory (and the Role of the State)," *Journal of Economic Behavior & Organization*, 56(3), 297–329.

Dunne, J. Paul and Ron P. Smith (2007), "The Econometrics of Military Arms Races," in Todd Sandler and Keith Hartley (eds.), *Handbook of Defense Economics*, vol. 2 (New York: Elsevier), 913–940.

Dunne, J. Paul, Ron P. Smith, and Dirk Willenbockel (2005), "Models of Military Expenditure and Growth: A Critical Review," *Defence and Peace Economics*, 16 (6), 449–461.

Durham, Yvonne, Jack Hirshleifer, and Vernon L. Smith (1998), "Do the Rich Get Richer and the Poor Poorer? Experimental Tests of a Model of Power," *American Economic Review*, 88(4), 970–983.

East, Maurice A. and Phillip M. Gregg (1967), "Factors Influencing Cooperation and Conflict in the International System," *International Studies Quarterly*, 11(3), 244–269.

Eck, Kristine and Lisa Hultman (2007), "One-Sided Violence against Civilians in War: Insights from New Fatality Data," *Journal of Peace Research*, 44(2), 233–246.

Ehrlich, Isaac and Zhiqiang Liu (eds.) (2006), *The Economics of Crime* (Northampton, MA: Edward Elgar).

Enders, Walter (2007), "Terrorism: An Empirical Analysis," in Todd Sandler and Keith Hartley (eds.), *Handbook of Defense Economics*, vol. 2 (New York: Elsevier), 815–866.

Enders, Walter and Todd Sandler (1993), "The Effectiveness of Anti-Terrorism Policies: Vector-Autoregression-Intervention Analysis," *American Political Science Review*, 87(4), 829–844.

(1995), "Terrorism: Theory and Applications," in Keith Hartley and Todd Sandler (eds.), *Handbook of Defense Economics*, vol. 1 (New York: Elsevier), 213–249.

(2000), "Is Transnational Terrorism Becoming More Threatening? A Times Series Investigation," *Journal of Conflict Resolution*, 44(3), 307–332.

(2006a), *The Political Economy of Terrorism* (New York: Cambridge University Press).

(2006b), "Distribution of Transnational Terrorism Among Countries by Income Class and Geography after 9/11," *International Studies Quarterly*, 50(2), 367–393.

Enders, Walter, Todd Sandler, and Jon Cauley (1990), "Assessing the Impact of Terrorist-Thwarting Policies: An Intervention Time Series Approach," *Defence Economics*, 2(1), 1–18.

Engene, Jan Oskar (2006), "TWEED Code Book," www.uib.no/people/sspje/tweed.htm (downloaded 6/6/08).

Epstein, Joshua M. (1985), *The Calculus of Conventional War: Dynamic Analysis without Lanchester Theory* (Washington, DC: The Brookings Institution).

(1990), *Conventional Force Reductions: A Dynamic Assessment* (Washington, DC: The Brookings Institution).

Faria, João Ricardo and Daniel G. Arce M. (2005), "Terror Support and Recruitment," *Defence and Peace Economics*, 16(4), 263–273.

Fearon, James D. (1995), "Rationalist Explanations for War," *International Organization*, 49(3), 379–414.

(2004), "Why Do Some Civil Wars Last So Much Longer than Others?" *Journal of Peace Research*, 41(3), 275–301.

Fearon, James D. and David D. Laitin (2003), "Ethnicity, Insurgency, and Civil War," *American Political Science Review*, 97(1), 75–90.

Fein, Helen (1993), *Genocide: A Sociological Perspective* (London: Sage Publications).

Feng, Yi and Jacek Kugler (eds.) (2006), "Special Issue: Empirical Studies in International Mediation," *International Interactions*, 32(4), 319–470.

Fetter, Steve (1991), "Ballistic Missiles and Weapons of Mass Destruction: What Is the Threat? What Should Be Done?" *International Security*, 16(1), 5–42.

Filson, Darren and Suzanne Werner (2002), "A Bargaining Model of War and Peace: Anticipating the Onset, Duration, and Outcome of War," *American Journal of Political Science*, 46(4), 819–838.

Fischer, Dietrich (1984), *Preventing War in the Nuclear Age* (Totowa, NJ: Rowman & Allanheld).

Flint, Colin (ed.) (2004), *The Geography of War and Peace: From Death Camps to Diplomats* (New York: Oxford University Press).

Florida Department of Corrections (2007), "Gang and Security Threat Group Awareness," article available at www.dc.state.fl.us/pub/gangs/index.html (downloaded 11/30/07).

Fox, Jonathan (2004), "Is Ethnoreligious Conflict a Contagious Disease?" *Studies in Conflict and Terrorism*, 27(2), 89–106.

Frank, Robert H. (2008), *Microeconomics and Behavior*, 7th ed. (New York: McGraw-Hill).

Frazier, Derrick V. and William J. Dixon (2006), "Third-Party Intermediaries and Negotiated Settlements, 1946–2000," *International Interactions*, 32(4), 385–408.

Frey, Bruno S. (2004), *Dealing with Terrorism – Stick or Carrot?* (Cheltenham, UK: Edward Elgar).

Frey, Bruno S. and Simon Luechinger (2003), "How to Fight Terrorism: Alternatives to Deterrence," *Defence and Peace Economics*, 14(4), 237–249.

Gardner, Roy (2003), *Games for Business and Economics*, 2nd ed. (New York: Wiley).

Garfinkel, Michelle R. (1990), "Arming as a Strategic Investment in a Cooperative Equilibrium," *American Economic Review*, 80(1), 50–68.

Garfinkel, Michelle R. and Stergios Skaperdas (2000a), "Conflict without Misperceptions or Incomplete Information: How the Future Matters," *Journal of Conflict Resolution*, 44(6), 793–807.

(2000b), "Contract or War? On the Consequences of a Broader View of Self-Interest in Economics," *American Economist*, 44(1), 5–16.

(2007), "Economics of Conflict: An Overview," in Todd Sandler and Keith Hartley (eds.), *Handbook of Defense Economics*, vol. 2 (New York: Elsevier), 649–709.

Gartzke, Erik, Quan Li, and Charles Boehmer (2001), "Investing in the Peace: Economic Interdependence and International Conflict," *International Organization*, 55(2), 391–438.

Gates, Scott and Håvard Strand (2006), "Modeling the Duration of Civil Wars: Measurement and Estimation Issues," Working Paper.

Gaver, Donald P. and Patricia A. Jacobs (1997), "Attrition Modeling in the Presence of Decoys: An Operations-Other-Than-War Motivation," *Naval Research Logistics*, 44(5), 507–514.

Geller, Daniel S. and J. David Singer (1998), *Nations at War: A Scientific Study of International Conflict* (New York: Cambridge University Press).

Ghosn, Faten, Glenn Palmer, and Stuart Bremer (2004), "The MID3 Data Set, 1993–2001: Procedures, Coding Rules, and Description," *Conflict Management and Peace Science*, 21(2), 133–154.

Gibler, Douglas M. and Meredith Reid Sarkees (2004), "Measuring Alliances: The Correlates of War Formal Interstate Alliance Dataset, 1816–2000," *Journal of Peace Research*, 41(2), 211–222.

Gibler, Douglas M., Toby J. Rider, and Marc L. Hutchison (2005), "Taking Arms Against a Sea of Troubles: Interdependent Racing and the Likelihood of Conflict in Rival States," *Journal of Peace Research*, 42(2), 131–147.

Gibney, Mark (ed.) (2007), "Special Issue: Refugee Flight and Return," *Conflict Management and Peace Science*, 24(2), 83–157.

Gleditsch, Nils Petter, Peter Wallensteen, Mikael Eriksson, Margareta Sollenberg, and Håvard Strand (2002), "Armed Conflict, 1946–2001: A New Dataset," *Journal of Peace Research*, 39(5), 615–637.

Glick, Reuven and Alan M. Taylor (2008), "Collateral Damage: The Economic Impact of War, 1870–1997," *Review of Economics and Statistics*, forthcoming.

Gochman, Charles S. and Zeev Maoz (1990), "Militarized Interstate Disputes, 1816–1976," in J. David Singer and Paul F. Diehl (eds.), *Measuring the Correlates of War* (Ann Arbor: University of Michigan Press), 193–221.

Goddard, Stacie E. (2006), "Uncommon Ground: Indivisible Territory and the Politics of Legitimacy," *International Organization*, 60(1), 35–68.

Goldstein, Lyle J. (2006), *Preventive Attack and Weapons of Mass Destruction: A Comparative Historical Analysis* (Palo Alto, CA: Stanford University Press).

Goodwin, Craufurd D. (ed.) (1991), *Economics and National Security: A History of Their Interaction* (Durham, NC: Duke University Press).

Gortzak, Yoav, Yoram Z. Haftel, and Kevin Sweeney (2005), "Offense-Defense Theory: An Empirical Assessment," *Journal of Conflict Resolution*, 49(1), 67–89.

Gowa, Joanne and Edward D. Mansfield (2004), "Alliances, Imperfect Markets, and Major-Power Trade," *International Organization*, 58(4), 775–805.

Grossman, Herschel I. (1995), "Insurrections," in Keith Hartley and Todd Sandler (eds.), *Handbook of Defense Economics*, vol. 1 (New York: Elsevier), 191–212.

Grossman, Herschel I. and Minseong Kim (1995), "Swords or Plowshares? A Theory of the Security of Claims to Property," *Journal of Political Economy*, 103(6), 1275–1288.

Guillemin, Jeanne (2005), *Biological Weapons: From the Invention of State-Sponsored Programs to Contemporary Bioterrorism* (New York: Columbia University Press).

Gurr, Ted Robert (1968), "A Causal Model of Civil Strife: Comparative Analyses Using New Indices," *American Political Science Review*, 62(4), 1104–1124.

Hall, Robert E. and David H. Papell (2005), *Macroeconomics: Economic Growth, Fluctuations, and Policy*, 6th ed. (New York: W.W. Norton).

Hammond, Grant T. (1993), *Plowshares into Swords: Arms Races in International Politics, 1840–1991* (Columbia: University of South Carolina Press).

Han, Sung Hun (2005), "Report on Critical Dimensions and Problems of the North Korean Situation (1995–2004)," *Peace Economics, Peace Science and Public Policy*, 11(1), article 5.

Hardesty, David C. (2005), "Space-Based Weapons: Long-Term Strategic Implications and Alternatives," *Naval War College Review*, 58(2), 45–68.

Harff, Barbara (2003), "No Lessons Learned from the Holocaust? Assessing Risks of Genocide and Political Mass Murder Since 1955," *American Political Science Review*, 97(1), 57–73.

Harpviken, Kristian Berg (ed.) (2003), "Special Issue on the Future of Humanitarian Mine Action," *Third World Quarterly*, 24(5), 773–908.

Harris, Geoff (1997), "Estimates of the Economic Cost of Armed Conflict: The Iran-Iraq War and the Sri Lankan Civil War," in Jurgen Brauer and William G. Gissy (eds.), *Economics of Conflict and Peace* (Aldershot, UK: Avebury), 269–291.

Harrison, Mark (2000), "The Economics of World War II: An Overview," in Mark Harrison (ed.), *The Economics of World War II* (Cambridge, UK: Cambridge University Press), 1–42.

Hartley, Dean S. III and Robert L. Helmbold (1995), "Validating Lanchester's Square Law and Other Attrition Models," *Naval Research Logistics*, 42(4), 609–633.

Hartley, Keith (2006), "Defence Industrial Policy in a Military Alliance," *Journal of Peace Research*, 43(4), 473–489.

Hartley, Keith and Todd Sandler (eds.) (1995), *Handbook of Defense Economics*, vol. 1 (New York: Elsevier).

(eds.) (2001), *The Economics of Defense*, vols. 1–3 (Cheltenham, UK: Edward Elgar).

Hausken, Kjell (2004), "Mutual Raiding of Production and the Emergence of Exchange," *Economic Inquiry*, 42(4), 572–586.

Hegre, Håvard (2000), "Development and the Liberal Peace: What Does It Take to be a Trading State?" *Journal of Peace Research*, 37(1), 5–30.

(ed.) (2004), "Special Issue on the Duration and Termination of Civil War," *Journal of Peace Research*, 41(3), 243–348.

Hegre, Håvard, Tanja Ellingsen, Scott Gates, and Nils Petter Gleditsch (2001), "Toward a Democratic Civil Peace? Democracy, Political Change, and Civil War, 1816–1992," *American Political Science Review*, 95(1), 33–48.

Henderson, Errol A. and J. David Singer (2000), "Civil War in the Post-Colonial World," *Journal of Peace Research*, 37(3), 275–299.

Hensel, Paul R. (2000), "Territory: Theory and Evidence on Geography and Conflict," in John A. Vasquez (ed.), *What Do We Know About War?* (New York: Rowman & Littlefield), 57–84.

Herbst, Jeffrey (2004), "African Militaries and Rebellion: The Political Economy of Threat and Combat Effectiveness," *Journal of Peace Research*, 41(3), 357–369.

Hess, Gregory D. (1995), "An Introduction to Lewis Fry Richardson and His Mathematical Theory of War and Peace," *Conflict Management and Peace Science*, 14(1), 77–113.

Hewitt, J. Joseph (2003), "Dyadic Processes and International Crises," *Journal of Conflict Resolution*, 47(5), 669–692.

Hirshleifer, Jack (1985), "The Expanding Domain of Economics," *American Economic Review*, 75(6), 53–68.

(1987), *Economic Behavior in Adversity* (Chicago: University of Chicago Press).

(1988), "The Analytics of Continuing Conflict," *Synthese*, 76(2), 201–233.

(1991), "The Paradox of Power," *Economics and Politics*, 3(3), 177–200.

(1995), "Theorizing About Conflict," in Keith Hartley and Todd Sandler (eds.), *Handbook of Defense Economics*, vol. 1 (New York: Elsevier), 165–189.

Hirshleifer, Jack, Amihai Glazer, and David Hirshleifer (2005), *Price Theory and Applications: Decisions, Markets and Information*, 7th ed. (Cambridge, UK: Cambridge University Press).

Hitch, Charles J. and Roland N. McKean (1960), *The Economics of Defense in the Nuclear Age* (Cambridge, MA: Harvard University Press).

Hoffman, Bruce (1998), *Inside Terrorism* (New York: Columbia University Press).

Holmes, Leslie (ed.) (2007), *Terrorism, Organised Crime and Corruption: Networks and Linkages* (Cheltenham, UK: Edward Elgar).

Houghton, Brian K. (2008), "Terrorism Knowledge Base: A Eulogy," *Perspectives on Terrorism*, 2(7), 18–19.

Howard, Russell D. and James J. F. Forest (2008), *Weapons of Mass Destruction and Terrorism* (New York: McGraw-Hill).

Iannaccone, Laurence R. (1992), "Sacrifice and Stigma: Reducing Free-Riding in Cults, Communes, and Other Collectives," *Journal of Political Economy*, 100(2), 271–292.

(2006), "The Market for Martyrs," *Interdisciplinary Journal of Research on Religion*, 2 (article 4), 1–29.

Iannaccone, Laurence R. and Eli Berman (2006), "Religious Extremism: The Good, the Bad, and the Deadly," *Public Choice*, 128(1–2), 109–129.

ICC International Maritime Bureau (various years), *Piracy and Armed Robbery against Ships: Annual Report, 2006 and 2007* (Barking, UK: ICC International Maritime Bureau).

Ihori, Toshihiro (1999), "Protection against National Emergency: International Public Goods and Insurance," *Defense and Peace Economics*, 10(2), 117–137.

International Institute for Strategic Studies (1974), *The Military Balance, 1974–1975* (London: The International Institute of Strategic Studies).

(2008), *The Military Balance, 2008* (London: Oxford University Press).

International Monetary Fund (2007), "World Economic Outlook Database, October 2007," www.imf.org/external/pubs/ft/weo/2007/02/ (data downloaded on 11/7/07).

Intriligator, Michael D. (1975), "Strategic Considerations in the Richardson Model of Arms Races," *Journal of Political Economy*, 83(2), 339–353.

Intriligator, Michael D. and Dagobert L. Brito (1986), "Arms Races and Instability," *Journal of Strategic Studies*, 9(4), 113–131.

(1988), "A Predator-Prey Model of Guerrilla Warfare," *Synthese*, 76(2), 235–244.

Isard, Walter (1969), *General Theory: Social, Political, Economic, and Regional with Particular Reference to Decision-Making Analysis* (Cambridge MA: MIT Press).

(1988), *Arms Races, Arms Control, and Conflict Analysis* (New York: Cambridge University Press).

(2000), "Formative and Early Years of the Peace Science Society (International)," *Conflict Management and Peace Science*, 18(1), 1–48.

Isard, Walter and Christine Smith (1982), *Conflict Analysis and Practical Conflict Management Procedures* (Cambridge, MA: Ballinger).

Ivanova, Kate and Todd Sandler (2007), "CBRN Attack Perpetrators: An Empirical Study," *Foreign Policy Analysis*, 3(4), 273–294.

Jackson, Matthew O. and Massimo Morelli (2007), "Political Bias and War," *American Economic Review*, 97(4), 1353–1373.

Jones, Daniel M., Stuart A. Bremer, and J. David Singer (1996), "Militarized Interstate Disputes, 1816–1992: Rationale, Coding Rules, and Empirical Patterns," *Conflict Management and Peace Science*, 15(2), 163–212.

Juergensmeyer, Mark (2000), *Terror in the Mind of God: The Global Rise of Religious Violence* (Berkeley: University of California Press).

Kadera, Kelly M. and Sara McLaughlin Mitchell (eds.) (2005), "Special Issue: Model Specification and Control Variables," *Conflict Management and Peace Science*, 22 (4), 273–363.

Kahler, Miles and Barbara F. Walter (eds.) (2006), *Territoriality and Conflict in an Era of Globalization* (New York: Cambridge University Press).

Kahneman, Daniel (2003), "A Psychological Perspective on Economics," *American Economic Review*, 93(2), 162–168.

Kemp, Geoffrey and Robert E. Harkavy (1997), *Strategic Geography and the Changing Middle East* (Washington, DC: Carnegie Endowment for International Peace, in cooperation with Bookings Institution Press).

Khanna, Jyoti and Todd Sandler (1996), "NATO Burden Sharing: 1960–1992," *Defence and Peace Economics*, 7(2), 115–133.

Khanna, Jyoti, Todd Sandler, and Hirofumi Shimizu (1998), "Sharing the Financial Burden for UN and NATO Peacekeeping: 1976–96," *Journal of Conflict Resolution*, 42(2), 176–195.

Kim, Suk Hi (2003), *North Korea at a Crossroads* (London: McFarland).

King, Robert G. and Charles I. Plosser (eds.) (2004), "Special Issue on Economic Consequences of Terrorism," *Journal of Monetary Economics*, 51(5), 861–1075.

Konrad, Kai A. and Stergios Skaperdas (1998), "Extortion," *Economica*, 65(260), 461–477.

Koubi, Vally (2005), "War and Economic Performance," *Journal of Peace Research*, 42 (1), 67–82.

Krain, Matthew (1997), "State-Sponsored Mass Murder: The Onset and Severity of Genocides and Politicides," *Journal of Conflict Resolution*, 41(3), 331–360.

Krause, Volker and Christopher Sprecher (eds.) (2004), "Special Issue on Alliances," *International Interactions*, 30(4), 281–397.

Kreps, David M. (1990), *A Course in Microeconomic Theory* (Princeton, NJ: Princeton University Press).

Krueger, Alan B. and Jitka Malečková (2003), "Education, Poverty and Terrorism: Is There a Causal Connection?" *Journal of Economic Perspectives*, 17(4), 119–144.

Krugman, Paul R. and Maurice Obstfeld (2009), *International Economics: Theory and Policy*, 8th ed. (Boston: Pearson).

Kuran, Timor (1989), "Sparks and Prairie Fires: A Theory of Unanticipated Political Revolution," *Public Choice*, 61(1), 41–74.

Lacina, Bethany (2006), "Explaining the Severity of Civil Wars," *Journal of Conflict Resolution*, 50(2), 276–289.

Lacina, Bethany and Nils Petter Gleditsch (2005), "Monitoring Trends in Global Combat: A New Dataset of Battle Deaths," *European Journal of Population*, 21(2–3), 145–166.

Laczko, Frank and Elzbieta Gozdziak (eds.) (2005), "Special Issue: Data and Research on Human Trafficking: A Global Survey," *International Migration*, 43(1/2), 1–343.

LaFree, Gary and Laura Dugan (2006), *Global Terrorism Database 1.1, 1970–1997* [Computer file]. ICPSR22541-v1. College Park, MD: University of Maryland [producer], 2006. Ann Arbor, MI: Inter-university Consortium for Political and Social Research [distributor], 2008–05–30.

(2007a), *Global Terrorism Database II, 1998–2004* [Computer file]. ICPSR22600-v1. College Park, MD: University of Maryland [producer], 2007. Ann Arbor, MI: Inter-university Consortium for Political and Social Research [distributor], 2008–06–16.

(2007b), *Global Terrorism Database II, 1998–2004: Codebook and Data Documentation* [Computer file]. ICPSR22600-v1. College Park, MD: University of Maryland [producer], 2007. Ann Arbor, MI: Inter-university Consortium for Political and Social Research [distributor], 2008–06–16.

LaFree, Gary, Laura Dugan, Heather V. Fogg, and Jeffrey Scott (2006), "Building a Global Terrorism Database," NCJ 214260, United States Department of Justice, National Institute of Justice, April 27, 2006.

Lai, Brian (ed.) (2007), "Special Issue: The Relationship between State Policies and Characteristics and Terrorism," *Conflict Management and Peace Science*, 24(4), 257–326.

Lanchester, Frederick W. (1916), *Aircraft in Warfare, the Dawn of the Fourth Arm* (London: Constable).

Landes, William M. (1978), "An Economic Study of U.S. Aircraft Hijacking, 1961–1976," *Journal of Law & Economics*, 21(1), 1–31.

Langford, R. Everett (2004), *Introduction to Weapons of Mass Destruction: Radiological, Chemical, and Biological* (Hoboken, NJ: Wiley).

Lapan, Harvey E. and Todd Sandler (1988), "To Bargain or Not to Bargain? That is the Question," *American Economic Review*, 78(2), 16–21.

Larsen, Jeffrey A. (2005), *Historical Dictionary of Arms Control and Disarmament* (Lanham, MD: Scarecrow Press).

Lee, Dwight R. (1988), "Free Riding and Paid Riding in the Fight Against Terrorism," *American Economic Review*, 78(2), 22–26.

Leeds, Brett Ashley (2003), "Do Alliances Deter Aggression? The Influence of Military Alliances on the Initiation of Militarized Interstate Disputes," *American Journal of Political Science*, 47(3), 427–439.

(2005), *Alliance Treaty Obligations and Provisions (ATOP) Codebook*, Department of Political Science, Rice University, available at http://atop.rice.edu/download/ATOPcdbk.pdf.

Leeds, Brett Ashley and Sezi Anac (2005), "Alliance Institutionalization and Alliance Performance," *International Interactions*, 31(3), 183–202.

Leeds, Brett Ashley, Jeffrey M. Ritter, Sara McLaughlin Mitchell, and Andrew G. Long (2002), "Alliance Treaty Obligations and Provisions, 1815–1944," *International Interactions*, 28(3), 237–260.

Levi, Michael A. and Michael E. O'Hanlon (2005), *The Future of Arms Control* (Washington, DC: Brookings Institution Press).

Levy, Jack (2008), "Preventive War and Democratic Politics," *International Studies Quarterly*, 52(1), 1–24.

Lewis, Bernard (2003), *The Crisis of Islam: Holy War and Unholy Terror* (New York: Modern Library).

Li, Quan (2003), "The Effect of Security Alliances on Exchange-Rate Regime Choices," *International Interactions*, 29(2), 159–193.

(2005), "Does Democracy Promote or Reduce Transnational Terrorist Incidents?" *Journal of Conflict Resolution*, 49(2), 278–297.

Long, Andrew G. and Brett Ashley Leeds (2006), "Trading for Security: Military Alliances and Economic Agreements," *Journal of Peace Research*, 43(4), 433–451.

Lucas, Thomas W. and Turker Turkes (2003), "Fitting Lanchester Equations to the Battles of Kursk and Ardennes," *Naval Research Logistics*, 51(1), 95–116.

Lund, Michael S. (1996), "Early Warning and Preventive Diplomacy," in Charles A. Crocker, Fen Olser Hampson, and Pamella Aall (eds.), *Managing Global Chaos: Sources of and Responses to International Conflict* (Washington, DC: U.S. Institute of Peace), 379–402.

Lynn-Jones, Sean M. (2004), "Preface," in Michael E. Brown, Owen R., Coté Jr., Sean M. Lynn-Jones, and Steven E. Miller (eds.), *Offense, Defense, and War* (Cambridge MA: MIT Press), xi–xxxvii.

Macnair, Elizabeth S., James C. Murdoch, Chung-Ron Pi, and Todd Sandler (1995), "Growth and Defense: Pooled Estimates for the NATO Alliance, 1951–1988," *Southern Economic Journal*, 61(3), 846–860.

Mankiw, N. Gregory (2007), *Principles of Economics*, 4th ed. (Mason, OH: South-Western).

Mansfield, Edward D. and Brian M. Pollins (eds.) (2003), *Economic Interdependence and International Conflict: New Perspectives on an Enduring Debate* (Ann Arbor: University of Michigan Press).

Marshall, Monty G. and Keith Jaggers (2007), *Polity IV Project: Political Regime Characteristics and Transitions: 1800–2006*, available at http://www.systemicpeace.org/polity/polity4.htm.

Marshall, Monty G., Ted Robert Gurr, and Barbara Harff (2001), "PITF Problem Set Codebook," Political Instability Task Force, available at http://globalpolicy.gmu.edu/pitf/pitfcode.htm.

Martin, Philippe, Thierry Mayer, and Mathias Thoenig (2008), "Make Trade Not War?" *Review of Economic Studies*, 75(3), 865–900.

Mas-Colell, Andreu, Michael D. Whinston, and Jerry R. Green (1995), *Microeconomic Theory* (New York: Oxford University Press).

McGillivray, Mark and Oliver Morrissey (2000), "Aid Fungibility in Assessing Aid: Red Herring or True Concern?" *Journal of International Development*, 12(3), 413–428.

McGuire, Martin C. (1965), *Secrecy and the Arms Race* (Cambridge, MA: Harvard University Press).

(1990), "Mixed Public-Private Benefit and Public-Good Supply with Application to the NATO Alliance," *Defence Economics*, 1(1), 17–35.

(2002), "Property Distribution and Configuration of Sovereign States: A Rational Economic Model," *Defence and Peace Economics*, 13(4), 251–270.

(2004), "Economics of Strategic Defense and the Global Public Good," *Defence and Peace Economics*, 15(1), 1–25.

Mearsheimer, John J. (1985), *Conventional Deterrence* (Ithaca, NY: Cornell University Press).

Merrouche, Ouarda (2008), "Landmines and Poverty: IV Evidence from Mozambique," *Peace Economics, Peace Science and Public Policy*, 14(1), article 2.

Mickolus, Edward F. (1980), *Transnational Terrorism: A Chronology of Events, 1968–1979* (Westport, CT: Greenwood Press).

Mickolus, Edward F., Todd Sandler, Jean M. Murdock, and Peter A. Flemming (2003), "International Terrorism: Attributes of Terrorist Events, *ITERATE*, 1968–2002 Data Codebook," Mimeo.

Minorities at Risk Project (2005), College Park, MD: Center for International Development and Conflict Management, http://www.cidcm.umd.edu/mar/ (retrieved 2/12/07).

Montalvo, Jose G. and Marta Reynal-Querol (2005), "Ethnic Diversity and Economic Development," *Journal of Development Economics*, 76(2), 293–323.

Mousseau, Demet Yalcin (2001), "Democratizing with Ethnic Divisions: A Source of Conflict?" *Journal of Peace Research*, 38(5), 547–567.

Murdoch, James C. and Todd Sandler (1982), "A Theoretical and Empirical Analysis of NATO," *Journal of Conflict Resolution*, 26(2), 237–263.

(2004), "Civil Wars and Economic Growth: Spatial Dispersion," *American Journal of Political Science*, 48(1), 138–151.

Murshed, S. Mansoob (ed.) (2002), "Special Issue on Civil War in Developing Countries," *Journal of Peace Research*, 39(4), 387–512.

Nafziger, Wayne and Juha Auvinen (eds.) (2003), *Economic Development, Inequality, and War: Humanitarian Emergencies in Developing Countries* (New York: Palgrave Macmillan).

Nalebuff, Barry and John Riley (1985), "Asymmetric Equilibria in the War of Attrition," *Journal of Theoretical Biology*, 113(3), 517–527.

National Air and Space Intelligence Center (2006), *Ballistic and Cruise Missile Threat* (Wright-Patterson Air Force Base, OH: National Air and Space Intelligence Center).

National Counterterrorism Center (2008), "2007 Report on Terrorism, 30 April 2008," www.nctc.gov/ (downloaded on 6/6/08).

Natsios, Andrew S. (2001), *The Great North Korean Famine* (Washington, DC: U.S. Institute of Peace).

Neary, Hugh M. (1997), "Equilibrium Structure in an Economic Model of Conflict," *Economic Inquiry*, 35(3), 480–494.

Nicholson, Walter and Christopher Snyder (2008), *Microeconomic Theory: Basic Principles and Extensions*, 10th ed. (Mason, OH: South-Western).

Niou, Emerson M. S. and Guofu Tan (2005), "External Threat and Collective Action," *Economic Inquiry*, 43(3), 519–530.

Nitsch, Volker and Dieter Schumacher (2004), "Terrorism and International Trade: An Empirical Investigation," *European Journal of Political Economy*, 20(2), 423–434.

O'Balance, Edgar (1964), "Middle East Arms Race," *The Army Quarterly and Defence Journal*, 88, 210–214.

O'Neill, Barry (1994), "Game Theory Models of Peace and War," in Robert J. Aumann and Sergiu Hart (eds.), *Handbook of Game Theory*, vol. 2 (New York: Elsevier), 995–1053.

O'Sullivan, Patrick (1991), *Terrain and Tactics* (New York: Greenwood Press).

Office of Technology Assessment (1993), *Proliferation of Weapons of Mass Destruction: Assessing the Risk* (Washington, DC: U.S. Government Printing Office).

Olson, Mancur and Richard Zeckhauser (1966), "An Economic Theory of Alliances," *Review of Economics and Statistics*, 48(3), 266–279.

(1967), "Collective Goods, Comparative Advantage, and Alliance Efficiency," in Roland McKean (ed.), *Issues of Defense Economics* (New York: National Bureau of Economic Research), 25–48.

Oneal, John R. and Paul F. Diehl (1994), "The Theory of Collective Action and NATO Defense Burdens: New Empirical Tests," *Political Research Quarterly*, 47(2), 373–396.

Oneal, John R. and Mark A. Elrod (1989), "NATO Burden Sharing and the Forces of Change," *International Studies Quarterly*, 33(4), 435–456.

Oneal, John R. and Bruce M. Russett (2003a), "Assessing the Liberal Peace with Alternative Specifications: Trade Still Reduces Conflict," in Gerald Schneider, Katherine Barbieri, and Nils Petter Gleditsch (eds.), *Globalization and Armed Conflict* (Lanham, MD: Rowman & Littlefield), 143–163.

(2003b), "Modeling Conflict While Studying Dynamics: A Response to Nathaniel Beck," in Gerald Schneider, Katherine Barbieri, and Nils Petter Gleditsch (eds.), *Globalization and Armed Conflict* (Lanham, MD: Rowman & Littlefield), 179–188.

Online NewsHour (2006), "The Darfur Crisis," posted April 7, 2006, to www.pbs.org/newshour/indepth_coverage/africa/darfur/rebel-groups.html (downloaded 11/30/07).

Peck, Merton J. and Frederick M. Scherer (1962), *The Weapons Acquisition Process: An Economic Analysis* (Boston: Harvard University Press).

Perkins, Ray Jr. (1991), *The ABCs of the Soviet-American Nuclear Arms Race* (Pacific Grove, CA: Brooks/Cole).

Picarelli, John T. (2006), "The Turbulent Nexus of Transnational Organised Crime and Terrorism: A Theory of Malevolent International Relations," *Global Crime*, 7 (1), 1–24.

Pickles, John (ed.) (2000), "Special Issue on Ethnicity, Violence, and Regional Change," *Growth and Change*, 31(2), 139–337.

Pindyck, Robert S. and Daniel L. Rubenfeld (2009), *Microeconomics*, 7th ed. (Upper Saddle River, NJ: Pearson Prentice Hall).

Plowes, Nicola J. R. and Eldridge S. Adams (2005), "An Empirical Test of Lanchester's Square Law: Mortality during Battles of the Fire Ant *Solenopsis Invicta*," *Proceedings of the Royal Society B*, 272, 1809–1814.

Polachek, Solomon W. (1994), "Peace Economics: A Trade Theory Perspective," *Peace Economics, Peace Science and Public Policy*, 1(2), 12–15.

Polachek, Solomon W. and Carlos Seiglie (2007), "Trade, Peace and Democracy: An Analysis of Dyadic Dispute," in Todd Sandler and Keith Hartley (eds.), *Handbook of Defense Economics*, vol. 2 (New York: Elsevier), 1017–1073.

Powell, Robert (2002), "Bargaining Theory and International Conflict," *Annual Review of Political Science*, 5, 1–30.

(2004), "Bargaining and Learning While Fighting," *American Journal of Political Science*, 48(2), 344–361.

(2006), "War as a Commitment Problem," *International Organization*, 60(1), 169–203.

Przemieniecki, John S. (2000), *Mathematical Methods in Defense Analyses*, 3rd ed. (Reston, VA: American Institute of Aeronautics and Astronautics).

Quackenbush, Stephen L. (2004), "The Rationality of Rational Choice Theory," *International Interactions*, 30(2), 87–107.

Raiffa, Howard (1982), *The Art and Science of Negotiation* (Cambridge, MA: Harvard University Press).

Ram, Rati (1995), "Defense Expenditure and Economic Growth," in Keith Hartley and Todd Sandler (eds.), *Handbook of Defense Economics*, vol. 1 (New York: Elsevier), 251–273.

Ramsay, Kristopher W. (2008), "Settling It on the Field: Battlefield Events and War Termination," *Journal of Conflict Resolution*, 52(6), 850–879.

Rapoport, Anatol (1957), "Lewis F. Richardson's Mathematical Theory of War," *Journal of Conflict Resolution*, 1(3), 249–299.

Rasler, Karen A. and William R. Thompson (2006), "Contested Territory, Strategic Rivalries, and Conflict Escalation," *International Studies Quarterly*, 50(1), 145–167.

Reed, William (2003), "Information and Economic Interdependence," *Journal of Conflict Resolution*, 47(1), 54–71.

Regan, Patrick M. and Aysegul Aydin (2006), "Diplomacy and Other Forms of Intervention in Civil Wars," *Journal of Conflict Resolution*, 50(5), 736–756.

Reiter, Dan (2003), "Exploring the Bargaining Model of War," *Perspectives on Politics*, 1(1), 27–43.

Richardson, Harry W., Peter Gordon, and James E. Moore II (eds.) (2005), *The Economic Impacts of Terrorist Attacks* (Cheltenham, UK: Edward Elgar).

Richardson, Harry W., Peter Gordon, and James E. Moore II (eds.) (2007), *The Economic Costs and Consequences of Terrorism* (Cheltenham, UK: Edward Elgar).

Richardson, Lewis F. (1939), *Generalized Foreign Politics* (London: Cambridge University Press).

(1960a), *Arms and Insecurity: A Mathematical Study of the Causes and Origins of War* (Pittsburgh: Homewood).

(1960b), *Statistics of Deadly Quarrels* (Pacific Grove, CA: Boxwood Press).

Rider, Robert (1999), "Conflict, the Sire of Exchange," *Journal of Economic Behavior & Organization*, 40(3), 217–232.

(2002), "Plunder or Trade?" *Defence and Peace Economics*, 13(1), 199–214.

Robinson, Julian Perry, Carl-Göran Hedén, and Hans von Schreeb (1973), *The Problem of Chemical and Biological Warfare, CB Weapons Today*, vol. 2 (Stockholm: Almqvist & Wiksell).

Roemer, John E. (1985), "Rationalizing Revolutionary Ideology," *Econometrica*, 53(1), 85–108.

Ron, James (ed.) (2005), "Special Issue: Paradigm in Distress? Primary Commodities and Civil War," *Journal of Conflict Resolution*, 49(4), 441–633.

Rosendorff, B. Peter and Todd Sandler (eds.) (2005), "Special Issue: The Political Economy of Transnational Terrorism," *Journal of Conflict Resolution*, 49(2), 171–314.

Rotte, Ralph and Christoph M. Schmidt (2003), "On the Production of Victory: Empirical Determinants of Battlefield Success in Modern War," *Defence and Peace Economics*, 14(3), 175–192.

Rowley, Charles K. (ed.) (2006), "Special Issue: The Political Economy of Terrorism," *Public Choice*, 128(1–2), 1–356.

Rueckert, George L. (1998), *On-Site Inspection in Theory and Practice: A Primer on Modern Arms Control Regimes* (New York: Praeger).

Russett, Bruce M. and John R. Oneal (2001), *Triangulating Peace: Democracy, Interdependence, and International Organization* (New York: W.W. Norton).

Saaty, Thomas L. (1968), *Mathematical Models of Arms Control and Disarmament* (New York: Wiley).

Sagan, Scott D. and Kenneth N. Waltz (2002), *The Spread of Nuclear Weapons: A Debate Renewed* (New York: W.W. Norton).

Sambanis, Nicholas (2000), "Partition as a Solution to Ethnic War: An Empirical Critique of the Theoretical Literature," *World Politics*, 52(4), 437–483.

(2002), "A Review of Recent Advances and Future Directions in the Quantitative Literature on Civil War," *Defense and Peace Economics*, 13(3), 215–243.

(2004a), "Poverty and the Organization of Political Violence: A Review and Some Conjectures," Unpublished manuscript.

(2004b), "What Is Civil War? Conceptual and Empirical Complexities of an Operational Definition," *Journal of Conflict Resolution*, 48(6), 814–858.

(2004c), "Expanding Economic Models of Civil War Using Case Studies," *Perspectives on Politics*, 2(2), 259–280.

Sample, Susan G. (2002), "The Outcomes of Military Buildups: Minor States vs. Major Powers," *Journal of Peace Research*, 39(6), 669–691.

Sandler, Todd (1977), "Impurity of Defense: An Application to the Economics of Alliances," *Kyklos*, 30(3), 443–460.

Sandler, Todd (ed.) (1992), "Special Issue: Terrorism, Guerrilla Warfare, and Insurrections," *Defence and Peace Economics*, 3(4), 259–358.

(2000), "Arms Trade, Arms Control and Security: Collective Action Issues," *Defence and Peace Economics*, 11(5), 533–548.

(2003), "Collective Action and Transnational Terrorism," *The World Economy*, 26 (6), 779–802.

Sandler, Todd and Daniel G. Arce (2007), "Terrorism: A Game-Theoretic Approach," in Todd Sandler and Keith Hartley (eds.), *Handbook of Defense Economics*, vol. 2 (New York: Elsevier), 775–813.

Sandler, Todd and Jon Cauley (1975), "On the Economic Theory of Alliances," *Journal of Conflict Resolution*, 19(2), 330–348.

Sandler, Todd and Walter Enders (2004), "An Economic Perspective on Transnational Terrorism," *European Journal of Political Economy*, 20(2), 301–316.

Sandler, Todd and John Forbes (1980), "Burden Sharing, Strategy, and the Design of NATO," *Economic Inquiry*, 18(3), 425–444.

Sandler, Todd and Keith Hartley (1995), *The Economics of Defense* (Cambridge, UK: Cambridge University Press).

(1999), *The Political Economy of NATO* (Cambridge, UK: Cambridge University Press).

(2001), "Economics of Alliances: The Lessons of Collective Action," *Journal of Economic Literature*, 39(3), 869–896.

Sandler, Todd and Keith Hartley (eds.) (2003), *The Economics of Conflict*, vols. 1–3 (Cheltenham, UK: Edward Elgar).

Sandler, Todd and Keith Hartley (eds.) (2007), *Handbook of Defense Economics*, vol. 2 (New York: Elsevier).

Sandler, Todd and Håvard Hegre (eds.) (2002), "Special Issue on Economic Analysis of Civil Wars," *Defence and Peace Economics*, 13(6), 429–496.

Sandler, Todd and James C. Murdoch (1990), "Nash-Cournot or Lindahl Behavior? An Empirical Test for the NATO Allies," *Quarterly Journal of Economics*, 105(4), 875–894.

(2000), "On Sharing NATO Defense Burdens in the 1990s and Beyond," *Fiscal Studies*, 21(3), 297–327.

Sandler, Todd and Kevin Siqueira (2006), "Global Terrorism: Deterrence versus Preemption," *Canadian Journal of Economics*, 39(4), 1370–1387.

Sandler, Todd, John T. Tschirhart, and Jon Cauley (1983), "A Theoretical Analysis of Transnational Terrorism," *American Political Science Review*, 77(1), 36–54.

Sarkees, Meredith R. (2000), "The Correlates of War Data on War: An Update to 1997," *Conflict Management and Peace Science*, 18(1), 123–144.

Sarkees, Meredith R., Frank W. Wayman, and J. David Singer (2003), "Inter-state, Intra-state, and Extra-state Wars: A Comprehensive Look at Their Distribution Over Time, 1816–1997," *International Studies Quarterly*, 47(1), 49–70.

Schelling, Thomas C. (1960), *The Strategy of Conflict* (Cambridge, MA: Harvard University Press).

(1966), *Arms and Influence* (New Haven, CT: Yale University Press).

(2006), "An Astonishing Sixty Years: The Legacy of Hiroshima," *American Economic Review*, 96(4), 929–937.

Schelling, Thomas C. and Morton H. Halperin (1961), *Strategy and Arms Control* (London: Pergamon-Brassey's).

Schmid, Alex, Albert Jongman, and Eric Price (eds.) (2008), *Handbook of Terrorism Research: Research, Theories and Concepts* (New York: Routledge).

Schneider, Gerald and Katherine Barbieri (eds.) (1999), "Special Issue on Trade and Conflict," *Journal of Peace Research*, 36(4), 387–496.

Schneider, Gerald and Vera E. Troeger (2006), "War and the World Economy: Stock Market Reactions to International Conflicts," *Journal of Conflict Resolution*, 50 (5), 623–645.

Schneider, Gerald, Katherine Barbieri, and Nils Petter Gleditsch (2003), "Does Globalization Contribute to Peace? A Critical Survey of the Literature," in Gerald Schneider, Katherine Barbieri, and Nils Petter Gleditsch (eds.), *Globalization and Armed Conflict* (Lanham, MD: Rowman & Littlefield), 3–29.

Schrodt, Philip A. and Deborah J. Gerner (2004), "An Event Data Analysis of Third-Party Mediation," *Journal of Conflict Resolution*, 48(3), 310–330.

Seiglie, Carlos (2007), "Efficient Peacekeeping for a New World Order," *Peace Economics, Peace Science and Public Policy*, 11(2), article 2.

Senese, Paul D. (2005), "Territory, Contiguity, and International Conflict: Assessing a New Joint Explanation," *American Journal of Political Science*, 49(4), 769–779.

Shelley, Louise I. (2006), "Trafficking in Nuclear Materials: Criminals and Terrorists," *Global Crime*, 7(3&4), 544–560.

Silke, Andrew (ed.) (2004), *Research into Terrorism: Trends, Achievements and Failures* (New York: Routledge).

Simons, Lewis M. (2006), "Genocide and the Science of Proof," *National Geographic*, 209(1), 28–35.

Singer, J. David (ed.) (1960), "Special Issue: The Geography of Conflict," *Journal of Conflict Resolution*, 4(1), 1–162.

(2000), "The Etiology of Interstate War: A Natural History Approach," in John A. Vasquez (ed.), *What Do We Know About War?* (New York: Rowman & Littlefield), 3–21.

(2007), "Nuclear Proliferation and the Geo-Cultural Divide: The March of Folly," *International Studies Review*, 9(4), 663–672.

Singer, Peter W. (2005), *Children at War* (New York: Pantheon).

Singh, Sonali and Christopher R. Way (2004), "The Correlates of Nuclear Proliferation," *Journal of Conflict Resolution*, 48(6), 859–885.

Siverson, Randolph M. and Harvey Starr (1990), "Opportunity, Willingness and the Diffusion of War, 1816–1965," *American Political Science Review*, 84(1), 47–67.

(1994), "Regime Change and the Restructuring of Alliances," *American Journal of Political Science*, 38(1), 145–161.

Skaperdas, Stergios (1992), "Cooperation, Conflict, and Power in the Absence of Property Rights," *American Economic Review*, 82(4), 720–739.

(1996), "Contest Success Functions," *Economic Theory*, 7(2), 283–290.

(2006), "Bargaining versus Fighting," *Defence and Peace Economics*, 17(6), 657–676.

Skaperdas, Stergios and Constantinos Syropoulos (1997), "The Distribution of Income in the Presence of Appropriative Activities," *Economica*, 64(253), 101–117.

(2002), "Insecure Property and the Efficiency of Exchange," *Economic Journal*, 112 (476), 133–146.

Slantchev, Branislav L. (2003), "The Power to Hurt: Costly Conflict with Completely Informed States," *American Political Science Review*, 47(1), 123–135.

(2004), "How Initiators End Their Wars: The Duration of Warfare and the Terms of Peace," *American Journal of Political Science*, 48(4), 813–829.

Small Arms Survey (2004), *Small Arms Survey 2004: Rights at Risk* (Oxford: Oxford University Press).

Smith, Adam [1776] (1976), *The Wealth of Nations* (Chicago: University of Chicago Press).

Smith, Alastair and Allan C. Stam (2004), "Bargaining and the Nature of War," *Journal of Conflict Resolution*, 48(6), 783–813.

Snyder, Glenn H. (1997), *Alliance Politics* (Ithaca, NY: Cornell University Press).

Solomon, Binyam (2007), "Political Economy of Peacekeeping," in Todd Sandler and Keith Hartley (eds.), *Handbook of Defense Economics*, vol. 2 (New York: Elsevier), 741–774.

Sorokin, Pitirim (1937), *Social and Cultural Dynamics* (New York: American Book Company).

Spolaore, Enrico (2008a), "Civil Conflict and Secessions," *Economics of Governance*, 9 (1), 45–63.

(2008b), "Size of Nations, Economics Approach to the," in Steven N. Durlauf and Lawrence E. Blume (eds.), *The New Palgrave Dictionary of Economics*, 2nd ed. (New York: Palgrave Macmillan). The New Palgrave Dictionary of Economics Online. Palgrave Macmillan. 23 June 2008 (www.dictionaryofeconomics.com).

Sprecher, Christopher and Volker Krause (eds.) (2006), "Special Issue on Alliances," *Journal of Peace Research*, 43(4), 363–502.

Stanislawski, Bartosz H. (2008), "Para-States, Quasi-States, and Black Spots: Perhaps not States, But Not 'Ungoverned Territories,' Either," *International Studies Review*, 10(2), 366–370.

Starr, Harvey and G. Dale Thomas (2002), "The 'Nature' of Contiguous Borders: Ease of Interaction, Salience, and the Analysis of Crisis," *International Interactions*, 28 (3), 213–235.

Stockholm International Peace Research Institute (2005), *SIPRI Yearbook 2005* (New York: Oxford University Press).

(2007), *SIPRI Yearbook 2007* (New York: Oxford University Press).

(2008a), "Multilateral Peace Operations Database," available at http://www.sipri.org (data accessed 5/5/08).

(2008b), "SIPRI Data on Military Expenditure," available at http://www.sipri.org (data accessed 10/16/07).

Tarar, Ahmer (2006), "Diversionary Incentives and the Bargaining Approach to War," *International Studies Quarterly*, 50(1), 169–188.

Taylor, James G. (1983) *Lanchester Models of Warfare*, vols. 1 and 2 (Arlington, VA: Operations Research Society of America).

Taylor, John B. and Akila Weerapana (2009), *Principles of Macroeconomics*, 6th ed. (Boston: Houghton Mifflin).

Tellis, Ashley J., Thomas S. Szayna, and James A. Winnefeld (1997), *Anticipating Ethnic Conflict* (Santa Monica, CA: Rand).

Thompson, William R. (2001), "Identifying Rivals and Rivalries in World Politics," *International Studies Quarterly*, 45(4), 557–586.

Tir, Jaroslav (2005), "Keeping the Peace after Secession: Territorial Conflicts Between Rump and Secessionist States," *Journal of Conflict Resolution*, 49(5), 713–741.

(2006), "Domestic-Level Territorial Disputes: Conflict Management via Secession," *Conflict Management and Peace Science*, 23(4), 309–328.

Toft, Monica Duffy (2006), "Issue Indivisibility and Time Horizons as Rationalist Explanations for War," *Security Studies*, 15(1), 34–69.

Tullock, Gordon (1974), *The Social Dilemma: The Economics of War and Revolution* (Blacksburg, VA: Center for the Study of Public Choice).

United Nations (1969), *Chemical and Bacteriological (Biological) Weapons and the Effects of Their Possible Use* (New York: United Nations).

United Nations High Commissioner for Refugees (2006a), *Helping Refugees: An Introduction to UNHCR* (Geneva, Switzerland: UNHCR Media Relations and Public Information Service).

(2006b), *Internally Displaced People: Questions and Answers* (Geneva, Switzerland: UNHCR Media Relations and Public Information Service).

United States Census Bureau (various years), *Statistical Abstract of the United States* (Washington, DC: U.S. Government Printing Office).

United States Government Accountability Office (2006), "Human Trafficking: Better Data, Strategy, and Reporting Needed to Enhance U.S. Antitrafficking Efforts Abroad," GAO-06–825 (Washington, DC: US Government Accountability Office).,

Usher, Dan (1989), "The Dynastic Cycle and the Stationary State," *American Economic Review*, 79(5), 1031–1044.

Vahabi, Mehrdad (2004), *The Political Economy of Destructive Power* (Cheltenham, UK: Edward Elgar).

Valentino, Benjamin, Paul Huth, and Dylan Balch-Lindsay (2004), "'Draining the Sea': Mass Killing and Guerrilla Warfare," *International Organization*, 58(2), 375–407.

Van Evera, Stephen (1998), "Offense, Defense, and the Causes of War," *International Security*, 22(4), 5–43.

(1999), *Causes of War: Power and the Roots of Conflict* (Ithaca, NY: Cornell University Press).

Van Ypersele de Strihou, Jacques M. (1967), "Sharing the Defense Burden among Western Allies," *Review of Economics and Statistics* 49(4), 527–536.

Vasquez, John A. (ed.) (2000), *What Do We Know About War?* (New York: Rowman & Littlefield).

Victoroff, Jeff (ed.) (2006), *Tangled Roots: Social and Psychological Factors in the Genesis of Terrorism* (Amsterdam: IOS Press).

Waldman, Don E. (2009), *Microeconomics*, 2nd ed. (Boston: Pearson Addison Wesley).

Wall, James A. Jr., John B. Stark, and Rhetta L. Standifer (2001), "Mediation: A Current Review and Theory Development," *Journal of Conflict Resolution*, 45(3), 370–391.

Wallace, Michael D. (1979), "Arms Races and Escalation: Some New Evidence," *Journal of Conflict Resolution*, 23(1), 3–16.

Walt, Stephen M. (1987), *The Origins of Alliances* (Ithaca, NY: Cornell University Press).

Walter, Barbara F. (2004), "Does Conflict Beget Conflict? Explaining Recurring Civil War," *Journal of Peace Research*, 41(3), 371–388.

(2006a), "Building Reputation: Why Governments Fight Some Separatists but Not Others," *American Journal of Political Science*, 50(2), 313–330.

(2006b), "Information, Uncertainty, and the Decision to Secede," *International Organization*, 60(1), 105–135.

Weiner, Myron (1996), "Bad Neighbors, Bad Neighborhoods: An Inquiry into the Causes of Refugee Flows," *International Security*, 21(1), 5–42.

Weiss, Herbert K. (1966), "Combat Models and Historical Data: The U.S. Civil War," *Operations Research*, 14(5), 759–790.

Wessells, Michael (2006), *Child Soldiers: From Violence to Protection* (Cambridge, MA: Harvard University Press).

Wiseman, Geoffrey (2002), *Concepts of Non-Provocative Defence: Ideas and Practices in International Security* (New York: Palgrave Macmillan).

Wittman, Donald (1979), "How a War Ends: A Rational Model Approach," *Journal of Conflict Resolution*, 23(4), 743–763.

(2000), "The Wealth and Size of Nations," *Journal of Conflict Resolution*, 44(6), 868–884.

Wolfson, Murray (1985), "Notes on Economic Warfare," *Conflict Management and Peace Science*, 8(2), 1–20.

(1987), "A Theorem on the Existence of Zones of Initiation and Deterrence in Intriligator-Brito Arms Race Models," *Public Choice*, 54(3), 291–297.

Wong, Kar-Yiu (1991), "Foreign Trade, Military Alliance, and Defence-Burden Sharing," *Defence Economics*, 2(2), 83–103.

Wright, Quincy (1942), *A Study of War*, vols. 1 and 2 (Chicago: University of Chicago Press).

Author Index

ABC News, 139
ACDA, 187, 189
Adams, Eldridge S., 184
Adams, Karen R., 181–183
Addison, Tony, 124
Alesina, Alberto, 155, 175–178, 179, 180, 184
Allison, Graham, 189, 220
Amegashie, J. Atsu, 82
Anac, Sezi, 245
Ancker, C.J., Jr., 184
Anderson, James E., 267
Anderton, Charles H., 7, 81, 83, 136, 153, 155, 172, 184, 185, 186, 210, 211, 220, 263, 264, 267, 268
Anderton, Roxane A., 81, 264, 267
Arce, Daniel G., 66, 146, 153, 184
Aslam, Rabia, 27
Auvinen, Juha, 124
Axelrod, Robert, 64
Aydin, Aysegul, 122

Balch-Lindsay, Dylan, 125
Ballentine, Karen, 113, 124
Banks, H. Thomas, 220
Barbieri, Katherine, 103, 119–120
Bartrop, Paul, 112
Bearce, David H., 94
Beardsley, Kyle C., 103
Becker, Gary, 14, 153
Beckerman, Stephen, 184
Bellany, Ian, 184
Bennett, D. Scott, 103, 245

Benoit, Emile, 14, 27
Bercovitch, Jacob, 125
Berdal, Mats, 124
Berman, Eli, 150–151
Betts, Richard K., 173
Bier, Vicki M., 154
Binmore, Ken, 14, 52, 66
Biswas, Bidisha, 103
Björnehed, Emma, 245
Bloch, Jean de, 101
Blomberg, S. Brock, 152–153
Boehmer, Charles R., 94, 97–98
Bogart, Ernest L., 100, 101
Bolton, Patrick, 184
Boulding, Kenneth E., 13, 102, 155–158, 159, 161–162, 164–165, 166, 179, 180, 183, 220
Braithwaite, Alex, 183
Brams, Steven J., 82, 221
Brauer, Jurgen, 13, 52, 102, 220, 221, 245
Bremer, Stuart A., 85, 86, 88, 93, 218
Brito, Dagobert L., 184, 185, 202–205, 216, 218, 220, 221, 267
Broadberry, Stephen, 103
Brown, Michael E., 14, 102, 184
Brück, Tilman, 154
Brunborg, Helge, 125
Brzoska, Michael, 220
Buchanan, James M., 184
Bueno de Mesquita, Bruce, 102
Buhaug, Halvard, 125, 180, 183
Bureau of Justice Statistics, 9
Bush, Winston C., 81, 267

Subject Index